DANGEROUS LEARNING

DANGEROUS LEARNING

The South's Long War on Black Literacy

DEREK W. BLACK

Yale
UNIVERSITY PRESS
New Haven and London

Published with assistance from the foundation established
in memory of Philip Hamilton McMillan of the Class of 1894,
Yale College.
Copyright © 2025 by Derek W. Black.
All rights reserved.
This book may not be reproduced, in whole or in part, including
illustrations, in any form (beyond that copying permitted by
Sections 107 and 108 of the U.S. Copyright Law and except by
reviewers for the public press), without written permission from
the publishers.

Yale University Press books may be purchased in quantity for
educational, business, or promotional use. For information, please
e-mail sales.press@yale.edu (U.S. office) or sales@yaleup.co.uk
(U.K. office).

Set in Janson type by IDS Infotech, Ltd.
Printed in the United States of America.

Library of Congress Control Number: 2024940508
ISBN 978-0-300-27282-6 (hardcover : alk. paper)

A catalogue record for this book is available from the British
Library.

This paper meets the requirements of ANSI/NISO Z39.48-1992
(Permanence of Paper).

10 9 8 7 6 5 4 3 2 1

In memory of my grandfather William Franklin Bunch, whose love of history I came to share only after he was gone but whose personal history long ago marked my own journey.

Contents

Preface ix

INTRODUCTION 1
1. The Spark 12
2. The Quarantine 36
3. The Word: David Walker 55
4. Arresting the Word 72
5. The Fire: Nat Turner 82
6. The South's Last Slavery Debate 96
7. The Blockade 117
8. A Gag in the Halls of Congress 138
9. The Tragedy of Silence 148
10. Southern Propaganda 166
11. Secret Learning 176
12. Black Literacy on Trial 190
13. A Rebirth of Freedom: Black Schooling in the Midst of War 208
14. Public Education for All 232
15. Burning Down the Schoolhouse 257
16. Our Chance to Break the Cycle 275

Notes 291
Acknowledgments 335
Index 337

Preface

IN 2020, FEW OUTSIDE the academy had ever heard of critical race theory. Even fewer could reasonably describe it. State legislators hadn't banned any books, pronouns, or ideas.

I started work on this book that year with no obvious agenda other than to share a story I found mesmerizing: enslaved individuals risking their lives to read and later filling freedmen's schools beyond their capacity. In a world where education is increasingly treated as a commodity, such a book might remind us that education is a human experience and literacy rests at its heart. Maybe some readers would connect the book with their own struggle with reading, their own moment of awakening through a special book, or their own journey to a more secure life.

But as the attack on public education took shape over the next year and terms like "critical race theory" grew familiar to the average person, I questioned whether a good story was enough to justify the book. I had spent the last two decades trying to make a difference for disadvantaged students—from litigating segregation and diversity cases to writing, testifying, and advocating on the right to education and its relevance to school funding, privatization, and federal policy. Telling a story, even one dramatic enough for the screen, seemed indulgent, and certainly irrelevant to the current crises consuming public education.

Though my self-doubt never fully lifted, over the next two years I saw connections emerging between the story of Black literacy and the current battles engulfing public education. I found eerily familiar cycles of progress and retrenchment revolving around the same thing—Black freedom through literacy. I found a time when some slaveholders and churches actively encouraged Black literacy followed by a time when they criminalized it, and then found a time when the South was dependent on Northern literature followed by one when it attacked Northern newspapers and textbooks as unsafe for public consumption, accusing them of perpetuating bias against the South. I instantly realized, in the story of Black literacy, William Faulkner's adage: "The past is never dead. It's not even past." And I finally saw the larger story that needed to be told, one that placed the current moment in sober context.

Deepening and adjusting the book rather than flattening the history involved its own lessons for the current moment. Few things are as exciting for me as discovering people or facts that upend conventional wisdom or demand more nuance. But I worried some of this book's discoveries and complexities might be an uncomfortable fit in a modern culture that increasingly insists on singular narratives—a Supreme Court that can do no right, an America that knows no flaw, a history that involves multiple perspectives but can validate only one. In today's world, details and ambiguities seem to infrequently matter, if at all. The only version of history that some will tolerate is one that serves their agenda—whether it be defending the status quo or shattering its foundations. This story could not be that.

The irony of having me at this project's helm and my insistence on its full narrative is that twenty-five years ago a seminal text in critical race theory, the supposed destroyer of white esteem, helped me find mine. Derrick Bell's *Faces at the Bottom of the Well* was the first book I ever read by a Black author. It made more practical sense—even as allegory—than most anything else I had previously read. A year later, I had taken up African American studies as an additional major and decided to abandon my plan to attend law school. But still struggling with my next step—and with no sense of Bell's importance or busy schedule—I wrote him an earnest letter seeking advice and dropped it in the mail. He responded to not one but two of my letters, offering insight, encouragement, and, finally, a copy of *Ethical Ambition: Living a Life of Meaning and Worth*, which helped me find my way back to law school but with a new goal.

Nothing I read from him ever suggested he was looking to indoctrinate. If so, I quibble or disagree with enough of his ideas to suggest he missed the mark. But if he was, as I thought, a scholar pushing us to expand our boundaries and consider things that, if true, would be hard for many to accept, he succeeded and changed me—and surely many more—for the better.

I can't project where I would be today had Bell not written *Faces at the Bottom of the Well*, had I not read it, or had he not been gracious enough to give his time to a random pen pal like me. I shudder to imagine where silencing the work of people like Bell might leave us. But the lessons I hope this book makes clear are the danger of silencing the opposition and the folly of painting with brushes so broad as to hide the truth or exclude others. To be clear, both sides of several current divides could stand to learn or refresh themselves on these lessons.

I hope this story might bridge some divides. It is at once distant to someone like me—a man raised in the overwhelmingly white rural foothills of East Tennessee—and yet it resonates. It is inseparable from public education in the South—my public education—what I called in my last book the intergenerational "inheritance that we all share, and one that is crucially important for kids like me who never could have hoped for an inheritance in the literal sense." Bringing together the threads of slavery, public education, and the current racialized debate surrounding public education serves to reinforce our common interest in preserving our shared inheritance. And if read with heart, this story has the power to connect people on a fundamental level. The personal stories of enslaved people's literacy journey, as I have pondered them, are the nearest thing we have to a holy testament to the intersection of literacy and humanity.

Introduction

On March 3, 1862, forty-one men and twelve women, all white, huddled along the edge of New York Harbor, waiting for a military steamship, the *Atlantic*, to carry them deep into troubled waters. Though the bustling harbor reflected business as usual, further south the country was ripping itself apart. Before they could board the *Atlantic*, they had to sign oaths of allegiance to the United States. The conflict would soon become a "great civil war, testing whether this nation, or any nation so conceived [in liberty], and so dedicated, can long endure." But on that March morning, President Abraham Lincoln and his allies still saw the conflict through a narrower lens—as the unavoidable price of saving the Union.[1]

This group of fifty-three already knew far more was at stake than a mere political union. They carried no muskets, bayonets, or knives. Instead, their bags were packed with Bibles, dictionaries, and reading primers. These "Gideonites," as the soldiers derisively called them, saw Lincoln's war as a fight for Black freedom and believed literacy was the key to unlocking it.[2]

They boarded the *Atlantic* on a promise that they could participate in an experiment to test Black autonomy. A major Union victory in the South Carolina Sea Islands had recently placed ten thousand Black people safely behind Union lines. Fewer than a dozen white Southerners remained. Per official Union policy, these Black people were "contraband" of war, a strange netherworld status between free and enslaved. A handful of individuals in the Lincoln administration were pressing for the chance to explore post-War possibilities in these isolated islands.

President Lincoln signed off on the experiment but had not uttered a word about emancipation. He was still publicly saying, "if I could save the Union without freeing any slave I would do it." Talk like that scared some volunteers away. At a public meeting shortly before the *Atlantic*'s voyage, several missionaries openly worried that Lincoln might return the people of the Sea Islands to slavery in some sort of truce to end the War. Those aboard the *Atlantic* did not discount this possibility, but the transcendent moral nature of their mission compelled them to act anyway. They believed that if Black people could prove themselves worthy of citizenship, they might one day have it.[3]

The missionaries' grand hopes rested largely on Brigadier General Edward Pierce. Unabashedly sympathetic to Black people's plight, Pierce had recently published an essay in *The Atlantic* magazine suggesting that the Union should enlist willing Black men in the War and prepare the rest for citizenship through education. Treasury Secretary Salmon Chase, Lincoln's rival for the 1860 Republican presidential nomination, hand-picked Pierce to oversee contraband affairs in the Sea Islands. Soon after taking the post, Pierce had written to the American Missionary Association, asking it to send teachers. Now they were coming.[4]

The missionaries' next six days aboard the *Atlantic* were fraught with danger and uncertainty. Though the passengers desperately wanted information, they extracted very little from officers who were more consumed with safe passage along a southern coast that—save Fort Monroe, a small island near Norfolk, Virginia—was controlled by the enemy. New orders or cannon fire could force them to retreat to New York at any moment.[5]

The tension finally eased on March 9, 1862, when the *Atlantic* docked in Beaufort, South Carolina, the Sea Islands' port of entry. Pierce greeted the passengers with a speech. "Never," he told them, "did a vessel bear a colony on a nobler mission, not even the Mayflower, when she conveyed the Pilgrims to Plymouth." The unprecedented work they would undertake deserved "the highest of all recognitions ever accorded to angels or to men, in this life or the next." While their white countrymen thought of Black people only as slaves or servants, the missionaries would show Blacks and whites to be equals. They would usher in a new birth of freedom in America through Black literacy.[6]

Standing in their way were four decades of Southern efforts to impose ignorance on the region. Two slave revolts—one in Charleston, South Carolina, in 1822 and the other in Southampton, Virginia, in

1831—had triggered a war on Black literacy that eventually engulfed the entire South. The revolt leaders were highly literate and leveraged the knowledge and communication ability that literacy provided to catalyze their followers. Between the revolts, a third Black man—free and living in the North—had written a manifesto and started shipping it into the depths of slavery's empire. He called on Black people, free and enslaved, to shake off the mental chains of slavery through education and seize freedom as their birthright by any means necessary.

Hysteria ensued across the South. White leaders were convinced that Black literacy was to blame for the rebellions and that the manifesto would provoke more. Literacy alerted Black people to Congress's slavery debates, sparked notions of revolution, inflated their expectations of a better way of life, and exposed them to contradictory biblical passages that, in white Southerners' view, would overwhelm their capacity to understand. The only safe course of action was to keep dangerous information secret.

By the early 1830s, all but a few Southern states had imposed severe sanctions on any enslaved person caught trying to read or write, as well as on any person, white or Black, caught teaching them. Some states went further, criminalizing literacy for free Black people, too. The punishment for a first offense was fifty lashes. For the second, in some states, it was death. And regardless of what state law dictated, those who held Black people in bondage claimed the right to take more aggressive measures. They chopped off fingers and hands, burned flesh with hot irons, and beat people to within an inch of their lives so that their punishments would serve to warn everyone who crossed paths with the victims.

The hysteria extended to books and newspapers, too. Even for white people, it was a crime to possess certain texts. At first, abolitionist newspapers were banned. But once abolitionist literature was expunged, governments in the South looked for new villains. Some leaders claimed that all Northern literature, including its magazines and textbooks, was infected with anti-Southern bias that would undermine the Southern way of life. As a replacement, they pushed textbooks and literature from the South, by the South, and for the South. By the mid-1830s, a pall of orthodoxy had descended over the region, constricting not only Black people's literacy but white people's access to information. The orthodoxy only grew more belligerent, more unpersuadable, and more repressive with time.

Yet despite every manner of oppression and brutality, Black literacy never fully died in the South. Black people did not need missionaries to convince them of literacy's worth. Some had been secretly teaching themselves since the literacy crackdowns. Decades of repression could not extinguish the skills that Black individuals acquired before the crackdowns and passed on to friends and family across the generations. Others painstakingly taught themselves with stolen books or scraps of paper. As forbidden fruit, secret learning took on special meaning in the enslaved community as the highest ability a person could wield, so powerful that some thought it akin to magic. As one of the first missionary teachers wrote, enslaved people in the Sea Islands "knew that there was power in letters." They had seen the devastating things "a scrap of writing sent from the master to the overseer" could do.[7]

Days after the Union victory in the Sea Islands, Black people began rekindling the flames of Black literacy. On St. Helena Island, they claimed a brick church that they had built with their own hands for white people a few years earlier to be their schoolhouse. When the missionaries arrived later, they saw Black people pursue education with a passion the visitors never could have imagined. Black people were eager, as one formerly enslaved woman explained, to put behind them the days of crawling "under the house an' lie on the ground to hear massa read the newspaper to missis." As another recalled, they wanted to move beyond memorizing—and later repeating to someone who could decode them—the letters of words that white people spelled out when they "didn't want me to know" something. Formerly enslaved mothers wanted their children to go to school as soon as they "could walk" and were "bitterly disappointed" if they weren't reading by the time they were three or four. One teacher, awestruck by the passion, described those early days of schooling as Black people's "first act on coming to the surface, a kind of instinctive head-shaking, and clearing of the eyes, after emerging from the waters."[8]

They crossed long distances by foot and boat daily, relocated permanently, and rearranged their schedules to ensure their children could attend school, making the first group of teachers far too small to meet the demand. The schoolrooms were, in the words of one teacher, "filled to overflowing with eager, expectant scholars," including their parents. Scenes like this would soon require teachers to abandon places like the Brick Church for buildings that could accommodate more students.[9]

While the Sea Islands' commanding officer, General Thomas W. Sherman, saw schooling as necessary "to enable the blacks to support and govern themselves in the absence and abandonment of their disloyal guardians," Black people saw something deeper. A middle-aged woman who arrived at a school with her children, grandchildren, mother, and grandmother—five generations of enslaved people, spanning from infancy to one hundred years of age—explained it most simply: "Us wants to larn, fur we've been in darkness too long, an' now we're in light, us want to larn."[10]

Over the next three war-torn years—in the Sea Islands and other communities—more teachers arrived, more schools were built, and more children and adults learned to read. Black people demonstrated the power of literacy and, with their teachers, laid the foundation for public education in the South. A generation of Black leaders rose from these communities in the years following the War to demand that the South do right by all its people. Though their immediate priority was to remedy the harms of slavery and elevate Black people to full citizenship, these Black leaders changed life's possibilities for all the South's children, Black and white. Poor and working-class white children had been, albeit to a much different degree, the victims of the slavocracy's anti-education policies too. During Reconstruction, a region that had long refused to provide public education for anyone suddenly tried to provide it for everyone. Southern states wrote public education obligations into their state constitutions, created new methods to finance the obligation, and exponentially increased the number of children, white and Black, attending school.

Yet for all these gains, Black education was still contested. Old ways of thinking died hard and sometimes not at all. A year after the War's end, Edward Pollard wrote *The Lost Cause* as a "vindication" of the "honor of the South" and declared: "Now 'a war of ideas' is what the South wants and insists on perpetuating." The War may have decided "the restoration of the Union and the excision of slavery," but it "did not decide negro equality" or any other issue pertaining to Southern "orthodoxy," which "Southern people will still cling to, still claim, and still assert in . . . their rights and views."[11]

The tamest opposition to Black literacy littered the newspapers with racist rants about Black people's intellectual capacity and maligned the public education system as social engineering designed to use white taxpayers' money to turn Black people against white people. The most violent opposition burned Black children's schools, intimidated students, and tarred, feathered, and fired shots at their teachers. The resistance understood that the public education system not only symbolized the rebirth of freedom and democracy but made it possible. If public education remained free, open, and adequate, it would be the gateway to Black citizenship and a functioning democracy.

When anti-literacy thinking returned to power following Reconstruction, it did not end the public education project but choked its funding and perverted its mission. In place of schools "open to all," Southern constitutions mandated segregation. In place of equitable funding systems, states shifted responsibility to local communities and gave white officials the power and encouragement to divert far more funds to white students than Black students. Southern leaders also began censoring what was taught in these schools, insisting that the War had been about Northern aggression, not slavery, and that the South had treated its slaves well. Any book of history or literature stating the contrary had to be expunged. With the law's blessing, segregated, unequal, and propaganda-based education would remain in place for the better part of a century.

A cyclical push and pull around Black literacy—and then the public education system—stretches from the 1820s to today, forming two distinct lines. One line reveals a Black freedom struggle perpetually anchored in the fight for education. In the antebellum period, literacy marked the line of freedom, practically and psychologically. After the Civil War, education represented a new type of permanent and, proponents hoped, uncontested freedom: citizenship. Twentieth-century civil rights advocates, seeking to end the Jim Crow era, placed education at the center of a renewed freedom struggle. Just like the *Atlantic*'s missionaries and Reconstruction's Black leaders, they believed that if they ended educational inequality, full freedom would follow across all aspects of life.

The Civil Rights Movement's seminal achievement, *Brown v. Board of Education*, stated it plainly. Echoing Thurgood Marshall and the NAACP legal team's arguments, the Supreme Court wrote:

> Education is perhaps the most important function of state and local governments. Compulsory school attendance laws and the great expenditures for education both demonstrate our recognition of the importance of education to our democratic society. It is required in the performance of our most basic public responsibilities, even service in the armed forces. It is the very foundation of good citizenship. Today it is a principal instrument in awakening the child to cultural values, in preparing him for

later professional training, and in helping him to adjust normally to his environment. In these days, it is doubtful that any child may reasonably be expected to succeed in life if he is denied the opportunity of an education.[12]

The nation now confronts another racial reckoning, and education is again taking center stage. Reoccurring police violence against Black people sparked the reckoning in 2020, but the focus soon shifted to public schools. Principals, teachers, and counselors increasingly questioned why law and policy have been so inept in addressing the needs of students of color and other disadvantaged students. Rather than wait for state and federal fixes, some educators attempted their own solutions, applying a stricter lens of equity to their own practices, diversifying the curriculum, adopting humane discipline policies, and making their spaces and programs more inclusive. These educators may not yet be in the majority, but they are trying to make *Brown*'s promise real with the tools at their disposal. Some even explicitly situate themselves within Black people's longer freedom struggle, calling their work "abolitionist teaching."[13]

A second historical line runs alongside the Black freedom struggle connecting the 1820s to today. It reveals white people perpetually resisting Black freedom (and, later, Black equality) through anti-literacy policies, attacks on public education, segregation, and now censorship. In the antebellum period, Southern states criminalized Black literacy, limited the movement of Black people who might spread knowledge, banned any literature perceived as seditious, intimidated postal workers and offices that might carry the literature, and started a propaganda campaign to publish purely Southern newspapers and textbooks—which meant literature that reinforced and staunchly defended slavery and all its tentacles. In the aftermath of the Civil War, those political strains quickly morphed into vigilante violence against Black schools and opposition to the public education project. During Jim Crow, the opposition reclaimed political power and turned public education against Black equality.

Three-quarters of a century later, *Brown* declared this assault unconstitutional, but the reprieve was only partial and short-lived. Much like the Reconstruction era, by the 1970s, violent resistance to school desegregation was reshaping mainstream politics. Having lost the 1960 presidential election on a moderate ticket, Republican nominee Richard Nixon tapped into Southern resistance during his 1968 presidential campaign. Speaking directly to the sympathies of Southern delegates to the

Republican National Convention, he criticized the practice of desegregation busing, saying that when a child was bused "into a strange community ... I think you destroy that child." The fault, he argued, rested with the courts. It was their job "to interpret the law, and not make the law." Only local school districts were "qualified" to make decisions about how best to educate students. With that type of talk, Nixon secured the support of staunch segregationists like Senator Strom Thurmond (who had set the length record with his filibuster of a desegregation bill in 1957) and flipped the South to the Republican ticket.[14]

Once in the White House, Nixon flipped the Supreme Court too. He handpicked four justices whom he believed would reshape or reverse the Warren court's approach to school desegregation. His appointments paid quick dividends. In 1973, the court held that racially imbalanced schools alone did not warrant a remedy; plaintiffs had to prove intentional discrimination was the cause of the segregation. The next year, another of the court's new evidentiary requirements blocked desegregation remedies that crossed school district boundaries—no matter how segregated that might leave schools. Those two holdings severely limited desegregation in the North and paved the way for its end in the South. The final nail in the coffin came in 1992 when demographic shifts became a justification for terminating desegregation orders. By 2004, *Brown*'s fiftieth anniversary, its gains had been lost and schools were as racially isolated as they had been when school desegregation began in earnest in the late 1960s.[15]

Despite the reversal of mandatory desegregation and more recent court decisions limiting even voluntary diversity efforts, white paranoia and hysteria have returned, dominating the daily news with stories eerily reminiscent of the antebellum period. Politicians and ideologues are targeting public education and its values as a source of cultural decay. In 2020, President Trump charged schools with spinning a "twisted web of lies" about the nation's racial history akin to "child abuse" and announced a counter-initiative to ensure "patriotic education" in schools. When his term ended a few months later, state legislatures picked up the baton and banned the supposed teaching of critical race theory, or any ideas that would make white students uncomfortable.[16]

Within a year, states were challenging public education in ways not seen since the massive resistance to school desegregation. Legislatures, governors, and local school districts were taking or considering action to ban books, allow parents to micromanage the education process, encourage families to exit the public school system, fine teachers for teaching objectionable concepts, and eliminate diversity, equity, and inclusion programs. In April 2022, Florida became the first to pass actual legislation in this vein, banning what its governor called "wokeness and Critical Race Theory" that indoctrinates and discriminates against students—particularly white students. That same month, Chris Rufo, a driving force in anti–critical race theory legislation across the country, delivered a speech at Hillsdale College arguing that the ultimate solution to indoctrination was to deconstruct the public education system and replace it with a system of "universal school choice" in the form of private school vouchers.[17]

By October 2023, eighteen states, primarily in the South, had passed legislation that restricts how schools teach and talk about race. Six states also banned or limited diversity, equity, and inclusion programming, either by legislation or executive action. More than half of states operated programs that used public funds to pay the private school tuition of students who opted out of public school. The American Library Association found that "2,571 unique titles were banned or challenged" in 2022 alone, a 40 percent increase over the previous year.[18]

Events at the local level present an uglier picture. Far-right individuals and groups have used outlandish untruths, unruly behavior, and death threats to intimidate school boards, superintendents, principals, and teachers who showed any ambivalence toward their agenda. In just a sampling of districts, Reuters documented 220 instances of threats, intimidation, and violence. "School officials or parents in 15 different counties received or witnessed threats they considered serious enough to report to police." Seeking to ward off such vindictiveness, some school districts began censoring and firing teachers accused of disturbing their students' racial mores in 2021.[19]

The occasional firing or statement, however, was not enough to stop the attacks. Frustrated with what they deemed a school system heading in the wrong direction and denying parents their rights, a group called Moms for Liberty organized to change the balance of power on local school boards. By 2022, the group claimed to have one hundred thousand members in forty-two states and to have flipped seventeen different districts. In Berkeley County, South Carolina, for instance, Moms for Liberty endorsed and helped elect six school board members, who then fired the district's Black superintendent and banned critical race theory within two hours of being sworn into office.[20]

In their bestselling *Battle for the American Mind*, Pete Hegseth and David Goodwin call on more parents to join the "insurgency" to save our children from Marxism, racial indoctrination, and anti-religion. Reminiscent of the 1840s when commentators scoured textbooks and newspapers for any hint of abolition or Northern bias, the current movement sees the enemy's bias hiding everywhere. "From kindergarten to twelfth grade," it is, as Hegseth and Goodwin put it, a "16,000-hour war, for our kids and our country." Consistent with the insurgency mentality, by December 2023, Donald Trump was promising, if reelected president in 2024, to root out Marxist hostility to "Judeo-Christian teachings" in public schools, terminate the "the radicals who have infiltrated the federal Department of Education," abolish teacher tenure, and "certify teachers who embrace patriotic values."[21]

In this environment, a new kind of silence is falling over the nation's classrooms. On newly sensitive subjects, teachers can't teach, librarians can't share books, and students can't learn—at least not freely at school. As Bernard Powers, the founding director of the College of Charleston's Center for the Study of Slavery, said, "A teacher who is faced with teaching the causes of the Civil War . . . might have trepidations as to what they can say and what they ought not to say." The consequence of getting it wrong would be losing their job.[22]

Rather than helping us find a common ground to bridge differences, public education policy is channeling our country's divisions. The historical parallels between these current events and the antebellum period raise disturbing questions. Is educational opportunity for students of color hopelessly constrained by a perpetual cycle of retrenchment? Can reasoned debate replace comforting dogma? Can public education rise above our divided politics and serve its democratic purposes when we need it most, or will it inevitably succumb to polarization?

The quest to rewrite our nation's racial narrative through education—the task envisioned at least a century and a half ago—remains unfinished, but not lost. If this book reveals anything, it is that no structure for repressing education was ever dominant enough to eliminate human agency. The story of Black literacy and freedom of thought is one of continual tension, with factions competing at every level to secure their vision of the world—or at least carve out a space for it.

More specific lessons emerge too. Knowledge truly is power—the power to keep a person enslaved in mind and body, but also the power to resist oppression, the power to seize the reins of self-government, and the power to warp society or reform it. But knowledge, or more precisely literacy, is also food for the soul. As today's world reduces education to a test score, a commodity, and job preparation, the antebellum period reveals it to be much more. Access to education transformed enslaved and formerly enslaved people's view of the world, its possibilities, and their position in it. As the country fights over young people's education again today, it should take stock of what is at stake, the damage it does when it fails our children, and the danger of politicizing something so essential.

History repeatedly illustrates that imposing or lifting educational roadblocks is one of the gravest decisions society can make. Decisions made two centuries ago still reverberate across generations. What follows are the most salient events in the war over Black literacy—some painful, some inspiring, some almost unbelievable. Viewed with a dose of humility, they offer not just a reflection of the past but a guide to the future.

CHAPTER ONE

The Spark

A T THE TURN OF the nineteenth century, white residents of Charleston, South Carolina, had a serious problem. Black residents had a tool.

The racial demographics of Charleston shifted dramatically between 1790 and 1820. Driven by the advent of the cotton gin in 1794, which made large-scale cotton plantations financially attractive, Charleston became America's premier slave trading port and South Carolina one of the largest consumers of enslaved people. While the Black population was generally stagnant in South Carolina in the 1780s, it grew from around one hundred thousand in 1790 to a quarter million in 1820, eclipsing the white population. The shift was even more dramatic in Charleston and the South Carolina low country. There, Black people outnumbered white people by more than two to one. A monopoly on power was not easy to hold under those conditions.[1]

More important, Black Charlestonians had a tool for overthrowing that power—not brute force but knowledge. White people could keep a brute-force threat at bay. Fabricated narratives convinced some Black people of the futility of rebellion. An oppressive thumb and constant surveillance frightened many of the rest.

But the written word offered literate Black people a subversive tool that white people could not easily control. Things that Black people weren't supposed to imagine could be absorbed and contemplated in secret through the written word. And once acquired, knowledge could be shared. A Black person who could wield the written word possessed the power to inspire, to intellectually challenge, and to convince others that Black equality was the natural order. Such a person could also communicate plans for rebellion.

The power of Black literacy traces back most directly to the Stono Rebellion, the largest revolt during the colonial period, which occurred just south of Charleston, near the Stono River, in September 1739 and eventually claimed the lives of around sixty people. The leader, an enslaved man named Jemmy, had reportedly been taught by his owner to read and write. Spain had extended a promise of freedom to any enslaved person who could escape to Spanish-controlled Florida, and historians surmise that Jemmy may have read about that promise. He apparently wrote out travel passes for other enslaved people to allow them to escape. He was leading some forty to sixty men to Florida when they all were killed in a battle with the South Carolina Militia.[2]

Whatever its actual role in the revolt, white people believed Jemmy's literacy was a catalyst. Aiming to stop the next Jemmy, South Carolina passed the Negro Act of 1740, which strictly regulated Black people's ability to travel, carry weapons, defend themselves against white violence, and contemplate insurrection or escape. Ad hoc tribunals, run by magistrates and white landowners rather than actual judges, were authorized to investigate alleged infractions and administer swift justice. Anything that might smack of insurrection was punishable by death.

The law also attacked the presumed underlying cause of the Stono Rebellion—Black literacy. "Having of Slaves taught to write or suffering them to be employed in writing," the act proclaimed, had led to "great Inconveniences." Therefore, anyone "who shall hereafter teach, or cause any Slave or Slaves to be taught to write, or shall use or employ any Slave as a Scribe in any manner of writing whatsoever . . . shall for every such Offense forfeit the Sume of One hundred pounds," the equivalent value of half a dozen horses. Though the law would remain on the books for the better part of a century, South Carolina initially did little to implement it.[3]

At that time, South Carolina was more a backwater colony than an organized governmental unit. Just twenty thousand white people lived in three cities on the coast and a handful of inland towns. Local custom and individual prerogative held more sway than law, particularly in the treatment of enslaved people. But once formally enacted, the Negro Act provided a backdrop for later events.[4]

Eighty years later, the Negro Act and its prohibition on Black literacy loomed large when another slave revolt shook Charleston and the nation. By then, the United States was independent, Charleston was a bustling international seaport, and though the country was increasingly divided over slavery, the South was entirely complacent in its power. A planned slave revolt larger than anything white Americans could have imagined caught them completely off guard.

In 1822, Denmark Vesey, a former slave, stood at the center of an audacious plan—in the works for months if not years—to overthrow the seat of slavery's empire. Charleston officials concluded that, were it not for a last-minute leak before the revolt, the city "would probably have been wrapped in flames," and "plantations in the lower country would have been disorganized, and the agricultural interests have sustained an enormous loss."[5]

For the first fifty years of his life—he was born around 1767—Denmark Vesey barely left a trace in the historical record. Even his birthplace, either the Caribbean or Africa's west coast, escapes certainty. The first record of his existence comes in 1781, when the slave trader Captain Joseph Vesey bought 390 enslaved people on the Caribbean island of St. Thomas and set sail for Saint-Domingue, what would later become Haiti. Denmark Vesey, then about fourteen, was one of them. Though Joseph's crew, noticing the boy's "beauty and intelligence," pulled him from the ship's bowels and gave him new clothes and food during the voyage, he was resold with the others when the ship arrived in Saint-Domingue. A year later, the purchaser forced Joseph to take the boy back because he was epileptic—or, some speculate, was able to fake it.[6]

Denmark Vesey then disappears from the public record for another seventeen years. The only traces are either indirect or retrospective. He spent a year or two at sea and grew to be Captain Vesey's trusted assistant. When Joseph abandoned the sea for the life of a Charleston businessman in July 1783, Denmark Vesey's life changed too. The other people Joseph enslaved likely maintained his residence in the countryside, but Denmark helped Joseph run an import-export business on East Bay Street in Charleston's wharf district.

Douglas Egerton, a leading Denmark Vesey expert, posits that Joseph may have taught the young man to read during this period. Joseph certainly had the aptitude and interest for it. He later spent a decade teaching reading, writing, and other subjects to children for the Charleston Fellowship Society. And while some whites feared any form of instruction for slaves, Joseph was probably not among them. He defied the slave owner archetype, affording Denmark Vesey a measure of economic and other freedom in Charleston, apparently never striking him, and in 1797 serving as a godparent to at least one free person of color. When Joseph began hiring Denmark out, he allowed him to share in the fruits of his labor rather than keeping them all for himself.[7]

It was also in Joseph's interest to teach Denmark. Joseph's commercial business was situated in a district that transacted with merchants from around the world. Denmark Vesey's highest value would have been in communication and business operations, not manual labor. As a literate person able to speak multiple languages, he could play an enormous role in facilitating the running of Joseph's business.

What is certain, though, is that in late 1799 Denmark Vesey used some of the money he earned to buy the winning ticket in the East Bay Lottery. The $1,500 he received allowed him to cross the most important line in America, going from slavery to freedom. Joseph Vesey released him for $600—a low price for a man in his thirties with Denmark's skills. He walked free with at least $900 to his name.[8]

If Joseph did not teach Denmark to read and write, his path to literacy likely began shortly after his freedom. Like so many others, he could have gone through the painstaking process of self-help, maybe reaching out to Joseph Vesey or free Black people who ran their own schools for supplemental assistance. Any of them would have directed him to reading primers, and then to the classics on which they based their schools. Whatever the details, Denmark Vesey possessed a level of literacy later in life that he could not have picked up overnight. He must have spent years developing his abilities.

Winning the lottery gave Vesey the time, space, and resources he would have needed to start—or jump start—his educational journey. He could pick up one of Charleston's multiple newspapers on his morning walk. Beyond shipping news, slavery notices, and mercantile sales, its papers included detailed reports on the workings of national, state, and local government. Congressional debates, diplomatic letters, executive orders, agency reports, and legislative texts were regular staples. If he was looking for a sharper political or cultural edge, he could find it in pamphlets and national papers, which arrived in Charleston's bustling port in a steady stream from across the country. Most notably, antislavery pamphlets—common in Philadelphia but scandalous in Charleston—filtered through the busy docks. Local officials stopped those they caught, but they could confiscate only a fraction of what was arriving.

White profiteers and Black sailors had only to slip the pamphlets into crates or knapsacks filled with other supplies.[9]

Charleston was also rich with books—classical literature, technical nonfiction, and political theory. Its library society, dating back to 1748, is the third oldest in the nation. By Vesey's day, the library stocked more than five thousand volumes of books and magazines on topics ranging from philosophy, religion, ethics, and government to science, literature, and history. These texts did not shy away from the hottest topics of the day—revolution, politics, and slavery. There was also a strong market for privately held books. Every day, bookstores announced new arrivals and individual owners offered their personal libraries for sale on the newspapers' front pages.[10]

Such a city fed Vesey's avid reading interests. He read so much that others called it studying. An obvious starting point for a man searching for universal truths was the Bible. Vesey was so engrossed in the Bible that he was known as "a man of the book." He eventually grew into a class teacher at the African Church—which later became the famous African Methodist Episcopal Zion Church.[11]

But unlike many others, Vesey did not stop with the Bible. He read a bit of everything. He followed the daily newspapers closely, even more so when they discussed slavery. He read antislavery pamphlets, searching for arguments he couldn't find in the papers. He also apparently read texts beyond the average reader: legal texts, political theory, history, and science. His cohorts testified that Vesey kept a large and varied library, and the stories they told about him suggested that he had a good knowledge of obscure world events, history, and classic literature.[12]

Newspapers and pamphlets were Vesey's mainstay, and the current events and ideas they conveyed influenced him as much as anything. He came of literary age during an era saturated with talk of revolution, freedom, inalienable rights, and equality. He lived through the aftermath of the Revolutionary War, the infancy of American democracy, and the extensive public debate around the drafting and ratification of the U.S. Constitution. He drew on these revolutionary ideas and writings for the rest of his life.[13]

Yet, while Vesey was technically free and his intellectual horizons expanding, his life grew more frustrating, not more fulfilling, with time. He married at some point and had children, but the law tightened around his family. All of his children and his wife were born enslaved. If it were simply a matter of desire and resources, Vesey might have purchased their freedom. But the legal context was changing for the worse. In December 1800, shortly after Vesey won the lottery, South Carolina rewrote the law under which he purchased his freedom. Money and the owner's assent were no longer enough. Freedom now required a magistrate and five white landowners to examine the person for "good character" and the ability to self-support. A court would then judge whether the evidence on those two issues was persuasive. South Carolina law would eventually require the General Assembly to approve each manumission.[14]

Vesey's personal freedom also began to narrow. In response to white paranoia over Charleston's growing Black population, the city restricted Black people's movement within its borders and required free Black people to purchase special work licenses. The city also increased the number of guards roaming the streets and permitted them to arbitrarily punish Black people for loud or offensive conversations. White people who murdered Black people, by contrast, needed fear nothing more than a fine.[15]

This reversal of fortune in Charleston felt even more perverse compared with developing events in Haiti, the place where Vesey had once experienced the worst of slavery. In 1801, General Toussaint Louverture and his forces liberated the eastern half of the island of Hispaniola and shared a new constitution that declared to the world that slavery "cannot exist ... on this territory" and "servitude is therein forever abolished. All men are born, live, and die free." When the rest of the island secured freedom three years later and renamed itself Haiti, it amended its constitution and announced itself as the world's first Black republic, "independent of any other power in the universe." Lest there be any doubt, the constitution added that "no white man of whatever nation he may be, shall put his foot on this territory with the title of master or proprietor."[16]

White Charlestonians had long worried that Haitian ideas would infect free and enslaved Black people "with the contagion of liberty." In 1793, when unrest had first begun in Haiti, Charleston officials tried to wall the city off from the contagion, holding ships flying a Haitian flag offshore, under threat of cannon fire, until the officials judged the ship safe to admit to the harbor. Even then, sailors could not disembark. A decade later, the city began tightening its restrictions on "inflammatory literature." On July 4, 1804, Charleston officials arrested a white immigrant for printing and selling copies of a pamphlet telling the story of Haiti's independence and kept him in jail for months after a local court found him guilty of "seditious and traitorous intentions." In 1809, authorities imprisoned a ship's steward when they learned that the ship had brought several hundred insurrectionary pamphlets to Charleston. They released him on the condition that he leave South Carolina and never return.[17]

For all their fear, Charleston residents still desperately wanted to know what was happening with their Caribbean trading partner, and the newspapers obliged with regular coverage of the Haitian Revolution and its political aftermath, from the detailed accounts of violence to revolutionary leaders' thoughts on freedom, slavery, and liberty. Following important developments, the news demand was so high that the *City Gazette* sometimes printed hundreds of copies above its normal run.[18]

Haitian leaders eventually used the newspapers to communicate directly with Black Americans. In a November 1817 letter reprinted in major newspapers, including the *Niles Weekly Register*, the most widely read magazine of the day, Haiti's secretary general urged Black Americans to immigrate to Haiti where they could "partak[e] of those blessings which the constitution we have given ourselves affords" rather than suffer "under the dominion of a barbarous prejudice" of white Americans. Haiti, he wrote, would "wait for them with open arms." He promised that "the government will pay the passages of those who have no means, at the rate of forty dollars per head." In 1820, Haiti's second elected president, Jean-Pierre Boyer, went a step further, offering homesteads to Black people who emigrated there. He made regular news over the next year as he expelled the last of the colonists and united the entire island under free Black leadership for the first time.[19]

Vesey followed all this intently. Each scrap of new information was like a communiqué from across enemy lines. He and other Black Charlestonians tore Haitian stories from the papers and carried them around in their pockets, ready to hand them out to comrades. And lest they miss something, enslaved men working in the offices of Charleston's newspapers would steal copies of papers when they contained "interesting extracts."[20]

Monday Gell, one of Vesey's most important co-conspirators, vividly recounted how Vesey had used Haitian news to draw him into his inner circle. After Vesey and another man marched into Gell's shop, the man accompanying Vesey produced a piece of newspaper from his pocket and told Gell to read it. The story was "about Boyer's battles in St. Domingo against the Spaniards." The two men told Gell that Black people "could do the same" in Charleston.[21]

Vesey and his closest associates were caught by what Julius Scott, a scholar of the era, calls a "common wind" out of Haiti that swept through and inspired Black people throughout the Caribbean and the Atlantic seaboard. Yet, as far as the white community was concerned, the only outward evidence of that common wind in Charleston was Black residents' burgeoning desire for an independent religious community. When the white Trinity Methodist Church voted to build a hearse house on ground occupied by a small Black cemetery in 1817, Black people who had been attending Trinity left in protest and began conducting their own services elsewhere. Their numbers quickly swelled.[22]

In the summer of 1818, the city broke up one of their services, arresting 140 attendees for violating a law that prohibited Black people from gathering for the "purpose of mental instruction" without a white person present to supervise them. Five of the attendees, presumably the leaders, were given the option of a month in jail or leaving the state. Eight others were to be whipped or pay a fine. A week later, a smaller group met in a private home in the suburbs. The city guard invaded the home and arrested them. A Charleston newspaper ran a story reminding readers that the law forbade Black people to assemble without a white supervisor.[23]

Events like these left Vesey incensed. According to one of Vesey's close associates, Vesey complained that Black people's "situation was so bad, he did not know how they could endure it." He even started complaining around white people, once decrying Black oppression in a white man's downtown shop. Vesey must have been considering the idea of rebellion around then, because one of his associates, Gullah Jack, purportedly "wanted to begin" the revolt right after "the negroes of the African Church were taken up."[24]

Other church members, however, wanted to avoid anything that would escalate tension, seeking a worship space that would not disturb neighbors or arouse white suspicions. They petitioned the state General Assembly for permission to purchase two lots to build a church. But the Charleston delegation to the General Assembly actively opposed the proposal, and prominent white Charlestonians wrote a letter to the General Assembly arguing that Black people did not need a church and that empowering them would only lead to more evil. The General Assembly never granted the petition.[25]

This steady stream of insults and injuries seems to have intensified Vesey's religious message. His main objective was to use his understanding of the Bible to challenge the premises on which white ministers justified slavery. They saw God's will and the institution of slavery as one and the same. They pointed to New Testament passages that seemingly endorsed slavery, like Paul's letter to the Ephesians instructing "slaves [to] obey your earthly masters with respect and fear and sincerity of heart, just as you would obey Christ." In his letter to the Colossians, Paul wrote that slaves should obey their masters "in everything," "not only . . . while they are watching." The apostle Peter went further, writing that slaves owe their obedience as much to "harsh" masters as to "good and considerate" ones.[26]

White ministers could easily attach those passages to Jesus's words: "do not resist an evil person. If anyone slaps you on the right cheek, turn to them the other cheek also." Jesus offered an analogous instruction regarding societal practices: "Give to Caesar what is Caesar's, and to God what is God's." The Sunday morning message to white and Black people was clear: the Bible recognized slavery as a legitimate social structure, and the slaveholder, even if evil, was not to be resisted.[27]

Vesey explained to his followers that the Bible's truth was not as simple as white ministers proclaimed. He turned a one-sided, authoritative endorsement of slavery into a debate. According to two of Charleston's magistrates, Vesey "rendered himself perfectly familiar with all those parts of the Scripture" that matched his purpose and "would readily quote them, to prove that slavery was contrary to the laws of God; that slaves were bound to attempt their emancipation." In front of a receptive audience, he could convince listeners that it was he, not white people, who faithfully spoke the word of God. The Old Testament was his sharpest tool.[28]

He grounded his teaching in the Israelites' path from bondage—a story that resonated in the minds of his followers. Witnesses against him would later testify that he had taught "how the children of Israel were delivered out of Egypt from bondage" and had always "identified their situation with that of the Israelites." This Old Testament deliverance story and its militant morals told a much different story than the New Testament. In it, Vesey found a God who stood on the side of the oppressed, not the oppressor, and who intervened in the world not to reinforce slavery but to free the Israelites from it. God consistently assured the Israelites that He would deliver their enemies into their hands if they would follow His will. And following His will did not mean turning the other cheek, fleeing from conflict, or suffering in silence. It often meant smiting those who stood against them, including women and children.[29]

According to one of Vesey's associates, he emphasized the verse in the Book of Exodus that dictated "he that stealeth a man, and selleth him, or if he be found in his hand, he shall surely be put to death." Vesey was infuriated that white ministers did not teach the Exodus story, much less this verse. The parallels to Black people in America were too clear to miss—God's position on slavery too explicit. The explanation was obvious. They intentionally distorted God's words for their own ends. For this, Vesey reasoned, God's judgment was righteous. Vesey longed to confront white ministers directly with this verse from Exodus and kill those who refused to acknowledge it and repent.[30]

With the Bible as his base, Vesey also began layering on everything else he had read and heard in the past twenty years about the American Revolution, the Haitian Revolution, political rhetoric, and classical literature. With this mix, he offered his own unique blend of biblical morals, libertarian theory, classical wisdom, and basic logic. In a shop near his home, Vesey often shared his thoughts with anyone who would listen. According to the shopkeeper, Vesey "would speak of the creation of the World in which he would say all men had equal rights, blacks as Whites."[31]

One of Vesey's associates testified that in more private settings he would press listeners with simple factual questions that led to an unassailable logic. Vesey would ask recruits: "Did His master use him Well? ... Did He eat the same as His master. ... Did his master not sleep on a soft bed. ... Did he ... sleep on as soft a bed as his master. ... Who made his master? God. Who made you—God—And then aren't you as good as your master if God made him and you, aren't you as free?"[32]

If the answer to that last question was yes, Vesey's logic dictated that Black people were entitled to take the same steps that Americans had taken to free themselves from British rule—and that Haitians had taken under French colonialism and slavery. If slavery is wrong, if you are equal in God's eyes to the white man who whips you, Vesey asked, "why don't you ... turn about and fight for yourself?" God required His people to take a leap of faith. If they did, Vesey promised, God would be with them.[33]

Vesey found the same moral in the classics. He was apt to tell the fable of Hercules and the Wagoner. When a farmer's wagon became stuck in mud, the farmer just stood there cursing his situation and calling on the gods for help. But Hercules appeared and rebuked the farmer: "Put your shoulder to the wheel, man, and urge on your horses. Do you think you can move the wagon by simply looking at it and whining about it? Hercules will not help unless you make some effort to help yourself." Black people were no different from the Greeks, Israelites, Americans, or Haitians. One Black man, who refused to indulge in Vesey's ideology but said he knew Vesey and his followers well, testified that Vesey told his followers that "if we did not put our hand to the work and deliver ourselves, we should never come out of slavery."[34]

American politics, interestingly, triggered Vesey's final ideological boost. The ongoing battle in Congress over the expansion of slavery reached a fever pitch when Missouri petitioned for statehood in 1819. Political control in the nation's capital and slavery's future hung in the balance. The Senate, with equal numbers of slave and free states, was deadlocked. Admitting Missouri as a slave state would hand the South a majority. Slavery could spread like wildfire through the territories and eventually swamp free states, forever putting them in the minority. Maine's petition to join the Union as a free state was also on the table, raising analogous concerns for the South.

Congress debated Missouri's statehood for two years. Vesey followed the debate via newspapers and pamphlets as closely as he had followed Haiti. Senator Rufus King of New York, a leading voice in the debates and one of the most accomplished statesmen of his day, captured Vesey's imagination. King characterized slavery as a "nefarious institution" that was "contrary to the laws of nature" and needed to be stopped. In the Missouri debate, King fashioned a creative legal argument that he hoped would reframe the way the nation understood slavery. It was not a political question that the current generation of legislators could resolve on an ad hoc basis, but a technical question governed by the constitutional compact the states agreed to in 1788.[35]

The Constitution acknowledged and accounted for slavery, but King emphasized that it did not affirm slavery as a general principle. Instead, the Constitution treated slavery as an exception to the general rules under which America intended to operate, and a contradiction beyond logical resolution. The contradiction was inherent in the constitutional provision that counted an enslaved person as three-fifths of a person for purposes of congressional representation. If slaves were persons, how could they count as anything less than a full person? But if they were property, as the South claimed, how could they count at all? And how could the Constitution afford some states extra voting power based on slave property when it did not afford political power based on any other property?[36]

These absurdities, King wrote, demonstrated the enormous "concession" the Constitution made on slavery, which ought not to be mistaken for a general rule. It was an exception, a limited agreement among the original thirteen colonies, accepted as "a necessary sacrifice to the establishment of the constitution." If Missouri or any other western state entered the Union as a slave state and took advantage of a three-fifths compromise never intended for it, it would wrest disproportionate political representation from free states. The original colonies would have never agreed to this. It wasn't the deal they struck. The only way to maintain the constitutional republic's foundational principles—equal representation, equal rights, and equal burdens—was for Congress to deny admission to any new slave state.[37]

The genius of this argument was that it removed the issue from the politics of the immediate moment. The issue was about far more than the people living in Missouri or any other territory. It was about honoring the equal rights of every person in the Union. The nation broke its democratic principle of equal representation once—to secure its constitutional founding. Doing so again would be an abomination.

This kind of talk, from no less than a U.S. senator, energized Vesey. He and Monday Gell held regular meetings to keep others abreast of the Missouri debates. Vesey added his own thoughts to the debates, grounding them in fundamental American principles. He blended phrases reminiscent of the Declaration of Independence with his own circumstances, proclaiming that "all men had equal rights, blacks as well as whites." In other instances, Vesey blended the Declaration's ideas with those of the Constitution. He rebuked Black men who cowered in the face of white men, telling them that Black people were "born equal." The Black man's problem, Vesey urged, was not Black inferiority, but that Black people were "deprived of our rights and privileges by the white people."[38]

Talk like this drove home the sharp conflict between the ideas America professed and slavery as Vesey's followers knew it. When a white church elder later pleaded with one of Vesey's lieutenants to repent for his actions, the lieutenant refused, explicitly describing Vesey's movement as falling squarely within the American liberty tradition and remarking that whites "applaud the leaders of the American Revolution, who resisted a small tax on tea; and rather than pay it killed tens of thousands, but what of the tax of our sufferings? Washington was a white man and you idolized him; but I, alas am a black man, and you hang me for the very act you applauded in him."[39]

Though they had yet to focus on Vesey, notable white Charlestonians began worrying about the possibility that Black people's self-prospects were shifting during the Missouri debates. After having largely ignored Black literacy for decades, they began raising the alarm. In 1820, for instance, 140 prominent Charlestonians, outraged that Philadelphia missionaries had arrived the prior year "for the avowed purpose of educating our Negroes," sent a petition to the General Assembly. It was an "evil, and one of the greatest magnitude," they argued, for "Schools or assemblages of [negro] slaves to be taught reading and writing, organized and conducted not only by Negroes and colored people and in some instances by white persons." Although the Negro Act of 1740 technically prohibited only teaching Black people to write, the petitioners believed that teaching them to read was "equally mischievous and impolitick and at variance with slavery."[40]

Their outrage, however, was far too naive and tardy. Vesey had been reading and writing for at least two decades, and his message in the community was already taking root. Literacy had long ago fundamentally transformed his thinking. He had evolved from a cabin boy and shop clerk to a dreamer, leader, and prophet, and had become part of something bigger than himself. Literacy had thrust him into conversation with the larger world. For two decades he had been part of a "mass ceremony" in which he and thousands of others sat down to read, knowing that they were consuming the same information and ideas and interacting with authors across a distant space. As an active reader, Vesey was continually situating himself within or in opposition to distant and nearby communities. He was in solidarity with the Northern abolitionists and Haitian revolutionaries, in defiance of Southern slaveholders, and in a curiously ambiguous relationship with American idealism. He no doubt pondered what kind of nation America was—this nation to which he supposedly belonged—and how he really fit in.[41]

With a newspaper in hand, Vesey could see America—specifically South Carolina and Charleston—for what it was and recoil. Slave owners' letters to the editor and petitions to the General Assembly spewed racist ideology without inhibition. Charleston city officials and the South Carolina General Assembly turned those ideological positions into laws, and the newspapers sympathetically reprinted the laws for all to see.

Even the most mundane parts of the daily newspaper assaulted him, maybe more deeply, as they depicted the cruel circumstances of Black people's lives as a matter of morally acceptable routine. Notices of slave sales, rewards for runaways, and punishment at the slave "workhouse" were as common as the coming and going of ships. Right on its front page, the *Charleston Courier* might announce a "Fifty Dollars Reward" for the "Negro wench Jenny." Deliver her to the "Jacksonborough Jail, or . . . the Work-House in Charleston." Living down the street from the workhouse, Vesey knew well that it was the place where the South Carolina Lowcountry broke and tortured its slaves, reunited runaways with masters, and held any unaccounted-for Black person—even those who claimed to be free but couldn't verify the fact—until eventually consigning them to slavery.[42]

Vesey decided to use his literacy to construct new meanings, create new problems, and posit new solutions. He had moved beyond reading as a mechanical skill for acquiring information and instead used it as a tool for critically understanding reality. And if he could critically examine the world around him, he might disrupt its existing hierarchy of power. No longer was he content—if he ever was—to serve as an empty vessel into which dominant society poured meaning. He engaged in an independent dialogue with texts and became the thinker, the teacher, the opposition. Literacy, as the historian Edward Pearson wrote, "created an incendiary mix" of "organic" ideas that Vesey used to "fashion 'new modes of thought' " that he could use to "overturn existing social relations."[43]

During the Missouri debates, Vesey hung on Senator King's arguments about the fundamental incompatibility of slavery with the American theory of government. He surely mused—or hoped—that the original and limited constitutional compromise was about to run its course. At one point, the House of Representatives passed a bill to block slavery in Missouri and set those currently enslaved there free. He may have hoped that some similar measure might aim at South Carolina one day. But when the bill to block slavery in Missouri died in the Senate, Vesey surely took it hard.[44]

A South Carolina law passed in December 1820, prohibiting any further importation of pamphlets like King's, would have only poured salt on Vesey's wounds. The law provided that

> if any white person shall be duly convicted of having, directly or indirectly, circulated or brought within this State, any written or printed paper, with intent to disturb the peace or security of the same, in relation to the slaves of the people of this State, such

person shall be adjudged guilty of a high misdemeanor, and shall be fined not exceeding one thousand dollars, and imprisoned not exceeding one year.

The law treated Black and white people alike on the first offense, but a Black person who broke the law a second time would receive fifty lashes and banishment from the state. If they reentered the state, they would "suffer death without the benefit of clergy."[45]

Charleston officials later claimed that Vesey had garbled the Missouri debates and misrepresented Congress as having freed slaves. Maybe he did, in an intentional effort to push his community closer to rebellion. Or maybe it was those who repeated Vesey's messages that garbled the Missouri debates. Either way, Vesey would have been fully aware of the bill's fate, and of the subsequent Missouri Compromise, in which Congress admitted Missouri as a slave state and drew an imaginary line extending west from the Tennessee-Kentucky border, treating everything below it as slave territory and everything above it (except Missouri) as free.[46]

Whatever hope Vesey held for a political or judicial solution to America's original sin likely died with the Missouri Compromise. That bill, which Vesey would have read about shortly after its passage in March 1820, made rebellion the only realistic option for the freedom Vesey insisted was Black people's birthright. If Congress was not coming to save Black people, the time had finally come for them to cast off their yokes and make the South let God's people go.

By that time, Vesey was ready to lead the Black community, like their own Black Moses. He was doing far more than just reading the Bible and teaching its basic tenets. He purveyed truth, connected ideas, and applied his own logic to written text. He was able to speak on matters of politics, religion, and law with an authority normally reserved for whites. Even whites acknowledged the stature he had obtained. Mary Beach, the daughter of the former pastor of Charleston's famous Circular Church and close associate of the current pastor, wrote that Vesey was "a man of superior powers of mind and the more dangerous for it."[47]

One Black man testified that Black people feared Vesey more than their own masters, yet not a single story exists of Vesey ever directly harming anyone. Black people more likely feared—if that is the right word—his intellectual power. Being in the room and hearing the radical words he spoke would have chilled the spines of most Black people.

They knew that simply entertaining Vesey's ideas was enough to land them in the workhouse, if not send them to the gallows. As one Black contemporary who survived the period later said, Vesey "was playin wid dynamite."[48]

It was precisely this capacity to leverage literacy into status, power, and knowledge that made a rebellion with Vesey at the lead so plausible. A prominent abolitionist, Thomas Wentworth Higginson, later asked the "ablest" Black Civil War soldiers "why there had been so few slave insurrections." Their answers were "always . . . the same. . . . They had neither the knowledge, nor the weapons, nor the mutual confidence to make any such attempt successful." Weapons and knowledge, however, were not the problem in Charleston. Black residents had the skill and freedom to make, secure, and hide weapons—and knew plenty about the logistics of the city. The problem, as in many other places, was belief. Vesey's critical literacy offered it.[49]

Vesey used his literacy to speak to hopes that enslaved persons normally dared not openly voice. He then elevated those hopes by sharing the alternative world and logic that he had fashioned in his mind. His planned rebellion was idea-based. It wasn't men making weapons or military tactics that pushed the rebellion forward; it was the ideas and emotions that Vesey evoked. He drew on multiple discourses—religious, logical, political, and moral—that flowed through his people, city, and nation to fashion a radical ideology that demanded Black freedom. And his natural audience took from it what they needed to find the courage to follow.

When the Missouri debates concluded, Vesey started calculating his steps toward rebellion. An associate, Frank Ferguson, invited Vesey to join a group relocating to Liberia on a chartered ship. He declined, Ferguson later testified, saying he wanted to "see what he could do for his fellow creatures." He then actively started pulling together the people, resources, and plans necessary to overthrow slavery in Charleston, hosting meetings at his house under the guise of Bible classes. Rolla Bennett, a man enslaved by the governor, testified that Vesey invited him to his home one evening, where he found a handful of other key co-conspirators already assembled. Vesey "told us, it was high time we had our liberty and he could shew us how we might obtain it." At first consisting of a small circle of co-conspirators, the meetings soon grew to include a few dozen men.[50]

Vesey was the only free man at these meetings. He believed that most free Black people were more interested in climbing the social ladder and separating themselves from other Black people than in helping their brethren. Given a chance, he thought, they would trade information to placate or cozy up to whites. Vesey was even suspicious of enslaved persons who maintained close relations with whites.

A "big book" lay at the center of the room during those evening meetings. Initiates presumed it was where Vesey wrote members' names when they joined. Its physical presence and heft quickened nerves. Insurrection was not just idle chatter; the ranks were not thin. Authorities later speculated that as many as nine thousand had agreed to join the cause. The most feared man in the revolt other than Vesey—Gullah Jack—claimed to have spoken to more than six thousand on the plantations. Vesey made sure that the big book—whether it contained thousands of names or none—stayed a secret. When authorities later raided his home, he had already burned it.[51]

Each man in Vesey's inner circle was responsible for developing his own social network on the Charleston peninsula. Outside the peninsula, they divided recruitment by islands and regions. This division of labor served more than efficiency: it was also a way to silo information. Vesey did not need to know the names of a lieutenant's recruits, and recruits did not need to know the inner circle or its overall plan. So long as they remained true to one another, the plan could survive even if one or more of its lieutenants were discovered. If caught, the one rule above all was to give no names.[52]

Vesey and his lieutenant Monday Gell also reached out to their revolutionary brothers in Haiti, again using the power of literacy. Everything Vesey read led him to believe that Haitian president Jean-Pierre Boyer might help. At the very least, he thought, Boyer would readily receive Vesey and his men if they fled to Haiti, and he hoped Boyer would also abide by Haiti's constitutional commitment to expel any slave owner who might follow them. Vesey and Gell prepared at least one letter to Boyer. A recruit who claimed to have visited both Vesey's and Gell's homes multiple times testified that Gell "was writing a letter to St. Domingo to go by a Vessel lying at Gibbes and Harpers wharf—the letter was about the sufferings of the Black and to know if the people of St. Domingo would help them if they made an effort to free themselves." They apparently sent the letter to Saint-Domingue in March 1822, before the planned summer revolt. They knew a cook on the ship whose uncle could present the letter to President Boyer. There is no indication they ever got a response.[53]

On one level, it did not matter. Merely sending the letter was galvanizing, particularly after Vesey read it aloud at an evening meeting. He was doing something no other Black man had imagined possible: appealing to the leader of a distant land, calling on another nation's power for assistance. This made his audacious plan more plausible and, in the eyes of its participants, more of a significant venture.

With recruits, belief, and a social network, Vesey started raising money for weapons and supplies. He passed a hat around at meetings, and a few in the inner circle donated money earned from skilled labor. By some accounts, the group amassed a stockpile of one hundred pikes, a few hundred bayonets, and a barrel of black powder—not enough to arm everyone, but more than enough to get started.[54]

The beauty of the plan was it did not require a massive armed force in the initial hours. Success rested on the element of surprise that secrecy, timing, and coordination would provide. At night, two small contingents—with guns stolen from their sleeping owners' homes—could easily surprise drowsy men at the downtown guardhouse and uptown arsenal and then sack a nearby store that sold guns. If they struck before anyone rang an alarm bell, the chances of stiff resistance were small. Equally important, they would simultaneously knock out the peninsula's only organized forces and take what they needed to overwhelm the rest of the city.

But getting weapons into the raiders' hands was no small task. Moving hundreds of Black people onto the peninsula and into position could rouse suspicion and doom the plan before it started. The solution was to take advantage of the natural rhythms of the weeks and seasons.

During the hottest parts of the summer, many white families abandoned Charleston for cooler and healthier conditions in the North, the upstate hills, or nearby Sullivan's Island. And on weekends throughout the year, Black people descended on the peninsula to attend church, take time off, or collect goods. On any given weekend, the peninsula's banks were littered with canoes of various sizes, capable of carrying anywhere from one to one hundred people. The same canoes could flood the peninsula with troops who could hide at friends' homes. On a predetermined night, they could flank the peninsula's shores, waiting offshore while the men already on the peninsula took the armories.

In the style of a general, Vesey was to lead a cavalry. Though the loud rumble of horses might rouse suspicion, Vesey believed that if they painted their faces white and wore long white wigs, these disguises would create enough ambiguity and confusion for his men to ride through the city killing anyone who might sound the alarm. If they could keep the city subdued for the ten or so minutes the others needed to secure and hand out guns, they would be nearly home free. Their armed men could then disperse through the city, ringing alarm bells to draw white people out. As soon as white men crossed the thresholds of their front doors, waiting insurrectionists would shoot or strike them down.[55]

This coordinated attack would overwhelm, decapitate, and isolate the peninsula. With the city brought to its knees, the larger force quietly assembling in the countryside could march into the city and occupy it, striking down anyone they passed along the way.

Escaping Charleston would be easy—loot the banks and seize ships in the harbor. With money and transportation, Vesey would call on the seafaring experience of his teenage years and sail to Haiti. Even if President Boyer had not responded, he had publicly announced it as a safe haven for Black people.

Vesey chose a historically significant day—July 14—for the rebellion. Thirty-one years earlier on that day, the French people stormed the Bastille in one of the most significant moments in the French Revolution. From Vesey's perspective, the stars were aligning to open a path to freedom.

Just six weeks stood between Vesey and the chosen day when the plan began to unravel. On May 30, an enslaved man came forth claiming another enslaved man, William Paul, had tried to recruit him for a slave revolt. City officials were incredulous. They delayed what one might have expected to be a mass inquisition for two weeks. Vesey lived only eight doors down from the main investigator and near other enslaved men who had been implicated, but they left him alone. They couldn't imagine that a free Black man—a relatively well-to-do one at that—could have any cause to join an insurrection, much less lead one. It wasn't until June 14 that city officials corroborated enough pieces of the wild story to believe it.[56]

Skepticism immediately turned into a witch hunt. Within days, city officers were filling the jail with suspects. On June 19, a tribunal formed and began trying men. A few days later, it was clear that all Vesey had dreamt and built had fallen apart. Over the next few weeks, the tribunal questioned or arrested nearly 150 enslaved men and persons of color. It found 67 guilty, ordering 35 hanged and the other 32 exiled from the United States. It recommended that eleven others be transported out of the state or country, even though it hadn't found them guilty of anything.[57]

Charleston workhouse where enslaved people were jailed and punished.
Courtesy of Library of Congress.

When Vesey stood before the tribunal on June 26, he was fully aware that America would not willingly let him or his people go, and fully resigned to the likelihood of death. He had always insisted that his men not say a word of their plans if a moment such as this ever came. Though all of them, save one, faltered in the end, Vesey kept his vow. He did not name a single person or confess a single fault.

Awaiting him in the jail's makeshift courtroom were two magistrates and five white landowners who had already broken several other men by torture, bribe, and the crushing weight of helplessness. An eighth man—a defense attorney—was nominally on Vesey's side but might as well have absented himself. He was either unwilling to do his job or Vesey refused to confide in him. Either way, Vesey decided to represent himself, raising his own objections and eventually questioning witnesses. Though the stakes could not have been higher or the environment more charged, Vesey remained calm and spoke with authority. The other side, however, made up the rules as it went, having all but predetermined his fate.[58]

Claiming that the Negro Act of 1740 gave it the power to depart "from the principles of common law and some of the settled rules of evidence," the tribunal dispensed with rules of evidence, prohibitions on hearsay, the testimony of accusers, and a jury. When anyone dared question its motives or procedure, the tribunal responded with outrage, even toward a sitting U.S. Supreme Court judge from South Carolina who urged a fair process.[59]

Even South Carolina's governor questioned the legality of the proceedings. In a letter to the state attorney general, the governor asked, "Can a Court of Justice, particularly in criminal cases, be held with closed doors? Can a prisoner be legally tried and convicted without being confronted by his witnesses and everyone of them? Can a corporation legally organize a court for the trial of Felons?" The attorney general's response was lengthy but singular: criminal laws exist to protect "freemen only.... Slaves are not entitled to these rights.... Slaves (according to our Institutions) have no civil rights." They could be tried and punished "in the most summary and expeditious manner." The attorney general admitted he had not even considered that the Negro Act of 1740 might be inapplicable to a free man like Vesey; instead, he assumed Vesey could be "treated by the laws in all respects in the like manner as slaves."[60]

Vesey had learned enough over the years to spot these flaws himself. In what he knew were his final days, he called on the same tools that had led him to that point. He stood tall, spoke confidently, and called on all he knew of justice, logic, and the law to challenge an illegitimate system. Vesey did not deny the charges against him; or if he did, the authorities hid his words from the historical record. Instead, in the face of enormously unequal power, he demanded that America live up to its principles. He insisted that officials disclose his accusers' names. He insisted that the court allow him to cross-examine white witnesses—and presumably the enslaved persons whose stories the white men were conveying. When these and other demands were refused, he insisted that the court was denying him a fair trial. With no awareness of the irony, the tribunal subjected Denmark Vesey to the exact thing that Americans had abhorred about British "justice" since the early 1700s: taking *ex parte* statements from witnesses and allowing only one-sided evidence to be presented in court. Several of the first state constitutions unsurprisingly prohibited the practice.[61]

Yet, Vesey's pleas were lost on the court, save a minor concession regarding the few Black witnesses who were brought in to testify. At Vesey's request, he, not his counsel, was allowed to cross-examine them. It took him a little while to get his footing. His questions initially waffled between a stern authoritative approach and what the tribunal saw as feigned "surprise and concern [at those] bearing false testimony against him." He soon fell back on his wit and assumed more careful tactics, resembling those of a skilled attorney. Thomas Wentworth Higginson, who investigated the trial for *The Atlantic* in the 1860s and apparently queried surviving witnesses, wrote that Vesey looked for small contradictions in witnesses' testimony, and when he "could not make them contradict themselves," he remained calm and trained "his whole mind composedly to the conducting of his defence."[62]

When the short trial closed, Vesey, in Higginson's account, "addressed the Court at considerable length, in which his principal endeavor was to impress them with the idea" that he had no reason "to join in such an attempt." He urged that "the charge against him must be false" and the witnesses testifying against him motivated by "great hatred." Had the tribunal afforded him an appeal to a proper court—to which a free man was entitled—he might have made something of his case or some committed attorney might have come to his aid, but his case was set to go no further than a summary judgment.[63]

All Vesey could do was assert rights that he knew existed in the U.S. Constitution, even if the tribunal refused to extend those rights to a Black man. He called on the tribunal to be better than it was, to treat him as the man he had grown to be, to apply fair rules. That he made these claims with calculated measure before a tribunal that held his life in the balance suggests that he still believed in the power of ideas. He believed words might still save him, or perhaps that they might inspire others. Only at that final decisive moment, when the tribunal rendered its judgment and sentenced him to death, was there any suggestion—a few tears—of weakness or doubt.[64]

The tribunal's final admonishment suggested its members had understood nothing of Vesey or his accusers' stories. He remained a mystery. The tribunal's words belied its confusion: "You were a free man; were comparatively wealthy; and enjoyed every comfort compatible with your situation. You had, therefore, much to risk, and little to gain. From your age and experience, you *ought* to have known, that success was impracticable. A moment's reflection must have convinced you, that the ruin of *your race*, would have been the probable result."[65]

The convenient social assumptions of the day blinded the court to the obvious. Vesey's plan was anything but implausible, and his situation anything but comfortable. A thoughtful court would have sought to answer

Denmark Vesey monument in Charleston. Courtesy of Brenda J. Peart/ Creative Commons, CC BY-SA 4.0 DEED, https://creativecommons.org/licenses/by-sa/4.0/.

fundamental questions: What led an old man who had been nonviolent for fifty years, and free for twenty, to suddenly strike against slavery? How was it that this man could inspire a revolt on a scale never attempted before? How could he involve potentially thousands of people over several months without a word of it leaking?

The answers lay on the surface of Vesey's life. He was one of four to five thousand free persons of color in South Carolina—most of whom lived in Charleston—and just one of sixty thousand Black people in the state. Countless others shared his frustrations, experienced worse oppression, and had more opportunities to respond with violence. Countless others had surely shared hushed conversations of rebellion or even made rudimentary plans.[66]

What set Denmark Vesey apart was his literacy. While he was far from the only literate Black person in Charleston, he was the one most deeply and fundamentally changed by it. He was certainly the one who used literacy to its maximum effect. It positioned him to know things that very few Black men of his time knew, to consider ideas and strategies that very few Black men of his time considered, and to say things that no other Black man dared say. The combination of literacy and courage gave him an authority that no other Black man held. And as a result, his memory resounded well beyond his time in the cries of freedom for generations to come. When Frederick Douglass implored crowds of Black men to join the Union Army in 1863, he offered a simple message: "Remember Denmark Vesey of Charleston."[67]

CHAPTER TWO

The Quarantine

TORTURED AND COERCED CONFESSIONS no doubt injected inaccuracies into Vesey's and others' trials. The number of white Charlestonians who already wanted to suppress Black freedoms in the city certainly created incentives to find danger and conspiracy where none may have existed. The first group of Black men jailed in the investigation would have had to give their inquisitors something—even if they had no real story to share. Vesey could have been a convenient fall guy.

In 1964, the historian Richard Wade posited that Vesey and his colleagues were just engaging in "loose talk" and became the "victims of an insurrection conspiracy conjured into being" by a handful of politicians determined to close the African Church. Douglas Egerton tried in 2002 to put this idea permanently to rest, arguing that its proponents relied on "flawed" premises and "faulty data." But Wade's theory was revived in 2020 by Michael Johnson, who dismissed the trial record as inherently unreliable and argued that Vesey's status as a communicant at the Second Presbyterian Church—which required a rigorous qualification process—was incompatible with his being a revolutionary.[1]

The decades-long consensus among leading scholars, however, is that the plan for an uprising was real. In an edited volume published in 2022 to mark the 200th anniversary of the Vesey affair, the historian James O'Neil Spady analyzed the trial record using modern techniques such as social network mapping and information triangulation to confirm the plot's existence. Manisha Sinha, in the book's foreword, charged skeptics with having "contrived" a "controversy." Egerton also noted that, curiously, they trained their skepticism only on the Vesey plot while ignoring narrative gaps in other slave uprisings.[2]

In confirming the existence of a conspiracy and Vesey's role in it, Spady has added at least one significant new finding. The plot, he emphasizes, is better understood as a "social movement" involving multiple leaders—six or more—of potentially equal importance, some of whom had their own independent networks. As the official trial narratives effectively conceded, in their rush to produce results the investigators may have only scratched the surface of the movement.[3]

Even if the record misrepresented some details in the Vesey affair—like how many people were involved, the imminency of attack, or some of the collaborators' roles—the most important facts are not in dispute: who Vesey was as a man, the literacy he acquired, his ideological leadership, Black people's desire for freedom and independence. Otherwise, it would have made little sense to lay a liberation story at his feet. And sadly, the truth of the Vesey affair did not matter for what followed. Nor did it matter whether white Charlestonians or the broader proslavery movement had a preexisting agenda, though they surely did.

What mattered was that white people feared such a story, would believe Vesey's plot was real, and were forever shaken when they heard of it. For them it was, as the final official report called it, "the most horrible catastrophe with which [South Carolina] has been threatened since it has been an independent state." White South Carolinians were so unsettled that the governor asked the federal military to secure the state for weeks after the plot was thwarted. Vesey's plot also triggered other responses that stood out in comparison with all revolt scares that preceded it.[4]

Earlier revolts produced laws that embodied a level of restraint—restraint born not of benevolence but of self-assurance. From South Carolina's 1740 Negro Act through the early 1820s, Southern states saw slave revolts as anomalies. It was the wayward or deranged individual, confused by too much freedom or information, who caused revolts, not any systemic risks inherent in the institution of slavery itself. There was thus no need to impose new restrictions on one's own slave, or for all states to adopt legislation.

South Carolina's 1740 act had addressed the most obvious factors leading to the Stono Rebellion—literacy, travel, and weapons—but it left other things untouched or ambiguous. Enslaved people could still gather in meetings, particularly for religious purposes, so long as they did not "disturb the peace." Applying the law in 1818, for instance, the South Carolina Supreme Court even sided with Black people after a slave patrol disrupted a religious meeting attended by both Black and white worshipers. Black religious instruction, including literacy, continued relatively unchallenged. White missionaries had long taught Black people to read and write, and nothing indicates that they ever stopped. Three years after the 1740 act, St. Philip's Church in Charleston opened the Charles Town Negro School for enslaved people, and within a month it had thirty students. Georgia copied South Carolina's literacy prohibition in 1755, but there, too, Black literacy continued to expand, particularly in Savannah.[5]

Vesey's revolt, however, awoke South Carolina, and eventually all the Southern states, from their slumber. By the end of the 1820s, the South saw the threat of revolt everywhere. Its source was knowledge: the ability to acquire it, spread it, and share it. Too many Blacks, however, already knew how to read for the South to fully isolate Black people from knowledge. Whites might slow the growth of Black literacy, but those who had already crossed the threshold would always pose a threat. As long as they could lay their hands on dangerous ideas, they could share those ideas with others. And as long as Northerners put dangerous words in print and sent their books and pamphlets to Southern ports, ideas of revolt could rapidly spread.

The South went from a society willing to tolerate a little Black literacy and a smattering of antislavery neighbors to a place of strict orthodoxy. In the several years following Vesey's revolt, South Carolina, Georgia, North Carolina, Virginia, Mississippi, and Alabama all passed new or additional restrictions on Black literacy and information sharing. Local ordinances and individual enslavers imposed their own restrictions in other instances. While Tennessee, for instance, never formally prohibited Black literacy, citizen groups and police in some locations blocked the practice anyway. During this same period, the borders and ports of the South were closing to free people of color from other states—Northern or Southern—and to books promoting Black freedom or equality. By early 1832, there was no more talk of moderating, slowing, phasing out, or ending slavery. Those who wished to remain in the South had but one option: to express full loyalty to slavery's empire.

The audacity and scale of Vesey's plans provoked a new level of fear, in part, because the white community shared and engaged with news of it so widely. State and local officials broadcast Vesey's plot in a way they had not done with previous uprisings. Smaller or distant revolts did not necessarily make the regional or national news. Even a notable revolt could run its course in the news quickly. In 1800, Gabriel Prosser's revolt in Richmond made national news, but Virginia's leaders were content to say less, rather than more, about it, lest the plot and the swift execution of its leaders reflect poorly on the state.

The Vesey affair followed a different trajectory. At first, Charleston officials kept the public in the dark, quietly investigating the matter and holding secret trials. But once the scope of the investigation expanded and public executions began to occur, the rough outline of the plot leaked, and the story spread throughout the nation. The ongoing investigation and trials generated streams of newspaper reports and commentary from Maine and Connecticut to Louisiana and Georgia.

Though historians account for the fact of these newspaper reports, they may inadvertently underplay the importance that the newspapers played in Vesey's revolt and the response. America was grappling with new technologies and services that, at times, seemed beyond its control. Increased and cheaper access to printing presses meant a larger staple of newspapers and pamphlets and a wider array of voices shaping the public narrative. When Vesey was tried, the country was just eight years away from the penny press, which made journalism and daily news reading the purview of the common person. The U.S. Postal Service was also subsidizing, with discount rates, the delivery of newspapers, pushing their circulation farther each year. The South, or at least its peculiar institutions and political hierarchy, struggled to adjust to an open exchange of information and ideas, wanting to leverage the technology to its own ends but not entirely sure what technology and information could do in other people's hands, particularly Black people. If elites could no longer control information and narratives, the status quo that accrued to their benefit might be in danger.

Once the trials were complete and Vesey's revolt apparently averted, recriminations began flying in all directions. Several Northern papers wrote of Vesey's plot as a natural outcome of oppression. The *Niles Weekly Register*, a national news magazine published out of Baltimore, argued, "We must admit that the slaves have a natural right to obtain their liberty, if they can; and hence those who best know what indulgence is, are the most desirous of being masters of their own conduct. The just man cannot blame the slave for seeking his freedom. . . . The system of slavery involves in itself a state of dreadful severity, for it is sustained only by force."[6]

Rather than concede fault in slavery, South Carolina governor Thomas Bennett pointed the finger at Northerners. In an official circular distributed on August 10, 1822, he emphasized that "materials were abundantly furnished in the seditious pamphlets brought into this state, by equally culpable incendiaries; while the speeches of the oppositionists in congress to the admission of Missouri, gave a serious and imposing effect to [Vesey's] machinations."[7]

Hoping to wrest back control of the story and defend themselves against charges of injustice, Charleston officials decided to release even more information about the plot. On August 13, the city council asked James Hamilton, the city intendant who had investigated the plot, to prepare "an account of the late intended insurrection in this city," sharing those facts "as may be deemed of publick interest." Hamilton must have already been at work because he released his forty-six-page report three days later. Covering scores of trials and death sentences, the report raised as many questions as it answered. So, two months later, in October, the court ordered that an official record of the trials be published. Two members of the tribunal that convicted and sentenced Vesey, Lionel Kennedy and Thomas Parker, authored an "Official Report of the Trials of Sundry Negroes," nearly two hundred pages in length.[8]

Like Governor Bennett's initial theory, these reports and the overall Southern response to Northern criticism of the trials homed in on Northern literature as the source of the problem. The reports fed the narrative, aiming to provide proof of this accusation and emphasizing that the conspirators' minds had been swayed by Senator King's objections to slavery in Missouri and by the other abolitionist writings available to them. Fearing that scandalous information was in fact the problem, Southern commentators began to caution against publicly discussing or debating the Vesey affair any further, lest the conversation spawn new threats.

The two reports on the tribunals were meant to justify to the world the mass executions of Vesey and his actual and suspected associates, but whites now saw danger in their continued circulation. In the wrong hands, they offered a blueprint for the next revolt. What was once openly traded on street corners was now to be burned or kept under lock and key in Charleston. Four decades later, Thomas Wentworth Higginson remarked that the reports were "amongst the rarest of American documents." As an army officer wrote when he discovered a copy of the official report stashed away in a Hilton Head attic in 1861, it must have been "thrown out and forgotten by the owner. All the copies which could be found were destroyed after its publication."[9]

The reports—before their destruction—made it clear that the problem was not just troublesome Northern literature but literacy itself. A few months after Vesey's trial, Thomas Pinckney, South Carolina's former governor, published a pamphlet purporting to explain what motivated Vesey's efforts. Although he castigated "indiscreet" Northeastern zeal for "universal liberty," he argued that South Carolina had a homegrown problem: "improper indulgencies" for Blacks, both enslaved and free. The "most dangerous of those indulgencies [was] their being taught to read and write; the first bringing the powerful operation of the Press to act on the uninformed and easily deluded minds; and the latter furnishing them with an instrument to carry into execution the mischievous suggestions of the former." Having been indulged for so long, this "dangerous instrument of learning" would now be difficult to check. Many free and enslaved Blacks had already acquired literacy, and "it is not only impracticable to deprive them of what they have attained, but as it is easily communicated, it is probably that, spite of all endeavors to the contrary, this evil will rather increase than diminish." The state's only hope was to change its racial demographics. It had to wean itself from Black laborers and replace them with free white immigrants.[10]

In the fall of 1822, Judge Henry William DeSaussure, the founder of the *Charleston Courier*, wrote a series of essays, which he republished as a pamphlet on the subject of next steps. As he saw it, South Carolina had three options: send its slaves "out of the country"; emancipate them and permit them "to remain in the country, with or without the civil and political rights of other citizens"; or retain them "in their present condition." For twenty pages, he debunked the practical feasibility of the first two alternatives, leaving the third as the only viable option. He needed but a page and a half to set forth his prescription: confine slaves "as much ... as possible to agricultural labours" and strictly prohibit their education. "It is as true as it is trite," he informed his readers, "that knowledge is power. Education therefore should on no account be permitted. I am aware that this may be considered a hard measure, to close the book of knowledge on the human mind, and shut it out from the delights of learning." But so long as Blacks were to retain their places, "it is a favour to them to keep them in ignorance, and contentment, with their lot." It was also risky, he warned, to allow Black people to gather alone for religious worship. They should always stay within earshot of "their masters," who must teach them "the mild doctrines of the gospel" and "instruct the slave to be obedient, and to serve industriously."[11]

In mid-November, a group of white Charlestonians, purporting to have engaged in an "attentive investigation into the origin, design and extent of the late projected insurrection" and given the matters "mature reflection," drafted a petition to the General Assembly in Columbia and started collecting signatures. The petition identified the problem as permissiveness toward Black people and allowing them the "means of enlarging their minds and extending their information." The petitioners pressed the legislature to shrink the state's Black population by forcing free people of color out of South Carolina and banning the further importation of slaves. Those who remained needed to live under a stern hand: No more hiring out of enslaved persons; no more quasi-freedoms; and no more roaming through the city at will for free or enslaved people of color. The petitioners wanted the state to fund and establish a military force in Charleston and to ban "under severe penalties, all persons from teaching negroes to read and write."[12]

James Hamilton, who had just won reelection as Charleston's intendant and state representative weeks earlier, championed the petition in the House and introduced a bill to match its demands. Hamilton was eager to jump into the spotlight. During the trials, Hamilton had prosecuted many Black people based on mere suspicion, with little to no respect for the process. Situating himself as having saved Charleston from calamity, Hamilton looked to ride the wave of the fear he had helped create in the summer to more political power in the fall. Though he had just won reelection to state and local office, Hamilton declared his candidacy in a special election to fill a recently vacated seat in the U.S. House of Representatives.

Multiple competing political agendas, including on matters beyond slavery, complicated the response to Hamilton's bill in the statehouse. Governor Bennett opposed the bill, sensing that Hamilton and others were exploiting people's emotional reactions to Vesey for their own political gain. Bennett agreed that Black literacy had been central to the flow of seditious ideas in Charleston, but he thought Hamilton's report had overdramatized Vesey's plot and overstated the danger. What Bennett believed had been a small group of active conspirators became for Hamilton the justification for a radical agenda to expel all free people of color from the state and prevent any other Black people—free or enslaved—from entering.

Bennett urged the legislature to focus on enforcing and updating the laws South Carolina already had on the books. He saw no reason to prohibit all gatherings of Black people. It was enough, he argued, to prohibit large and unsupervised assemblies. So long as the meetings were small or supervised by whites, they were not a danger. Similarly, Black education was not an inherent evil—it just needed to be limited to the basics of Christianity. The major need, he argued, was more state officers to monitor compliance with the law.[13]

Bennett and Hamilton, ironically, cancelled each other out by reaching for too much, but in different directions. In addition to requiring substantial new tax revenues, a cadre of new state police officers would have shifted vast new power to Bennett and away from local authorities. Hamilton's removal proposal would have come with an even larger cost for a state so heavily invested in Black plantation labor and the slave trade. In the end, the General Assembly did not adopt either man's agenda. Hamilton's bill failed. And while Charleston got funds for a military installation—now known as the Citadel—to defend itself from revolts, the governor didn't get his policemen.[14]

The historian Lacy Ford also correctly points out that simmering divisions between the low country and the mountainous upstate stymied Hamilton's repressive legislation. With far fewer enslaved people, the upstate was less prone to overreaction and less likely to simply let slave owners of the low country have their way—a story that would play out many more times from South Carolina to Virginia over the next two decades.

Unwilling to leave their fate entirely to the state capital, white Charlestonians took matters into their own hands. Shortly after the public execution of Vesey and his co-conspirators, they looked for other targets. A mob burned down the African Church, displacing nearly three thousand members, according to the church. Then the city went after the church's leaders. Though the investigation never directly implicated him, the city questioned and jailed Reverend Morris Brown, only releasing him on the condition that he permanently leave Charleston in late 1822. A number of other church elders followed, seeing no future for themselves in Charleston. Daniel Payne, who lived through the oppression in Charleston, wrote that it "did not stop" until "our Church in that State was entirely suppressed." Local authorities similarly sought to repress and close Black schools. Once an open city that offered the closest thing to freedom Black people might find in the deep South, Charleston began to close. Black freedoms, Black churches, and Black literacy became the enemy. Independent Black worship and learning ended—at least as far as white authorities knew.[15]

These measures also gave the South Carolina legislature time to rethink its options. After rejecting Bennett's and Hamilton's approaches, the legislature latched on to the theory that while dangerous ideas were the source of revolts like Vesey's, those ideas came from Northerners, and "South Carolina had to take drastic action to prevent outside influence from poisoning and corrupting the minds of slaves." It found an easy target—Black sailors—whom legislators suspected of carrying poisonous Northern ideas into the state.[16]

In what came to be known as the Negro Seamen Act of 1822, South Carolina closed its borders to Black immigration and the revolutionary ideas it might spread. Lest they consort with Haitians or Northerners—or Southerners who had consorted with such persons—any free person of color who left the state could not return. But that is not to say South Carolina wanted free people of color to remain in the state either. All but telling them to leave, the state required free persons of color to pay a fee of fifty dollars a year (more than a thousand dollars a year in today's terms).

The real jolt to the status quo, however, occurred in the harbor. Under the new law, "any free negroes or persons of color" arriving in the state on "any vessel" were to be "seized and confined in jail until said vessel shall clear out and depart from this State." The ship's captain would have to pay the expense of detaining Black sailors. Captains who violated the law faced a $1,000 fine. And any Black persons whom the captain left behind in Charleston—or for whom the cost of detention was left unpaid—faced the unimaginable: they would be sold into slavery.[17]

The 1822 act set off a firestorm of controversy—local, national, and international—that continued through the Civil War. In 1787, one of the major accomplishments of the U.S. Constitution was to place the national economy under the federal government's control and tame interstate competition that undermined the whole economy. States retained sovereignty on many local matters, but commerce and travel that crossed state or national borders were not among them. Congress had the explicit power to "regulate commerce with foreign nations, and among the several states," and individual states were prohibited from arbitrarily restricting access to their ports with extra fees, duties, or inspections.[18]

The Quarantine

But the constitutional compact was also about individual rights. Before the Civil War, the Constitution secured very few individual rights against state interference, but it did protect one very important right: Americans had the right to come and go as they pleased, and cross any state boundaries they pleased, without fear of reprisal or targeted discrimination. The Constitution guaranteed that no matter where a citizen of one state went, he was "entitled to all privileges and immunities of citizens in the several states." And if he decided to stay, the new state had to give "full faith and credit" to any relevant "public acts, records, and judicial proceedings of every other state."[19]

The Negro Seamen Act trampled on all these lines. What had been a purely local matter—how a state dealt with people it enslaved—suddenly became a national and international problem. Interstate and international shipping businesses depended on free men of color for their operations. Like the young Denmark Vesey, these Black sailors possessed invaluable knowledge of languages, commerce, the sea, and the ports. Their faces were familiar sights in ports all over the eastern seaboard, the Caribbean, and the Gulf Coast. When they stepped off a vessel, white and Black men alike greeted them, did business with them, and relied on their word.

It was implausible to ask these men to step off their ships in Wilmington, North Carolina, and wait to be picked up on some later voyage north. Nor could a ship simply skip Charleston and head to Savannah instead. Charleston was the central hub. The indignity of sitting in jail was no better. More important than the jobs they had to do, these men held citizenship in their home states or countries. Massachusetts, for instance, had abolished slavery in its 1780 constitution. Several Northern leaders took the position that Blacks were now citizens in free states. South Carolina countered that the citizenship argument was convenient, if not spurious, given that these Northern states continued to exclude Black men from military service and voting. But state citizenship in Massachusetts, it would seem, was a matter for Massachusetts to decide, not South Carolina.[20]

If Massachusetts declared Black men citizens, the Constitution barred South Carolina from excluding them from its borders or treating them like slaves—much less re-enslaving them—simply because they arrived in Charleston's port. When South Carolina persisted, it ripped the scab off the wounds from the Missouri Compromise. During the Missouri debates, Northern senators sought to deny Missouri admission to the Union because its constitution barred free Blacks from immigrating there. The federal Constitution, they argued, prohibited even a slave state from doing that. Congress ultimately approved the Missouri Constitution anyway, but only under the condition that Missouri would not enforce the provision in any way that might conflict with the privileges and immunities clause of the U.S. Constitution. Summarizing the debate, Michael Schoeppner, a leading historian of the era, explains that "those who believed free blacks to be citizens would read the provision as a limitation on Missouri's power to restrict them. Those who denied the existence of black citizens saw the provision as an empty one."[21]

Now, South Carolina had enacted a law that could not be reconciled with the U.S. Constitution. South Carolina did not care. Rather than just declaring that its Black residents were not citizens, it claimed the power to treat Black citizens from other states and nations much like slaves when they passed through South Carolina. In other words, South Carolina's approach to Black citizenship and rights would trump every other state and nation's approach when those citizens entered South Carolina's waters. The number of Northern and international vessels passing through Charleston's busy port—and the fact that they regularly employed free Black sailors—made the Negro Seamen Act a recipe for international and domestic conflict. Even if the United States acknowledged and allowed slavery, one of its major trading partners did not. Britain had abolished the international slave trade in the 1770s and had been sending ships with Black sailors into U.S. ports—fully in accordance with U.S. law—for decades.

South Carolina recognized, however, that its argument could come back to bite it. If it could ignore Massachusetts's position on Black citizenship in Charleston, then Massachusetts could ignore South Carolina's position on slavery in Boston. The tension, along with its impact on commerce, was immediately obvious to some leading statesmen and jurists in South Carolina. The Negro Seamen Act's proponents responded by justifying the law in terms of a state's right to protect the health, safety, and welfare of its citizens, not to intrude on other states' prerogatives. All the federal Constitution's provisions about commerce and travel aside, states had always retained the power to quarantine visitors and goods that posed a health threat. South Carolina—and any other state—could, for instance, force a visitor infected with or exposed to cholera to remain in quarantine any time it wanted.

The Negro Seamen's Act, its advocates argued, was simply placing Black sailors in the same category as it had always placed potentially sick people, just on a different presumption—that Black men coming from other jurisdictions carried a higher risk of having been infected with revolutionary ideas regarding slavery. The federal government had long recognized states' rights to quarantine passengers and goods that might pass on contagion or pestilence, and there was even precedent for applying this rationale to slavery. Early in the Haitian Revolution, in 1793, Charleston authorities had quarantined a Haitian ship, the *Maria*, on the pretext that the ideology of Black liberty would spread if it was not contained. The fear of revolution on U.S. shores was palpable enough that even skeptics conceded to the quarantine. Now, following Vesey's revolt, with its apparent Haitian connections, Charleston's elites, prodded by Hamilton, believed that the contagion had returned and was directly threatening Charleston, if not the entire state. Vesey would not have spared a single white life. South Carolina had the right to defend itself against this contagion.[22]

The controversy escalated in January 1823 when Charleston authorities began jailing free Black men on British and American ships. A coalition of Northern shipmasters petitioned Congress to intercede on behalf of "native citizens of the United States," whom South Carolina was stripping of their "liberty." The state was also, they claimed, interfering with the shipmasters' right to secure these men's services. Congress, however, had no interest in engaging the issue so soon after the massive fight over Missouri. The issue fell to the courts.[23]

A ship out of Philadelphia arrived in Charleston in January carrying two Black crew members—a cook and a steward. The Charleston sheriff boarded the vessel, forcibly removed the two men, and took them to jail. Their captain, Jared Bruce, filed suit in South Carolina state court on their behalf, arguing that the men had been jailed in violation of the U.S. Constitution. Both the trial and appellate courts rejected the constitutional claim, but the appellate court ruled in the Black men's favor on other grounds. The court presumed, incorrectly, that the crew members were slaves rather than free men and ruled that the Seamen Act did not apply to them. While clearly a relief to those two men, the decision announced no principle that would deter the state from imprisoning other Black sailors.[24]

But when Charleston began seizing foreign citizens as well, international diplomacy kicked into gear. In February, Great Britain's foreign minister complained to Secretary of State John Quincy Adams that a "vessel under the British flag has experienced a most reprehensible act of authority under the operation of the law." After conferring with President James Monroe, Adams assured the foreign minister that "measures were taken by the Government of the United States" to resolve the matter and ensure that it would not reoccur. Though no official communiqués survive, Charleston authorities apparently got the message. Arrests effectively ceased. The sheriff and harbormaster stopped boarding vessels, particularly British vessels, to inspect for Black passengers.[25]

South Carolina's governor and the legislators who had pressed for the Negro Seamen Act were incensed. They believed that aggressively policing Black life and closing the harbor to free Blacks and outside ideas were essential to white citizens' safety. With the sharp initial fear from Vesey's revolt receding, they were concerned that the state was falling back into its slumber.

To draw attention to the issue, a private group of citizens, dominated by prominent Charleston residents, formed the South Carolina Association on July 24, 1823, with the purpose of ensuring "the due enforcement of those laws" regarding "the negro population, their number, employments, habits, and peculiar characters." The organizers included several who had helped prosecute Vesey and his co-conspirators. A little more than a year after Vesey's plot, they complained, the remedial state law already "lay dormant on the statute book," leaving "all the methods of corrupting our negroes ... as operative ... as ever." By November, the association claimed more than three hundred members and took direct aim at the legislature, petitioning the Senate to show "OBEDIENCE TO THE LAWS."[26]

Whatever impact the South Carolina Association had on the statehouse, its members held sway in Charleston. During the summer of 1823, they managed to undermine the truce that Adams had seemed to secure early in the year. The British ship *Homer* had arrived in Charleston's harbor in March 1823 and remained there. Then, at some point in the summer, Charleston officials came aboard, seized Henry Elkison, a Black British man, and carted him to jail. The local British Consul tried to intercede, but to no avail.

Elkison turned to the federal courts. The case landed with Justice William Johnson Jr., a U.S. Supreme Court justice who also presided in the federal trial court of Charleston. Elkison couldn't have drawn a better judge. Months earlier, Johnson had publicly expressed concern over how state and local officials had dealt with the Vesey affair—from the process surrounding the slave trials to the substance of the Seamen Act itself.

Johnson wasted no time in reaching a decision in Elkison's case, issuing his opinion on August 1, 1823. He found the Seamen Act to be a clear violation of federal law. The power South Carolina claimed, he wrote, could not "be exercised without clashing with the general powers of the United States to regulate commerce." The United States' power over international and interstate commerce "is a paramount and exclusive right," so exclusive as to "sweep away the whole subject and leave nothing for the state to act upon." Constitution aside, the "seizure of this man, on board a British ship, is an express violation of the commercial convention with Great Britain in 1815." Yet, Johnson indicated that he could not issue the precise relief that Elkison requested: release from jail. Only a state court, he explained, could issue a writ of habeas corpus to a state jail under these circumstances.[27]

Leaving Elkison in jail did not spare Johnson any barbs. A long string of local newspaper essays attacked him from every imaginable angle. His personal character, legal acumen, grasp of the facts, and logic all came under question. Written under the pseudonym Caroliniensis, a series of essays published in the *Charleston Mercury* accused him of "fanaticism, false charity, [and] fashionable humanity," and of favoring the British Empire, "a cruel and unnatural parent" out to "destroy her own children." One essay in the series equated him with a Northern agent who sought to force South Carolina to accept thousands of free Blacks into the state's jurisdiction and allow them to "reside and remain as merchants."[28]

Though powerful in its logic, Johnson's opinion was effectively a dead letter the day he announced it. South Carolina had no intention of changing its position toward Black sailors. Three days after publishing his opinion, Johnson wrote to Thomas Jefferson, seeking counsel. He admitted to "gloomy doubts crossing my mind respecting the Destiny of our beloved Country. Those who cannot govern us may perhaps succeed in dividing us. . . . My Ears are shocked at Times by Expressions that I hear on the subject" of disunion. Recalling the violence and divisions accompanying the Missouri debates, he worried about new pushes for disunion, and whether he, a loyal Southerner, could remain in the South. Johnson said he had already received "a Warning to quit this City."[29]

The tension surrounding the case was palpable all the way to Boston. A month after Johnson's opinion was published, John Quincy Adams attended a formal dinner for thirty or so statesmen and military men. When the conversation at one table turned to Johnson's decision, tempers flared. Only a change of subject prevented things from spiraling further. By

January 1824, Charleston officials were stirring trouble again. They jailed four Black British sailors traveling on the *Marmion*, setting off another round of furious international diplomacy. This time everyone got involved: President Monroe, John Quincy Adams, the U.S. attorney general, British officials, South Carolina governor John Wilson, and the offending Charleston officials. Attorney General William Wirt, relying on Justice Johnson's opinion, advised the secretary of state that the Seamen Act violated both the Constitution and U.S. treaties. But Governor Wilson was more emboldened now than before.[30]

By November he was taking the position that South Carolina was not bound by the Constitution or international treaties because the "law of self-preservation" superseded both federal and international law. The state's first responsibility was "to prevent, if possible, such encroachments as eventually would lead to the injury and destruction of all the citizen holds most dear." In discharging that responsibility, "South Carolina has the right to interdict [people] whose organization of mind, habits, and associations, render them peculiarly calculated to disturb the peace and tranquility of the State, in the same manner as she can prohibit those afflicted with infectious diseases, to touch her shores." It needed no federal or international permission for interdiction. South Carolina and its people "alone" could "judge" when the "peace and security of the community" were at risk.[31]

When he addressed the legislature in early December, he unleashed more fiery words of disunion and violence. Any attempt to interfere with South Carolina's rights of "sovereignty and independence" would lead to calamity. "There would be more glory in forming a rampart with our bodies . . . than to be the victims of a successful rebellion, or the slaves of a great consolidated Government." The South Carolina House and Senate offered up their support with their own resolutions, declaring the Seamen Act an exercise of the power of "domestic police absolutely necessary to insure the safety of the citizen" and echoing the governor's logic regarding self-preservation as a right that can never "be renounced" or made subservient to any other "Power whatever."[32]

This states' rights argument, a self-serving justification for suppressing Black people in the aftermath of Vesey's plot, became the foundational logic animating Southern resistance to Black equality for the next century and a half—from the Civil War through the Civil Rights Movement, and sometimes even today. Michael Schoeppner correctly highlights that rather than "inconsequential laws reflecting over-reactive"

Southern hysteria, South Carolina's Seamen Act was the vessel through which the South first fully tested its theories regarding "the contours of federal commercial authority, the limits of state policing power, and, most importantly, conceptualization of U.S. citizenship."[33]

South Carolina's theory of expansive state authority vis-à-vis the federal government immediately took hold outside the state. Earlier in the year, on February 6, 1824, Georgia had proposed an amendment to the U.S. Constitution that would codify Southern states' rights to exclude Black seamen: "No part of the Constitution of the United States, ought to be construed, or shall be construed to authorize the importation or ingress of any person of color into any one of the United States, contrary to the laws of such state."[34]

The rule of law—if it had ever really existed in the South—was eroding in the service of slavery. Justice Johnson, who had sought to uphold it in the summer of 1823, began to see how little it would mean in South Carolina. A year after his opinion, in a letter to John Quincy Adams lamenting the continued enforcement and escalating violence of the Seamen Act, he shared the story of Amos Daley, a Black man from Rhode Island who had come through Charleston. Local authorities did not just jail him. They lashed him like a slave, twelve times. Such violence, Johnson warned, would have no bounds in the hands of a Southern power that increasingly disregarded any rules not of its own making. South Carolina authorities claimed "the power of inflicting, in the most summary manner, twelve thousand lashes, should they think proper."[35]

Even as a Supreme Court justice, Johnson wrote that he felt "destitute of the power necessary to" protect the constitutional rights of men like Daley. South Carolina would respect no judicial power or authority that ordered the end of these atrocities. And the South Carolina Association's influence was rising beyond any legal authority's control. "The district attorney," he pointed out, "is himself a member of the association; and they have, further, the countenance of five other officers of the United States in their measures." Johnson felt he could do nothing but "look on and see the Constitution of the United States trampled on by a set of men." He pleaded for Adams to bring the matter to the attention of the president, who might issue "an official remonstrance." No word from the president ever came.[36]

Meanwhile, white South Carolinians were circling the wagons. South Carolina's government had to stay united and vigilant against outside influence. The national contest over Missouri in the 1820s and the

Whitemarsh Seabrook. Courtesy of South Carolina Governor's Mansion.

federal dispute over the Seamen Act had shown that the North was unsympathetic to Southern interests.

Fearing that the battle line might soon move from interstate commerce and travel to slavery itself, proslavery theorists began working on their ideological defenses. Whitemarsh Seabrook, a rising political star from one of the most prominent slaveholding families in South Carolina, laid down an important foundation in his 1825 pamphlet *A Concise View of the Critical Situation and Future Prospects of the Slave-Holding States, in Relation to Their Coloured Population*, which would shape proslavery arguments for the next decade and eventually send him to the state senate and governorship.

The pamphlet warned that "the tenure by which we hold our slaves, is daily becoming less secure, and more the subject of acrimonious animadversion." This "crisis" had started with the Seamen Act, Seabrook wrote, but it would not end there. Nothing less than "our property, and ... Southern influence in the national councils" hung in the balance. Once the Missouri debates made the idea of Black freedom a topic of discussion in polite company, abolitionist talk freely proliferated. Now it was moving federal power not only against the spread of slavery but against its continuation where it was long established.[37]

The signs were everywhere: an 1823 Ohio resolution, which four other states had joined, calling for the "gradual, but entire emancipation of slaves"; petitions and proposals in Congress to send emancipated slaves to colonies in Africa; and continued federal efforts to thwart the Seamen Act. The press and religious leaders were fueling these efforts by portraying slavery as contrary to Christianity and democracy and by making it possible for people to casually discuss emancipation. The abolitionists knew, Seabrook wrote, that none of their radical measures would succeed, but that wasn't their point. They aimed to slowly soften Congress to other antislavery measures in the future. And Great Britain looked on from afar, sowing "the seeds of disunion."[38]

Seabrook's primary contribution was to buttress the states' rights claim against shifting political winds. The South's dominion over slavery, he argued, did not rise or fall with the contagion theory but was rooted in the national Union and Constitution themselves. Southern states had entered the constitutional compact on the premise that other states—even if a supermajority—could not attempt "to alter the conditions of our society, or fundamentally to change the form of our government." Otherwise, Southern states never would have yielded their sovereignty to the Union. This fact, Seabrook emphasized, made calls to abolish slavery by constitutional amendment—even if enslavers received "equitable remuneration"—an express breach of the "political contract" states had entered. A monarchy might exercise such power, but never a republic.

Having put to rest, in his own and many of his readers' minds, the question of whether the South had a right to enslave people, Seabrook argued that the only open question was how the South might treat the people it enslaved. Here, too, it was important to resist Northern liberalization. "Our history has verified the melancholy truth, that one educated slave, or coloured freeman, with an insinuating address, is capable of infusing the poison of insubordination into the whole body of the black population." Once educated, "he will intentionally misrepresent facts, and draw with a deeper colouring the lineaments of those baneful pictures, with which he may be furnished." It was true of the Stono Rebellion and it was especially true of Vesey. The "injudicious speeches on the Missouri question animate[d] Vesey in his hellish efforts." The debates, and a misreading of the word of God, had served as "guidance" and had infected him with the "most 'wild and frantic ideas of the rights of man.' "[39]

Seabrook also fired a warning shot at the press. He professed fidelity to the freedom of the press in one line, only to limit it in the next: freedom of the press should apply only to literature within the scope of accepted Southern norms. It was the "solemn duty of every citizen" to check the "unbridled fanaticism" of writing that threatened the tranquility and "permanency of our happy institutions." The same applied to religion. "So long as [its] influence shall be confined to its legitimate sphere," it was a virtue. "But whenever some direful cause shall propel it beyond its proper orbit, ... obedience to its admonitions" is no longer warranted.[40]

Seabrook closed with a point many now deny: the nation's wealth—North and South—was built on slavery. In 1823, Southern cotton, rice, and tobacco accounted for three-fifths of the nation's exports. This tide of Southern goods lifted all boats. It caused more ships to be built in the North, more goods to be manufactured, more employees to be hired. Louisiana and South Carolina each produced more exports than all the Northeastern states combined. The North, thought Seabrook, was in no position to judge or bully the South.

Saber rattling—from Charleston's elites to the governor's mansion—ultimately carried the day. After Johnson's fleeting decision, no one—not Congress, the president, or the courts—interceded in South Carolina. It enforced the Seamen Act unhindered and rebuffed calls to moderate it. The federal government grudgingly accepted South Carolina's premise that the Seamen Act was not a restriction on commerce or on individual rights. It was simply a quarantine law pursuant to state police power—something the Constitution did not reach. As to how South Carolina treated the people it enslaved, abolitionists could not muster nearly enough support to pass a constitutional amendment or prompt legislative action by states. Sadly, Seabrook was right. Slavery was too deeply intertwined with the national economy and abolition too radical for the average white man—North or South.

Although Vesey had aroused South Carolina to extreme action, the rest of the South did not feel the same fear. Other states supported South Carolina's states' rights claim, but they did not see the need to suppress literacy in their own Black populations—at least not yet.

CHAPTER THREE

The Word
David Walker

SIX YEARS AFTER VESEY'S execution in 1822, another man, David Walker, picked up, at least ideologically, where Vesey left off. Rather than the sword, Walker used the written word, authoring the most revolutionary antislavery document America had ever seen, *Walker's Appeal to the Coloured Citizens of the World*. Southern commentators damned the document as a threat to their way of life and very existence. Even a Federalist-aligned Boston newspaper, the *Columbian Centinel*, called it "one of the most wicked and inflammatory productions that ever issued from the press."[1]

But for Blacks, North and South, it was a call to unity and action as powerful as Thomas Paine's call for the American Revolution in *Common Sense*. Walker's biographer, Peter Hinks, wrote that the *Appeal* gave Black people "the courage to take a public stand" against slavery and the rising tide of new anti-Black policies coming out of the North and South. Looking back on it a full fifty years later, Frederick Douglass saw *Walker's Appeal* as the polestar of the Black freedom movement. It had "startled the land like a trumpet of coming judgment." Though Walker's name is relatively obscure today, his *Appeal* ranks alongside the writings of Martin Luther King Jr., James Baldwin, Malcolm X, and Frederick Douglass in political significance.[2]

Walker, however, arguably stands alone in one key respect. Others' writings grew out of and intermingled with a Black oral tradition whose lineage is so deep and wide as to evade starting and ending points. But Walker, many would argue, is the fountainhead of the African American literary political community—or what Robert Levine, a scholar of African American literature, more specifically calls "Black Literary Nationalism." Other Black authors and advocates preceded him, but Walker was the first to truly nationalize Black identity and politics through writing.[3]

Walker's path to prominence, though not as dramatic as Vesey's, was shrouded in its own mystery. He was born in Wilmington, North Carolina, in 1785 to a free woman of color and an enslaved father. Legal status followed the mother in North Carolina, so Walker was free—but his freedom was no wider than Vesey's. In some respects, it was narrower. Wilmington, resting at the mouth of the Cape Fear River, had much in common with Charleston. Both were trading ports that relied on skilled Black labor and drew free Blacks looking to eke out a living. But Wilmington was much smaller than Charleston, with a smaller Black population. It offered fewer economic opportunities, less capacity for a self-sufficient Black community, and greater leverage to whites to impose their will. And Wilmington's restrictions could be harsher. For instance, enslaved people were not even allowed to purchase items from whites without written authorization.[4]

Even less is known of Walker's life in Wilmington than of Vesey's in Charleston. Sometime between 1815 and 1820, he left Wilmington for Charleston, presumably in search of better employment. He apparently did not have the skills of a carpenter, blacksmith, or drayman—typical employments for a Black man in a Southern city of Wilmington's size. But Walker was highly literate and socially oriented. His skills, or possibly the allure of a community and religious associations that might move the dial on Black freedom, made Charleston a better fit.[5]

He likely crossed paths with Vesey in Charleston. Even if Vesey didn't know Walker, Walker surely would have known Vesey—and his leading associates—given the attention he drew to himself. The cadre of literate Black men in the city may have numbered as few as several hundred, and probably no more than two thousand. Many in this group earned Vesey's disdain for cozying up to whites at the expense of their brethren, but Walker would not have been one of those, making the likelihood of their acquaintance stronger. The harder question is whether Walker constructed his view of racial justice before or after he came to Charleston. Either way, Charleston—and likely Vesey—fed Walker's passion.[6]

Walker, curiously, never publicly acknowledged a connection to Vesey. He didn't even comment generally on Vesey's or others' trials or executions. But Walker was not the only one to stay silent. Vesey's church, the Charleston branch of the African Methodist Episcopal Church, also remained carefully silent after Charleston's head of police tried to tie the church to Vesey's plot, burned it to the ground, and jailed its members. Walker had his own personal connection to the church. When he left Charleston, not long after Vesey's execution, the best evidence suggests he went to Philadelphia, the church's national headquarters—the same place to which Reverend Morris Brown and other church members fled. In Philadelphia, Walker apparently developed a relationship with the head of the African Methodist Episcopal Church, Bishop Richard Allen, whom Walker later held up as an exemplar in his writings. Walker's and others' silence about Vesey suggests an agreement—maybe for their mutual safety—not to speak openly of the Vesey affair (which Vesey himself had always urged).[7]

Clearer is that Walker left Philadelphia for Boston in late 1824 or early 1825. Within a year, he opened his own business, selling used clothing, a few blocks west of Faneuil Hall and north of the Old State House. He was successful enough to buy his own home—one large enough that he eventually rented rooms to boarders. By 1826, he was climbing the social ranks in Boston's Black Masonic Lodge, Prince Hall, earning initiation as a first-degree member in July and a master in August. Moving in the lodge's circles, he built relationships with Boston's Black elite, who notwithstanding their small ranks had been protesting slavery for decades.

Walker, however, wanted to expand his network and advocacy beyond the lodge—and beyond Boston, for that matter. Newspapers were the perfect venue. Droves of white newspapers were already circulating across the country, printing matters of immense importance to the Black community, like the Missouri statehood debates. But Black voices—particularly those of former slaves—were excluded from their pages. Hearing from the very subjects of the debate—Black people—was considered irrelevant. When Secretary of State Henry Clay, for instance, proposed to colonize free Blacks in Africa, Black leaders were skeptical if not hostile, but their voices never appeared in popular print. The only debate that seemed to matter was that among white people.

In 1827, Walker joined a small cadre of men working to build the foundation for a regional and national Black press. The prime movers included

Samuel Cornish, the minister of the first Black Presbyterian Church in Manhattan, and John Russwurm, the third Black person to graduate from an American college. Disgusted with the white presses, they founded the country's first national Black newspaper, *Freedom's Journal*. But getting the project off the ground required resources and collaboration outside their home base in New York City. They reached out to David Walker in Boston, and four weeks before the first issue went to print, Walker hosted a meeting in his home to encourage local Black leaders to support the *Journal*. At the meeting's end, Walker and his invitees promised their "utmost exertions to increase its patronage." Walker dove into the project, acting as a subscription agent for the paper in Boston and other cities. Two years later, Cornish and Russwurm split due to editorial and political differences, and Cornish started another Black newspaper called *The Rights of All*, which Walker also circulated.[8]

The immediate hope of Walker and his cohorts was to use the newspapers to oppose the colonization movement. They needed to offer a full-throated denunciation of colonization and its underlying premise—Black inferiority. The more this notion festered unchecked, the worse it would be for all Blacks. *Freedom's Journal* asserted what colonizers would not admit—that colonizers saw all Black people as slaves in some form and considered even free Blacks unfit for citizenship. None, they believed, should remain in America. Colonization might sound benign on the surface, but at its core, as Walker and his colleagues saw it, it was a capitulation to the South's hardening positions on slavery.

Newspapers like *Freedom's Journal* served a longer-term purpose, too: building a national Black political community. Denmark Vesey had received information and ideas from people outside his orbit through newspapers and books, but it was a one-way street. He was always on the outside looking in. *Freedom's Journal*, conversely, was by Blacks, for Blacks, and about Blacks. The inaugural issue, which came out on March 16, 1827, made its nationalist design clear: "It is our earnest wish to make our Journal a medium of intercourse between our brethren in the different states of this great confederacy." The written word, not secret meetings or word of mouth, would "link together the disparate and scattered African American communities of the early Republic" and allow them to use the paper "to plead our own cause." For the first time, there would be an open and wide-ranging regular communal conversation about the problems confronting the Black people.[9]

As an agent working to expand the paper's circulation, Walker began building the knowledge and relationships that would later allow him to breach the South's information silo. He made connections that could take a pamphlet from Boston to Baltimore, Wilmington to Charleston, Savannah to New Orleans, and everywhere in between. He got to know the people who could place stacks of pamphlets in another person's arms at a Southern port, to be carried inland by river or horse, where another person might read the pamphlet eagerly, pass it on, or read it aloud to an audience. By 1828, he was part of a network that could tap into hundreds if not thousands of people. *Freedom's Journal*, for instance, had nearly fifty distribution agents who circulated the paper in fourteen states. From there, the web could expand in unknowable ways. Walker's biographer writes that, by late 1828, Walker was "riding a surge of faith that it was an unusually auspicious time" to connect America's Black communities in a conversation about their collective future.[10]

As soon as circulation for *Freedom's Journal* hit its stride, Walker's mind turned toward the possibility of something more dramatic than newspapers and short essays. Weekly or monthly circulars might prod the community and elevate its knowledge across time, but Walker believed that Black people—and white people who would listen—needed something more stirring to motivate them to do something about their situation. Walker sensed that the overall American identity was up for grabs and saw literature as a way to shape it.

Speaking of American identity development during this era, the historian David Waldstreicher observed that a nation "is never just an idea or a thing; it is also a story, an encompassing narrative or set of competing narratives with the potential to crowd out other narratives that may have rather different political implications." When Walker got into the newspaper business, the American narrative was still undergoing competition and transition. The most familiar narrative of the late 1700s had centered around liberty, republicanism, rugged entrepreneurship, and the democratic ideals of a fledgling nation. The War of 1812 wobbled that narrative, but the war's end in 1814 stabilized the United States' northern frontier and helped coalesce the nation once again around a common destiny. Yet, the debates surrounding the Missouri Compromise of 1820 exposed the national consensus as paper thin. Not only did the question of slavery in the territories sharpen regional divisions, the words of men like Senator Rufus King exposed the contradiction between slavery and American democracy. Following Vesey's thwarted 1822 insurrection, the problem only seemed to deepen—the South hardening its position, slavery expanding, and the North imagining that compromise would resolve rather than prolong national conflict.[11]

The problem, as Paul Starr, a scholar of sociology and public affairs, observes, was that this contradiction rested at America's "most fundamental, constitutive level," with opposing principles "entrenched in the structure of both state and society." In America's nascent years, those principles managed to coexist, but the expansionist aspirations of the North and the South would inevitably bring the contradiction to a salient head. Over time, "neither freedom nor slavery alone but the contradictory relation between them," Starr writes, would define "what America became."[12]

Walker saw this contradiction as clearly as anyone and sensed the country was at a turning point. Either those who would not countenance slavery would stand up and be counted, or the United States would become wedded to perpetual slavery and Black inferiority as necessities for a successful white democracy. Walker was determined to stand up.

Exactly when Walker arrived at his plan to leverage America's identity crisis is unclear, but he spent several months in 1829 researching and crafting a theory for Black freedom that called America's given identity into question. He was going to write a Black freedom manifesto and share it, not just among the Northern Black elite, but among the South's enslaved people as well. Walker's idea was the natural evolution of Vesey's efforts. He was what white slaveholders were seeking to avoid when they burned churches, burned transcripts of Vesey's plot, and spoke of literacy's evils. Vesey had proved the power of the word to expand one man's intellect and equip him for leadership. Walker wanted to prove the power of the word to spread an idea to Black communities across the country, unite them in their political thinking, and spur them to action. Such a man had the potential to inspire countless more like Vesey.

Walker decided to model his manifesto on seminal American political documents. He would include a preamble and four articles that mirrored the U.S. Constitution. He would assert inalienable human rights and call for a revolutionary response to degradations and humiliations that mirrored the Declaration of Independence. But he also wanted to write something entirely unique: a moral analysis of slavery, freedom, and dignity that gave Black people the right to meet violence with violence.

He knew that when white people saw something so audacious, they would draw the unmistakable connection between it and the Denmark Vesey affair, particularly given that Walker would draw on both the Bible's deliverance message and America's liberty narrative to validate Black humanity and justify violence. Walker, however, was more dangerous than Vesey. He was going to air his grievances to the world. He would not move in the shadows or allow himself to be circumscribed by time or space. He was going to put pen to paper, paper to press, press to seaports, and call the whole Black race to arms, not just his acquaintances. Whites could reject his logic and denigrate his intellect all they wanted. If the *Appeal* resonated with just a fraction of its audience, the South would have a fight on its hands that made Vesey's revolution look like a schoolyard rumble.

But Walker knew that if anyone was going to take him seriously, he needed some standing or legitimacy. Walker expected "to be held up to the public as an ignorant, impudent and restless disturber of the public peace." Writing in the style of the Constitution and Declaration might help, but that was far from enough, particularly for an unknown Black man with no credentials. What he lacked in credentials, Walker would have to make up with skill and self-assurance. A text written with the style, knowledge, and adeptness of a learned man, he hoped, might speak for itself. Rather than rely on pure emotion or internal musings, he would wrap his thoughts in a standard mode of argument that reached back to the ancient world. As Stephen Marshall, a scholar of American political thought, writes, Walker sought to "ground his authority by surveying the geographical, social, racial, moral, and philosophical boundaries of the polity."[13]

As to geography, Walker would write in the vein of Alexis de Tocqueville or James Bryce, basing his argument on his travel throughout "a considerable portion of these United States" and coming to the conclusion that the "coloured people of these United States ... are the most degraded, wretched, and abject set of beings that ever lived." The morals and philosophy of his argument would draw from the nation's most sacred texts and concepts—the Bible, the Constitution, the Declaration of Independence, and a republican form of government. History and current events would do the rest, offering voluminous detailed facts to substantiate his conclusions about race and society.[14]

On September 28, 1829, after presumably months of writing, David Walker dropped his bombshell, reigniting the passions Vesey had aroused and starting a war of words between himself and the white world—a war that had implications for both Black and national identity. The full title of his manifesto was *Walker's Appeal to the Coloured Citizens of the World, But in Particular, and Very Expressly, to Those of the United States of America*. The title alone—with its reference to citizenship—said more than enough to provoke outrage.

Frontispiece to David Walker's *Appeal*. Courtesy of Library of Congress.

For the past decade, the question of Black citizenship, though a distant second to slavery, had also stoked political controversy. Vesey, of course, focused on slavery in the debate over Missouri's admission to the Union, but Congress separately debated whether Missouri could deny free Black people the same right as other citizens to enter the state. Whatever the U.S. Constitution might allow regarding slavery, Senator David Morril of New Hampshire argued, it did not "prescribe one class of citizens" from another. "Color no more comes into consideration to decide who is a citizen than size or profession." Moreover, free Black men "have fought your battles; they have defended your country; they have preserved your privileges." Surely, they have not "lost their own" in the process. Representative William Eustis of Massachusetts, who had served as James Madison's secretary of war, made a similar argument in the House, reminding his colleagues that enslaved people had "shed their blood" in the Revolutionary War under the "condition" that they would be "made freemen." It would be unconscionable to now say "you are not to participate in the rights secured by the struggle, or in the liberty for which you have been fighting." He added that the U.S. Constitution doesn't begin with "We the white people." In the end, however, "the racial white identity of the nation" and narrow originalist thinking carried the day. Congress allowed Missouri not only to enslave people but to deny free Black people their rights of citizenship. And, of course, South Carolina's Negro Seamen Act had made a mockery of Black citizenship throughout 1823. Even in the nation's capital, Black people could be arbitrarily jailed and condemned to slavery unless they affirmatively proved their free status. In 1826, for instance, Gilbert Horton, a free Black man from New York, spent weeks in a District of Columbia jail and was only released after a high-profile campaign by William Jay, the son of former governor and Supreme Court justice John Jay. When Walker was writing in 1829, Haiti was the only Western country in which Black people had explicit citizenship.[15]

Against this backdrop, Walker meant to stun Blacks and whites by unabashedly claiming citizenship for Blacks in his title. By treating Black citizenship as a given, Walker was directly challenging the national identity that many white thought-leaders were trying to build. And that he was doing it as a Black man on behalf of Black people—not as a white representative in Congress—was crucially important. Daring to address Black people as "citizens" was an act of citizenship in itself. Walker was engaging in political activity whether America liked it or not and, thus, inserting Black people into a conversation from which whites aimed to exclude them. Though white people would not acknowledge it, Walker was doing what America's political heroes had long extolled as the highest form of republicanism—using one's intellect and voice to shape American democracy, in the written form no less.[16]

Thomas Jefferson had singled out civic participation as a defining feature of American democracy. Jefferson argued that American democracy did not bow to aristocracy, elitism, or authoritarianism, but only to the reasoned judgment of its people and their capacity to judge. Reflecting on Walker in relationship to other political leaders, Melvin Rogers, a historian of politics, wrote, "The battle for America's soul" was "waged through [one simple] question: Who among us will be more persuasive?" Democratic legitimacy derives from our collective judgment, not brute force. Understanding as much, Walker dove into the debate.[17]

Walker asked no one's permission to question America's laws, leaders, religion, and democracy. He knew, and his writing would demonstrate, that he had the capacity to sit in judgment. Whether he was the most persuasive was a matter for his fellow citizens to decide. But the very act of stepping into the public debate should, according to Jefferson, have conferred on him standing as a citizen.

When Walker released the *Appeal*, he also became the first Black man to publicly challenge white hierarchy—and not just in the abstract. He named names and confronted the nation's greatest idols. And when he stood intellectually toe-to-toe with white giants, he did not simply disagree; he threw blows. And who better to strike—and thus draw attention—than the author of the Declaration of Independence and one of America's most revered statesmen, Thomas Jefferson? Walker called out Jefferson nineteen different times over the course of his seventy-five-page manifesto.

Jefferson's presidency had ended in 1809, but he continued to play an outsized role in national and Southern affairs. His longtime political ally and secretary of state, James Madison, held the presidency from 1809 to 1817, and then Jefferson's mentee, James Monroe, held it from 1817 to 1825. Jefferson had also continued to build his intellectual legacy, founding the University of Virginia in 1819, planning its design and curriculum over the next few years, and leading the institution when it finally opened in 1825 until he died in 1826.

Jefferson, though deceased, remained the perfect target for Walker because of his slaveholding past and because he had authored what many considered one of America's most important books, *Notes on the State of Virginia*. Though the book addressed a wide range of topics—natural history, society, politics, religion, and law—it had served as an academic, or rather pseudo-academic, defense and justification of slavery. Jefferson famously posited that Black people were inherently inferior to white people. Roman slaves, he argued, demonstrated intellect and artistry beyond that of American slaves, and the reason was that Roman slaves were white. Any Black achievements in America were on account "of their mixture with whites."[18]

This intellectual difference, he speculated, had a biological basis. Pointing to the larger animal kingdom, he argued that just as "different species of the same genus, or varieties of the same species, possess different" traits and characteristics, so too do racial groups. Black people's unique traits and characteristics made them "inferior to the whites in the endowments both of body and mind." This was simply the natural order of things, and it posed "a powerful obstacle to the emancipation of these people." Walker believed that this assertion, coming from Jefferson, had "injured us more, and has been as great a barrier to our emancipation as anything that has ever been advanced against us."[19]

One can sense Walker's blood rising as he responded to Jefferson's claim that God made Blacks inferior. Refusing to defer to Jefferson's status, Walker wrote bluntly, "We will not take his say so for the fact." He urged Blacks to buy a copy of *Notes on the State of Virginia* and read it for themselves. A full accounting of the facts would show that Jefferson was wrong, but this accounting should not be delivered by a white man. "We, and the world wish to see the charges of Mr. Jefferson refuted by blacks themselves." Therein, he wrote, lay the first step in rebuilding Black identity: "unless we try to refute Mr. Jefferson's arguments respecting us, we will only establish them." The *Appeal* embodied Walker's refutation of Jefferson and Black inferiority in both word and deed.[20]

Walker also denounced the notion that America could exclude Black people from its fruits and claim to be a just society. To move forward, the country had to see how slavery was corrupting its democracy. Naively conceived as a circumscribed institution in the 1787 Constitution, slavery had grown dramatically, changing the nation as it did. The constitutional compromise on slavery was a "curse" on the nation, disfiguring everything it touched. Slavery was now entrenched in the country's religious, legal, economic, cultural, and political institutions. Slaveholders told themselves that Blacks were an "inheritance" from God and that it was their right to marshal government power to protect that inheritance. The North, too, had grown too rich from the benefits of cheap labor to wish to disturb the status quo.[21]

Walker worried that America might already be beyond redemption. In the service of slavery, it routinely used its democratic ideas to justify deeply undemocratic ends. "Can there be," he wrote, "a greater absurdity in nature, and particularly in a free republican country" than slavery? Yet, it was increasingly becoming the economic and political foundation on which the country stood. "At the close of the first Revolution in this country," Walker wrote, "there were but thirteen States in the Union, now there are twenty-four, most of which are slave-holding States, and the whites are dragging us around in chains and in handcuffs, to their new States and Territories to work their mines and farms," enriching their children "from one generation to another with our blood and our tears."[22]

Walker framed the *Appeal* as a last-ditch plea for America to awaken from its self-delusion and write a new identity. Toward that end, the *Appeal* made hypocrisy its recurring theme—and the worst kind was religious hypocrisy. Walker echoed Vesey's theology: God stands with the oppressed and abhors slavery's brutality, and "this side of eternity," His righteous judgment would fall swiftly on those who practiced slavery as well as those who benefited from it. But the most original part of Walker's argument moved beyond vague prophesies of deliverance to call attention to white religious contradictions in the here and now.[23]

White leaders, he explained, clearly believed God's word applied to Black people: they literally built places for them to sit in church. But as soon as Blacks started worshiping outside those reserved spaces, "the wretches would burst in upon them and drag them out and commence beating them ... so unmercifully ... that they would hardly be able to crawl for weeks and sometimes for months." White pastors preached a gospel of "peace and not of blood" in the same sermons where they asserted that slaves "must do their to duty to their masters or be whipped." Even in the North, churches chastised intemperance, infidelity, and breaking the Sabbath, but hardly said a word about slavery, which, by comparison, made "all those other evils" look like "nothing."[24]

Walker went so far as to question whether "the preachers and people of America believe the Bible." Didn't Jesus say, "All power is given unto me in Heaven and in earth. Go ye, therefore, and teach all nations, baptizing them in the name of the Father, and of the Son, and of the Holy Ghost"? Jesus's command, Walker emphasized, did "not show the slightest degree of distinction," but applied to all people. Yet rather than teach and baptize in God's name in Africa, America had gone to Africa "and learnt us the art of throat-cutting, by setting us to fight, one against another, to take each other as prisoners of war, and sell to [America] for small bits of calicoes, old swords, knives, & ... to make slaves for you and your children." How could Christian societies send missionaries across the world to "display their charity, Christianity, and benevolence" but degrade their Black neighbors? Until they "do justice at home," God would not "accept their offering" abroad.[25]

Walker also cut more specifically into the contradiction of "this Republican Land of Liberty." America's democratic rhetoric proceeded as though slavery did not exist or matter. Thomas Paine's *Common Sense*, for instance, barely mentioned it. And while the front pages of American newspapers regularly decried the inhumanities that Turks visited on the Greeks in the 1820s during their fight for independence from Ottoman rule, those very same papers had no shame in advertising slaves for sale.[26]

Walker even turned the Declaration of Independence against America. In the *Appeal*, he republished its opening paragraphs, which announced the "self-evident" truths "that all men are created equal" and "endowed with certain unalienable rights," including the entitlement of "one people to dissolve the political bands which have connected them with another." Americans, he demanded, must "compare your own language ... with your cruelties and murders inflicted ... on ... men who have never given your fathers or you the least provocation." The "long train of abuses and usurpations" of which the Declaration spoke were not "one hundredth part as cruel and tyrannical" as those Black Americans suffered. By the Declaration's logic, Blacks have the "right" and "duty" to "throw off such government."[27]

As in his religious critique, Walker grounded his republican argument in specifics. American slavery and discrimination went beyond that of ancient Rome—which Americans held up as the model republic—or of Egypt, whose evil God punished. Rome never prevented slaves from buying their freedom; Egyptians never claimed slaves were outside the human family or prohibited them from marrying others. America denied these rights and more to the people it enslaved. It often did not treat free Blacks much better, denying them the right to serve on juries, hold public positions, or marry outside their race. Even when it formally allowed free Blacks a privilege, such as owning property, whites could trample on it in practice—for instance by stealing Black men's property.

The white notion of Black intellectual inferiority made no sense either. If slaves were "incapable of acquiring knowledge," why beat them for trying to read? If slaves were "void of intellect," why go to lengths to stop them from trying to inform themselves? If Black freedom was a ruse, why outlaw the presence of free persons of color and fear their relationships with enslaved persons? Why weren't white superiority and Black inferiority self-evident enough to drown out abolitionist pamphlets? White people, Walker wrote, knew the truth. Keeping Black people "ignorant and miserable" was the only way they could maintain slavery and white supremacy. Enforced "ignorance . . . produces a state of things, Oh my Lord! too horrible to present to the world. Any man who is curious to see the full force of ignorance developed among the coloured people of the United States of America, has only to go into the southern and western states of this confederacy."[28]

On this point, however, Walker also turned his gaze to Black people, whom he sometimes described in terms that were not much more flattering than the insults spewed by slaveholders. He all but conceded Black inferiority as a practical, but not inherent, reality, and regularly spoke of enslaved people as "wretched" or "brutes" whom whites had degraded to "the most profound ignorance and stupidity." But if ignorance and degradation were how whites kept Blacks enslaved and suppressed, education was the way out.

Although some found these depictions too callous, Walker felt that ceding the facts of Black degradation and ignorance served an empathic purpose—to move the locus of contest from the fact of Black ignorance to its cause. The state of Black America had nothing to do with natural inferiority, he argued, and everything to do with the enslavers' bloodlust, greed, and barbarity. Whites' "greatest earthly desires" were to systematically disfigure Black capacity and intellect.[29]

Slaveholders' own words proved the point. Walker quoted one slave owner as saying that "a n[*****] ought not to have any more sense than enough to work for his master." The same man had threatened that if anyone tried to teach his slaves "to spell, read or write, he would prosecute him to the very extent of the law." The logic was clear: "the more ignorant they can bring up the Africans, the better slaves they make." Those who advocated returning Blacks to Africa were not much different. As a prominent member of the Colonization Society said of enslaved people, "the more you cultivate their minds, the more miserable you make them in their present state. You give them a higher relish for those privileges which they can never attain, and turn what we intend for a blessing into a curse." Therefore, "if they must remain in their present situation, keep them in the lowest state of degradation and ignorance." Whites might wax eloquent and cite Jefferson on Black inferiority, but these voices belied the truth. Walker argued that the enslavers withheld information and constricted learning because to do otherwise would "awaken ... his ignorant brethren, whom they held in wretchedness and misery" and expose the enslavers' "infernal deeds of cruelty."[30]

The antidote was education, and it rested in the hands of Blacks themselves—if they would seize it. Walker called on learned Black men to teach others and share what they knew. Education was not an individual asset but a communal one. Those who had it were duty-bound to share it as they would share any other skill.

Getting there, he believed, required not just effort but a change in mindset. Black people lacked more than knowledge; they lacked the "desire and motivation to know." Subjugation, he claimed, had taken away the desire to learn. Some simply had no sense of what it meant to be educated. A father "who knows no more than what nature has taught him" thinks his son is a success when he is "able to write a neat hand." The son-turned-student "struts about, in the full assurance, that his attainments in literature" will carry him for a lifetime, even though he has "scarcely any learning at all!!!" Walker claimed that only a fraction of the Black students he examined had anything beyond a rudimentary education. He implored them to "seek after the substance of learning."[31]

Such learning would awaken Black people to their individual and communal interests alike. An awakened people would reject their current station in society, appreciate whites as the enemies they had become, and act. According to Walker, no man of any "good sense and learning would submit himself, his father, mother, wife and children, to be slaves" to their "wretched" white oppressors. "I would crawl on my hands and knees through mud and mire, to the feet of a learned man, where I would sit and humbly supplicate him to instill into me, that which neither devils nor tyrants could remove, only with my life."[32]

Walker clearly believed that education was first and foremost a matter of personal dignity and awareness, but in the public sphere, he believed education was also fitness for the citizenship he was trying to claim for Black people in the title of his manifesto. A title was not enough. Against the premise of Black colonization—that Black people were not fit for citizenship—they needed to justify their political worth.

America—the idealized notion of it—had long depended on an informed citizenry, and literacy was a predicate to information. As James Madison remarked, "a popular Government, without popular information, or the means of acquiring it, is but a Prologue to a Farce or a Tragedy." Walker believed that Black people could use education both to resist slavery and to justify Black citizenship. Educated Black people, like him, could perform the acts of citizenship, even if formally denied its privileges. As Peter Thompson, a professor of American history, wrote of Walker's argument, the "best way to secure and extend rights of citizenship—of both the US and the world—was to act as citizens." And that, in Walker's words, would make "tyrants quake and tremble on their sandy foundation."[33]

Walker was posing a crossroads for both Black and white people. One path, on which Black people "shall arise from this death-like apathy" to claim their "natural right" to be free, paralleled Vesey's. If white people refused to repent, the path would not be civil. So long as we are enslaved, Walker said, "we cannot be your friends." Blacks would have little choice but to "root some of you out of the very face of the earth!!!"[34]

In closing, Walker dared white people to consider the *Appeal*'s logic "and tell me if their declaration is true—viz, if the United States of America is a Republican Government." But when white people first saw the book in late 1829, they struggled even to get to the substance. The notion of Black intellectual inferiority ran so deep that some questioned whether Walker could have authored such a persuasive document. The *Appeal*, some argued, represented too much knowledge, skill, and literacy for a Black man. The author of an essay in the *Boston Daily Courier* found it implausible that Walker had authored the *Appeal*. Even abolitionists initially rejected his authorship.[35]

An essay in William Lloyd Garrison's *The Liberator* was friendlier than others, saying it wasn't that Walker "is a man of color" that raised doubts but that the *Appeal* showed evidence of more background "reading than could have fallen to the lot of that man. . . . He could never have read all the authors quoted in his book, and seen of what true greatness consisted, and then bestowed such unbounded praise upon" Bishop Richard Allen. And the "excellent criticisms" Walker launched at the "most talented men of the age" required a "greater degree of education than we have any reason to believe he possessed."[36]

The book's details, however, matched Walker's life story and authorial voice. And when Boston authorities confronted him in his shop, he made no attempt to shift responsibility for the *Appeal* to anyone else. Instead, the investigator reported, "he openly avows the sentiments of the book and authorship." Walker did not let the public or private harassment distract or dissuade him from pressing his case. In subsequent editions of the *Appeal*, he wrote, "if any are anxious to ascertain who I am, know the world, that I am one of the oppressed, degraded and wretched sons of Africa. . . . If any wish to plunge me into the wretched incapacity of a slave, or murder me for the truth, know ye, that I am . . . at your disposal. I count my life not dear unto me, but I am ready to be offered at any moment." Come and get me.[37]

No honest white person could read his *Appeal* without doubting the lie America was telling about Black people. No Black person could read it without feeling that Walker had shattered the lie. That's what made the *Appeal* so dangerous in the eyes of white people. It gave Black people a lens through which to focus their own desire for dignity. When Walker shipped that lens South in the final month of 1829, it was all but a declaration of war on slavery, with Black literacy as the primary weapon. That would soon make Black literacy public enemy number one in the South. The slaveholding establishment would see no option but to marshal its troops.

CHAPTER FOUR

Arresting the Word

Though *Walker's Appeal to the Coloured Citizens of the World* probably first arrived in Charleston, officials in Savannah were the first to seize copies of it—around Christmas in 1829, three months after Walker published it. Whether they were expecting the *Appeal* or simply caught it with their normal suspicion of Black seamen and potentially incendiary outside literature is unclear. Walker officially published the *Appeal* in September, but the first print run was limited and apparently shared only among trusted associates. Subsequent print runs that winter included changes in response to evolving events. Analyzing the South's response to the *Appeal*, Kim Tolley notes that Southern officials may have been expecting it for weeks. "Active social, religious, and business networks," she writes, "bound Northerners and Southerners together. News traveled relatively quickly from North to South and back again through personal letters, business dealings, religious conference meetings, newspapers, and other outlets."[1]

Regardless, the moment the first copies arrived in plain view south of the Mason Dixon line, in December 1829, local authorities seized them and arrested those in possession. Vesey's plot was, by then, seven years old, but the fear it provoked remained seared in their memories. Vesey had shown what a literate Black man could do in back alleys and dimly lit rooms. Walker's *Appeal* could do exponentially more by reaching into every Black community in the South. Mixed with those memories was an ongoing state of political hysteria in Georgia over a series of recent fires in Augusta. Thirteen fires had broken out that year—two in February, six in April, and five more in the fall—bringing to the surface a persistent fear that slaves would sow chaos with fire rather than directly attack whites. That April, when the fires seemed too frequent to be coincidental, the city instituted martial law. In November, the city went out of its way to make an example of two Black women, sentencing them to death for a stable fire even though its cause—an argument between the women—had no relation to any larger plot.[2]

Georgia's legislature was debating the fires when word arrived that officials in Savannah had seized sixty copies of Walker's *Appeal*. The news came in a letter from Governor George Gilmer, along with a copy of the *Appeal* so the members could appreciate the danger for themselves. Gilmer implored the legislature to pass legislation to block further importation and circulation of the *Appeal* quickly. He expected a challenge from the federal government, but "when the torch is ready to be applied to our Houses, and the assassin's dirk drawn upon our breasts, it is not a time when we can take in our defence to dispute [it] with casuists in other States."[3]

Both houses passed legislation within a single day, and Gilmer signed it immediately. The general strategy was similar to South Carolina's—close Savannah's harbor to Black seamen. But Georgia's law was more comprehensive and aggressive, attacking Black literacy and the feared intersection between seamen, literature, and Black literacy.

The legislature styled the law as intended to "Quarantine in the several sea ports of this State, and to prevent the circulation of written or printed papers within this State calculated to excite disaffection among the coloured people of this state, and to prevent said people from being taught to read or write." It required a forty-day quarantine of all free Black people arriving in Georgia ports from another state or country, a measure it described as "necessary and essential to the welfare and safety of the good people of this state." The legislature perceived these outsiders as so dangerous that Black Georgians could not board any boat that carried even one free Black man, and if they somehow communicated with such a person, they would be jailed and "whipped," up to "thirty-nine lashes."[4]

The primary targets, however, were Walker's *Appeal* and other works like it. If any person—Black or white, free or enslaved—"shall circulate, bring ... [,] assist," or in any manner be involved with "any printed or written" materials designed to excite "insurrection, conspiracy or resistance among" Black people, they "shall be punished with death." The act

Georgia State Capitol building in Milledgeville, where Walker's *Appeal* was debated. Historic American Buildings Survey, L. D. Andrew, photographer, January 3, 1937. Courtesy of Library of Congress.

further made it a crime for any person "to teach any other slave, negro or free person of colour, to read or write either written or printed characters." Leaving no stone unturned, the legislature went after printing presses, too, prohibiting Black people—free or enslaved—from "the setting of types in any printing office in this State." Merely possessing the skill posed too great a risk.[5]

Governor Gilmer knew, however, that legislation in his state was not enough to solve the problem. The *Appeal* had already breached the port and would probably do so again, save some drastic measure that shut down commerce. It would be better to attack the problem at its source. Gilmer and Savannah mayor William T. Williams wrote separately to Boston's mayor, Gray Otis, urging him to stop Walker. Mayor Otis sent someone to Walker's place of business to investigate, but when Walker said he intended to continue printing and shipping the *Appeal*, Otis didn't stand in his way. He wrote back to Gilmer and Williams and explained that Walker was "a free black man" who had done nothing wrong. No federal or Massachusetts law prevented him from speaking his mind. Although "all sensible people regretted what he wrote and what he was doing—he could not be stopped legally." Otis even goaded the Georgians a bit, telling them Walker "openly avows the sentiments of the book and

... declares his intention to be, to circulate his pamphlets by mail, at his own expense, if he cannot otherwise effect his object." The most Otis would do was to alert Boston's ship captains to Georgia's laws.[6]

Mayor Williams next pressed Governor Gilmer and U.S. Senator John Forsythe to prevail on Congress. By Williams's logic, if the federal government claimed the power to open Charleston's harbor (in contravention of South Carolina's Negro Seamen Act), then it had the power to close Boston's harbors to prevent Walker's *Appeal* from ever leaving Massachusetts. Whatever the merits of restricting seamen, the federal government had to see Walker's *Appeal* as a direct threat to Georgia. He was literally calling enslaved people to violence against whites. Even white abolitionist leaders distanced themselves from Walker's violent rhetoric.[7]

It was, ironically, other Southern political leaders who nipped the idea of congressional intervention in the bud. South Carolina's position—and soon Georgia's—was that Congress could not interfere with a state's quarantine measures or its domestic dealings with slaves. Asking Congress to intercede in Massachusetts undermined this position. The South would have to deal with Walker itself.

Some Georgians offered private bounties. Henry Highland Garnet, a famous abolitionist who wrote the first biographical sketch of Walker, reported that "a company of Georgia men ... bound themselves by an oath, that they would eat as little as possible until they had killed the youthful author. They also offered a reward of a thousand dollars for his head, and ten times as much for the live Walker." Southern planters later reportedly offered rewards ranging from $3,000 to $30,000 "to any one who would take the life of Walker."[8]

Friends urged Walker to flee to Canada, but he refused, telling them, "I will stand my ground. Somebody must die in this cause. I may be doomed to the stake and the fire, or to the scaffold tree, but it is not in me to falter if I can promote the work of emancipation." He would, in fact, die a year after publishing his *Appeal*. Many suspected foul play, maybe poison, but no evidence confirmed it, only the rumor that Walker was found slumped over dead several blocks from his home and business. Garnet then repeated the rumor two decades later in his brief sketch of Walker's life. Peter Hinks, in his full-length biography of Walker, indicates that the only available sources of evidence "strongly support a natural death from a common and virulent urban disease of the nineteenth century." Nothing in Boston's papers or city records suggests any foul play. Instead, the records indicate that several people, including Walker's daughter, Lydia, died the week before him of lung sicknesses.[9]

Regardless of what befell Walker, he was not the only one who faced danger. Southerners aggressively attacked anyone who might be sympathetic to him. Mere accusations put lives at risk. The best-documented story involved Elijah Burritt, a newspaper publisher in Milledgeville, then the capital of Georgia. When he heard about Governor Gilmer's message to the legislature regarding the *Appeal*, Burritt asked the governor's office for a copy of the book to read and report on. The office agreed on the condition that he return the copy the next morning.[10]

Covering the flurry of legislative activity around the *Appeal* that day, Burritt did not have time to actually read it. But knowing he had something important on his hands, he wrote two letters the next afternoon—one to Mayor Williams in Savannah, and the other to Walker himself. Written just hours before the legislature took a vote on its seamen and literacy laws, Burritt's letter to Walker projected that the legislature would most definitely "pass some law in relation to matters involved in [the *Appeal*'s] circulation." And though he had not yet read the *Appeal*, he was sure such a law would make it "a theme of considerable discussion and serious interest." So, like any good newspaper man, he asked Walker to "forward to me one or more copies." Unsure how or whether Walker would respond, Burritt made the same request of Mayor Williams.[11]

He then wrote a column catching his readers up on the legislative discussion. Burritt was careful. Saying too much would provoke "excitement on a question of so deep a stake and momentous delicacy." Saying nothing would disserve public safety.[12]

Williams responded quickly to Burritt's letter, informing him that the police were holding the city's one copy of the *Appeal*. Two weeks later, Burritt found twenty copies—not the one or two he had hoped for—waiting for him at the post office. The signature on the accompanying letter all but assured his fate in Georgia—"your friend, David Walker." Officials issued a warrant for Burritt's arrest on February 11, even though he had written to Walker before the new law went into effect and never did anything with the copies other than share a few with local authorities. Nevertheless, officials carted him to jail on February 12. His attorney found a defect in the charging papers and secured his temporary release from jail, but his reputation was beyond repair and Burritt knew updated charges would follow. He saw no choice but to leave his family and business behind and flee north. A grand jury indictment in early March assured he would never return.[13]

In July, the sheriff sold Burritt's newspaper at auction. His former co-editor, who some scholars suspect was scheming against him the whole time, purchased the paper's assets and opened another in its place. Burned financially and emotionally by the affair, Burritt pursued an entirely different passion in Connecticut, devoting the rest of his life to astronomy.[14]

A similar string of events occurred in Virginia. A week after the *Appeal* arrived in Savannah, officials discovered a man circulating copies in Richmond. He was carrying a letter from Walker. The presence of the *Appeal* that far inland—as well as the letter's contents—suggested that Walker had a network that was moving the pamphlet through ports and cities. Richmond's mayor forwarded the *Appeal* to Virginia's governor, William B. Giles, who immediately alerted the Virginia legislature on January 7, 1830.

Unlike Georgia's lawmakers, the Virginia legislature discussed the issue in closed session. Openly discussing David Walker and Black uprisings was thought to increase the likelihood of unrest. Only after the secret session concluded did the public receive any notice—and then only of the final resolution, not the substantive debate. An essay in the *Niles Register*, a national weekly magazine out of Baltimore, mocked Southerners: "How much is it to be regretted, that a negro dealer in old clothes, should thus excite two states to legislative action." The *Richmond Whig* chafed at being shut out of the legislative debate.[15]

When the bill surfaced in the public record, it revealed a different approach from Georgia's or South Carolina's. Fires and seamen were apparently of far less concern than Black literacy and information sharing. The bill's first section went straight for Walker's *Appeal* and similar materials that might follow, making it a crime for "any white person, free negro, mulatto or slave, [to] print or write, . . . or knowingly circulate . . . any paper, pamphlet, or book, advising insurrection or rebellion amongst the slaves in the state, or the tendency of which shall be to excite insurrection or rebellion." For free persons of color, the first offense was punishable by a $500 fine, the second by a year in jail. First-time enslaved offenders received thirty-nine lashes. The second offense carried death.[16]

The bill's remaining sections attacked literacy in a broader and more detailed manner than any previous laws, which had always been limited in some respect. In the past, a law would target slave literacy but not free

Black literacy. Or it would target writing but not reading, or general education but not religious education. Virginia's new bill specified the contexts in which Black literacy might arise and barred them all.

One section prohibited free Blacks from assembling anywhere—day or night—to learn "reading or writing." Other sections prohibited enslaved persons from learning to read and write and explicitly intruded into slaveholders' prerogatives. Where prior literacy restrictions were typically treated as inapplicable to slaveholders, the Virginia bill sought to prevent slaveholders and missionaries from using religion as a ruse. It prohibited "the owner, master, or overseer of any slave" from sending enslaved persons to "any Sunday school . . . to be taught to read or write."[17]

This infringement on religion and slaveholders' discretion was probably the bill's downfall. Missionaries and religious organizations had been teaching enslaved people to read since colonial days and had resisted legislative restrictions on these activities since at least 1800. Delegates from the mountainous western part of the state, with much smaller slave populations, were particularly sympathetic to religious and autonomy interests and less susceptible to fearmongering. Despite the closed session and lightning-fast consideration, the bill passed the House of Delegates only by the narrowest margin—81 to 80. The Senate voted it down, 7 to 11. Those margins, however, suggested that a less aggressive bill or a change of circumstances might produce a different result—and circumstances were changing.[18]

The circulation of Walker's *Appeal* in Southern states was not under control. Places like Charleston tried to put up a good façade, assuring the public that the police were barricading the city against incendiary pamphlets. But the first official seizure of the book proved the opposite. Southern states were not even looking at the right suspects. An unassuming and apparently apolitical white man had slipped copies into the city.

Edward Smith, a white steward on the brig *Columbo* out of Boston, appeared to be the most unlikely of couriers. Before the *Columbo* left Boston, a well-dressed Black man boarded and asked Smith to do him a favor. According to the trial court's summary of Smith's confession, the Black man asked him to "bring a package of pamphlets to Charleston . . . and . . . give them to any negroes he had a mind to, or that he met." He told Smith to do it "privately" and not to "let any white person know any thing about it." Smith claimed that he didn't know what was inside the pamphlets. He just accepted the task, presumably for money. He did not peruse them until he left port and was immediately frightened. When he arrived in Charleston, he anxiously handed copies to the first Black people who boarded the vessel. After they passed word of Smith's stash, other Black men approached him in the city.[19]

It is not clear if Smith came under surveillance, but the police captain overheard him discussing Walker's *Appeal* with a free Black man. The man asked for a copy; Smith said he had given them all away but could get more in Boston. No doubt the man who had given him the first package would oblige with more. On hearing this, the captain arrested him, and a grand jury indicted him for "falsely and maliciously contriving . . . to disturb the peace and security of this State" with "false and scandalous Libel" that would "move a sedition among the Slaves." A jury found him guilty, and the court fined him $1,000 and sentenced him to a year in prison.[20]

But for every man caught, an unknown number evaded detection. Knowing as much, the prosecuting attorney in Charleston sent a letter to Boston's mayor warning that Charlestonians were ready to commit "every article of Massachusetts manufacture . . . to the flames" and "cut off all [future] commercial Intercourse with Boston" if he did not stop the flow of Walker's *Appeal*.[21]

North Carolina proved more porous than South Carolina, with wider—or at least better known—pathways into Wilmington. Having lived there for three decades, Walker knew Wilmington's docks, rivers, and neighboring towns well. Wilmington authorities were convinced that the *Appeal* was circulating underground in and around the town. Insurrection rumors spread throughout 1830 and set the region on edge. It was not clear what white officials could do to stop the book's infiltration. In nearby New Bern, a court ordered a county patrol to seize weapons from Blacks, including weapons held with slaveholders' permission.

Walker's network evaded detection until summer. Finally, in August, authorities sighted copies of the *Appeal* in Wilmington. A few weeks later, a copy surfaced in New Bern's slave community, having also come through Wilmington. Finding the book in the hands of enslaved people further alarmed whites, who worried that slaves might start to seriously consider how best to secure their own freedom. The town called a meeting to discuss strategies for suppressing an insurrection. To assist in any necessary defense, the adjutant general sent two hundred muskets from the state arsenal to New Bern.[22]

Panicked letters from around the state began arriving at the governor's office. A letter from the Fayetteville police indicated they were trying to get ahead of things by sending secret agents into the Black community to gather information. A letter from New Bern claimed a slave had confessed to a conspiracy, saying that someone had brought the *Appeal* from Wilmington and that a stash of weapons had been readied for an uprising on Christmas Day. Although the confession was almost certainly coerced, other evidence strongly suggested that Walker did have an agent circulating large numbers of his pamphlet in the region. Authorities traced sightings of the *Appeal* to a man named Jacob Cowen, "who acknowledged," according to a Wilmington magistrate, "that he had received 200 copies of said Pamphlet from the author for the purpose of being distributed among the slaves of this place."[23]

As these stories poured in, Governor Montfort Stokes urged the North Carolina legislature to act. When the legislative session started, in November, he shared Walker's "incendiary publication" with its members, telling them that it had also "been circulated very extensively in the Southern country." The book's discovery across the South, he warned, should "leave no doubt upon any rational mind, that a systematic attempt" to sow sedition among slaves was afoot, and that the means were "well calculated to prepare the minds of that portion of our population for any measure, however desperate." North Carolina was as much at risk as anywhere. According to Stokes, some free Black people were already acting as "agents for the distribution of seditious publications." Danger having now arrived on North Carolina's doorstep, it would be "criminal" for the legislature not to act.[24]

The state's General Assembly, like Virginia's, went into secret session. Very little is known of the proceedings, other than that an antiliteracy legislator requested a copy of Walker's *Appeal* from the governor in hope of using it to provoke decisive legislative action. Representatives from western North Carolina had reservations about draconian antiliteracy laws. And at least a few citizens assailed the secrecy. But a legislative committee reported that an extensive conspiracy to provoke slaves was afoot. The response made one thing clear: rising fears fanned by the *Appeal* outweighed any reservations.[25]

The legislature passed two aggressive laws by a substantial margin. Using nearly the same language as in Georgia, it criminalized the transportation and circulation of materials with the "tendency ... to excite insurrection, conspiracy or resistance in the slaves or free negroes ... within the State, or which shall advise or persuade [them] to insurrections, conspiracy or resistance." It even criminalized mere talk of such matters, prohibiting people from orally sharing the contents or knowledge of Walker's *Appeal*. First offenses against these sections carried a year in prison. Repeat offenders got "death without benefit of clergy."[26]

A second North Carolina law directly connected Walker's goals with Black literacy. It was the power to open minds that made literacy dangerous—Walker's point of emphasis throughout the *Appeal*. The law's preamble declared that reading and writing have "a tendency to excite dissatisfaction in [slaves'] minds and to produce insurrection and rebellion." The legislation prohibited anyone—white or Black—from teaching or attempting to teach "any slave ... to read or write." And to prevent indirect assistance or self-teaching, it also prohibited giving or selling "slaves any books or pamphlets." Free whites and Blacks would face imprisonment, but in a concession to slaveholders, enslaved persons were to be whipped, not imprisoned or executed. Shocked at the sweep of the two laws, the *Greensborough Patriot* wrote that "it has become an indictable offense to *dream* on the subject of slavery; and much more so *write* or *speak* on a subject so exceedingly 'delicate.' "[27]

When North Carolina's secret legislative session closed for Christmas on December 9, 1830, its members surely thought they had secured the state, just as South Carolina had thought in 1822 and Georgia in 1829. Virginia, having failed to pass its anti-literacy legislation, knew it still had business to do and resumed session early in 1831 with a simpler approach. Its new bill retained prohibitions against teaching free Blacks to write and made it a crime to "assemble with any slaves for the purpose of teaching." But it said nothing of slaveholders, implicitly conceding its provisions did not apply to them. The law passed on April 7, 1831.[28]

That concession also revealed that Virginia thought itself safe enough to recede into prior patterns of life. None of these states had any idea that, just above the North Carolina–Virginia border, a storm of ideas even more radical than Walker's was gathering. Before the next year ended, more blood would flow than in any other uprising in Southern history. David Walker's future had arrived.

CHAPTER FIVE

The Fire
Nat Turner

O N SUNDAY, AUGUST 21, 1831, a dozen or so enslaved men in Southampton, Virginia, gathered for a secret meeting in the woods. They prepared a feast—brandy and a freshly slaughtered pig—that matched the meeting's grand purpose. The next day would hold a new beginning—either death or a radically different life. At this night's end, there would be no turning back.

Nat Turner was the last to arrive. His tardiness stoked anxiety and drama in the camp. He entered with a salute, conveying resolute seriousness, and made his proposal—the one the men anticipated and to which they quickly assented. After a few hours' rest, they would begin.

They waited for the countryside to fall sound asleep before moving from the woods into cultivated fields. Their first stop was the home of Joseph Travis, the man who enslaved Turner. Turner entered the house by way of a ladder propped next to a second-floor window, then came downstairs and let the others in through the front door. To avoid waking neighbors, they used hatchets and axes as their weapons. Nat struck first, his blow glancing off Travis's head and waking him up. When Travis rose in terror, one of Nat's men finished him. They killed Travis's wife and two children before they woke. They left, remembered that the Travises had a baby, reentered, and took its life in the cradle. Turner had said to spare no one. Then they exited the house again, this time carrying guns, leaving five dead bodies behind.

Turner and his men snaked their way through the countryside for the rest of Monday, stopping at sixteen houses, and killing every white person they found. The Black people they recruited. The group swelled and thinned along the way. Some lost heart while others found it. At its largest, Turner's group consisted of forty men on horses, with perhaps twenty more on foot. They took between fifty and sixty lives.[1]

Their fate was sealed by day's end. Between the one white person who narrowly eluded death and the enslaved people who refused to join the cause, word of the revolt, as the historian Vincent Harding puts it, leapt "like fire from one blanched and trembling set of lips to another." Moments after the first solitary church bell signaled distress, Harding writes, the "clashing sound of church bells" could be heard "across the county," meaning the militia was on its way. That realization triggered the first wave of desertion among Turner's men. After a midday clash with the militia, their ranks numbered a third of their original size.[2]

Though battle weary and wounded, the remaining members regrouped, hid for the night, and prepared for an attack on a large plantation early the next morning, hoping that success there would draw recruits and rebuild momentum. But they had lost the element of surprise. Armed white community members confronted Turner's group at the plantation. The militia arrived not long after. Only five rebels avoided capture or death. By nightfall, Turner was alone. Everyone else was dead or in custody.

He remained at large for weeks, during which passions ran high. Many white people feared the worst—that David Walker had inspired Turner, that the plot reached beyond Southampton, and that subsequent slave uprisings in North Carolina were connected. These fears were fueled by a letter to Southampton officials penned under the pseudonym "Nero," claiming that a cadre of Northern Blacks had armed themselves and were coming south to avenge the "indignities and abuses" of slavery. Their leader was purportedly already there, visiting "every Negro hut and quarters" to mobilize them.[3]

Whatever credence Southampton afforded Nero, three thousand Virginia militiamen stood on high alert across the state to ensure that Turner's revolt would go no further. But as time passed, some speculated that Turner had fled the county, probably the state. In fact, he remained in the local woods he knew best, hiding in crevices during the day and venturing out for food at night.

When he stepped into plain sight on October 27, nine weeks after the revolt, it was surely by design. Nathaniel Francis, a slaveholder and

Discovery and capture of Nat Turner. Courtesy of The New York Public Library.

childhood playmate of Turner, was inspecting stacked supplies of food for his livestock when Turner suddenly appeared in front of him, close enough to touch, with what Francis described as a "smiling countenance." Francis, shocked, drew his shotgun and fired. The bullet narrowly missed Turner, tearing a hole through his hat. Turner fled.[4]

Fifty men with dogs were on his tail in no time, but his backwoods prowess proved greater than theirs. No one spotted him for another three days. Finally, he peeked his head out again—this time from a hole dug beneath a fallen tree. But the man who took aim did not fire. Turner announced himself by name—"I am Nat Turner"—and said, "Don't shoot, and I will give up."[5]

His captors marched him to Jerusalem, the county seat. Wearing clothes still stained with the blood of his victims, Turner was lucky to finish the march. During his weeks on the run, inquisitions and trials had named him as the revolt's leader and inspiration. Scholars estimate that whites had summarily killed between one and two hundred Black people, based merely on suspicion of participation in the revolt or sometimes just sympathy with it. Some were shot at random. Other killers mutilated suspected rebels' bodies and, in several instances, left decapitated heads on display in prominent places as a warning. Vigilante violence was prevalent enough that Richard Eppes, the Virginia militia's commanding officer, ordered the end of any further violence against Black people and pledged to "punish . . . , if necessary, by the rigors of the articles of war" anyone "who may attempt the resumption of such acts."[6]

Whether fearing Eppes's order or hoping to see Turner tried, the angry crowd that followed Turner on his march to Jerusalem permitted him to arrive safely at the courthouse on October 31—though his final steps required a more perilous pass through a crowd gathered at the courthouse. But the crowd, and the officials who held him, seem to have wanted something different from what the residents of Charleston had wanted from Denmark Vesey. The question was not *what* Turner had done but *why*. Seemingly out of nowhere, he had produced the bloodiest—and soon the most notorious—slave revolt in U.S. history. Charleston made sense as a place of revolt, but Southampton didn't.

Aside from slavery, Southampton had very little in common with Charleston. No white elite to speak of, no upwardly mobile and organized free people of color, no autonomous and independent enslaved labor. Southampton's Black community was religious but hadn't started its own church or dared to seek political leverage. And though Southampton's enslaved community got information through the grapevine, Turner apparently never saw Walker's pamphlet—or the similar ones that followed.

From white people's perspective, Turner himself was an unlikely candidate for an insurrection leader as well. He was born enslaved on October 2, 1800, and was traded from one owner to another three times and hired out to a fourth. He was a stranger to travel, urbanization, and radical ideas. He briefly tasted freedom, running away to the woods only to come home—not out of hunger or fear but because he believed it was God's will that he obey his earthly master.

He spent almost every moment in his rural community, where, unlike in Charleston, whites rather than Blacks set the tenor of activity, leisure, and religion. Playing the role of an obedient, upright, Christian slave to a tee, he didn't drink alcohol, didn't court women, and held fast to God's rules. His physical presence was far from imposing. More important, he didn't exude Vesey's or Walker's confrontational persona.

When Turner arrived at the Jerusalem jail, he eagerly answered everyone's questions, even speaking to the throngs that had encircled him on his march. Starting on October 31, he sat and talked for three days with Thomas Gray, the young lawyer assigned to defend him. Those conversations offered a mesmerizing story of race, religion, and literacy. Turner's narrative was so cogent, so articulate, so awe-inspiring that after it appeared in print as Turner's "confession," readers openly wondered whether Gray had dressed it up. They could not fathom that such words could come from a slave.[7]

Turner's trial began early in the morning on November 5, 1831, two days after he concluded his confessions to Gray. Though he admitted to leading the killing, he pleaded not guilty because, he said, "he did not feel so." In fact, when asked if he felt regret, he said no; he would do it again.[8]

The prosecutor called only two witnesses—one to identify Turner as the person he saw leading the rebels and another to confirm that Turner confessed to one of the killings. Gray offered no defense, and a panel of magistrates swiftly sentenced Turner to death. Before adjourning, the magistrates asked Turner if he had any final words. "I have made a full confession to Mr. Gray," Turner answered, "and I have nothing more to say."[9]

The words Turner shared with Gray were more than a confession. They were an affirmative statement. He answered the questions Gray posed but navigated the conversation toward his own ends, which needed describing far more than the revolt. Saying he knew that Gray and others wanted "a history of the motives which induced me to undertake the late insurrection," he told his story with no prompting. To understand his motives, he said, you had to "go back to the days of my infancy, and even before I was born." Turner's narrative spoke to his life trajectory, purpose, and aspirations. It offered a different view of the world than whites were accustomed to hearing. Since childhood, he said, he knew he was destined "for some great purpose."[10]

This belief was part fantastical, part practical. The first hint of his great purpose came when "the Lord had shewn me things that had happened before my birth." His parents and others in the community were "greatly astonished" that a child could know such things. The other hint was what he shared with Vesey and Walker—literacy—though his road to it was shrouded in mystery.[11]

Turner said he learned to read and write "with the most perfect ease, so much so that I have no recollection whatever of learning the alphabet."

When someone gave him a book as a plaything to appease his crying as a young child, he took it. But rather than fiddle with it in ignorance, he "began spelling the names of different objects." This was another "source of wonder," particularly among Black people.[12]

Others, sensing he was special, began encouraging his learning. Turner used his spare time to reflect on "many things that would present themselves to my imagination." When white children left their books behind, he would devour them, gathering more fodder for his imagination. He had such "uncommon intelligence for a child" that even the man who enslaved him remarked that Turner "had too much sense to be raised" as a slave and "would never be of any service to any one as a slave."[13]

Though he could not confirm when or how Turner learned to read, Gray wrote that, on a number of subjects, Turner "possesses an uncommon share of intelligence, with a mind capable of attaining anything." Though deprived of "the advantages of education, . . . he can read and write, . . . and for natural intelligence and quickness of apprehension, is surpassed by few men I have ever seen." Gray did not say Turner was smart for a Black man but smart when compared with all men.[14]

The gift of literacy, as with the other Black revolutionaries who preceded him, was foundational to everything Turner became. It marked him as unique, gave him power, propelled his mind in different directions, and fueled his leadership. His literacy also raised issues that could not be reconciled short of revolt.

Turner and others eventually came to believe that his great purpose in life was as a prophet. With the willingness to ponder God's word until it moved him, Turner espoused uncanny biblical insights and interpretations that astounded his peers. And no other Black person in his community was in a position to seriously challenge him.

An enslaved person who could read, Stephen B. Oates notes in his biography of Turner, was "a very important fellow." Turner used the text he interpreted—the Bible—to claim his intellectual and spiritual authority in the community. Such a prized skill garnered "respect bordering on deference" in the enslaved community. While others could offer their competing worldviews, supporting one's position by reading or quoting scripture often made for an unanswerable argument.[15]

Turner was acutely aware of the power his literacy and biblical interpretation afforded him. He told Gray that because he could read at a young age, the community came to place "confidence" in his "superior judgment." Over time, he leveraged this respect to his advantage. "Knowing the influence I had obtained over the minds of my fellow servants ... by the communion of the Spirit whose revelations I often communicated to them, ... they believed and said my wisdom came from God." He cultivated their belief so that, in time, they would follow his lead.[16]

The problem with a prophet, though, is that he must go where the Word and Heavenly Father lead him, not where his earthly master wishes. If those paths ever parted, Turner would either have to defy God or face the hard reality of whips, shackles, and Virginia's unflinching legal stance on slavery. And he did not believe God intended him to be a slave—at least not for life. Slavery was a period of tribulation that he had to undergo before being freed of it.

Turner also confronted the basic contradiction of his human existence. Slavery was a personal affront. Turner knew he might be more intelligent than any man he knew. Black and white people knew it, too, and set him on a pedestal at an early age. He was the darling of the Black community, yet somehow set apart from it. He spent significant time playing with white children. Stephen Oates suggests that the special treatment his first owner, Ben Turner, afforded him—encouraging his literacy, praising him, and letting him mix with white children—may have given Turner the expectation that he would emancipate him someday. Instead, the title to him passed through several hands.[17]

When Nat was twelve years old, Ben Turner separated him from his white playmates and sent him to toil in the field. This brutal awakening made it clear that his life experience would follow his race, not his intellect. As his intellect continued to turn, the risk of sharing it rose. Freely speaking his mind—boldly or naively—Turner once told his later enslaver, Thomas Moore, "that blacks ought to be free, and that they would be free one day or another." Moore lashed him—another shocking reminder of the gulf between his intellect and his situation.[18]

Such violence surely engendered resentment, but slavery also meant living under the thumb of men who were beneath him in intelligence. Turner's life was a perfect example of the raging internal conflict that Walker described in his *Appeal*. Although Walker believed that slavery disfigured enslaved people's intellect and character, he thought those who escaped ignorance would not accept the servile station assigned to them. They would rather die than live out their lives enslaved. As Walker wrote and Turner felt, "your freedom is your natural right."[19]

The great question facing Turner was how to reconcile this conflict. He devoted vast amounts of time to fasting, reading, and searching for an answer. In his mid-twenties, he found a pious way of life and built his existence around it. Yet the chasm between the man he believed he was meant to be and the life of slavery remained a tormenting and insoluble problem.

Finally, he saw past the Bible's explicit rules and found an answer in Jesus's Sermon on the Mount. Jesus instructed his followers to lay aside the worries of food, clothing, and the fleeting pleasures that pagans chase. Putting biblical text in his own words, Turner said the solution was to "Seek ye the kingdom of Heaven and all things shall be added unto you."[20]

This passage haunted Turner for two years. He reflected and prayed on it daily, at one point experiencing a visitation by the Holy Spirit as he plowed, hearing Jesus's words as if spoken aloud to him: "Seek ye the kingdom of Heaven and all things shall be added unto you." Turner believed God was now calling him to his great purpose.[21]

His first instinct was to flee from slavery so that he could finally "fulfil the purpose for which ... I felt assured I was intended." He tried but didn't go far, staying in the woods for thirty days until he received a second message, which shocked him. The "Spirit appeared to me" and chastised him for setting his "wishes ... to the things of this world, and not to the kingdom of Heaven." Turner had allowed his worldly desires to cloud his understanding of God's will. The Spirit instructed him to "return to the service of my earthly master." Blending a quote from the book of Luke with personal instruction, the Spirit added: "For he who knoweth his Master's will, and doeth it not, shall be beaten with many stripes, and thus have I chastened you."[22]

When he returned, some in Turner's community questioned why a man with "any sense" would willingly "serve any master in the world." His status fell some. If this was the brand of insight he was selling, many wanted none of it. Some began to talk behind his back.[23]

But Turner began shifting his persona from an especially intelligent, religious man to a prophet on the verge of something big. His next vision, at least in his own mind, unmistakably signaled a new consequential stage in life. He "saw white spirits and black spirits engage in battle." With thunder rolling, they fought alongside streams flowing with blood under a darkened sun. In his confession, Turner didn't explicitly say that the vision foreshadowed a racial contest over slavery, but that was clearly the image.[24]

In 1828 he began a period of what he called self-perfection. To the extent an enslaved person could, he withdrew from his community to purify his behavior and body, ponder God's will, and maybe inspire mysticism regarding his absence. He claimed he saw physical signs—drops of blood on unharvested corn and cryptic text on the leaves in the woods—that he believed indicated "the great day of judgment was at hand."[25]

Other signs came from the heavens. On May 12 he heard a noise in the heavens and saw the Holy Spirit loosened and Christ laying down the "yoke he had borne for the sins of men." It was now for man—for Turner—to "take on" Christ's yoke and fight. The scripture anchoring the Spirit's message connected to the tension that had burdened Turner his entire life. "The time was fast approaching," the Spirit told him, "when the first should be last and the last should be first."[26]

This final message resolved his life's mystery. It made sense of God's promise to work great things through him. Yes, he was born a slave, and his talents had been squandered and repressed by slavery—a slavery to which God had told him to submit. But now he recognized that it was for him to make the apocalyptic battle of Black and white in the sky manifest on earth. This battle would lift Black people from their place in life and put white people in their own. He only needed a precise moment to strike.

A solar eclipse in February signaled it was time for Turner to "arise and prepare myself, and slay my enemies with their own weapons." Having kept his visions secret for half a decade, he believed the eclipse removed "the seal ... from my lips, and I communicated the great work laid out for me ... to the four in whom I had the greatest confidence"—the four who prepared the final meal the night before the revolt began.[27]

But when Turner fell ill the day before he planned to carry out God's final judgment on slavery—July 4—the men paused while Turner awaited health and another sign. Once again that sign came from the sun. On August 13, 1831, the sun appeared bluish green (apparently the result of debris in the atmosphere from an eruption at Mount Saint Helens). A week later, Turner and his men's bodies would drip with blood.

The reasons enslaved people revolt are as obvious as they are many. Yet revolts—much to David Walker's frustration—were rare. Virginia, for instance, enslaved half a million people annually by 1860—a quarter of the country's entire enslaved population—but experienced just two significant slave revolts in the nineteenth century. Those who did revolt experienced doubt, fear, strategic questions, and power struggles. It isn't immediately obvious why enslaved people in Southampton followed Turner.[28]

The visions he shared did not necessarily inspire confidence. They gave Black people every reason to consider him a madman and to think that revolt would lead only to a quick death. Turner was also long on visions, short on plans. He had no weapons cache, rallying points, provisions, communication strategy to enlist additional followers, demarcated route, or endgame other than to reach Jerusalem.

What were his followers to do when word of revolt spread to the white community, as it surely would? There were not enough enslaved people or guns in Southampton to hold off the militia that would encircle Jerusalem. A few in his community had to recognize that Turner had no real plan. The revolt sprang more from desperation than from any considered strategy. Wiser and cooler heads would have cautioned against it.

An earlier revolt in Richmond, Virginia, in 1800 faced the same dilemma. Its leader, Gabriel Prosser, had a plan and weapons, but members of his group were still unsure. In their final meeting, Gabriel's brother, Martin, drew on God's authority and the Israelites' emancipation story to quiet the resistance and inspire action. But one man voiced serious doubt, saying he "heard that in the days of old, when the Israelites were in Servitude to King Pharoah [sic], they were taken from him by the Power of God,—and were carried away by Moses—God had blessed them with an Angel to go with him." But if God was their source, he went on, they had better stop now. God had given signs to the Israelites, but "I could see nothing of that kind in these days."[29]

Martin quieted this man's doubt much as Vesey would have in Charleston. Because he could read and cite text, he could claim greater biblical authority than the objector. "I read in my Bible," Martin replied, "where God says, if we will worship him, we should have peace in all our Lands, five of you shall conquer a hundred and a hundred, a thousand of our enemies." The detractor apparently had no response. The man who could read and interpret text had the final say. All might have an equal claim to an opinion, but the opinions of those who could read the Bible carried more weight. Their interpretations were the foundation of what James Sidbury, a historian of race and slavery, calls "textual communities" whose members trusted their literate brethren "to interpret God's word reliably."[30]

Turner, Vesey, and Prosser, as well as all those secretly reading Walker's *Appeal* from pulpits across the South, fell within this tradition. But Turner stands apart from Vesey and Prosser in his singular focus on the

Bible. Vesey drew on multiple texts, and one needed not buy into Vesey's religion in order to follow him. His liberty and democracy arguments were just as compelling as his religious ones. Even for the religiously inspired, Vesey and Prosser didn't require much imagination. All their followers had to do was connect a basic biblical narrative to a parallel world they could see and touch. Vesey and Prosser also had relatively well-wrought battle plans.

Turner, however, relied on vague biblical allegory and asked his community to believe things that only he could see. They had to make a leap of faith and trust in things they could not fully appreciate or understand. Though textual mastery gave Turner a large measure of authority, some surely wanted more assurances. He closed that gap with a personal story that his community knew, and then interweaved it with biblical text. Old Testament prophets, God's miraculous intervention in the world, Christ's coming, the promise of Christ's return to judge the living and the dead, and the apocalyptic visions that accompanied Christ would have been familiar to Turner's community. Rather than add conflicting or extraneous prophecies to those familiar narratives, he cultivated a personal story that paralleled the Bible.

Turner presented himself as God's prophet—the one preceding Christ's return—and leveraged enough personal details to convince many in his community. Of particular importance was the notion that God had called Turner before birth. The scripture told of God calling several other prophets—Jeremiah, Isaiah, and John the Baptist—in the same way. The community would have remembered, for instance, the story of God telling Jeremiah that "before I formed thee in the belly, I knew thee; and before thou camest forth out of the womb I sanctified thee, and I ordained thee a prophet unto the nations." The notion that Turner fell within this prophetic lineage had a ring of truth given his early literacy, the expectations of his greatness, and his apparent knowledge of events that happened before his birth.[31]

God had also communicated with prophets—Samuel and Ezekiel—through the Holy Spirit and visions. A community open to prophets would have also been open to the idea that God spoke to Turner through visions. His literacy allowed him to connect the two and use his independent and unchecked scriptural interpretations to blend his persona with God's will. As a presumptive part of the biblical story itself, he claimed a direct line of communication with God. And that communication, open only to his interpretation, became prophecy.

Turner's actions fit the mold. His asceticism, moral austerity, spiritual retreats, and falling ill on the eve of revelation all had a biblical character. Following Christ's instruction to "lay not up for yourselves treasures upon earth, where moth and rust doth corrupt, and where thieves break through and steal," he disdained property. He "was never known to have a dollar in his life," yet never wanted for anything. God, he could say, was keeping His promise to His obedient servant.[32]

Turner's literacy, persona, and standing reinforced one another. Were literacy or religion removed from his story, his life would have unfolded quite differently, his revolt maybe not at all. The same is true of Vesey and Prosser. And Walker's name lived on not because of what he did but because of what he wrote.

Revolt required more than rage. Premeditated revolt—particularly if it involved a substantial number of people—demanded a leader with insight and a careful touch. Few enslaved people had access to the information they needed to answer questions of what to do after the initial violence. Remaining in place was a death sentence. Facing a vast unknown geography was overwhelming. Without information or literacy, revolt meant fighting a battle and then rushing into a hostile territory with no map and no way to read the signs.

Vesey got his community past those uncertainties with his sense of the world and plan for tackling it. He had traveled the world and kept abreast of its developments through reading. He could correspond with people outside his immediate orbit—even outside his country—and these connections inspired confidence in his leadership. Walker never directly plotted a revolt, but his literacy, worldliness, and network ran deep and were far more threatening than violence. He announced his intentions and still could not be stopped.

Until Turner, enslavers had allowed themselves to think that Vesey and Walker were products of a freedom to which Black people were ill-suited. With no white man to direct him, they thought, Vesey got ideas in his head, distorted God's word, misunderstood politics, and fraternized with other self-important Blacks. In his confusion, he poisoned enslaved people's minds and indulged his misguided ideas. White slave owners were livid when Walker freely contested their narrative, but it was Turner's revolt that wrecked their delusions. He was not part of a larger conversation or network. He was born and died enslaved. He lacked worldly expertise. And while he may have heard of Vesey through the slave grapevine, there is no indication he read anything about him, had access to Walker's *Appeal*, or was subject to outside influence. A dose of charisma and a shot of literary interpretation were enough to change his and his community's trajectory.[33]

Turner smashed the stereotype of the master-slave relationship. After remaining loyal—even unusually loyal—to his enslavers for the better part of three decades, he was moved toward violence not by ideas some other Black man planted but by ideas originating in his own mind—as a result of engaging with a text white men put in his hand. And what most set Turner apart from Vesey and Walker may be what Turner didn't say.[34]

Turner had no outward politics. Although he clearly sought an end that would have had political consequences—Black freedom—his motivation and rhetoric were purely religious. As a Virginian, he had heard of Thomas Jefferson and the Declaration of Independence, experienced July 4 celebrations, and understood their symbolism. But in his confession, he never even hinted at a political inspiration, American or otherwise. While his religion was superficially the same as Vesey's and Walker's—the deliverance story and God's righteous vengeance—Turner's was personal and mystical, to such an extreme extent that some questioned his sanity. Was he a fanatic, a prophet, or a huckster expertly playing the role? We can have no clear answer.[35]

The most direct evidence of Turner's inner thoughts comes from Gray, a white man who would have struggled, over three short days, to understand him. Gray portrayed Turner as a compelling figure, but one whose full measure was impossible to convey in writing. In his own confession, Gray admitted he wasn't sure whether Turner was crazy or so shrewd that he played all those around him.

Whatever the truth of men like Turner, Vesey, and Walker, something fundamental changed with the publication of *Walker's Appeal* and the events of Turner's revolt. The "slavery question," as historians and politicians have so frequently called it, can encompass too much and submerge important threads in the process. Repressing Black literacy was, no doubt, part of intentionally consolidating the larger slavery agenda. In Vesey's day, the repression of literacy might have intermingled with ulterior motives and provided a convenient rhetorical target. But Walker and Turner made Black literacy a distinct issue and threat in its own right.[36]

Attacks on Black literacy would never again just be subterfuge for something else, nor would its danger be speculative. These men unquestionably proved the importance and power of Black literacy, and it required its own special precaution, regardless of slavery's larger trajectory. And the fact that Black literacy would, for decades, persist as an issue of special concern in the context of an institution that was most directly empowered by violence and physical brutality stands out. Literacy was Black people's power. It would take a concerted movement to stop it.

CHAPTER SIX

The South's Last Slavery Debate

NAT TURNER'S REVOLT PUT an end to any rational discussion around race in the deep South. Though Southern states had been sympathetic to South Carolina's response to Vesey, it largely stood alone for the better part of a decade in its urgent concern over Black literacy. David Walker's *Appeal* spreading across the South forced some states to admit that they were no different from South Carolina. Yet other states still held fast to old assumptions, thinking they could wait out this crisis, if it even was one.

For the states that took Vesey and Walker seriously, Turner's revolt was a shot of post-traumatic stress. They realized their response to Walker's *Appeal* had not ended the war. The remaining states saw that war was spreading—through violence or the printed word—to every part of the South. Southern states would have to stand together or die alone. In what they believed was a fight for survival, a core group of Southern states—particularly South Carolina, North Carolina, Georgia, and Virginia—stood together and cast the die for a civil war a generation later. From the positions they drew and the tone they took, there could be no retreat.

Simply to be south of the Mason Dixon line was to be compelled to a regional order in support of slavery—which was a relatively new phenomenon. Using geography as his lens, Lacy Ford, in *Deliver Us from Evil*, captures the diversity of Southern thought regarding slavery across time. During the first two decades of the 1800s, from Virginia to Georgia, the coastal regions in those states increasingly favored a proslavery economic and political order and wanted to expand it westward. The mountainous regions in those states took more moderate positions and sometimes blocked proslavery agendas. By the 1830s, however, the proslavery forces in these states managed to force their political order on the entirety of their respective states. That made the most important dividing line the one between the Lower and Upper South. Many whites in Tennessee, Kentucky, and Maryland, for instance, remained ambivalent toward slavery and the presence of free people of color. Yet, even there, violent opposition would eventually shrink the increasingly small pockets of open and rational thought.[1]

Sharing borders with more moderate states and home to its own competing political camps, Virginia's evolution captures these shifts best. In the immediate aftermath of Walker's *Appeal*, Virginia had been unsure whether to entrench itself or engage rational discussion. Two starkly different ways of life and geographies coexisted in the state. The coastal and piedmont areas were heavily dependent on slavery, but the western part of the state was not. Eastern Virginia enslaved 416,350 people and was home to 40,000 free Black people. The western half of the state enslaved about 100,000 people, but the numbers fell as one moved further west.[2]

The northwestern part of the state, which later became West Virginia, shared a border, a mountain range, and a good deal of culture with Pennsylvania and Ohio. The entire Black population—free and enslaved—in Virginia's Allegheny region numbered only 16,600. A hotbed of abolitionist sentiment rested just across the border in Pennsylvania, and Ohio had introduced a constitutional amendment to end slavery during the controversy over South Carolina's Negro Seamen Act.

Virginia's voice on slavery carried national importance. Virginians had controlled the White House and helped set the national political climate for decades. Thomas Jefferson's *Notes on the State of Virginia* remained one of the most widely read and authoritative pieces on slavery. More important, Virginia was home to almost a quarter of the entire nation's enslaved population. It enslaved more people than Louisiana, Mississippi, Alabama, and Tennessee put together. Charleston may have been the port through which most enslaved people arrived, but Virginia is where most came to toil.[3]

Turner's revolt provoked a hurried public conversation in Virginia that seemed little different from those occurring south of Virginia. But behind closed doors, leaders were questioning the institution's viability. That winter, the conversation would burst into the public view and turn into the most deliberate discussion of slavery in the nation's history, what Joseph Clarke Robert characterized in his recounting of the debates as the "line of demarcation between a public willing to hear the faults of slavery and one intolerant of criticism." It would be the last such debate south of the Mason-Dixon line before slavery was ended.[4]

On August 23, 1831, in the midst of Turner's revolt, Virginia governor John Floyd wrote in his diary that "this will be a very notable day in Virginia." He then returned to the task of suppressing the insurrection. He sent a cavalry troop, an artillery troop carrying one thousand guns, and two infantry companies to Southampton. Five days later, he received word that the rebels had killed sixty-one people. The following days brought news of arrests and possible insurrections elsewhere.

With Turner still at large, Floyd tried to retain his composure. Striking a hopeful note, he wrote that while Virginia had suffered "the most inhuman butcheries the mind can conceive of, men, women, and infants, their heads chopped off, their bowels ripped out, ears, noses, hands, and legs cut off," other enslaved people had been moved "to defend their masters and to give information of the approach of the hostile party." Five days later he was less sanguine. The state militia commander in Northampton County, on the eastern side of the Chesapeake Bay, informed him that "the negroes in that county are in a state of insubordination and intend to create an insurrection.... Guns have been found among them and some they were compelled to take from them by force." In his final diary entry that day, he worried that Walker's vision for the South was unfolding before his eyes. "I fear much this insurrection in Southampton is to lead to much more disastrous consequences than is at this time apprehended by anybody," he wrote.[5]

By the end of September, Floyd had regained his bearings. Outwardly, he kept the state on full alert and armed, but he sensed things were settling down. Speaking of the western counties, he wrote: "I know there is no danger ... as the slaves were never more humble and subdued." He even showed mercy to Black people accused of revolting. Believing that they had been convicted in haste or on thin evidence, he commuted some sentences and shortened others.[6]

Moderation on slavery, especially in the aftermath of a revolt, was not typical for Southern governors. But Floyd had spent his youth isolated from the most virulent influences and biases of slavery. He was born just south of the Ohio River, in Kentucky, and raised in the western reaches of Virginia, land that would become West Virginia. He left there for college in Pennsylvania, where he lived under the care of Dr. Benjamin Rush—a Founding Father and signer of the Declaration of Independence—who openly decried slavery. These experiences led him to question the supposed racial inferiority of Black people.

As a young man and aspiring politician, however, Floyd either sidelined his views or was not sufficiently convinced of them. He married into a prominent family that owned slaves and, as a U.S. representative, remained quiet during the Missouri debates. Yet given how strongly Virginia's other representatives favored admitting Missouri as a slave state, Floyd's silence may offer a clue to what he was thinking. By the fall of 1831, with slavery wreaking havoc on the fabric of Virginia's society, Floyd seemed to tire of the institution. That November he promised himself that "before I leave this Government, I will have contrived to have a law passed gradually abolishing slavery in this state."[7]

He did not, however, come at the issue as a staunch abolitionist. Having long been more than willing to tolerate slavery, he was motivated by more practical concerns. He saw enslaved populations as a threat to the state's security, and he wanted to make the world safer for white people. On that point, he sometimes aligned with proslavery forces, arguing that Northern agitators like William Lloyd Garrison were making things worse.

On January 1, 1831, Garrison, a white journalist in Boston, had begun publishing a weekly newspaper, *The Liberator*. He framed it as a frontal attack on slavery and promised to press his cause "till every chain be broken, and every bondman set free! Let southern oppressors tremble—let their secret abettors tremble—let their northern apologists tremble—let all the enemies of the persecuted blacks tremble."[8]

Garrison had spent the previous two years publishing a different newspaper, *Genius of Universal Emancipation*, which favored a gradual approach. Now he asked "pardon of my God, of my country, and of my brethren the poor slaves, for having [been] so full of timidity, injustice, and absurdity." *The Liberator* would brook no compromise with truth and justice. "Tell a man whose house is on fire," he wrote, "to give a moderate alarm; tell him to moderately rescue his wife from the hands of the ravisher." *The Liberator* quickly became the nation's most widely circulated abolitionist paper.[9]

If Virginia couldn't catch Turner, Garrison made a convenient substitute target. When authorities found copies of *The Liberator* circulating in Virginia, Floyd went on the offensive, calling Garrison's disavowal of

Masthead of *The Liberator.* Courtesy of Wikimedia Commons.

violence a façade. Garrison's paper, he said, was published "with the express intention of inciting the slaves and free negroes in this and the other States to rebellion and to murder the men, women and children of those states." He could not believe "there is no law to punish such an offence." It was absurd, he argued, that "a man in our States may plot treason in one state against another without fear of punishment, whilst the suffering state has no right to resist by the provisions of the Federal Constitution." If these threats were not checked, "it must lead to a separation of these states. . . . The law of nature will not permit men to have their families butchered before their eyes by their slaves and not seek by force to punish those who plan and encourage them to perpetrate these deeds." It was his and the General Assembly's duty to find a solution during the next legislative session. "Something must be done," he urged, "and with decision."[10]

Floyd began coordinating with other governors. On November 19, 1831, he wrote to South Carolina's governor, James Hamilton—the Charlestonian who had prosecuted Denmark Vesey, dramatized it in a pamphlet, and leveraged it for political power for years in the legislature—in order to enlist Hamilton in a master plan. He started by diagnosing the problem in a way he knew would resonate with Hamilton. Floyd was "fully persuaded" that "the spirit of insubordination" and revolt came from "the Yankee population," not enslaved people themselves. The Yankees "began first, by making them religious" and then "telling the blacks God was no respecter of persons" and that "all men were born free and equal." They then persuaded "our females . . . that it was piety to teach negroes to read and write." When Blacks began assembling on their own for religious purposes and reading "the incendiary publications of Walker, Garrison, and [others]," things spiraled out of control.[11]

Floyd's proposal reflected ideas Hamilton had pushed in South Carolina a decade earlier. Floyd promised to recommend a series of slave laws to the Virginia legislature, including laws that would "confine the Slaves to the estates of their masters—prohibit negroes from preaching—absolutely to drive from this State all free negroes." He also wanted to use the state's annual surplus revenue to compensate slaveholders for putting enslaved people to work on state projects—in a sort of rent-to-own arrangement that would eventually allow the state to lease enslaved people to work outside the country. He saw this as "the first step to emancipation" and hoped South Carolina and Georgia "may be disposed to co-operate."[12]

Though no other governors expressed interest in this scheme, Floyd sensed a path forward in Virginia. In a written address opening the Virginia General Assembly's new session on December 6, 1831, Floyd asked for action as dramatic as anything any state had done since the Constitution was adopted. Since the General Assembly had last met, he wrote, "grave and distressing" events had placed "your country" in "crisis." Now all eyes were "upon you. ... You alone possess the power of accomplishing all the great objects which the public desire, and much of the future welfare of this Republic depends upon your present deliberations." Turner's revolt was quelled, he assured his readers, but evidence suggested that "the spirit of insurrection was not confined to Southampton; many convictions have taken place elsewhere, and some few in distant counties." Using the post office and local agents to spread seditious materials, "unrestrained fanatics in some of the neighbouring States" had brought this madness to Virginia.[13]

The problem at home was Black preachers—literate Black preachers in particular. They had been "the most active among ourselves, in stirring up the spirit of revolt." The average slave would normally give little thought to insurrection, but "those preachers have a perfect understanding" of potential plots in other counties and "have been the channels through which the inflammatory papers and pamphlets, brought here by the agents and emissaries from other States, have been circulated amongst our slaves." Under the guise of religious worship, they have been reading these inflammatory tracts to their flocks. Therefore, Floyd argued, "the public good requires the negro preachers to be silenced, who, full of ignorance, are incapable of inculcating any thing but notions of the wildest superstition, thus preparing fit instruments, in the hands of the crafty agitators, to destroy the public tranquility."[14]

Floyd then turned to free people of color. Even if a "slave is confined by law to the estate of his master, . . . the free people of colour may nevertheless convey all the incendiary pamphlets and papers with which we are . . . inundated." Virginia had been too indulgent toward free Black people, he argued, and it was now "indispensably necessary" to remove them from the state. In the "spirit of kindness," however, he would confer one "last benefit" on them—an annual appropriation to pay for "their removal from this Commonwealth."[15]

Though aggressively proslavery in many respects, Governor Floyd's letter to the assembly carefully crafted a public proposal that could undercut slavery by effectively buying out slaveholders. In doing so, he opened the door to the most open legislative debate the South would see on the abolition of slavery. It was not the only such debate, but the others were all narrower in scope. Slaveholders had long wielded dominant power in the South, but missionaries, mountaineers, Northern transplants, and rational thinkers constituted a critical mass that could question and sometimes moderate Southern states' slavery policies.

South Carolina, for instance, temporarily shut down its international slave trade in 1787, believing that planters had placed the state's economy in jeopardy by recklessly running up debt to purchase slaves. Other Southern states did the same in the following years. But when the slave trade reopened in the early 1800s and the enslaved population in many places overtook that of whites, slavery became at once both a threat to white safety and an institution that the wealthy believed they could not live without. Walker's *Appeal* and Turner's rebellion brought this dilemma to a head.[16]

The Virginia General Assembly responded to Turner's revolt in predictable fashion. After reading the governor's remarks on the subject, the House of Delegates ordered five hundred copies of the governor's message to be printed and appointed a select committee of thirteen members to study the state's options. The committee needed to work fast. The House was already receiving petitions to take more dramatic action. Moments after the select committee was appointed, other members read petitions from their constituents that called for the immediate removal of free people of color from the state. That option, along with other obvious ones—like oppressive regulation of Black people and more military might—were certainly on the table. But the full body was eager to hear from the committee sooner rather than later.[17]

On December 14, while the committee was still working in private, Delegate William Roane, the grandson of Founding Father Patrick Henry, introduced a petition before the full House of Delegates from the Quaker community in his Richmond district calling for "the ultimate manumission of the slave population of Virginia." He assured his colleagues that he did not support abolition, but given recent events, the legislature and, thus, the committee had to consider all options. Another delegate instantly rose in opposition, arguing that the issue of abolition was outside the committee's charge and could not be considered.[18]

That objection was a gut check for the 120 most powerful men in Virginia. They could rule the topic of emancipation out of order and avoid discussing the question as a full body or in committee. Governor Floyd had seen that maneuver coming and had been working hard behind the scenes to avoid it. The discussion "must come," he wrote in his diary, "if I can influence my friends in the Assembly to bring it on." The day after Christmas, he closed his diary entry much as he had at Thanksgiving: "I will not rest until slavery is abolished in Virginia."[19]

By a vote of 93 to 27, the House rejected the motion to cut off discussion of abolition. All eyes were on its next move. By then, forty different petitions, signed by two thousand people, had rolled into the General Assembly since Turner's revolt. Virginians wanted action on slavery; they needed leadership. But it was not clear they would get it.

The tension was palpable when the legislature resumed its work in the new year. On January 7, the *Richmond Enquirer* wrote that there were but "two great subjects before the Committees." One was much needed internal improvements of the state. The other related "to the colored population of the State." The stakes could not be higher, the *Enquirer* fretted:

> We may shut our eyes and avert our faces, if we please. . . . But there it is, the dark and growing evil, at our doors; and meet the question we must, at no distant day. God only knows what it is the part of wise men to do on that momentous and appalling subject. Of this I am very sure, that the difference—nothing short of frightful—between all that exists on one side of the Potomac, and all on the other, is owing to that cause alone.—The disease is deep-seated—it is at the heart's core—it is consuming, and has all along been consuming our vitals, and I would laugh, if I could laugh, on such a subject, at the ignorance and folly of

the politician, who ascribes that to an act of the government which is the inevitable effect of the eternal laws of nature. What is to be done. Oh! my God—I don't know, but something must be done.[20]

The free press, if it still existed, had to tell the truth: the state's enslaved population was rising, its white population shrinking, and the trend would only accelerate. The paper confessed little hope that the current legislature could find a solution, but it had to try. "Our wisest men," it implored, "cannot give too much of their attention to this subject—nor can they give it too soon."[21]

That appraisal revealed another fissure. Some politicians and commentators believed that the issues should not be discussed at all—not in the legislature and definitely not in the papers. Responding to the *Enquirer*, an essay in the *Whig* argued that slavery had been with the nation since its founding and nothing could be done with it now. "Agitation" around slavery would only "stimulate the blacks to fresh acts of violence, with the hope of obtaining their freedom by exciting the fears of the timid, and by the aid of modern philanthropists." Better to stay silent on such a "delicate subject."[22]

Accusing the *Enquirer* of having breached that rule and taken up "intermeddling with what belongs to others," the *Whig* urged readers to respond by "discontinuing the use of that paper." That attack on a competitor triggered personal threats. The *Enquirer* reported that the *Whig*'s piece prompted not only calls to "muzzle the Liberty of the Press," but calls for "vengeance . . . to be invoked upon our bodies." This talk, it suggested, was more dangerous than talk of abolishing slavery. Without a free press and open debate, the republic would slide into demagoguery and tyranny. Virginia did not turn back. As one commentator wrote, "The seals are broken, which have been put for fifty years upon the most delicate and difficult subject."[23]

A few in the House took one more shot at ending debate. Arguing that it was "not expedient to legislate on the subject," William Goode, representing a district near Southampton, moved to preclude the select committee "from consideration of all petitions, memorials and resolutions, which have for their object of the manumission" of enslaved persons. The committee's work, Goode argued, stoked dangerous passions "throughout the country." The morality of slavery, he said, was beside the point: Virginia could not "confiscate the property of citizens." Indulging the notion that it could do so would disrupt the market and devalue property.[24]

Blacks, too, he reminded his colleagues, were listening closely. "They are not an ignorant herd of Africans. On the contrary, they are an active and intelligent class, ... weighing every movement of the Legislature." Any sign of weakness from the legislature would encourage violence. Seeing the fear Turner's insurrection wrought, enslaved people had reason to hope that another insurrection "would force upon the State a measure for their emancipation." But Goode believed emancipation was a fool's errand. Ending debate immediately was the only way to avoid inflating "expectations which were doomed to disappointment."[25]

Goode's motion to terminate the select committee's work backfired. What might have stayed quiet instead went to the House floor. As soon as Goode laid his motion on the table, Thomas Jefferson Randolph (the late president's grandson) was ready with an amendment. He struck one line in Goode's resolution and replaced it with another that would require the legislature to "inquire into the expediency of submitting to the vote [of the people] that the children of all female slaves, who may be born in this state, on or after the 4th day of July, 1840, shall become the property of the commonwealth" and would, upon reaching adulthood, be hired out until they generated enough funds to pay for their removal "beyond the limits of the United States." Randolph, as William W. Freehling writes in *The Road to Disunion*, "nervously stepped forward where his grandfather had faltered back" and proposed gradual emancipation and colonization.[26]

Samuel McDowell Moore of Lexington, a mountainous part of the state, followed Randolph's lead, saying he hoped "the time has not yet come when we are prepared" to shut down the legislature just because a newspaper might express an opinion about its work. So far, the House had only referred some petitions to a committee. Now, Goode would have the House disband the committee for no reason other than that the press was reporting on the matter. The people of Virginia, he emphasized, had petitioned their government for solutions regarding slavery, and the House owed it to them to consider their appeals.[27]

As for the issue of slavery itself, Moore echoed arguments David Walker had raised two years before. Slavery, Moore believed, was a curse, and American slavery—its racialization, rigidity, and aggressive oppression—was the worst in human history. Like Walker, he argued that slaveholders knew that education and slavery were incompatible and were trying to keep enslaved people as ignorant as possible. But because "slavery is a violation of . . . natural rights," they could do nothing to stop revolts. Turner's was just one of many to come. Having absorbed the American credo of inalienable rights and the idea that "all men are by nature free and equal," the growing enslaved population would soon rise to seize their freedom, leaving the land "everywhere . . . red with human blood."[28]

Thomas Jefferson Randolph closed the day with a simple plea: let the people have the final word on slavery, not delegates in dark rooms. It was too late for Virginia to avoid debate. The "public mind" was awakened "to the grave circumstances of our condition" and demanded "eradication" of the evil plaguing it. That eradication would come by either legislative solution or "the bloody scenes of Southampton and St. Domingo."[29]

The proslavery contingent used the evening following Randolph's speech to regroup, responding the next morning with full force. James Gholson, representing another community near Southampton, was their messenger. Disgusted by the previous day's debate, he argued that the subject "should never be openly discussed, until we are ripe for prompt and energetic action." The Founding Fathers, he emphasized, had considered the subject only "with closed doors and secret journals." But with open debate forced upon him, Gholson launched into a daylong diatribe that laid the foundation for several weeks of proslavery argument.[30]

The issue, Gholson said, was not morals but property rights. Both the Virginia and U.S. Constitutions recognized a "binding obligation" that "private property shall not be taken for public use without just compensation." But this "sacred principle" had roots deeper than constitutional language. It rested on "the principles of justice—it is the very ligament which binds society together." Without property rights, "there is no civilization—no government," only a "state of nature." Drawing a comparison to the future benefits of real estate, he argued that those rights extended not just to current slaves but to the yet unborn children of enslaved mothers. Landowners had always had "a reasonable right to its annual profits; the owner of orchards, to their annual fruits; the owner of brood mares, to their product." So too did "the owner of female slaves" have a right "to their increase."[31]

Although Gholson conceded that public necessity could justify infringing on property rights under certain circumstances, he rejected the notion that slavery posed an inherent risk of insurrection. Literacy and newspapers were the threat, he argued, not slavery. "Incendiary publications" were "infusing into the minds of our slaves, a spirit of restlessness and insubordination. These are the true authors of all our apprehensions and unhappiness." Instead of attacking slavery, the legislature should marshal "all the powers at its command" to extinguish these publications. Northern states had to do their part, too. "Among civilized Governments in friendship with each other," Gholson explained, when a citizen of one power incites rebellion in another, the first government must punish the citizen under its own laws, "deliver him up to the injured Government to be punished," or be prepared to "incur the consequence." In this instance, the consequence was an "appeal to war."[32]

Gholson ended by pointing out a fatal practical flaw in Randolph's proposal. Randolph claimed that slavery was a public safety threat, but his proposal would leave slavery intact for a generation. Only a fool, Gholson sneered, would assume that enslaved people would somehow be dissuaded from plotting sedition by the promise of freedom for some other group in the distant future. Such a policy might even further inflame them.

As the day was closing, William M. Rives, a descendant of Virginia's early wealthy colonial families, questioned the political standing of people like Gholson. Elite planters, Rives argued, had held the state's democratic process in a death grip for decades, intentionally limiting education not just for Black people but for poor and middle-class whites as well. It was no coincidence, he surmised, that Northern states "liberally extended" education and suffrage while Virginia "warmly opposed and curtailed" those rights. Suppressing the common white man allowed the planters to more easily extend slavery.[33]

On the third day, William Brodnax of Dinwiddie held the floor for most of the day. Brodnax chaired the select committee working on the current dilemma. The committee's report was due any day and the assembly was eager for any hint of its contents. Equally important, Brodnax had commanded the state militia that quelled Turner's rebellion. He was also a slaveholder, the owner of a 1,600-acre plantation and enslaver of a hundred people. Rather than whip up fear, he sought to offer a realistic assessment of the danger and propriety—from the slaveholder's perspective—of abolition.

For the first half of the day, Brodnax hid where he stood. He had wanted the committee to finish its work, but the legislature had "passed the Rubicon," making the committee report pointless and stoking more emotions than any issue since the American Revolution. When he finally reached the merits, he said he could not concur with Randolph's gradual emancipation or Gholson's willingness to do nothing. Randolph's assault on private property would "tear up by the roots all the ligaments that bind society together." Yet no reasonable "human being" could "doubt or deny" that slavery is "a transcendent evil."[34]

The chasm between the two positions compelled him to "listen to 'the still small voice' of reason and moderation" and "examine frankly and fairly, the arguments and principles of others" regardless of political party or region. He first chided the proslavery camp for trying to shut down "a full and free discussion." His willingness to break ranks and side with democratic dialogue signaled possibility, even if not a solution. He was, he claimed, "anxious to demonstrate to the world" that the legislature is "not afraid to discuss" the issue of slavery "without any affectation of mystery or concealment." And that discussion should extend beyond the legislature—it should continue in the press, the streets, the taverns, by the fireside. "The time has passed," he said, "when there can be any 'sealed subject' in this country. The spirit of the age will not tolerate suppression." The debate was already feverish across the world. "We might as well attempt to put out the light of the sun" as try to stop it.[35]

He asked the assembly to hold up a mirror, to neither exaggerate nor underrate what it saw, and to be unafraid "to examine into our real situation." The ruin of the state would come not from debate but from avoiding reality. Most slaveholders were like patients suffering from "chronic diseases" that they refused to acknowledge. But when he, as a slaveholder, took a hard look at the institution, he saw four things.[36]

First, emancipation required colonization. A Black population half-free, half-enslaved would bring too many practical problems. Second, Virginia could not eliminate the individual right to private property or undermine its value. Third, no slave should ever "be taken from its owner, without his own consent, or an ample compensation for its value."[37]

Had Brodnax stopped there, the difference between his position and Gholson's would have been hard to discern. He was giving almost no ground to the other side. And if this was the most that a "reasoned" slaveholder would accept, it belied a deeper truth—that slavery could only end through war. Enslavers might acknowledge slavery as an evil cancer, but they would rather suffer cancer to the bitter end than accept treatment. Surgery was its own form of death. A region mired in this mindset could not save itself. But Brodnax did not see it that way. He was optimistic: "I do believe a ray of light has dawned," insufficient on its own to illuminate a solution, but that "if steadily pursued, will . . . lead us to safety. . . . I do believe that measures of incalculable benefit may be adopted, entirely consistent with those great principles which I have assumed."[38]

His optimism led to his fourth point—his willingness to recognize "a single exception" to the inviolable rules of property: "absolute necessity." It "is a hard rule, but an inevitable one. When the public safety and prosperity obviously require the deprivation of private property, the sacrifice must be submitted to." The exchange for that submission is "just compensation." Whether this concession was purely self-serving or a pragmatic middle ground, it was further than many slaveholders would go. Even during the Denmark Vesey trials, slaveholders had demanded that the state release convicted slaves back to them, so that they could decide their fates.[39]

Brodnax, however, spoke with more urgency regarding necessity than Randolph—something only a man with a vested interest in slavery could do without being shouted down. He assured the assembly that while there was never any danger that the Turner rebellion would overwhelm armed white forces, such "scenes of inconceivable horror" would inevitably recur if the course of slavery did not change. Although he disagreed with the details of Randolph's plan, "I do most heartily agree with him in the conviction, that prudence and policy . . . require that something should be done to stay this onward evil."[40]

The first step Brodnax proposed was to remove free people of color. This idea proceeded on the stereotype of free Blacks as mischievous gossips who set bad examples. At best they were a mirror in which enslaved people could see the contradiction of their own circumstances. But more important, Brodnax believed, the state needed to rebalance its racial demographics. By his calculation, if Virginia deported six thousand free Black people each year, within ten years "there would not be left one single free negro in Virginia." Their removal would cancel out the growth of the enslaved population and allow white labor and a more productive economic system to reestablish themselves. Virginia could achieve his goal for about $200,000—just 30 cents per white Virginian.[41]

Removing free Blacks, however, was only a demonstration of concept. If the state could do that, it could accomplish Brodnax's "ulterior object" of removing slaves. The details on that ulterior object were vague. Brodnax proposed that the state purchase six thousand enslaved people a year "at fair prices" and deport them. "There are a number of slave-holders at this very time," he claimed, "who would voluntarily surrender their slaves," and another group that "would cheerfully compromise with the state for half their value." If the state facilitated the process, it could end slavery in Virginia within eighty years.[42]

With the few moments left in the day, James Bruce of Halifax rose to pour water on Brodnax's plan. Virginia, he said, was trapped by circumstances. Even the "mind of the immortal Jefferson" could not see a way out of slavery, and the House's weeks of debate had only confirmed the impossibility of finding a workable solution. The House should just admit defeat now.[43]

The fourth day settled into shorter speeches that repeated prior arguments. The only notable exceptions were those urging humility and good faith efforts. These speakers did not claim to be wiser than Jefferson, or certain that a solution would be found, but they believed in trying—at this auspicious moment in particular. A delegate from a district outside Richmond, for instance, vowed to put "the best interests of his country" first, even if it meant the end of his political career, and pleaded for others to do the same. Though debating abolition felt like a "dream," it was all too real. Public discussion of the issue would "roll on by the force of its own intrinsic weight and importance." He did not know the proper course, but he rejected the notion that there was not "wisdom enough in this ancient Commonwealth, to devise some safe, some just, and some practicable scheme of emancipation"—or "patriotism enough to adopt that scheme at almost any sacrifice." It was the legislature's duty to let the debate continue until it found an answer.[44]

Something else, however, was starting to bubble over—regional differences that could tear Virginia apart. The western part of the state, which enslaved very few people, still carried wounds from a recent legislative reapportionment that included enslaved people in the population count and, as a result, shifted substantial power in the General Assembly to the eastern slaveholding counties. Now, eastern delegates were arguing that representatives from the western parts of the state did not even have the right to vote on slavery's future because they had no vested interest in it.

Charles Faulkner, a western delegate, confronted this tension head on. Slavery—or its abolition—was deeply important to every Virginian's future, and he was incensed that easterners were suggesting otherwise. The state's internal improvements—railroads, canals, and other infrastructure—depended on taxes that fell across the entire state. Whatever taxes slavery did or did not contribute affected everyone's tax burden and the state's capacity to improve itself. Slaveholders, therefore, could not claim to be the only interested parties. But then Faulkner went a step further and denounced what he saw as wildly overstated natural rights theories of property. Men, he argued, did not hold slaves "by any patent from God ... but solely by virtue of the acquiescence and consent of the society in which they live." And when property began to "jeopardize the peace, the happiness, the good order—nay, the very existence of society—from that moment, the right by which they hold their property is gone."[45]

Just as slaveholders had been drawing lines in the sand for days, Faulkner had now drawn a new one that further widened the gap between abolitionists and the slavocracy. He was saying that slaveholders were only entitled to compensation if Virginia took their property for public use; Virginia owed them nothing if extinguishing slavery was necessary to protect society from destruction.

On January 16, 1832, the fifth day of debate, the select committee issued its report: "It is INEXPEDIENT for the present legislature to make any enactment for the abolition of slavery." It offered no explanation for its conclusion.[46]

Those who wanted to stop the committee had won a battle, but they lost the war. The full House would still debate the resolution. One of the first delegates to speak on the proposal proved the committee's judgment of inexpedience premature, if not wrong.

A slaveholding delegate, William Roane, confirmed that slaveholders were willing to give up the institution. Though he had never "revolted at the idea or practice of slavery" or believed in the "natural equality of men," he considered slavery "as much a correlative of liberty as cold is of heat." None of that, however, mattered given the dangers facing Virginia. Those dangers left the state with but one solution: to start reducing its number of slaves and compensate slaveholders for their loss of property. He was for it.[47]

As the following days settled into irreconcilable talking points that suggested the legislature might never agree on anything, some began to argue for putting the issue to the voters. This, of course, unsettled the slaveholders even more. Asking the voters was worse than debating the subject in the legislature because it would endorse the legitimacy of abolition as a policy option. After that, each side restated its property rights arguments, but the abolitionists got the better of it. William Preston of Montgomery County, for instance, turned slaveholders' own sources against them. The federal Constitution, he pointed out, recognizes slaves as "persons," not property, for purposes of apportioning legislative seats.

And Virginia's constitution never referred to Black people as property but spoke only of equal and independent men. Men became "property" only by statute. But if a statute could declare a man to be property, it could just as easily declare him not to be property. A statute cannot permanently divest a man of his "natural and unalienable rights.... The slave has a natural right to regain his liberty."[48]

George Summers of Kanawha added that slaves were distinct from all other property. Property claims in conventional items could be "founded in natural right, and acknowledged by the consent of all mankind," but slaves "become property only by force: they are retained [as] such, by force and necessity." As another delegate said, "It is very easy to see that a man is a man; but there is more difficulty in showing that a man is property." You can't enslave a man in Massachusetts, "because he is a man." And he remains a "man in Virginia" no matter what a statute may proclaim.[49]

But by this point, the tenor of the debate had changed. Finger pointing replaced substance. Rather than attack or defend the press, the delegates attacked each other. And as Charles Faulkner's comments had foreshadowed a few days earlier, the debate increasingly became a contest of east versus west, slaveholder against yeoman farmer, person against person. The more that happened, the more those on the receiving end of barbs talked of dividing the state.

One delegate threatened that if the west pushed abolition down the east's throat, eastern slaveholders would take their slaves and leave. Another delegate swore that if the east continued to force slavery on the state, he would vote against every statewide improvement project. The rising acrimony drained Governor Floyd of his optimism. On January 20, he wrote in his diary that the growing "bad and party feelings" were fueling "erratic tendencies" that "must be checked." A day later, he wrote that "the debate begins to be carried on in an angry tone. It is not good."[50]

Having listened to his proposal being pilloried and altered for two weeks, Thomas Jefferson Randolph tried to cool tensions by saying his proposal would not emancipate anyone. He only wanted a committee to inquire into the subject. It could produce a bill in due time and submit it to the voters—or not. Randolph was moderating his prior position, as Brodnax had, by speaking in opposition to both sides of the property debate—not because he did or did not see enslaved people as property but because both sides' absolutism ignored the legal reality. In truth, he said, some Virginia and national laws "consider slaves as exclusively persons," while others consider them "as exclusively property." Some treat them as "both." Both sides, he urged, must allow that the issue was not property or persons, but exigencies. And the exigency was not confined to Virginia.[51]

Slavery was not just an internal Virginia issue. It was a national issue that could divide the North from the South as it was dividing east and west Virginia. This prospect carried grave danger, in which slave revolts would be the least of their worries. Randolph offered his own prophecy, delivered with as much gravity as Vesey's, Walker's, or Turner's: "There is one circumstance to which we are to look as inevitable in the fullness of time; a dissolution of this Union. God grant it may not happen in our time, or that of our children; but sir, it must come, sooner or later; and when it does come, border war follows it, as certain as the night follows the day." When white Virginians "march to repel the invader," the enslaved population behind them would seek the "arms and asylum" the North would surely promise. And as the North entered the South "with black troops, ... burning with enthusiasm for the liberation of their race," they would "roll forward, an hourly swelling mass," until the South was paralyzed—its "families butchered," its "homes desolate," and its "power gone." Whatever strength the South might hold now, it could not win a "war with these disadvantages" and would ultimately be forced to accept "peace upon any conditions that an enemy may offer." The question Virginia had to ask itself was whether it was "prepared to barter the liberty of our children" to preserve slavery.[52]

Randolph's prophecy did not chasten the slaveholders any more than the last decade's violence had. Each side moved toward concrete motions, resolutions, and votes in an effort to put the debate to rest. On January 24, one resolution threw down a dare for the proslavery contingent:

> It is expedient to apply to the General Government, to appropriate annually, a part of the Revenue of the United States, to the use of such States as may be disposed to remove the whole or any part of their colored population, to be applied to the purchase of slaves within each State, at a fair price, and to defraying the expense of colonizing such slaves, and other colored persons, beyond the limits of the United States.[53]

If the financial strain of paying slave owners for freeing slaves was the impediment, Virginia could seek help. Given that the U.S. government's revenue would soon reach tens of millions of dollars a year, the federal government could easily purchase fifty thousand slaves at $200 per person and end slavery in Virginia within a few short years. The next morning, a delegate moved to amend the select committee's resolution with one single word. Rather than declare abolition "inexpedient," the resolution declared it "expedient."[54]

The next proslavery delegate responded with the only measure he could: a motion to postpone any further action on the report. Though the House was no doubt tired after weeks of debate, the motion failed, 60 to 71, lifting hopes that maybe the votes were there to move toward abolition. But then the resolution to declare abolition "expedient" failed by nearly the same margin. Either the House was actually undecided on slavery or abolition was doomed.

A softened proslavery proposal answered that question. A new motion to amend the select committee's resolution acknowledged "the great evils arising from the condition of the coloured population of this commonwealth" and emphasized that the House had tried to devise a plan for the removal of slavery but could find no plan within its power and means. Thus, further action by the House on this matter "should await a more definite development of public opinion." This motion passed by a margin of just four votes. A nearly identical vote margin approved the report as amended.

As the legal historian Alfred Brophy writes, these final votes pointed in "two directions, as did much of southern thought on slavery at the time—both an awareness of the evils of the institution and an awareness of the difficulty, perhaps even the impossibility, of doing anything significant about it at that moment." Randolph saw the narrow votes as a sign that the abolition movement was gaining strength. He was wrong.[55]

Virginia had cracked open the door to abolition once, but it would not do so again. Floyd, Randolph, and their allies had pushed their cause to its apex. True believers had won the indulgence of people thoughtful enough to listen and had carried on an open and deliberate conversation about changing the course of racial history in the Commonwealth of Virginia. But from there, Virginia slid downhill to a place worse than where it had started. The road it had traveled so inflamed east-west tensions that the state would not even survive as an undivided political unit. Having arrived at a crossroads, different groups wanted to take radically different paths.

With the prospect of abolition gone, Governor Floyd turned his attention to that crossroads. People talked of "dividing the state" inside and outside the legislative halls. When the abolition debate closed, Representative Goode, speaking directly to the governor, confided a very bleak perspective: "that the Eastern and Western people were not at all the same people, that they were essentially a different people, that they did not think alike, feel alike, and had no interests in common, that a separation of the State must ensue, and rather than have the subject of abolition again debated he would be glad for a separation. Both sides seem ready to separate the State if any one would propose it." Writing in his diary, Floyd sadly admitted, "I think that event from appearances highly probable."[56]

Talk of slavery did continue in the assembly, but only in the service of buttressing the status quo. By March 1832, Virginia's legislature appeared no more open-minded than that of any other Southern state. On the 15th, it consolidated and amended its acts "concerning slaves, free negroes, and mulattoes" by cracking down on the things it thought led to slave revolts. The new provisions treated literate slaves, the Bible, and reading as a dangerous mix—even more dangerous when Black people came together in an unsupervised group.[57]

The new laws prohibited Black people, free or enslaved, from preaching or holding assemblies "for religious or other purposes, either in the day time, or at night." The first offense carried thirty-nine lashes, the second deportation for enslaved persons and enslavement for free persons. Anyone in attendance faced similar punishment, but to resolve the issue that had torpedoed a prior version of the bill the year before, it provided that nothing in the law would "prevent the masters" from taking enslaved people to "any place of religious worship, conducted by a white minister" or hiring a free white person "to give religious instruction to their slaves."[58]

To avoid concerns over the commerce clause that Black seamen acts faced in South Carolina and Georgia, Virginia did not aim to throw Black sailors in jail; it simply made it illegal for free or enslaved Blacks to be employed on any ship leaving a Virginia port. The state also criminalized the writing, printing, or circulating of "any book, pamphlet or other writing, advising persons of colour within this state to make insurrection, or to rebel." The first offense was stripes, the second "death without benefit of clergy." Seditious speeches would be treated the same way.[59]

Once Virginia proved incapable of throwing off the institution of slavery, there was little hope for the deep South. A flurry of legislative activity spread across the Southern states. Alabama, which had passed an anti-literacy law in 1831, passed an anti-pamphlet law in 1832 and went further than any other state in making the first offense punishable by death. In 1833, the Alabama legislature further strengthened its anti-literacy law. At that point, the only Southern states without anti-literacy laws were the border states and Florida. Tennessee appears to have been the only future Confederate state to allow formal education for Black people.[60]

Consistent with that spirit, at Tennessee's constitutional convention in 1834, East Tennesseans tried to revive the emancipation debate that had died in Virginia, but to no avail. The committee tasked with considering emancipation petitions concluded, with language similar to Virginia's, that the issue was beset by too much "impracticability" and "inexpediency." Having seen Virginia's failure, it knew that merely discussing the matter would lead to the "destruction of that harmony among members, the preservation of which, was so necessary for the accomplishment of the great work the people of Tennessee sent the Convention here to perform."[61]

Tennessee did not want to follow the path of the lower South. But the disappointing resolution of the Virginia debate signaled that things there were about to get even worse. Although border states like Maryland and Delaware might persist with more moderate approaches to questions about slavery, free people of color, and Black literacy, slavery advocates in an increasingly aggressive core group of Southern states, from Georgia to Virginia, would set the course for both the region and the nation.

CHAPTER SEVEN

The Blockade

VIRGINIA'S COMPROMISE, ALLOWING BLACK people to receive religious instruction, did not sit well further south. Shortly after Turner's revolt, South Carolina's legislature and local governments began receiving petitions, too. Far from advocating compromise, the petitioners saw all religious instruction, worship, and literacy that involved Black people—free or enslaved—as a source of evil and a threat. What had once been a concern about Black people and their motivations now came to include certain white people as well. The slavocracy, as abolitionists and newspapers like *The Emancipator* labeled Southern culture and power in the 1830s, began to frame religion that advanced the mental uplift of Black people—even if led by white people—as subversive. Examining the legal history of religious assembly laws, Nicholas May writes that "placing the Bible in the hands of slaves" came to be seen as "the first step to abolition."[1]

Also provoking fear was the growing recognition that some Southern religious leaders sympathized with Black people's plight and, though they eschewed violent rhetoric, shared some ideas in common with men like Vesey and Walker. Some of these leaders were even attracting a few slaveholders to their cause. Charles Jones, for instance, a wealthy slaveholder and plantation owner just below the South Carolina–Georgia border, was gaining influence in the Presbyterian synod covering the two states. At the synod's 1831 meeting in Columbia, Jones and his allies called for Presbyterians to expand religious instruction among the enslaved population. He was already instructing enslaved people on his plantation and wanted others to do the same.

Jones might have gone unnoticed if he had limited his remarks to doing God's will and reading the Bible. But he also questioned why slaveholders feared teaching "the whole Bible" to the people they enslaved. Anyone familiar with the official reports on Denmark Vesey would have drawn the connection to Vesey's criticisms of white religious leaders. But Jones went even further, suggesting an openness to abolition. If emancipation somehow gradually resulted from preaching the whole Bible, he told his listeners, he would accept it as the "work of the Almighty, the effect of the Divine principles of his word." He even mused that emancipation might be the "easier, . . . safer way." The synod, acutely aware of the political danger, explicitly disavowed Jones's notion that the "end of religious instruction will be emancipation." But neither did it entirely close the door, affirming that "come what may," the synod would obey God's will and spread His teaching.[2]

Over the next year, Jones and the synod drew enough adherents to catch the attention of local officials. A grand jury in Columbia petitioned the South Carolina legislature to bar people like Jones from teaching Black people to read and write under the pretext of religious instruction.[3]

At the same time, free people of color in Charleston were reestablishing the education societies and projects that the Vesey backlash had suppressed. Having lived through the backlash, however, they were careful not to draw attention or step outside the bounds their white neighbors would tolerate. Most notable among these education leaders was Daniel Payne. Born free in 1811 in Charleston, Payne came of age during the aftermath of Vesey's trial. He was a member of Vesey's African Church community and well aware of Vesey's plot and the ideas and stories that inspired it. His boyhood dream was to fight on the battlefield for Haiti.[4]

Payne's real passion, however, was education. At eighteen, not fully appreciating the challenges, Payne started a small school. The enrollment did not match his ambitions, and he soon had to close the school for want of resources. As Payne tells it in his autobiography, a wealthy slaveholder inadvertently persuaded him to try again, patronizingly asking if he knew "what makes the difference between the master and the slave? Nothing but superior knowledge." Payne resolved that he would "rather go and obtain that knowledge which constitutes the master" than work for one. More important, he would aim to share that knowledge with other Black people. When he reopened his school in 1830, student enrollment took off. A wealthy Black businessman, Robert Howard, erected a school building in his backyard to support the growing enrollment.[5]

During a time of racial paranoia, men like Payne made for easy targets. Whitemarsh Seabrook first made a name for himself with his inflammatory defense of slavery and South Carolina's Seamen Act. In subsequent years he rose through the political ranks, serving in the South Carolina House until he won election to the state senate in 1829. At the time Nat Turner led his revolt, Seabrook had his eyes on the governor's mansion and saw that his response to Turner's revolt could help his prospects.

By then, Seabrook's assault on slave literacy had been going on for a decade, so his push for a new round of repressive legislation surprised no one. He proposed to restrict all Black literary and religious gatherings, whether of free or enslaved people. Black literacy would be prohibited even if approved by the enslaver. Whatever theoretical good might come from religion and literacy among the enslaved, Seabrook and his sympathizers were more worried about literacy as a gateway to insurrection. The missionary and religious societies promoting literacy had to be quashed.

Seabrook introduced an anti-literacy and anti–religious gathering bill in the South Carolina Senate in November 1833. It passed, as did a companion bill in the House. But the legislators who had voted against the bill on religious grounds managed to bog it down during the reconciliation process, preventing the final joint vote needed for it to become law. Stung by the maneuver, Seabrook took his case to the court of public opinion, releasing "An Essay on the Management of Slaves, and Especially on Their Religious Instruction."[6]

Well into the 1830s, as the historian Larry Tise writes, "hardly any Southerner bothered to pen a defense of slavery or to launch a systemic critique of abolitionism." Seabrook aimed to fill that void and respond to the winds of fear and liberalism sweeping through the South. In Seabrook's estimation, both sides of the Virginia slavery debate had been indecisive and divisive. That the proslavery forces had even allowed the debate to proceed showed that their resolve was softening. And one talking point that he found especially troubling reverberated through both sides: slavery was an evil. Slavery survived in Virginia and would survive elsewhere too, but it had done so only because enslavers could not agree on a practical way to abolish it.[7]

Seabrook meant his lengthy essay as a tonic for the weak-kneed enslaver. Rather than retreat in response to the Turner and Walker crises, slaveholders must, he wrote, enforce "proper discipline of our coloured population." And he wanted to make one point very clear: "slavery is not inconsistent with the laws of nature or of God." God had "established and sanctioned" it. Slavery also, he argued, facilitated a division of labor that made society and economic development possible.[8]

As to laws, Seabrook wanted to have his cake and eat it too. On the one hand, he argued, the federal government had no power, direct or indirect, to interfere with the "master and bondsman" relationship. The state, on the other hand, was free to interfere. Maybe the essay's most surprising claim was that "the right of the master to his slave is not . . . absolute. The relation between them is limited and restrained by the laws of the state."[9]

From a rule-of-law perspective, the truth of those lines is obvious. As slavery's skeptics pointed out in the Virginia debates, the state never gave slaveholders unfettered control over their "property." The law, for instance, treated killing an enslaved person as murder. But for Seabrook to argue that the state could interfere with slavery itself was another matter. This logic supported a new idea: that the state had to defend the institution of slavery both from the federal government and from individuals who might corrupt the institution. He believed the state could and should nullify federal actions that interfered with this state responsibility, both as a matter of public safety and to buttress and reinforce slavery itself. In his hierarchy of values and power, slavery took precedence over both federal power and individual liberty.

Then Seabrook turned to individuals. "Whoever believes slavery to be immoral or illegal" and aims to reform it, he wrote, "is practically an enemy to the state. Such a person is utterly unfit to fulfil the obligations of his trust" as a representative of the people. The best thing such a person could do was to "emigrate with his property to the land of" the abolitionists.[10]

Having laid down those ideological markers, Seabrook set out his policy agenda for keeping enslaved people "in strict subordination" through a system of rules, rewards, and escalating punishments. Religious instruction was a powerful Trojan horse to be demolished before it unleashed its terror. Attacking religion, however, required nuance: he would have to isolate the problem of religious instruction without assailing pastors or religion in general.

Seabrook applauded the important role that clergymen play, calling them "the most useful class in society." But their role in society had clear boundaries, and violating those boundaries would "endanger the peace and happiness of the community." Some clergymen, he charged, had become entranced by abstract, theoretical notions of justice that called for "applying the same rules to the black as the white man." Rather than preach God's word, they were challenging the distinctions on which society rests, threatening the peace, and fostering insubordination.[11]

Seabrook wanted the white community to do what had so enraged Denmark Vesey: teach the Bible selectively. It was preposterous, he argued, to assume that "the spiritual welfare of the blacks demand[s] that their religious knowledge should be co-extensive with that of their owners." A slave's instruction should be limited to the "points essential to his salvation." Anyone who shared the entire Bible with Black people deserved "a room in the Lunatic Asylum." The Bible's contradictory ideas would not lead an enslaved person to the truth. It would only confuse and "unduly excit[e]," leaving "him a wild and restless fanatic—an enemy to himself, and useless, if not dangerous to his master." In short, he would be "irretrievably ruined."[12]

Groups like the Georgia–South Carolina Synod were flirting with danger. It was already difficult, Seabrook scoffed, "to convert the educated man to the practical duties of the Gospel." How could clergymen possibly convert "the vulgar and illiterate?" The religion of "the freemen of this country" was simply inapplicable "to those in servitude." But if the zealots' goal was to "enslave the owner and to liberate his bondsman," there was no better way to accomplish it than "schools for negro children." Seabrook even objected to handing out hymn books during service. Remember and tremble, he said, for religious literacy and authority had made the Vesey and Turner revolts possible.[13]

Seabrook then trained the same logic on slaveholders. No individual, he wrote, had a right to act in ways that put his entire community at risk. Despite their general authority over the people they enslaved, plantation owners could not—with or without the backing and encouragement of the clergy—decide for themselves whether to educate their slaves. To allow religious opinion to decide this matter would be to substitute "an ecclesiastical government for the civil system."[14]

The most Seabrook would tolerate was oral religious instruction. Even that was appropriate only under narrow circumstances: only in church services, only during the day, only on Sundays, only involving people from a single plantation, and only led by clergy who believed in the legitimacy of slavery. As an extra check, clergymen who were not slaveholders would need two slaveholders present.

When Seabrook's pamphlet started gaining attention and traction, the clergy began organizing. They met with the Charleston City Council, sent a memorial to the legislature, and urged everyone not to overreact. Seabrook, they argued, was seizing on isolated historical events to push unjustifiable general principles. Religious instruction had done more to promote "faithful" and "subordinate" servants than any other program, and Seabrook's proposals would put an end to this work, particularly in Charleston. There weren't enough white preachers and overseers in Charleston to supervise its vast Black population.[15]

But the facts hardly mattered. Seabrook's brand of politics was ascendant. The legislature elected him lieutenant governor in 1834, and in December of that year, over the religious community's objections, a bill was passed that barred any person, regardless of race or status, from teaching or assisting "any slave to read or write." White offenders faced six months in jail and Black people, free and enslaved, faced "fifty lashes." The law did not, however, ban free Blacks from reading or writing, or ban Black preachers. The restrictions on Black gatherings enacted after Vesey's plot were apparently enough. They just needed to be taken seriously.[16]

The religious community, however, did not give up. After the law passed, 122 slaveholders petitioned the legislature for relief, explaining that there were many places where "this law could not be enforced. A jury could not be made [to] see how the teaching of the scriptures, or any book strictly religious, could jeopardize any interest human or divine.... Does chivalrous South Carolina quail before gangs of cowardly Africans with a Bible in their hands?" This religious backlash was formidable enough to demand a response.[17]

Representative Edward Laurens, who had championed the law in the House, published his own essay. His logic differed slightly from Seabrook's. Whereas Seabrook asserted infallible principles, Laurens focused on evolving circumstances. Until recently, he said, Black literacy had been harmless, maybe even positive, especially as it was largely confined to the Bible. Even if they read other material, Black people would have been hard pressed to find abolitionist writings. But now "there is hardly a publication" coming into South Carolina's ports from the North or abroad that "does not contain ... inflammatory matter." With each passing day, new societies were emerging "whose object is to 'ameliorate' the condition of those in slavery."[18]

South Carolina's new law, he said, was not born of a general objection to Black literacy or religion. No doubt, literacy allowed some to "draw the pure waters of life from the fountain of inspiration." But in a time of countless false prophets, there was too much risk that enslaved people would be led astray. For now, the law was a necessary defense against abolitionist agitation. Well-intentioned religious instruction would have to be an unfortunate casualty of war.[19]

Even though the final law allowed oral instruction, the message was clear: the menace of Black literacy must end. Schools that had peacefully served free Black children for years quickly closed. And unlike earlier panics, when enforcement had moderated after the initial fervor passed, South Carolina was about to plunge the entire nation into controversy in a way not experienced since the Missouri Compromise.

Rather than Black men preaching revolt or freedom, this time the Southern hysteria was triggered by white Northern abolitionists. Believing the time had come to organize and press their agenda, they called a national convention in Philadelphia in December 1833, which was attended by more than sixty delegates, representing various societies and organizations. They agreed to form a new national organization, the American Anti-Slavery Society.

The society's first act was to release a formal declaration, in the style of the Declaration of Independence. Employing arguments both religious and democratic, it declared in its first line that God "hath made of one blood all nations of men to dwell on all the face of the earth." The next lines placed American slavery in historical context. Half a century ago, the document explained, a "band of patriots" had thrown off the British yoke and established a "TEMPLE OF FREEDOM" based on the principle that "all men are created equal" and endowed with inalienable rights. But the enterprise of "our fathers" would remain "incomplete" until slavery was abolished and all people were free. According to scripture, it continued, any "American citizen who retains a human being in involuntary bondage as his property is . . . a MAN STEALER."[20]

Yet unlike the patriots who birthed the American project, the Anti-Slavery Society intended to work within the law. Clearly separating itself from Vesey, Walker, and Turner, the society explicitly rejected violence as a means to its ends. Instead, it would appeal "to the consciences, hearts, and interest of the people to awaken a public sentiment throughout the nation." But as a sign of just how entrenched the notion of states' rights was, the society conceded that Congress lacked the power to eliminate slavery. The Constitution reserved that power to the states. Yet democratic processes still offered a solution. If states held the power, that was where the Anti-Slavery Society would take the fight.[21]

In a war of words, the nation's laws were on their side. "American citizens have the right to express and publish their opinions" on slave laws, the declaration continued, in "any and every State and Nation under Heaven; and we mean never to surrender the liberty of speech, of the press, or of conscience." They would send "publications to the South." There was nothing "incendiary" about exercising the rights of speech and press to prove the government wrong or to "prove Slavery to be a moral and political evil." It was, in fact, their civic duty.[22]

The society would "send forth agents" to spread its message, circulate antislavery periodicals, enlist the pulpit and press in their cause, and boycott products made from slave labor. All their hopes rested on the First Amendment. They were not anarchists, as Southerners charged, but citizens who wanted to preserve the Union and its Constitution precisely because it "restrains Congress from making any law 'abridging the freedom of speech or the press.' "[23]

For all its bluster, the Anti-Slavery Society's first year was modest. With a budget just over $1,000—almost exclusively from member donations—it printed five thousand copies of its *Slavery Report*, giving away half and keeping the rest on hand. Ironically, it was Southern states' paranoia that gave the society energy and focus.[24]

When Southern states escalated the war of words through censorship, they revealed a weakness. If the Southern politicians really believed that their way of life depended on blockading the South against antislavery ideas, rhetoric, and literature, it made sense for abolitionists to test that belief. What better way to agitate the South than to flood it with abolitionist newspapers? At its 1835 annual meeting, the American Anti-Slavery Society's executive committee devised what would become known as the Postal Campaign. It would compile a mailing list and raise funds for a huge run of papers and postage. The executive committee contributed half of the necessary funds right there at the meeting and asked members and friends to do the rest—raise public awareness, send donations, and volunteer to help with distribution and identifying names for the mailing list.[25]

The project was a perfect recruiting tool. More than three hundred local antislavery societies formed and joined the national organization, bringing the total number of antislavery societies in the country to 523. Only half of them reported their membership numbers, but those that did counted 27,182 members. Those numbers also created a base from which to grow the budget for antislavery activities. The national budget for 1835 was twenty-five times larger than it had been two years earlier. The organization spent most of this on publishing: 25,000 copies of the *Slavery Report* each month, as well as 20,000 copies of *Human Rights*, 15,000 of *The Emancipator*, and 15,000 of *The Slave's Friend*. Counting quarterly and special publications, the American Anti-Slavery Society printed 1,095,800 abolitionist papers in 1835—making it quite possibly the largest publisher in the country.

Scouring city directories, church memberships, and other publicly available lists, the society collected the names and addresses of politicians, clergymen, and other notable figures across the South. Its Southern mailing list reportedly included more than twenty thousand people. By July 1835, it had sent 175,000 antislavery papers through the New York Post Office alone. The inundation and agitation were more than the South could tolerate. As the historian Clement Eaton put it in *Freedom of Thought in the Old South*, the region lost the "poise necessary to deal with the negro problem with an open mind." It turned aggressive, at times violent, toward not only Black people but white people too.[26]

Sending stacks of abolitionist newspapers south reopened a festering wound. In 1831, *The Liberator*'s initial circulation in the South, coming so soon after Nat Turner's revolt, had led many Southerners to think that William Lloyd Garrison, the paper's editor, had instigated the revolt. They tried to shut him down. The Vigilance Association of Columbia, South Carolina, offered a $1,500 reward for anyone caught circulating the paper in the state. One of South Carolina's U.S. senators, Robert Y. Hayne, demanded that Boston's mayor prevent Garrison from spreading a "contagious disease" designed to incite "our Slaves to insurrection." If he didn't, Hayne threatened, South Carolina would pursue "measures of self protection, which may interrupt the harmony which has heretofore subsisted between the several States of this confederacy." If a smattering of abolitionist papers had provoked that much passion in 1831, Southern emotion might rage out of control this time.[27]

On July 29, 1835, the steamship *Columbia* arrived in Charleston from New York "overburthened" with antislavery tracts: *The Emancipator*, *The Anti-Slavery Record*, and *The Slave's Friend*. The tracts were not stowed as regular cargo, however, but stuffed in U.S. Postal Service mailbags. The

Charleston Southern Patriot, reporting that same day, labeled the Postal Campaign a "monstrous abuse of the privilege of the public mail" and demanded that something be done to stop "the moral poison with which these publications are drugged." It would be "impossible to answer for the security of the Mail in this part of the country," the paper threatened, so long as the poison continued to flow.[28]

By the time the *Charleston Southern Patriot* story hit the stands, a large portion of the antislavery papers had already gone out for delivery. The first Charlestonians to receive them marched straight to the Charleston Post Office and returned them. That afternoon, members of the South Carolina Association—the vigilance society formed in the aftermath of the Vesey affair—confronted the Charleston postmaster, Alfred Huger. Huger was of two minds. On the one hand, he was a slave owner by birth and had stayed sufficiently within the political mainstream to win three terms in the South Carolina Senate. On the other hand, he had opposed Southern nullification of federal tariffs, and though much of America retained provincial loyalties, he believed in the Union's importance. Those Union loyalties had earned him an appointment as postmaster.

When the vigilantes demanded that Huger surrender the incendiary pamphlets, they surely expected that he would hand them over, but he refused. With no leverage but his spine, he managed to broker a truce. He would set aside the offending mail and hold it until he received word from the U.S. postmaster general, Amos Kendall. That was enough to pacify, at least temporarily, the association members, but as the afternoon wore on, a couple hundred angry men—including, as Huger called them, some of the city's "most respectable men"—assembled around the post office hurling threats. The city guard eventually broke up the mob, but the reprieve was fleeting.[29]

Not long after ten at night, men from another vigilance society, the Lynch Men, pried open one of the post office windows and entered. True to his word, Huger had sorted the offending mail into separate bags. The men found the bags and took them away. This smash-and-grab at the city's heart must have drawn a curious audience, but apparently no one tried to stop them.

Reporting the break-in the next day, the Charleston papers' only criticism was to call it "premature." The men should have waited for Postmaster General Kendall, who would surely have dealt with the antislavery tracts. In the meantime, the *Charleston Southern Patriot* urged a

Attack on the Charleston Post Office. Courtesy of Library of Congress.

legal solution—grant postal workers the authority to open packages suspected of carrying antislavery literature, so they could seize and destroy it. Otherwise, Southern states would "take the law into their own hands." The *Charleston Courier* hoped that the event would "open the eyes of our northern friends to the necessity of some energetic step to prevent the ... criminal [acts] of northern fanaticism" because "mob violence" in response could easily reach "dangerous excesses."[30]

Dangerous excess arrived the next day. A raucous crowd marched through the city displaying the fruits of the robbery, finally coming to rest on the training field at the Citadel—the military installation created after the Vesey affair to defend the city against slave revolts. The organizers hoisted a signal balloon for anyone who missed the procession or the morning newspaper announcing the rally.

A large bonfire, fueled by abolitionist literature, raged as the crowd increased. By night's end it numbered between two and three thousand—the city's largest public event outside a formal holiday in many years.

"Am I Not a Man and a Brother?" Antislavery imagery depicted on a broadside poster, New York, 1837. Courtesy of Library of Congress.

Ready to take the war to the North, the crowd burned three abolitionists in effigy: William Lloyd Garrison, Arthur Tappan (a primary financier of the Postal Campaign), and Samuel Cox (a New York City minister whose congregation was at the center of the antislavery movement). An artist's rendering of the night depicted a fire in the background and a pilfered post office in the foreground. A bounty tacked next to the broken window offered $20,000 for Tappan.

This night was only a beginning. More antislavery pamphlets were already en route to Charleston. Postmaster Huger hoped for a solution that didn't involve break-ins, capitulation, or firing the shotgun he now carried as he transported the mail from the docks to his office. He wrote to the postmaster general on August 1, pleading for help. "The Whole

Civil authority," he explained, was "in favour of arresting the Mail." With the antislavery tracts uniting white men of every party, creed, and ideology, it would take "a military force greater than the Undivided population of Charleston" to protect the mail. Yet he vowed to defend the mail "until I am overpower'd" and urged that Northern postmasters segregate the mail before sending it South, putting normal mail in bags labeled "Nothing but Letters" and tracts in bags marked "Suspicious."[31]

Charleston's leaders called a city hall meeting on August 3. It drew one of the largest—and apparently most esteemed—crowds in the city's history, filling the room and spilling outside. On one level, the meeting was civil and businesslike. The city appointed a twenty-one-member special committee to investigate the matter and report back. The committee members believed they could trust Huger. He was a Carolina man and had pledged to hold the obnoxious mail until he got further instructions. But the threat of violence lurked in the background. Civic leaders would try to resolve things civilly, but if things did not go to their liking, the "responsible and respectable" citizens would "abate the nuisance ... with the least possible violence."[32]

With pressure mounting, Huger sent a flurry of letters to the New York postmaster, hoping he would leverage his connections with the postmaster general—whose instructions, he prayed, would come soon.

August 6 was a lucky day. Though no instructions arrived, neither did any antislavery tracts. Huger fired off yet another letter to New York, saying that when the tracts inevitably arrived, he would hold them unless instructed otherwise. He had no other choice. Under orders from the special committee, Charleston's chief judicial officers would accompany the mail from the harbor to the post office every day to make sure he did not distribute any "Seditious Pamphlets." If he tried, they had promised to arrest him in the street.[33]

Two days later, another batch of "incendiary publications" arrived, provoking more threats. The police guarded the mail as it left the post office for delivery, demanding, with each bag, Huger's personal assurance that no antislavery pamphlets were going out. If they learned he had missed or hidden something, they would start ripping open all the mailbags to check.

This threat raised a new concern. If police started opening and examining mail, the whole postal system would fall apart. They would compromise a lot more than antislavery material if they began peeking into people's personal lives and maybe even pilfered money and checks.

The commercial transactions that fueled Charleston's wealth would grind to a halt. Again, Huger wrote to the postmaster general, pleading for direction before the special committee held its next public meeting. Guidance never came.

Internal documents suggest that many in Andrew Jackson's administration knew what they should do but refused to stand on principle. When the postmaster general finally responded to Huger, it was in an open letter for the world to see, appearing in newspapers on August 11, 1835. He had examined the law and was "satisfied that the Postmaster-General has no legal authority to exclude newspapers from the mail, nor prohibit their carriage or delivery on account of their character or tendency." Congress, he presumed, had withheld such a power, lest it be "perverted and abused" to the detriment of the free press. Yet neither was the postmaster "prepared to direct you [Huger] to forward or deliver the papers" in question. The Jackson administration would do nothing. The postmaster's rationale would have sounded familiar to Southerners: local communities had a right to something resembling nullification. "We owe an obligation to the laws," he wrote, "but a higher one to the communities in which we live, and if the former be perverted to destroy the latter, it is patriotism to disregard them." The postal service was meant to serve communities, not undermine them. If newspapers contained insurrectionary commentary, the postal service should afford them no aid, directly or indirectly, by circulating them.[34]

This tortured logic surely reflected the thinking of President Jackson, who sympathized with the Charleston rioters. In an August 9 letter to the postmaster general, Jackson had called antislavery advocates "monsters" who stirred up the South and "ought to be made to atone for this wicked attempt, with their lives." He fully approved of holding the papers, with one caveat. If any of the addressees were real subscribers to an antislavery paper, the "Postmaster ought to take the names down" and publish them so that the local citizens could punish them.[35]

This resolution did not satisfy Charleston's leaders. On August 11, the same day the postmaster general released his letter to Huger, the city council unanimously adopted twelve recommendations from its special committee. In a clear criticism of Virginia's recent debate, it resolved that "labored argument on the subject of slavery" was not acceptable. "The people of this State permit no discussion ... of rights, which she deems inherent and inseparable from the very existence of the State." Slavery was a "domestic question, belonging exclusively to the citizens" of slaveholding States. No one had a right to interfere with slavery in another state, much less to incite sedition. Non-slave states had a duty to put down antislavery societies and their current activities. And lest the U.S. Postal Service be "converted into an instrument" of sedition, Congress should prohibit it from transporting "any seditious Papers" into a state whose laws forbade them.[36]

At home, Charleston's city council urged the state legislature to give local officials explicit authority to seize and destroy seditious materials. But South Carolina could not resist Northern aggression on its own. Charleston called for a convention of Southern states to develop a regional strategy for dealing with the Northern agitation. Finally, the city council requested that the clergy close schools for free Black children, even though state law did not require it.

The Charleston City Council and committee meetings were the first of hundreds that took place across the South in the weeks following the postal standoff. Though other cities lacked Charleston's theatrics, the fervor ran just as high. White Southerners were outraged that antislavery advocates dared to spread messages that might provoke more revolts. City after city held meetings, many copying Charleston's recommendations. These meetings collectively represented the largest grassroots movement to that point in Southern history—what Susan Wyly-Jones, in her detailed cataloguing of the meetings, calls "an unprecedented anti-abolitionist panic whose intensity far exceeded the actual threat."[37]

The size, vigor, and strategy of these meetings are somewhat surprising. About two-thirds of Southern whites did not hold any slaves. And plantation owners with huge economic stakes in slavery made up only a fraction of those who did hold slaves. As the Virginia abolition debate and steady flow of petitions there revealed, white people were often split as to how best to respond to slavery concerns—and in some places, were decidedly against slavery.

The Postal Campaign dramatically shifted those dynamics, hardening and consolidating proslavery advocates' stance. The Virginia debate revealed how regionalism could inflame one group against another. Still, standing face-to-face in the same room, knowing each other well, and contributing to a shared tax base could bind disparate regions within a state. But the only obvious thing binding the North and South was the abstract notion of the Union, and the tariff crisis of 1828 had hit the South hard and thinned its allegiance to the federal government.

Another factor unifying a belligerent South was that the Postal Campaign brought the contest home to communities. Prior slave revolts could seem anomalous, distant, or theoretical, but the Postal Campaign shoved antislavery into people's faces. It directly touched thousands of individuals, who surely touched thousands more, making this threat feel real in a way others perhaps did not. And as real as the threat was, it was more elusive to target.

A clearer racial identity had also accompanied prior threats. It was a Black man who wrote the *Appeal*, and it was Black men who revolted. But now white men were involved, writing abolitionist literature and using federal workers to deliver it. Their Southern emissaries, agents, and religious leaders were also white, meaning the threat could blend in and strike without notice. Safety required suspicion of white outsiders—and of some local whites, too. Locals who wanted to avoid trouble needed to toe the party line, self-censor, or flee.

Public meetings were the perfect place to show where one stood. Robert Gage of South Carolina wrote that "Yankees" living in the South feared their neighbors' prejudice and were "constantly getting up ... and giving out expressions of opinions against the abolitionists," which were "very violent at times." These meetings functioned as "ritualistic displays of white unity and the communal means of enforcing race control," Wyly-Jones writes. "They reflected Southern fears both of outside intrusion and of vulnerabilities within the slave system." Collectively, they served to "unite the region socially and politically behind its domestic institutions."[38]

Attendees and onlookers also recognized that vigilance committees would punish and purge antislavery sympathizers. New laws authorized them to snatch suspects and haul them to court, where, according to locals, some judges condemned suspects without any meaningful semblance of a trial. Gage, writing to his brother, reported that "several have been tried before Judge Lynch[,] condemned and hung without a word." Even seemingly moderate locations violently rooted out potential sympathizers. In Nashville, for instance, a vigilance committee skipped the judicial process altogether and declared a suspect guilty on the spot. After whipping him twenty times, the committee banished him from the state. A newspaper account suggested that had the committee not acted firmly and swiftly, the crowd of onlookers would have killed the suspect.[39]

Some local committees wrote violence into their founding documents. A vigilance committee in Georgia resolved to "omit the use of no means in our power, to bring all such culprits to condign punishment." Committees also urged their communities to form or reestablish volunteer militias to help police antislavery activities. These committees saw themselves as a new governing order with virtually unlimited power to enforce and preserve slavery.⁴⁰

Southern newspapers fell in line too. Covering the Charleston postal affair from more than four hundred miles away, the *Richmond Enquirer* gave daily updates and by early August, just days after news of the affair spread, was calling for a vigilance committee in Richmond to track suspects and emissaries in the area, seize mail, and quarantine ships that might carry the "moral pestilence." Interference with the South's "domestic institutions," it warned Northerners, was the "rock on which the Union may probably split." The Constitution established a union of equals and barred its Northern member states from saying anything about the South's "ownership in the Slaves." Northern Unionists who did not wish to risk "torrents" of "blood ... in the South" were urged to "put down these Incendiaries," their "poisonous presses," and the "system of Agitation ... in all its branches and divisions." Speaking on behalf of the entire South, the *Enquirer* closed with the prediction that further escalation would turn fellow citizens into "aliens, rivals, enemies."⁴¹

With the issues still burning months later, President Jackson felt compelled to address them in his 1835 annual message to Congress. The crisis clearly weighed on his mind. In his opening lines, Jackson sought to capture the country's historical arc: the nation, he said, had survived infancy to achieve "unexampled growth and prosperity." It now ranked among the most important nations on earth and no longer need fear "external foes." The present danger was from within. Writing obliquely, but clearly enough for all to understand, he said that "internal dissension" has "so often blasted the hopes of the friends of freedom." Countries can be "strong and successful when united against external danger" only to fail "in the more difficult task of properly adjusting their own internal organization."⁴²

Toward the end of his written remarks, he spoke more plainly. Congress needed to turn its "attention to the painful excitement produced in the South by attempts to circulate through the mail inflammatory appeals addressed to the passions of the slaves ... and ... calculated to stimulate them to insurrection, and to produce all the horrors of a servile war." Here Jackson was operating from the same ideological frame as the Charleston City Council or the *Richmond Enquirer*. He expressed indignance and regret "at conduct so destructive to the harmony and peace of the country, and so repugnant to the principles of our national compact," and warned that peace "depends" on adherence to "those compromises of the Constitution upon which the Union is founded." These constitutional compromises, in Jackson's estimation, placed slavery above all other rights, including the right of a free press. Although he dropped his earlier suggestion that agitators who interfered with the South deserved death, he spoke of them as domestic terrorists whose actions were "wicked" and required retribution.[43]

Jackson asked Congress to "take such measures as will prevent the Post Office Department ... from being used" to interfere with Southern rights, including "severe penalties" for offenders. Riding politically high in his second term, he might have gotten his new law passed were it not for Senator John Calhoun. Calhoun wanted to silence the abolitionist papers as much as anyone, and he agreed with Jackson that government must do it. But he did not want to concede authority—even if it might help the Southern cause in the short term—to the federal government. Federal power to censor the mail, he believed, could also be turned against the Southern states' rights—and against slavery—in the future. Aiming to temper the president's proposal, he referred it to a special committee that he himself would chair.[44]

The committee moved quickly, issuing its final report on February 4, 1836. It concluded that Congress lacked the power to stop abolitionists from using the mail to spread their message. That conclusion was astounding, given the messenger, and interesting in its logic. Calhoun did not think abolitionists had an unfettered right to spread their newspapers, but he thought that the power to stop them fell within "the reserved rights of the States." This distinction was essential, he argued, because it would allow Southern states to decide for themselves what was incendiary. Giving that discretion to federal officials would leave the South powerless to protect itself. But state discretion would allow Southern states not only to block mail but to enlist the postal service in enforcing state laws. The federal government would become the South's subservient partner.[45]

While Calhoun's legal reasoning on state primacy was debatable, he was correct as to the First Amendment's limits on Congress. At the time, the full meaning of the First Amendment's protection of free expression—"Congress shall make no law" restricting free speech and the press—had yet to be developed by the courts. Its meaning was more a function of popular historical understanding. The first major test of the First Amendment had come in 1798, when Congress narrowly passed the Sedition Act to prohibit citizens from printing, uttering, or publishing

John Calhoun in 1846. Bequest of Vincenzo Botta, 1895. Courtesy of The Metropolitan Museum of Art.

"false, scandalous, or malicious writing" against the federal government. James Madison, the father of the Constitution, railed against the Sedition Act as a violation of the First Amendment. The public saw it that way, too. Thomas Jefferson defeated John Adams for the presidency in 1800, in part, because Adams had signed the Sedition Act. That controversy, Calhoun wrote, had "conclusively settled the principle that Congress has no right, in any form, or in any manner, to interfere with the freedom of the press."[46]

But his second step was a leap. While Congress couldn't restrict the press, he argued that states could. The Constitution had "left that important barrier against power under the exclusive authority and control of the States." Because "the internal peace and security of the States are under the protection of the States themselves," states had to have the power to determine what disturbed their internal security. "The General Government," he went on, "is bound to respect the measures adopted by [states] for that purpose, and to co-operate in their execution." Congress had not only to "respect" Southern states' restrictions on antislavery pamphlets but to assist in their enforcement.[47]

The problem with Calhoun's logic is that, taken to its natural extreme, it would paralyze Congress any time a Southern state disagreed with its actions. Even when exercising a constitutionally valid federal power, Congress would be unable to overrule states' notions of danger, no matter how misguided. This was the very contradiction that caused the standoff over South Carolina's Seamen Act—where South Carolina sought to trump federal power over commerce. Calhoun was now pushing the same contradiction regarding freedom of the press. Calhoun justified his position by saying that the Constitution prohibited Congress from abridging speech not because speech was essential to democratic governance but because states alone could determine when speech was dangerous. The only role for Congress was to help states expand their power over speech and other forms of expression.

Working on this logic, Calhoun's committee proposed a simple bill. Congress should prohibit postal workers from "knowingly" receiving or transmitting any materials "touching the subject of slavery, addressed to any ... State, Territory, or District, where by the laws of said State ... their circulation is prohibited." When a postal service employee discovered offending mail, they were to hold it for one month and then destroy it, unless someone claimed it.[48]

The Senate debated the bill for months, and it seemed some version or combination of Jackson's and Calhoun's proposals would pass. "Not a word, not a whisper," Vermont congressman Hiland Hall lamented, had been uttered against Calhoun's bill. Even Northern politicians, no doubt uncomfortable with the aggressive mail campaign, remained silent. Finally, on March 25, Hall broke the silence himself and produced a report detailing the practical and constitutional problems with restricting the mail. He thought the House would debate it, but when he tried to speak, the chair ruled him out of order.[49]

That may have been a mistake by slavery's defenders. Just as the motion to stifle debate in the Virginia General Assembly had backfired, the opposition to Calhoun's bill began to grow. In June, after debating for months, Calhoun's bill failed, 25 to 19, in the Senate. Calhoun was right on one thing—the First Amendment prohibited Congress from censoring the mail—but Northern politicians opposed his move to permit censorship by states. Even if they disliked the antislavery advocates' tactics, they balked at requiring postal workers to help Southerners censor the mail. The president's proposal didn't go anywhere either.[50]

That July, Congress passed a law overhauling the postal service's structure and operations. The motivation had nothing to do with antislavery literature, but nestled in the law were two provisions rebuking Jackson and Calhoun's approach. The first provision authorized fines and jail time for postmasters who "unlawfully detain" mail or prevent its delivery. The second increased the fine and jail time—as many as five years—for stealing mail.[51]

But while Jackson and Calhoun lost the battle, they won the war. As the Charleston postal raid revealed, postal policy is set on the ground as much as in Washington. Congress had put a new law on the books, but Southern postmasters ignored it: they detained and destroyed abolitionist material as they saw fit and never suffered any reprimand. The Anti-Slavery Society eventually gave up sending bulk mailings to the South and instead began lobbying Congress. Even if the First Amendment meant little in South Carolina, they thought, surely its protections would mean something in Washington, D.C.

CHAPTER EIGHT

A Gag in the Halls of Congress

I F THE FAILURE OF the Postal Campaign had a silver lining, it was that Congress, in rebuffing Jackson and Calhoun, reaffirmed its commitment to the First Amendment. Abolitionists had reason to believe they might make themselves heard in Congress even if not in the South. The Constitution was clearly on their side. However stridently the Southern states might proclaim their right to seize literature they deemed seditious, constitutional text explicitly guaranteed people's right "to petition the Government for a redress of grievance." In the 1830s, advocates leveraged this right for all it was worth, redirecting all their energy into an antislavery Petition Campaign.[1]

The idea of petitioning Congress to end slavery was not new. Benjamin Franklin, in his role as president of the nation's first abolitionist organization, the Pennsylvania Society for the Abolition of Slavery, had done so in 1790. Declaring slavery at odds with God's design and America's "Political Creed," the petition called on Congress to secure the "birthright" of all men, regardless of color, to the "blessings of liberty." Nothing was more essential to the national welfare than "restoration" of Black people's liberty—and the national welfare was, of course, Congress's constitutional responsibility. Since then, abolitionist societies had periodically petitioned Congress in this vein, but when the Postal Campaign flagged, the abolitionists decided to take the petition strategy to another level. Throughout 1835, even as the Postal Campaign dominated public attention, the American Anti-Slavery Society sent more than one hundred thousand petitions to Congress. The society thought it might have an issue it could win.[2]

The ultimate hope of the American Anti-Slavery Society was to end slavery nationwide, but the challenges—from the practical to the constitutional—were obvious. So the society narrowed its focus to a goal that might be within its reach: abolishing slavery inside the District of Columbia, where states' rights did not apply. There, the Constitution granted Congress "sole and exclusive" control over local "government."[3]

When new petitions began pouring into Congress in 1835, the first question was the procedure for addressing them. Should they be read aloud, debated, tabled, sent to a committee, voted down, or rejected altogether as a matter of process? Before the new antislavery offensive began, Congress had quietly ignored the petitions with whatever procedure was expedient. But in the wake of the Postal Campaign, both sides saw an advantage in forcing the issue.

The political firestorm began rather politely. On Wednesday, December 16, 1835, Maine congressman John Fairfield, who was serving his first term in Congress, presented a petition from 172 women praying for the abolition of slavery in the District of Columbia. He hardly mentioned the substance of the petition, asking only that it be referred to the Committee on the District. Then, following the normal protocol for abolition requests, he moved to table the petition he had just introduced, a move that would let it die without ever being discussed. But congressional rules required that it first receive an official reading.[4]

As the final words of the petition sounded out, William Slade, a budding abolitionist, jumped in before anyone could call for a vote to table it. He moved for the petition to be printed. Fairfield's motion to table, however, took precedence, and by a vote of 180 to 31, the House tabled the petition. Slade rose a second time, politely suggesting that many of the votes to table were merely a courtesy to the congressman who made the motion. Surely those members would not deny him the similar courtesy of laying the petitioners' "views before the House and the country." Abolition, he said, was among the nation's most important issues, one that regularly came before Congress and occupied countless citizens' "anxious attention." Whatever the petition's merits, it was due the courtesy of a printing.[5]

The chair interrupted Slade before he could go any further. The merits of the petition were not yet a proper matter of discussion, and Slade's comments crossed that line—he was to address them no further.

When Slade resumed, he cited precedent for his request. Seven years earlier, the House had printed a memorial from D.C. slaveholders, who had detailed the evils of slavery and asked for a remedy. In 1833 the Senate had printed the same petition again. Slade had piqued some interest, but not enough: his modest motion to print failed, 169 to 49. But those in the know recognized it for what it was—a test balloon in a new battle.[6]

Two days later, on Friday morning, another abolition petition was presented, but the slavocracy was ready for a fight. The normal process of referring the petition to a committee and then tabling it now seemed too risky for slavery's defenders. Congressman James Hammond from South Carolina said it was improper for Congress to receive the petitions at all, much less read, print, or refer them. Congress should "put a more decided seal of reprobation on them, by peremptorily rejecting" them.[7]

Hammond's motion, however, was too aggressive for some more moderate Southerners, most notably the Speaker of the House, James K. Polk of Tennessee. Polk said he was not aware of Congress ever having refused to merely receive a petition, and under House rules, all petitions had to lie on the table for at least a day. Hammond snapped back that no rule prevented the House from rejecting petitions. Receiving them, he said, only invited "fanatics" to continue assaulting Southerners' rights, but voting to reject them would end the petitions once and for all.[8]

With the House teetering on chaos, Speaker Polk took out his rule book and read the House's provision on petitions to the body. It precluded debating the merits of a petition on the first day, so Hammond's motion would have to wait. Hammond and his sympathizers countered that an abolition petition received in error could not take precedence over any other matter. When Polk ruled Hammond's motion to reject the petition out of order, his supporters formally challenged the ruling. With that, the Speaker lost control: his ruling would go before the whole body.

The Speaker was sinking in Southern eyes. A Georgia congressman made matters worse for Polk by pointing out that Polk had let the congressman from Maine hold forth on his motion to print but was now denying Hammond the same courtesy. Suddenly alerted to the disparate treatment, Hammond lost whatever cool he had, vowing he would never again sit idly by when petitions from "ignorant fanatics" arrived in Congress.[9]

Several other Southerners joined the debate. Balie Peyton, of Tennessee, sharpened Hammond's fumbling motion to reject into a clear rationale. If a petition contained a "matter improper for legislation," Peyton said, the House should immediately reject it. Because abolition petitions "asked Congress to do what every man in the country knew it had no power to do," Congress could not receive such a petition or lay it "on the table for one day." That meant Hammond's motion to reject was completely in order and took precedence. There, finally, rested the Southern logic: because Congress lacked the power to abolish slavery, it was improper for it to receive petitions to do so.[10]

Having crystalized the issue, Peyton demanded that Congress decide it "at once." Otherwise, a "flood of petitions" large enough to "cover the tables of that Hall like the locusts of Egypt" would arrive just to be received. Working himself into a fit hotter than Hammond's, Peyton denounced prior motions to table as evidence of his colleagues' weak spines. The people in this room, he thundered, must declare right now that Congress has "no power whatever to interfere with the question" of slavery.[11]

The debate turned into an angry free-for-all. Motions, reframed motions, withdrawn motions, renewed motions, appeals, and motions to reconsider prior votes flew everywhere. Soon the conversation was so muddied that members no longer knew what they were debating. The increasingly raucous Southerners would not quiet down until Hammond was given a vote on whether to reject the abolition petition.

Rejecting the petition, however, was a radical step, even for those who had long been tired of the petitions. Representative Samuel Beardsley of New York, for instance, was a bitter foe of the antislavery movement. Just months earlier, he had led a mob into an antislavery convention and forced it to adjourn. But he pleaded with his fellow congressmen not to reject the petitions: the right to petition is "a sacred right, guaranteed to the citizens of the United States by the constitution, and ... one, therefore, the House [is] bound to respect." He had no problem taking up Hammond's motion, but he was against it in substance and would move to table it, too.[12]

By Friday evening, the House was where it had started, voting on a motion to table the abolition petition with which the day had begun. But when the petition was read aloud, everything broke loose again. A congressman who had warned the body two days earlier not to discuss Slade's motion to print rose, all but wagging his finger, to say I told you so. The South's cardinal rule, he believed, still stood: the less said on this subject the better. Southerners were only hurting their cause by forcing this wide-ranging conversation. The lopsided vote denying the earlier request to print petitions showed clearly that the House had no interest in taking up abolition. Hammond's motion was pure theatrics, the congressman continued, which showed only that there were fanatics on both sides who wanted to inflame the debate.

In that, they succeeded. The debate showed no sign of ending. The House could not even agree to adjourn. But the fracturing of a majority once committed to basic order and tabling petitions suggested that Hammond was gaining ground. With a new approach still up in the air, however, late in the evening, the body finally decided to adjourn until Monday. Hammond used the weekend to devise an idea to cut through the procedural morass. On Monday he proposed a resolution, rather than a motion, by which he hoped the House would agree to reject all future antislavery petitions. This might have resolved the procedural problem, had it passed, but the procedure debate was only a proxy war. On the substance of their disagreement, the members were as divided as ever.

Both sides saw the process for dealing with abolition petitions as a symbolic fight, but one in which a victory would give them leverage on more substantive matters. Slavery hardliners were going to fight with everything they had to make their point. As one congressman put it, rejecting the petition would be "hailed in the South as the greatest omen that the permanency of this great and glorious Union was about to be secured." Constitutionally speaking, he added, the right of petition only entailed delivery of a petition to Congress, not its actual consideration. Once a representative presented an abolition petition to Congress, nothing else was due. Exhausted and clearly making no progress, the House adjourned for a week.[13]

Time off, however, did nothing to heal the wounds. The petition issue festered until it absorbed the Senate too. When the next antislavery petition arrived in the Senate, on January 7, 1836, John Calhoun pounced. He was not about to get caught in a procedural morass, and immediately called on the Senate to reject the petition. His argument was efficient. Congress could not receive the petition because it slandered half the states in the Union, addressed a subject beyond Congress's power, and called for the body to violate the Constitution.[14]

By eliminating confusion and cross-motions, however, Calhoun only allowed senators to speak longer and more freely on the substance. Some had clearly been researching the issue since it arose in the House. One senator had combed through congressional records for the response to Ben Franklin's 1790 petition. Congress deliberated Franklin's petition for several days before finally resolving that it had "no authority to interfere in the emancipation of slaves, or in the treatment of them within any of the states." But that history lesson did little to speed the debate, which dragged on for days.[15]

In late January, a slightly altered take on Hammond's proposal showed where the camps stood. A new, competing House resolution stated that "the subject of the abolition of slavery in the District of Columbia ought not to be entertained by Congress," and any future petitions "ought to be laid upon the table, without being referred or printed." This resolution got no closer to passing than Hammond's, but it smoked out irrational Southern obstructionism. Southerners didn't just want to win the debate—which this new resolution would have effectively signaled—they wanted to banish the possibility of debate and render views contrary to slavery impossible to voice in the halls of Congress.[16]

Some Southern congressmen, clearly stung by the previous summer's Postal Campaign, took an extreme stance toward the Petition Campaign. Francis Pickens of South Carolina claimed that the issue wasn't the efficient administration of congressional business but the proliferation of "societies upon societies" whose sole purpose was "producing a change, a deep and vital change, in the domestic institutions of the southern states." The fault, as he saw it, lay not with abolitionists alone but with the entire North: "There is scarcely a common newspaper, a magazine, or review that comes from the North, but what brings something of prejudice and denunciation against us." Even its schoolbooks were seeded with "innuendo or insinuation, calculated to train up our children to believe that the inheritance of their fathers is full of evil and iniquity." The North, Pickens complained, was using all its clout and moral power to undermine slavery.[17]

Though the debate over abolition petitions was more than a month old at that point, Pickens was the first to focus on the question of whether Congress could actually abolish slavery in the District of Columbia. His basic premise was that the original states would have never given Congress the power to do so, since such a power, if exercised, would shock the country and endanger slavery everywhere. Therefore, the Constitution's language granting Congress "exclusive legislation" power in the district "cannot mean absolute and unlimited legislation." States could not have given Congress the power to abolish slavery in the district, even if they wanted to, because slaveholders' property rights took precedence.[18]

The Southern representatives in the House allowed Pickens to pound his fist and take all the time he wished, even rolling his speech over into the next day. Finally, Representative Samuel Hoar of Massachusetts, a Harvard-educated lawyer, could not listen anymore. When Pickens slowed for a breath, Hoar cut him short: "What of the framers' intent?"[19]

Pickens, said Hoar, had carried on for hours without saying a word about constitutional intent. His soliloquy, Hoar quipped, "had much elegant declamation, but very little argument." The petition on the table, Hoar emphasized, spoke solely to abolition in the district, and that issue was governed by the Constitution, "not by remote probable consequence." The Constitution gave Congress power, "as clear as the English language could convey it, to legislate on the subject of slavery within the District." And no one could cite any provision in the Constitution to cast doubt on this plain reading.[20]

With minor variations, these same arguments were replayed for the next two months, whenever a new stack of petitions reignited the fire. Around March, by either consensus or exhaustion, the Senate finally began moving toward a truce. After a Pennsylvania Quaker petition for abolition carried over for a few days, Calhoun tried to quash it by renewing Hammond and Peyton's argument that there was a distinction between the right to present a petition and the right to have it received. Allowing anything more than presentment would encourage abolitionists to "encroach upon the rights of the Senate."[21]

Many in the Senate did not buy Calhoun's argument, but they were ready to reach some compromise. Senator Henry Clay of Kentucky—who had so inflamed David Walker with his efforts to colonize free people of color—led the way. The Senate, he said, had to put aside its emotions regarding slavery for a moment and focus on the basic, inviolable constitutional right to petition government. He saw no plausible way for Congress to legitimately refuse petitions. Most of his colleagues—Northerners and Southerners—agreed. So, over Calhoun's lengthy objections, the Senate received the Pennsylvania petition by a vote of 36 to 10. This vote was the prelude to a long-term solution.

Clay then proposed that the Senate receive such petitions but automatically reject their requested action. His proposal explicitly stated that receiving an abolition petition did not imply that Congress possessed or lacked the power to grant it. Instead, the Senate would reject petitions based on its judgment that abolition was "inexpedient." That word—*inexpedient*—had been the same one to spark abolitionists in Virginia's debate. This time, ironically, it triggered slavery's defenders, who worried that what is inexpedient today might become expedient tomorrow. Clay, however, was willing to compromise—the very thing Calhoun insisted the South could not do—to address that concern. When James Buchanan of Pennsylvania proposed an amendment to Clay's resolution that, rather than deeming abolition "inexpedient," simply provided that the "prayer of petition shall be rejected," Clay agreed.[22]

Calhoun seethed as he felt the fight quickly seeping out of the Senate. Rejecting petitions, he believed, opened a dangerous precedent. If the Senate could receive and then reject petitions, it could also consider and act on them. He saw Clay's approach as "pregnant with consequences of the most disastrous character." The Senate disagreed. By a vote of 34 to 6, it decided to receive and immediately reject all future abolition petitions.[23]

This resolution of the issue in the Senate did nothing to tame emotions in the House, where debate dragged on with no end in sight. President Jackson feared it was endangering the Union itself and asked Vice President Martin Van Buren to find some way to bring the petition debate to an end. Eyeing his own presidential run and needing Southern support, Van Buren, a New York Democrat, looked to pacify the South. His solution was to refer abolition petitions to a select committee, which would then report back that Congress had no power to interfere with slavery. As the historian William Freehling put it, Van Buren and the Northern Democrats who supported him were willing to "gag antislavery for the sake of slavery, Union, and ... Martin Van Buren's hope of carrying the South."[24]

Van Buren got a South Carolinian, Henry Pinckney, to introduce the proposal. Rather than slam the door in the face of petitioners, as Calhoun and Hammond had wanted, Congress would receive them. But it would eliminate the ambiguity of tabling them. Each petition would draw the same response: under its limited constitutional authority, Congress could not, and therefore never would, do anything about slavery. But this was still too gentle for the hardliners. Committee referral lacked the symbolic rebuke of a refusal to receive.

The hardliners saw Pinckney as a traitor. When he first broached the compromise, one of them stood and "hissed" at Pinckney, calling him "a deserter from the principles of the South." The attack eventually crossed the line of decorum, and Speaker Polk ordered the belligerent congressman to take his seat. Fuming, the congressman refused the order—and a second order, too—taking his seat only after Polk appealed to the whole body for support.[25]

To avoid a bruising floor debate with the hardliners, Pinckney maneuvered to get the debate sent to a select committee, which he would chair. During its deliberations, the committee incorporated enough of Hammond's and Calhoun's ideas into Pinckney's proposal to secure a unanimous vote to send its final report to the House floor. The committee proposed a resolution that "Congress possesses no constitutional authority to interfere in any way with the institution of slavery" in any state. In the District of Columbia, however, it merely provided that "Congress ought not interfere in any way." But all abolition petitions would be treated the same: Congress wouldn't debate or vote on them. They would be received and automatically tabled, and no further action—not even a committee referral—would ever be taken, thus precluding any discussion of their substance.[26]

Though not the preemptory gag that Hammond or Calhoun pressed for, this was a gag nonetheless. The petitions would move unceremoniously through Congress. No one would read them. No one would print them. No one would discuss them. And this, Pinckney reasoned, was the strongest gag that could be had in the House—because a gag required Northern Democrats' votes, too. While Northern Democrats were sympathetic to the South on abolition, they weren't willing to eviscerate the First Amendment any further. When the votes were tallied, the House approved Pinckney's revised gag, 117 to 68.

Despite the hardliners' dismay and Northern Democrats' sense that they had saved the right to petition, it is hard to paint the final result as anything other than a resounding victory for the South and a loss for the right to petition government. May 18, 1836, was the last day that Congress would dare speak of abolition for the better part of a decade. Petitions would continue to arrive, but when Speaker Polk sounded the final gavel on May 18, he silenced their voices. The gag order remained in place for seven years. It would take a former president, returned to Congress as a representative—John Quincy Adams—to break the silence.

A procedural mechanism for dispensing abolition petitions, inconsequential for fifty years, had suddenly brought Congress to a standstill in 1836. That it took six months to find a workable compromise revealed how extreme the South was becoming and signaled that worse was to come. That Congress managed a compromise did nothing to hide the fact that the body had profoundly changed. An increasingly powerful Southern contingent was no longer concerned with practicality, collegiality, reasoned debate, or constitutional principle.

A belligerent South was uniting to leverage power. In its demand for ideological purity, it would roll over the Democratic Party and undermine the Union if necessary. Taking the South's side would no longer be enough. Ascendant hardliners demanded that all Southerners—and Northern Democrats if they wanted Southern votes on anything at all—commit fully to uncompromising slavery principles that Southern leaders insisted were necessary for their survival. Talk of abolition wasn't just inexpedient or unwise. The mere mention of it was insufferable and, supposedly, unconstitutional.[27]

CHAPTER NINE

The Tragedy of Silence

SOUTHERN RESISTANCE TO ANTISLAVERY societies' postal and petition campaigns quickly grew into a regime of silence and suspicion coupled with propaganda. Silencing incendiary and aggressive ideas wasn't enough. It became necessary to silence any discussion even implying that slavery was a subject of reasonable debate. The South would fill that silence with its own version of history, law, economics, and custom.

Debates like those in the Virginia General Assembly in 1832 and the U.S. Congress in 1836 were no longer acceptable. To discuss slavery was to question it, and the South had come to believe that any questioning endangered its "right" to slavery. History offered a stern warning, too. Published transcripts of the Missouri debates in 1820 had helped inspire Denmark Vesey. There was but one solution. As the South Carolina newspaper the *Columbia Telescope* ironically put it in 1835, "let us declare through the public journals of our country, that the question of slavery is not, and shall not be open to discussion," and anyone who dared "lecture us upon its evils and immorality" should have "his tongue ... cut out and cast upon the dunghill." The satire, however, passed uncomfortably close to reality: North Carolina law forbade "all such publications as may have a tendency to make ... slaves discontented with their present condition."[1]

The South insisted that the North keep silent as well. Southern legislatures and vigilance committees directly petitioned Northern governments to pass their own laws prohibiting the printing and circulation of abolitionist papers. In 1836, the Alabama, Georgia, Kentucky, Mississippi, North Carolina, and Virginia legislatures all passed resolutions to that effect. Louisiana and Missouri followed in 1837 and 1838. All of the resolutions called for criminal punishments, not just civil injunctions or fines.[2]

Several Southern states even indicted Northern abolitionists and publishers. As early as 1831, a North Carolina grand jury indicted the Massachusetts publisher of *The Liberator*. Four years later, even though officials "admitted the offender was not in the state when his crime was committed," an Alabama grand jury indicted Robert Williams for "being a wicked, malicious, seditious, and ill-disposed person, and . . . feloniously, wickedly, maliciously, and seditiously contriving, devising and intending to produce conspiracy, insurrection and rebellion among the slave population"—or, more simply, because he "distributed, circulated and published . . . The Emancipator" in Tuscaloosa county. Alabama governor John Gayle forwarded Williams's indictment to New York governor William Marcy and issued a "demand" that he extradite Williams. Gayle's theory was as expansive as those that had silenced debate in Congress. He correctly pointed out that the Constitution and federal laws regarding fugitive slaves gave Southern slaveholders authority to reclaim their property in Northern states and seek their help in doing it. He argued that the same logic and laws applied to people like Williams who "evaded" Southern laws pertaining to slavery and remained "at large" in the North.[3]

A year later, even the District of Columbia was attacking the press, subjecting Reuban Crandall to a ten-day trial for circulating antislavery papers. By 1839, merely planning to petition Congress to abolish slavery—what a majority of Congress had deemed a constitutional right during the Gag Rule debates—triggered the prosecution of Lysander Barrett in Virginia. All she had done was collect signatures. She escaped punishment on a technicality—that she was not proven to be a formal "member or agent of an abolition or antislavery society"—but others in the future would not. The Virginia legislature clarified the law, authorizing one-year jail sentences and $500 fines (roughly $18,000 in today's dollars) for "any free person who, by speaking or writing, shall maintain that owners have not right of property in their slaves."[4]

When Northern states pointed out that their state constitutions protected free speech, Southern states accused them of breaching the U.S. Constitution. The national compact, they insisted, guaranteed them the right of slavery. North Carolina's resolution of 1835, for instance, was relentless in its logic. Each American state was "sovereign and independent" when it joined others in union. They joined with a limited purpose in mind—mutual "protection from the encroachments upon their rights and privileges, made by the king and parliament of Great Britain." Consistent with this limited purpose, each state had "recognized the right of its citizens to hold slaves." Though they later altered the terms of their confederation by adopting the Constitution, that Constitution "contains no grant of power to any department of the government to control the people of any state in regard to its domestic institutions." States could not, some half century after the fact, disclaim this national compact. Southern states were entitled to non-interference from others on slavery.[5]

Nor could Northern states hide behind their free speech laws as an "excuse" to ignore abolitionist agitation. The national compact, North Carolina insisted, took precedence and precluded Northern states from passing local laws to "disable themselves" from complying with the compact. Northern states had a duty to rescind any state constitutional provision that might prevent them from adhering to the non-interference principle. Several other Southern states passed similar resolutions and, along with North Carolina, forwarded them to Northern legislatures and officials. These resolutions articulated the most robust imaginable concept of states' rights—one that operated exclusively in one direction. It was never suggested that non-interference required Southern states to defer to Northern free speech principles.[6]

Southern claims did not end there. Not only did they believe slave laws were the supreme law in their own states and immune from federal interference, they also considered these laws supreme beyond their borders. "States' rights," in their version, required Northern states to enforce the Southern slavery position.

Carried to its natural conclusion, this logic was absurd and impracticable. Each state could not be simultaneously supreme. That was one of the problems the Framers of the Constitution intended to fix by granting the federal government the power to resolve interstate disputes. And when the federal government acted within the scope of that explicit power, the Constitution declared its actions supreme. The newfound Southern position left no place for this federal role.

This logic partly rested on the notion that the South was not, contrary to appearances, asking the North to limit free speech. Southern legislators insisted that they too believed in free speech. But their understanding of it was clearly different from that in the North—and full of exceptions. They claimed that the First Amendment's guarantees of freedom of speech and the press only protected freedom to speak without prior restraint, not freedom to speak without consequence. If someone said something defamatory, states could subject them to civil fines. And when someone said, printed, or published something incendiary, states could subject them to criminal consequence.

The question was, what counted as incendiary? The South insisted that stirring up its Black population crossed that line. On most matters of debate, Southern leaders were content to let the North have its version of free speech. But on slavery, there was to be no debate.

When Northern legislatures refused to go along, Southerners were incensed and their congressmen became the agitators. Having silenced abolition petitions, Southern congressmen then sought to reopen debate—but on their own terms. In 1836, a month after the Senate dispatched its abolition petitions, Calhoun condemned Northern state legislatures for their inaction. "Not a step has been taken," he railed, "not a law has been passed" to restrict abolitionist literature in the North.[7]

Two years later, Calhoun was still insisting, even more loudly, that the North should enforce Southern norms. In 1838 he introduced a series of resolutions designed to spur Northern action. One resolution declared that slavery was "inherited from [states'] ancestors, and existing at the adoption of the constitution," that it was "recognized as constituting an important element in the apportionment of powers among the states, and that no change of opinion or feeling ... can justify ... open and systematic attacks thereon." When one part of the Union attacked another on slavery, the federal government was obligated to stop it.[8]

While antislavery organizing and literature remained legal in the North, it wasn't because Northern politicians favored antislavery societies. The North proclaimed general fidelity to free speech, but its tolerance for abolitionist speech was hardly less cramped than the South's. When the antislavery lawyer Alvan Stewart, in his first published speech on slavery, described the public atmosphere in the North in 1835, he could easily have been talking about Charleston or Richmond. Hostility to antislavery speech, he wrote, was a stubborn fact of "daily experience. ... Each man may discuss slavery ... in the silent chambers of his own heart, but must not discuss it in public." Tar and feathers awaited those who dared suggest abolition. According to Stewart, free speech in the North was an "abstract right of discussion" to be exercised in a manner "disconnected with time [and] place." An abolitionist's abstract discussions of slavery were off limits "if a majority of his neighbors differed with him." Unchecked free speech on such matters could be had only in "the solitude of the wilderness, or loneliness of the ocean."[9]

Men as high ranking as the governor of New York, or "gentlemen of property and standing," as antislavery literature dubbed them, actively intimidated abolitionists. Anywhere abolitionist activity went in the North, its opponents soon followed—often with violence. Mobs invaded antislavery meetings, shouted them down, and forcefully ran them out of the buildings where they assembled. The violence, as Leonard Richards writes in his award-winning book on the subject, reached its "high tide between 1834 and 1837." Relying on newspaper accounts, Richards documents "157 Northern mobs" during that period, with sixty-four in 1836 alone.[10]

In a single day, October 21, 1835, "gentlemen of property and standing" broke up antislavery meetings in three separate cities—Boston, Montpelier, and Utica. A sitting member of Congress, Samuel Beardsley of New York, was at the center of the Utica confrontation. In advance of the meeting, he remarked that "the disgrace of having an Abolition Convention held in the city is a deeper one than that of twenty mobs; and that it would be better to have Utica razed to its foundations, or to have it destroyed like Sodom and Gomorrah, than to have the Convention meet here." When the antislavery society met, Beardsley, leading a group of twenty-five men, barged into the meeting and demanded an "apology ... for proceedings which we know ... are intended to exasperate the members of our National Union against each other" and bring about "the dissolution of the American Union." If they refused to apologize, he warned, "any unpleasant circumstances" that "should follow" would not be his responsibility. Recognizing that Beardsley's group was "inflamed with strong drink as well as passion," the antislavery society members had no safe option but to adjourn. But in the days and weeks to come, "insults and threats of violence" would continue to follow "them wherever they were met in the streets of Utica and at the hotels where they had quartered themselves."[11]

The worst and most frequent threats, however, were reserved for the movement's leaders: Arthur Tappan, Lewis Tappan, and William Lloyd Garrison. They co-founded the American Anti-Slavery Society in 1833 and fueled the organization with their own special contributions for years. The Tappan brothers were successful New York City businessmen, without whose wealth the movement might have floundered. For instance, they almost single-handedly funded the Postal Campaign of 1835. Even before that, Whitemarsh Seabrook called them out in his anti-literacy rants as primary instigators of the political movements to undermine slavery.

The Tappans suffered multiple attacks in the 1830s, and they lived under the constant threat of property damage, kidnapping, and death. In October 1833, two thousand people surrounded a chapel where Arthur Tappan had called a meeting to form a New York antislavery society. The mob tried to force its way through the iron gates shielding the chapel, shouting "$10,000 for Arthur Tappan." In 1834, a mob ransacked Lewis Tappan's home, dragged his furniture into the street, and set the furniture on fire. When Arthur went to the mayor's office to plead for help, he was "cursed" and told by an officer that "he had better leave" because the police could not "protect him if it is known that he is here."[12]

That same year, a mob attacked the brothers' store. The most the police did was redirect the rioters, who apparently left the store to indiscriminately attack Black people and their homes. In 1835, after what Arthur Tappan called "apathy" and disingenuous half-measures by the police, a mob attacked the brothers' store again and set fire to it. Throughout the 1830s, Southerners regularly issued bounties for Arthur's head. In 1835, a $100,000 bounty reportedly awaited anyone who would kidnap him and bring him south to stand trial for his crimes. A ship was said to be on standby in the New York harbor to carry him away.[13]

Arthur was eventually forced to keep armed guards to protect his property and his life. But knowing guards could only do so much to protect his and his family's safety, Arthur moved his family to their summer house in New Haven in the late 1830s. When he joined them there, violence followed. During one visit, Tappan narrowly eluded the grasp of Southerners who were staying at a hotel near his home, armed with bowie knives and pistols, intending to attack him and stop an antislavery meeting.[14]

Garrison, a journalist, made a more visible target than the Tappans and had fewer resources. Recruited to co-edit *The Genius of Universal Emancipation* in his mid-twenties in 1829, he spent most of his adult life at the front of the fight for abolition. He rose to real national prominence in 1831, covering the Southern response to David Walker's *Appeal* and Nat Turner's revolt in his newly founded paper, *The Liberator*. Cataloguing Southern violence and abuses, he spared no criticism in calling out Southern officials by name and deed. Though Southern legislators and newspapers directed violent vitriol back at him, he refused to stop.

Public officials in his hometown of Boston were, fortunately, more sympathetic to abolitionist activity than those in New York, but Boston was far from safe. Many Bostonians bought into Southern rhetoric regarding antislavery and criticized Garrison and his allies for putting the Union at risk. In October 1835, a false rumor spread that a notable British abolitionist, George Thompson, was to speak at a meeting of the Boston Female Anti-Slavery Society, which Garrison was supposedly to host at Stacy Hall, a small meeting space that adjoined Garrison's newspaper office on Washington Street. On October 21, the same day that Congressman Beardsley's mob broke up the antislavery meeting in Utica, Boston's *Commercial Gazette* ran a story announcing that "friends of the Union" were offering $100 to the person "who shall first lay violent hands on Thompson, so that he may be brought to the tar kettle before dark."[15]

That night, a thousand people assembled outside Stacy Hall, trapping Garrison and thirty female abolitionists inside. The mayor arrived midway through the meeting and attempted to defuse the situation. He entered the building and convinced the women that they could brave the "throngs" outside. Hoping also to ease the men's way out, he assured the mob that Thompson was not inside. The mob, however, had come for Garrison too and refused to disperse.

Garrison eventually tried to escape through a second-story window into the back alley. But when watchers spotted him sliding down a rope dangling from the window, the mob quickly filled the alley. Rioters swarmed onto the shed where Garrison landed, coiled a rope around him, and lowered him into the crowd below. As he recounted in a speech in Stacy Hall commemorating the event twenty years later, "I was dragged bare-headed through the lane into State street, where my clothes were nearly all torn from my body, the intention being ... to carry me to the Common, and there give me a coat of tar and feathers, a ducking in the pond," and more.[16]

Seeing the mob parading Garrison along a route approaching the front of City Hall, the mayor assembled his constables to attempt a surprise rescue. Just as the mob approached City Hall's entrance, the mayor and constables burst out, wrested Garrison away from his captors, and whisked him into the building. Now even angrier, the mob remained, as Garrison said, "bent on my seizure." Dispersing them was out of the question. With the mob still trying "once more to get possession of my person," Garrison spent the night in the only safe place the city could offer—a jail cell. Only under the "ruse" of a court calling him to appear for the prior day's disturbance was he able to safely leave City Hall. From there, the judge quietly discharged him.[17]

William Lloyd Garrison. Courtesy of Library Company of Philadelphia.

Cities like New York, Boston, and Philadelphia were the only places offering even token resistance to anti-abolitionist violence. Elsewhere, abolitionists were often on their own. Elijah Lovejoy, a newspaper publisher in St. Louis, Missouri, lost his life defending his right to speak on slavery. His newspaper, the *St. Louis Observer*, covered a wide variety of local and national news in the early 1830s, including slavery. Starting in 1834, he occasionally called out the barbarity of slavery as inconsistent with religion but still distanced himself from the likes of Garrison. Lovejoy criticized proposals to free enslaved people as "unwise" and instead favored "gradual abolition" over a long period of time as "safe, practicable and expedient." Readers apparently tolerated his occasional criticism of slavery, merely asking that he "let a certain subject alone." He eventually, however, reached an impasse with his community.[18]

On May 5, 1836, a mob lynched a Black sailor who was accused of killing a white deputy. After condemning the mob and insisting its members be brought to justice, Lovejoy began receiving threats. Though the rioters were eventually charged, the judge's response only infuriated Lovejoy more. Judge Luke Lawless declared that "the case is beyond the reach of human law." Instead of punishing the rioters, the judge condemned Lovejoy for publishing material that served no purpose other than to incite revolt. Escalating tensions soon forced Lovejoy to flee St. Louis for Illinois. When he tried to bring his printing press with him, a mob followed him across the Mississippi River and destroyed his press as it sat on the dock. The violence persisted in Illinois. Vandals destroyed his new presses several more times over the next year. On November 7, 1837, an armed mob intercepted Lovejoy's newest press as it was arriving and intended to burn his office. When Lovejoy came outside to confront them, he was shot and killed.[19]

Most Illinois politicians and officials wanted to look the other way. Meaningful reproaches of mob violence were rare. But a twenty-eight-year-old Illinois state representative named Abraham Lincoln took notice. Realizing he largely stood alone, however, he spoke carefully. Speaking to the Young Men's Lyceum of Springfield in 1838, he lamented the "outrages committed by mobs.... Whenever the vicious portion of population shall be permitted to gather in bands of hundreds and thousands, and burn churches, ravage and rob provision-stores, throw printing presses into rivers, shoot editors, and hang and burn obnoxious persons at pleasure, and with impunity; depend on it, this Government cannot last." His solution was simple: "Let every man remember that to violate the law, is to trample on the blood of his father, and to tear the charter of his own, and his children's liberty.... Let reverence for the laws be breathed by every American mother ... in short let it become the political religion of the nation."[20]

Violent opposition to antislavery thought in the North did start to decline in 1837, but the decline was more a function of antislavery activity receding than Northern forbearance. Antislavery societies and their primary financiers had burned through a lot of cash in their postal and petition campaigns, only to be hit hard by a nationwide financial panic in 1837 that brought six years of economic depression. As antislavery resources dried up, declines in newspaper circulation and membership rates followed. Anti-abolitionists, however, remained ready to attack, even during the decline.[21]

One of their most aggressive acts of violence occurred in 1838. Having struggled to find a safe and proper meeting place for years, the Pennsylvania Anti-Slavery Society constructed and finally opened Pennsylvania Hall in Philadelphia on May 14, 1838, what E. C. Prichett and others called in their dedication remarks the "Temple of Free Discussion." Four days later, the building was a smoldering heap of ashes. On the evening of May 18, a group of rioters had overtaken the police, broken open the doors, smashed out the first- and second-floor windows, pushed all the furniture into a heap, and set the building on fire. A group of "thousands" stood and watched the building burn.[22]

Destruction of Pennsylvania Hall by anti-abolition rioters. Courtesy of Library of Congress.

Further south, ironically, discussions of slavery were more ordered and less violent, but not for a good reason. By the mid-1830s, few people dared to say anything a neighbor might find objectionable. Those inclined toward antislavery either fled north or gave no outward indication of sympathy. Critics of slavery had always been a small minority in the South, but they had always existed, and in the early 1800s their numbers seemed to be growing. One scholar identified more than one hundred antislavery societies operating in the South in 1827. Some claimed only a handful of members, while others were substantial.[23]

The North Carolina Manumission Society, for instance, claimed 1,600 members in 1826—and they weren't secretive either. The society actively petitioned the state to liberalize its slave code. In the years following Turner's revolt, however, antislavery views grew less acceptable. By 1833, notes the historian Gordon Finnie, "hostility toward any kind of antislavery activity was so bitter ... that emancipationists were severely flogged, repeatedly intimidated, and frequently forced to leave the state." Antislavery societies quickly faded into obscurity or disbanded. When the North Carolina Manumission Society held its annual meeting in 1834—just eight years after its membership reached 1,600—only twelve people risked attending. It never met again.²⁴

Individual lives, however, most vividly capture the South's evolution. Francis Lieber was recruited to the region in the 1830s but left on very different terms in the 1850s. A German political philosopher trained at the University of Berlin and the University of Jena, he arrived in Boston in 1827. He first directed a gymnasium—physical education being cutting-edge educational theory at the time—and after it failed, wrote and edited the thirteen-volume *Encyclopedia Americana*, published in Philadelphia from 1829 to 1833. In 1836, he was invited to take up a professorship at South Carolina College, in Columbia, South Carolina. Opposition to his ideas almost derailed his appointment.

Conservatives scoured his record and found the *Encyclopedia Americana*'s entry on slavery, where Lieber had described the practice as an "atrocity" that persisted based on the "idea" that dark skin color was a natural mark of degradation. He questioned whether the South was degraded more by "colour or slavery." When his opponents leaked the information to the press in the summer of 1836, Lieber was forced to respond, denying that he was an abolitionist in an interview with Columbia's *Telescope* and affirmatively defending himself in an editorial in the same paper.²⁵

Sensing that the entire institution's reputation was at risk with state officials and the families who sent their children there, five prominent college trustees rushed to clear Lieber's name by collecting recommendations and endorsements from the "profoundest scholars and distinguished men in Europe and America." Even a Supreme Court justice and author of one of the era's most influential constitutional commentaries, Joseph Story, attested to Lieber's character. He was, the trustees argued in a twenty-page pamphlet, one of the finest, most "eminently qualified" professors Carolina could hope to hire, one who "would elevate the reputation of any University in our country" and help the college "rise from its ruins like the lately dilapidated walls of the edifice—in renovated grace and beauty—to become the PRIDE and ORNAMENT, the BLESSING and GLORY of THE STATE."²⁶

Lieber's appointment survived. But his feelings toward slavery are hard to fathom. Despite having called slavery an "atrocity," shortly after arriving he purchased two enslaved persons, reasoning in his diary that "where slavery exists, it is far better" that slaves be owned by men like him, who could "do something for them." Under his roof, "they shall be treated as kindly as anywhere," and he would keep family units together. But these good intentions were not enough to block slavery's corrupting effects. Lieber didn't provide the idyllic safe harbor he supposedly aspired to. He came to think of the people he enslaved as a financial investment and their lives subject to his needs rather than their own. When a person he enslaved, Betsy, died in 1841, for instance, he hoped she had "gone to a better state" but lamented his own economic loss as "great."[27]

Yet he never accepted the state's increasingly aggressive rhetoric on slavery, or its demand for conformity. He began to struggle with his choices and sought a double life. On the surface, he was still a slaveholder who maintained cordial relationships with men like Senator Calhoun and contributed articles on economics to proslavery journals. But privately, he was increasingly disturbed by the horrors he saw. Like an investigator preparing a dossier, he compiled files and clippings on slavery's atrocities. He began mixing in circles he knew were sympathetic to abolition. Apparently desperate to leave the South's contradictions behind, he begged Senator Charles Sumner—whom he had mentored in Boston and with whom he maintained a clandestine relationship—to find him a job in the North.

By the mid-1840s he was contemplating some sort of public advocacy. Silence had grown difficult. In 1849, he wrote five letters under the pseudonym Tranquillus and planned to release them as open letters to John Calhoun. The first ones, echoing the language of moderate Virginia delegates in 1831 and 1832, questioned the economics, safety, and stability of slavery. Lieber wanted to persuade, not berate. In the first letter, speaking as someone with "many affectionate ties" that "unite me individually to" the South, he worried that "the more she regrets slavery, and the less she sees how to cure the evil, the greater is her irritation." The South's distaste for abolitionist tactics was, in his estimation, leading it to discount sound logic and imperil the Union. "If the existence of slavery depends on the acquisition of more and more territory, it is by its nature at war with all free countries, and its doom will appear far sooner than very many friends of man have had the heart to hope."[28]

In the second and third letters, he even more directly contested the logic and legality of westward expansion. In the fourth, he took a more moralist tone. Just "because . . . the law declares the slave to be the property of his master, slavery is not purely an institution of property. It is also a personal one. It is this fact, this indissoluble union of property with person in the deplorable institution of slavery which causes all the difficulty . . . , infallibly bringing consequences in its train which those that love freedom are unwilling to encounter."[29]

By the fifth letter, hostility had shouldered restraint aside. Addressing Calhoun, he wrote, "It is not the North that is against you. It is mankind, it is the world, it is civilization, it is history, it is reason, it is God, that is against slavery." He even took a note reminiscent of Walker: "You preach that the Bible is the book of salvation, but you are obliged to forbid millions even to learn to read. Other people have established lately institutions for the instruction and melioration of even idiots, and everywhere the subject of general school education forms one of the highest questions of national policy, but you must condemn millions to ignorance."[30]

Shortly after he began writing them, he shared one of the letters with a colleague, who warned him to keep them private. Lieber knew the consequences if his authorship leaked. That was, in part, the point. He confided to his diary that he wanted to release the letters and "hoped at times" that he would be "discharged over the slave issue." Yet the pressure to remain silent was too strong, and the consequences of disclosure too dangerous. He never released the letters.[31]

Two years later, with calls for Southern secession growing louder, Lieber again felt it necessary to express his thoughts. He wrote a series of essays under a pseudonym, and this time he released them in a friendly newspaper. He came at slavery more indirectly than in the letters to Calhoun. Rather than criticize the institution itself, he criticized the idea of Southern secession. Then, edging a step further into view, he released a letter under his own name that questioned the constitutionality of secession and warned of the economic consequences. But he only danced so close to the flame. He stopped short of critiquing slavery.[32]

Finally, after two decades of hiding, Lieber grew reckless, probably intentionally. He publicly came out in support of John Fremont, the antislavery Republican, in the 1856 presidential election. That drew a series of attacks that also rekindled concerns over his 1828 encyclopedia entry on slavery. Lieber got what he long claimed to want—an end to his torment in the South—though not in the way he expected. Believing that supporters on the board of trustees would beg him to stay, he submitted his letter of resignation—and they accepted it.

In his new home, as a professor of "political science" (a term he coined) at Columbia College in New York City, Lieber no longer had to keep his views on slavery private or his criticisms of Southern society indirect. In letters to George Stillman Hillard, an associate editor at the *Boston Courier* and former law partner to Charles Sumner, he called Southern leaders "malcontents," bullies, "ungodly," agents of disunion, and ambassadors of "tyranny." Lieber's importance, however, is not in what he said or thought about slavery. (He would write major works on other subjects, including the laws of war and democratic leaders' emergency powers.) As a person who owned slaves, his condemnation is ambiguous, and in any case, others said it as well or better. But his twenty years in South Carolina show the extent to which the space for discussion in the South had vanished, leaving public discourse contingent, shrunken, cramped. A shadow fell upon the South and only darkened over time.[33]

Once a place willing to tolerate thoughtful discussion of slavery, the South actively ran off its few remaining open thinkers in the 1840s and 1850s. As the historian Clement Eaton writes of the period, "presidents or professors could not express any sympathy with the antislavery movement without serious danger of losing their jobs."[34] In 1849, after it came to light that he had voted for a candidate who favored emancipation, Howard Malcolm was forced to resign from Georgetown College in Kentucky. Sherwood Hedrick, whose family held slaves, was similarly dismissed from the University of North Carolina for questioning the economics of slavery. Hedrick was flung into the spotlight for a response he gave to a student's question in class. Hedrick opined that John Fremont, the Free Soil Party nominee, was the best candidate for president in 1854. He tried to save his job with a public letter explaining that his positions were "once advocated by Washington and Jefferson," and warranted "argument" rather than "denunciation." When a vote to terminate him was called, only a single faculty member, Henri Herrisse, dissented. After the vote, Herrisse went public, publishing an essay saying the state could "eliminate all the suspicious men from your institutions of learning, ... But as long as people study ... and think among you, the absurdity of your system will be discovered and there will always be ... protest against your hateful tyranny." Closing your schools altogether "is the only means which ... you" have "some chances of success." Herrisse resigned not long after.[35]

The important question so easily overlooked in this period—in part because we know that Southern ideological escalation ended in war—is why the South became so militaristic so quickly when it came to suppressing abolitionist materials and open dialogue. Some, and not only in the North, saw slavery as an economic or philosophical issue to be studied. This is what motivated Whitemarsh Seabrook's early defense of the institution in 1825. Seabrook and others may have rattled their sabers to some extent, but in those years it was only bluster. If they casually threatened disunion, they did it to dramatize their economic, historical, and political arguments. Slavery in their view was a matter for serious debate, in which one might logically engage adverse arguments and refute them point by point.

That is not to say that Southern arguments in defense of slavery ever made much sense. Politicians like Calhoun claimed that antislavery writings caused them emotional distress and sullied their good names. The notoriously fragile Southern sense of honor manifested itself in many ways. A Southerner might very well draw a weapon against someone who insulted him, but to demand that third parties, much less states, intercede on one's behalf seemed like a sign of weakness more injurious to one's honor. And a right of free speech that protected only flattering opinions, not offensive or unpopular ones, was no right at all.

The other claim—that abolitionist writings and talk posed a threat to safety—was more logical. Vesey had clearly been influenced by newspapers. And though Walker's *Appeal* likely bore no actual link to Turner's revolt, the temporal connection was close enough to make the Southern response understandable. Yet, beyond these isolated—albeit dramatic—events, the Southern rationale quickly falls apart. Enslaved people's dissatisfaction was a function of the conditions under which they lived, not of distant authors describing those conditions to them. And if the South—as it claimed—really treated enslaved people better than Europe and the North treated their laborers, the South should have had no more fear of social uprisings than Northern or European manufacturers did.

Something else was clearly going on. Even as the revolts receded into the past, Southern demands for silence expanded. In other places and times, ideological repressions tended to fade, not escalate, after a crisis passed. And it wasn't as though abolitionists were trying to sneak papers into the hands of enslaved people or excite insurrection. Antislavery advocates aimed their postal and petition campaigns primarily at white politicians. Yet the veil of silence in the South was shockingly comprehensive. Southern states and local communities didn't just ban talk of insurrection and antislavery writing. They effectively banned any talk or writing about slavery that didn't amount to a defense of the institution. A whole spectrum of thought existed in the area between abolitionists and the slavocracy, and very little of it presented a plausible public safety concern. But the South—through law and custom—silenced all of it. For all its dramatic rhetoric, what the South feared was not insurrection but any objective, reasoned, or thoughtful discussion of slavery.

This fear flowed from a fundamental belief that, ironically, Southerners shared with the Northern abolitionists—belief in the power of persuasion. The abolitionists thought they could change the nation through written and oral advocacy. They didn't need guns or formal political power. They didn't even need many resources—they only needed pens, paper, and a printing press. The written word was their weapon. With it, they could draw crowds, prod the people's consciences, change souls, and provoke action. They believed they could change Southerners from the inside out by convincing them they were living in sin.

It is tempting, given how history unfolded, to paint the abolitionists as naive dreamers who thought slavery could be ended without a war. But the South didn't see them that way. Calhoun recognized the threat they posed. It wasn't that his honor was irreparably injured or his life in any remote danger. What he feared was that abolitionist ideas might resonate in open minds, be shared with others, and generate conversations that could lead the South to reform itself. What he feared was that, in the mental combat of constitutional interpretation, historical narrative, and economic analysis, some of his allies might decide he was wrong and abandon him—and along with him, an entire way of life and entire personal and social identity that he had dedicated himself to defending. Slavery's survival did not come from discussing or thinking about it, but by insisting that discussion and consideration were illegitimate. Testing the logic of the original national compact threatened slavery, so the Calhoun faction could insist only on a singular understanding of the compact that precluded further discussion. The reason to silence abolitionist speech was, quite simply, to take "slavery off the Southern political agenda."[36]

Though this stance surely made sense to the slavocracy, it may have been the mistake that sealed the region's fate decades before the Civil War. As Lieber wrote in one of his unsent letters to Calhoun, "If you fear discussion, if you maintain the south cannot afford it, that every man who differs from your community, or who sees deficiencies in the institution must be hushed, then you admit at the same time that the whole institution is to be kept up by violence only." But closed-mindedness ran counter to the spirit of the times, and if violence alone could support slavery, then "violence will be its end." When the South refused to debate slavery, it was—whether it knew it or not—putting itself on a war footing. The North at first responded with appeasement, but unless Northerners intended to eventually bend the knee to the South, the South's refusal to entertain conversation could only end one way.[37]

Slavery had always been the antithesis of democracy, but shutting down white people's ability to debate slavery was the end of the façade of white democracy. A republican form of government couldn't survive in such silence. Silence gave the people no political choice but to accept the policies that those in power—through violence or a political majority—offered them. In Virginia, for instance, this would have meant the General Assembly's 1831 debate could never have happened.

With Southern emotions flaming, Congress didn't dare take legislative action against the South. In any case, many Northern politicians would have questioned such legislation as an invasion of states' rights. Yet a moment's reflection reveals how preposterous this position was. Would Congress permit a territory to enact laws that denied free speech to its citizens? Would it admit such a territory as a new state in the Union? A state that would brazenly deny the right of free speech is not a government for or by the people—not a republican form of government that the Constitution obligates Congress to guarantee in each state. It's a jurisdiction premised on repression.

James Madison, for all his compromises on slavery, clearly recognized this problem and tried to head it off. The U.S. Constitution, which he principally drafted, in 1787, focused exclusively on federal power. It granted the federal government a limited set of enumerated powers. In 1791, the first ten amendments to the Constitution, also Madison's handiwork and otherwise known as the Bill of Rights, protected individuals' rights only against federal, not state, intrusions. But he pressed for one exception.

In conjunction with the limits the new amendments placed on federal power, Madison sought one for states—a prohibition against infringing speech or the press. This right was too precious to leave to the vicissitudes of state governments. Some states that opposed the federal Constitution, he pointed out, had "no bill of rights" in their state constitutions, or guaranteed these rights in ways that were "defective" or "absolutely improper." These states were as likely to "abuse" the people's "invaluable privileges" of speech and press as the federal government—and this abuse could not be squared with the "common ideas of liberty" that the U.S. Constitution guaranteed.[38]

As a check against majoritarian power in state governments, Madison proposed an additional amendment: "no State shall violate the equal right of conscience, freedom of the press, or trial by jury in criminal cases; because it is proper that every Government should be disarmed of powers which trench upon those particular rights." These rights were so vital that they justified "double security"—against the federal and state governments. The House favored this amendment, but the Senate rejected it.[39]

We can only imagine how differently the debates in Congress and the South might have evolved in the 1830s if not for that decade's tragic silence. The South's addiction to slavery would have ensured a strange relationship with the rule of law, but the North would just as surely have seen the South's states' rights and speech arguments differently. It might have been in a position—or at least made an effort—to protect men like Jones, Lovejoy, and Lieber, even if it was not yet ready to protect the people the South enslaved.

CHAPTER TEN

Southern Propaganda

THE SOUTH'S IDEOLOGICAL ASSAULT was multifaceted. Most obviously, it shut off the exchange of ideas involving slavery, cowed dissent, and forced retreat. But it also encouraged sycophants to fill the silence. Southern leaders realized silence was not enough. The more the region closed itself off to the outside world, the more it needed a propaganda machine. That machine fed the Southern identity a poisonous diet for three decades. And once the slavocracy was speaking only to itself, the capacity to sort fact from fiction, reason from sophistry, policy preferences from constitutional principle, disappeared.

Pamphlets and tracts defending slavery and extolling its supposed virtues started to proliferate. If the North could have abolitionist newspapers, the South was determined to have slavery newspapers. The increasing circulation of proslavery thought, however, did not necessarily translate into new substance. Slavery always had its defenders. The real change was the new guard's aggressiveness. It wanted to create an airtight echo chamber from the schoolhouse to the post office.

Southern culture and identity became inseparably intertwined with slavery. No matter how diverse the tapestry of Southern life and experience, slavery was now spun into every strand. The South increasingly saw its defense of slavery as a defense of its entire way of life. With that mindset, quashing abolitionist papers was not enough. Censorship might silence explicit antislavery voices, but it wouldn't silence subtler voices that threatened Southern culture in other ways.

In addition to attacking antislavery thought, the South grew suspicious and hostile toward any idea or author who was not homegrown. Starting in the mid-1830s, proslavery thought leaders established new journals and magazines with the express purpose of speaking to this instinct. In August 1834, for instance, the *Southern Literary Messenger* published its first issue, stressing that the South needed to "assert our mental independence" from the North. While "hundreds of similar publications thrive and prosper north of the Potomac, . . . shall not one be supported in the whole south?" If it were always a consumer and never a producer, the South would "be doomed forever to a kind of vassalage of our northern neighbors."[1]

Framing the problem, however, did not solve it. Independent Southern thought would require serious effort and a new infrastructure. The South was starting at square one. Its public education system was grossly underdeveloped compared with the North's—at the primary, secondary, and higher education levels. Even calling it a "system" of public education would be too generous. Public schooling was limited to a smattering of free schools for poor children and the occasional privately run academy that charged tuition. For most people in the South, public education remained a nascent idea. It wasn't that Southerners lacked interest in public education, but that the plantation elites who controlled state policy had no interest in seeing their property taxed for that purpose. They were content to educate their own children, but no one else's.

Higher education fared no better. Few saw a need to support it through taxes or attendance, making it almost exclusively the domain of the wealthy. The sense among most citizens was that college was pointless for men destined to be farmers and women destined to be housewives. Wealthy people who thought otherwise could educate their children in the North.

But as the friction between the North and South intensified, Southern politicians, leaders, and commercial interests became self-conscious about the South's educational ineptitude. They knew the economic, political, and ideological independence they yearned for required education. Some put the problem in the direst terms, describing the Southern education movement as preparation for disunion. Sensing, if not yet desiring that moment, they felt the South had to be as ready to educate itself as to clothe and feed itself.

Lucian Minor, who later became dean of the William and Mary School of Law, captured the sentiment well. In an 1835 address at

Hampden-Sydney College, he argued that the only remedy to the ongoing assault on the South's republican form of government was "to enlighten the people." Yet enlightening the Southern people was no easy task. The South's "mental culture" lagged far behind the North's. The challenge, he said, began with resources. The North devoted substantial funds, buildings, and people to education while the South devoted almost none. Minor's prescription was straightforward: establish and fund a system of "common schools" for all (white) children. Commercial associations echoed Minor's proposal, emphasizing that education was crucial to the South's economic development. Lack of education held the economy back. More education would unleash it.[2]

This push was ideological as well as practical. Building a system of Southern education was also about escaping Northern influence. The antislavery campaigns had so unnerved Southerners that anything sounding remotely not of the South was met with suspicion. It had to be purged.

The idea of homegrown education had a rich lineage. Believing that public education was a predicate of a functioning democracy, Thomas Jefferson had spent much of his life promoting common schools and higher education in Virginia. But he too had drawn a line between Southern and Northern education. In 1821 he had written to General James Breckenridge warning that Virginia had fallen into the trap of "trusting to those who are against us in position and principle, to fashion in their own form the minds of affections of our youth." Families were sending their sons to Northern seminaries where they were, according to Jefferson, "imbibing opinions and principles in discord with those of their own country. This canker is eating on the vitals of our existences, and if not arrested at once, will be beyond remedy." At the time, these sentiments may have sounded only like special pleading for Jefferson's beloved, yet struggling, University of Virginia. A generation later they inspired the Southern higher education agenda.[3]

From the 1830s onward, however, the South's education agenda encompassed every aspect of education at every level. Southern leaders increasingly worried about who would teach in their elementary schools and colleges and who would write their textbooks. Northern authors and teachers, they believed, could never deliver what Southern children needed. Even worse, they were likely to injure those children. As Mississippi's governor implored, "let us have our own schools, academies, colleges, and universities. Let us rear and educate our own teachers; and above all, let us prepare and publish our own school books." If their sons "are to live in the South, and follow Southern occupations," he insisted that they must "receive Southern educations."[4]

Southern leaders rationalized this homegrown education regime with the notion that, as Charles DeBow put it, "southern life, habits, thoughts, and aims are so essentially different from those of the North, that here a different character of books, tuition, and training is absolutely required, to bring up the boy to manhood with his faculties fully developed." Writing in 1842 for a magazine newly established to promote Southern literary genius and its peculiar institutions, the *Southern Quarterly Review*, Supreme Court justice Joseph Story argued that the problem was deeper than just culture. Northern modes of thought were being "incorporated with every species of knowledge taught in schools," including the law, and would continue to grow into "a mighty stream, whose taste and color is seen and known, in the mingled waters of the mighty ocean of the affairs of life." Nothing was more important for the survival of Southern institutions, he argued, than to ensure that "correct theories" be taught in school and modeled in law.[5]

Charles DeBow would become one of the loudest and most influential voices in this conversation. In 1846 he founded *DeBow's Review*, a monthly magazine on agriculture, commerce, and all things Southern. Over the next decade, it became the most widely circulated periodical in the South, continuing to operate until 1884. Initially, he was its sole author, and he always remained the primary one, but the magazine eventually included contributions by other thought leaders, politicians, businessmen, and publishers—men like Francis Lieber, James Hammond (who had shepherded the final gag order in Congress), and Edmund Ruffin (one of the South's foremost proslavery theorists).

DeBow's theory of Southern education was more specific than some others. He argued that students needed to "learn what the constitution really is, how it became so, the perils that have threatened and do threaten it, the fanaticism that has attacked it." All this, however, was predicated on states' rights as a fundamental principle. And states' rights were in turn predicated on the right to enslave people. DeBow argued that "southern thought must be a distinct thought," and its core was slavery: "Domestic slavery must be vindicated in the abstract, and in the general, as a normal, natural, and, in general, necessitous element of civilized society, without regard to race or color."[6]

Aside from the singular issue of slavery, the Southern education movement primarily defined itself in reaction to the North. A good

Southern education was an education that wasn't Northern and that appreciated the South as superior. That sense of self triggered, among other things, a textbook purge. For the better part of a decade, starting in the mid-1840s, political leaders, news outlets, and pro-Southern associations pored over schoolbooks looking for Northern bias. The *Southern Quarterly Review* pleaded for schoolbooks "free from objectionable matter" and declared Northern textbooks "not only offensive but actually poisonous to the mind."[7]

DeBow's Review spent years making sweeping denunciations of Northern textbooks. It anointed itself the public's watchdog, conducting detailed reviews of textbooks and publishing its findings. It devoted many magazine pages to reviews of individual textbooks in which it recounted objectionable passages, quoting and critiquing them at length. These reviews by DeBow and others created enough fear to reach the upper levels of government. In 1859, for instance, Mississippi governor Albert Brown gave a public address with a Northern schoolbook in hand, detailing the book's various faults and reading aloud five separate offending passages. His assessment was blunt. Northern textbooks were "pure, unadulterated abolition" and were turning "the school-room [into] an anti-slavery lecture room."[8]

Many commentators, however, were unnerved about more than just the comments touching on slavery or directly assailing the South. They could find slights in nearly any book or subject. DeBow insisted that geography texts, for instance, were full of Northern bias, pointing out that when they discussed farming, these books typically featured crops found in the North rather than the South. Books that heaped praise on Northern universities without recognizing Southern ones were similarly biased—never mind that Southerners themselves considered their higher education systems to be grossly underdeveloped. Such slights were enough to render a book unsuitable for Southern use.[9]

From DeBow's perspective, there were only two types of books—those that promoted the South and those that undermined it. He concluded that "all Northern and European books teach abolition either directly or indirectly." And "the indirect method is more dangerous.... It consists in inculcating doctrines at war with slavery, without expressly assailing the institution." Northern books insidiously instilled their worldviews across a wide range of seemingly unrelated subjects. As far as he was concerned, every book written in the "last twenty or thirty years" by someone other than a Southerner was in some fashion inculcating abolition. The only solution—the "all important" solution—was for Southerners to "write our own books. It matters little who makes our shoes," but "we cannot safely delay writing our own books for one hour." *DeBow's Review* called on state governments to step in and ensure that Southern schools used only Southern books.[10]

State leaders, commentators, and commercial conventions began taking concrete steps toward that goal. The challenge, however, was not necessarily publishing resources or vision. DeBow himself was quite successful in publishing Southern books, and others had made serious financial investments in hope of spurring more. In 1836, for instance, Duff Green, a former Jackson administration insider and close political ally of John Calhoun, had announced the formation of the American Literary Company. The company planned several publishing ventures, but its principal aim was to "prepare a new series of elementary school text books, elevate the general standing of literature, and 'render the South independent of Northern fanatics.' " The mission clearly had backing: the company started with a $500,000 capitalization—the equivalent of about $16 million today.[11]

Rather than resources, the real challenge was finding textbook authors. Most textbooks are written by professors, but the South's underdeveloped higher education system meant that qualified professors were in short supply. And the experts the South did have tended to carry high teaching loads and lacked the time for serious research and publishing.

The leaders of the Southern education movement hoped to rebalance those odds. They recruited authors, established prizes for people who wrote Southern textbooks, and leveraged their social networks to elevate the prestige of textbook writing. In 1853, the Southern Commercial Convention, an association devoted to developing and promoting strategies for enhancing the Southern economy, passed a resolution emphasizing the importance of Southern textbooks and calling for a concerted plan to further their publication. It eventually got some states to institute their own prizes for textbooks. But if a lack of authors was the primary barrier, the South also had to focus on changing its system of higher education. In 1857, DeBow implored the University of Virginia—in his opinion the South's best educational institution—to hire more professors and free up their time from teaching so that they could write textbooks.[12]

One leader in the school literature reform movement, Reverend C. K. Marshall, gave a series of addresses in 1856 calling on Southern state legislatures to increase their available prizes for textbooks—from $5,000 to $10,000 in each state—and also to come together to finance and choose the best books. Quality, however, was not necessarily the barometer of success. Speed of publication and fidelity to the Southern way of life were more important. Marshall admitted that these books "might not be as good, after all, as the [states] desired, but ... being free from lies, perversions, anti-scriptural dogmas, sophistries, and withal, highly respectable, [they] might be esteemed not only as safe, but an advancement." To ensure that teachers had no choice but to use these books, he urged that every Northern book found in a Southern schoolhouse should be burned.[13]

While Northern authorship would damn a book, Southern authorship did not ensure its warm reception. The slavocracy read Southern books with critical eyes, too. A Louisiana professor and former school superintendent named D. Barton Ross, for instance, edited a school textbook titled *The Southern Speaker*, which came out in 1857. The *Southern Literary Messenger* dismissed it as "not by any means what a 'Southern Speaker' should be" because Ross had "not made a sufficiently wide selection from Southern writers. A work of this kind, designed for the Southern youth, should not only be entirely free from the poison of antislavery, but it should give the student some adequate idea of what the South has done in literature." Southern students must not grow up thinking, explicitly or implicitly, that "the intellectual wealth of the Southern States is inferior to that of New England." The only possible explanation for the book's relative neglect of Southern writers was that Ross must not be "very well acquainted with the literary production of his own section of the Union." The *Messenger* had come to expect such "injustice" from Northerners, but for Ross "to ignore the literary wealth of the South" was " 'most intolerable and not to be endured.' "[14]

The Southern movement began to turn on its elementary school teachers in the same way. Calls to purge Northerners from the teaching ranks were common. The premise was the same as with schoolbooks: anyone not from the South was not fit to teach Southern youth. For instance, Mississippi Governor Albert Brown embedded disdain for Northern teachers in his denouncements of Northern textbooks. One textbook, *The Elements of Moral Science* by the president of Brown University, particularly offended him, and he apparently went on the prowl to find a teacher using it. When he found one, he questioned her. She responded that she had taped the book's objectionable pages together to prevent students from reading them. But he didn't believe her, he said, because she was a "yankee."[15]

For all the complaints and suspicions, there is no evidence of mass firings, probably because it would have meant shuttering schools. As a transitional measure, some communities publicly pledged not to hire any more Northern teachers. An official resolution at the 1853 Southern Commercial Convention seconded the idea, recommending "to the citizens of the States here represented" that they employ only "native teachers in their schools."[16]

Southern leaders, however, knew that refusing to hire Northern teachers was impracticable. So long as its college system lagged behind, the South could not produce a fraction of the teachers it needed. While it might speed the production of textbooks, maybe even relying on Northern presses to print them, a Southern teaching core required more infrastructure. So, at the same time leaders were calling for Southern books and common schools, they were also calling for "normal schools" to train teachers. Governor Brown put normal schools ahead of common schools as a state priority, understanding that the former were a predicate to the latter. "We can never have proper school books until we educate our own teachers," he told the faculty, trustees, and students at Madison College. "We do not expect books on theology from lawyers, nor books on law from preachers." The only long-term solution was to create fountainheads for the production of teachers. Everything else the South wanted could flow from there.[17]

In the short term, however, Southern families were in a bind. DeBow, Brown, Marshall, and others could paint glorious pictures of the future of Southern education, but families with growing children could not wait for it. Those with means had long sent their young men to Northern academies and universities. Virginians alone filled a large fraction of the seats at the North's most prestigious institutions. And it was not just moderates or those wanting to emulate Northern elites who sent their children there. Several of the leading Southern figures responsible for shutting down abolition discussions in the Virginia Assembly, blockading the Postal Campaign, and gagging the petitions were educated at the Ivies. Whitemarsh Seabrook and James Gholson, for instance, had gone to Princeton, and John Calhoun to Yale.

By the 1840s, however, Southern leaders were making a concerted movement to dissuade these families. Young men crossing the Mason-Dixon line to study were entering a den of "enemies" where they would be bombarded on all sides with abolition—from culture and newspapers to friends and leaders. Both the professor and the preacher, the firebrands warned, would indoctrinate these young men with an anti-Southern view of the world.

In his 1858 address "Southern Education for Southern Youth," William Stiles charged that everything taught in Northern schools, churches, and the culture is in "violent hostility to our institutions." It was impossible that Southern youth could go North and "survive without inhaling seeds of moral corruption and decay." Foreshadowing a tragic future that was fast approaching, he compared the political situation to that of warring ancient Greek states. Would the rude and hardy Spartans have sent their children for cultivation and refinement in Athenian schools? Would the learned Athenians send their children to Spartan barracks for combat training? Doing so would have been "an act of consummate folly." The same held true in the United States, Stiles said. Southern institutions were "based upon slavery" and Northern ones on "what they are pleased to call freedom." For Southern boys to receive a Northern education would not only "unfit them for their native institutions" but "implant in them a deadly hostility" toward the South, "which nothing but its destruction could possibly appease."[18]

Southern leaders called on families to preserve their way of life by bringing their children home from the North. Even if the South could not meet their educational wants, this was a small price to pay for cultural survival. As DeBow wrote, it was better for their sons to remain ignorant plow hands than to be fed "doctrines subversive of their country's peace and honor"—doctrines that would set them at war with the fundamental principles of Southern society. But the South could offer no alternatives to a Harvard, Yale, or Princeton education, and Southern attendance at Northern schools remained steady. Rather than sacrifice their children's education, most families were willing to trust that their children could survive the cultural assault.[19]

The contradiction of the era was that leaders who had long ignored and even discouraged education suddenly became preoccupied with its importance. In the years after the Vesey and Turner incidents, the South had focused on denying Black people education and information because it believed these to be the gateways to freedom, power, and insurrection. The unintended consequence was that by underfunding and undervaluing public education, it had held back its white population, too. Not until the South began to take a war footing toward the North did it appreciate the damage it had done to itself. It was dependent on the North to supply its educational needs and had no immediate path to self-sufficiency. The multilayered pipeline of students, teachers, professors, books, and institutions—even with perfect coordination and full resource deployment—would have taken a generation to become self-perpetuating.

The South had also begun to realize—though it would never admit it—the wisdom of the abolitionists. People who could artfully wield the pen didn't need guns. Written ideas could take hold and spread. If there was any truth in the South's diagnosis of Northern literature, it was that while the abolitionists had failed in the formal political arena during the 1830s—having their mail and their petitions gagged—they had succeeded in changing culture. By the 1840s, books, papers, and institutions all showed their influence, and Northern politics would soon follow the path its literature had carved out. Years behind the abolitionists, the South tried, albeit less successfully, to replicate the abolitionists' strategy. An 1843 issue of the *Southern Quarterly Review* summarized it best: "He who commands the avenues, through which the minds of a people may be reached, exercises over them a power greater than that of the mere written law. In this reading age, that avenue is the press; and . . . 'he who writes a people's books, need not care who makes their laws.' "[20]

CHAPTER ELEVEN

Secret Learning

However many laws they passed, and however much revenge they exacted, the Southern states could never stamp out Black literacy. The roots were too deep, the desire too feverish. Black literacy already had a good head start before the crackdowns came. Churches and missionaries had been teaching enslaved people to read the Bible since the eighteenth century, and Black individuals—free and enslaved—had been self-teaching ever since their ancestors first felt literacy's pull.

But reconstructing this history is particularly hard and can only be gleaned from afar. Save those Black people who escaped slavery—and the much smaller fraction who then found a venue to publish their narrative—the story of Black literacy mostly emerges through the eyes of white people. Their "paternalism," as the historian Heather Andrea Williams writes in *Self-Taught*, clouds the story at times, forcing us to "read between the lines, to pull out people who are mentioned only in passing." Even the most basic facts, like how many enslaved people learned to read, are elusive.[1]

The historian Antonio Bly did a study of notices of runaways in Virginia newspapers from the 1730s until the Revolution. These notices often mentioned enslaved persons' skills, including literacy. Bly found that 3 percent of runaways were literate in the 1740s, rising to 7 percent in the 1760s. In New England, where slavery was still legal at the time, literacy among runaways approached 10 percent. While literate enslaved people were probably the most likely to run away—because they had greater access to the information and skills that made escape possible—these numbers surely undercount their literacy. First, some notices would not have bothered to mention it. Second, enslaved people who acquired literacy often feigned ignorance, so enslavers would not have known to mention it. Regardless, scholars estimate that slave literacy ranged from 5 to 10 percent into the 1800s.[2]

In cities and among free Black people, the rates could be higher. Black elites in Charleston ran their own schools from at least the turn of the nineteenth century until they were shut down in 1835. As the city's free Black population grew, so did its aspirations. Among the first outward signs of those aspirations were social societies that pooled resources for community uplift and made education one of their primary functions. In 1790, Black Charleston's upper crust formed the Brown Fellowship Society with the express purpose of providing education for the children of society members. A half dozen similar education societies formed in Charleston over the next two decades.[3]

Some of the new societies offered education to students other than just their members' children. In 1803, for instance, the Brown Fellowship Society's leaders founded the Minors Moralist Society, aiming to educate poor and orphaned Black children, some of whom were enslaved. The founders recruited fifty members to the society, each of whom paid a membership fee of five dollars and monthly dues of twenty-five cents to support the program, which operated for decades.[4]

Expanding capacity also translated into qualitative improvements in the education the societies could provide. By 1807, the Brown Society had the resources to formalize its education mission. It built a school on the property of Richard Holloway—a successful Black businessman—and hired Thomas Bonneau as the headmaster. Bonneau developed a course of study resembling what Thomas Jefferson had proposed as leadership training. Under Bonneau's tutelage, students learned to read and write but moved on to a classical style of education, studying ancient history, the *Columbian Orator*, and the art of speech. The school was so popular that Bonneau had to hire two men to assist him. It became the foundation for a broader education movement, and its students didn't just bend their learning and talents toward individual attainment. Many served as the next generation's leaders and teachers, in Charleston and elsewhere. Although schools like Bonneau's started as an effort to elevate the position of the Black elite, the contributions their students made as adults gave them a far wider impact.[5]

For a time, it seemed that Black schooling and education would only continue improving. Charleston's rapidly expanding Black population, the relative freedom Black Charlestonians enjoyed, and the support of white and Black churches fostered an environment where education—formal and informal—grew naturally. But Vesey's plot changed those dynamics. After 1822, white authorities began attacking religion and literacy as central facilitators of Black unrest.

When they destroyed the African Methodist Church where Vesey and his colleagues had worshipped, forcing church leaders to flee the city forever, the Charleston authorities hoped that Black congregants would return to white churches, where the white clergy would once again indoctrinate them in the worldview that Vesey spent years contesting. By suppressing Black schools and literacy as well, they believed they could put all subversive agitation behind them.[6]

But eliminating Black education proved harder than expected. For one thing, white churches ran schools, too. Their leaders may have been fine with closing down independent Black schools, but they did not want to close their own. Once the initial reaction to the Vesey affair had passed, the churches began to outmaneuver the firebrands. Charleston adopted an anti-literacy ordinance in the immediate wake of Vesey's trial, then lifted it the next year. The pro-literacy churches held enough sway in Charleston that opponents had to appeal to the state legislature for help, begging the General Assembly to block what the city was willing to tolerate. They wanted to severely penalize anyone, including the churches, who taught "negroes to read and write."[7]

In 1826, a memorial from the Charleston City Council to the South Carolina House of Representatives reported that a Charleston grand jury had investigated a number of "schools publicly kept for the instruction of persons of Colour in reading and writing" and found them "injurious to the Community." The city council wanted to permanently close those schools and others, but it was difficult because state law only prohibited the instruction of slaves, and "it is impossible to distinguish between the free and the slave of our colored population." The only remedy, they urged, was "the absolute prohibition of all Schools for the instruction of Colored persons." Neither the state nor Charleston obliged them. State legislators, still fighting to uphold the Seamen Act against federal objections, had their own problems, and attacking Black literacy would trigger an unnecessary fight at home.[8]

These mixed politics afforded Black Charlestonians the space to continue their education efforts and societies, some of which flourished.

In 1830, for instance, shortly after Bonneau passed away, his colleagues formed the Bonneau Library Society in his honor and kept it going for at least fifteen years. One of Bonneau's former students, Daniel Payne, eclipsed, or at least equaled, Bonneau's pre-Vesey school with one of his own in the post-Vesey world. Years later, in the North, Payne served as the sixth bishop of the African Methodist Episcopal Church, vastly increasing its membership, expanding educational training for ministers, and helping to found Wilberforce University in 1856.[9]

Payne was born free in Charleston in 1811. Education, according to his autobiography, marked nearly every major step of his life. His father, a remarkable man in his own right, began teaching Payne to read as a toddler. When his father's premature death left four-year-old Payne and his mother in hardship, the Minors Moralist Society partially came to the rescue by offering him a spot in its school. Payne sped through the school's curriculum, catching the attention of Thomas Bonneau, who then took him as a student at his school for the city's Black elite.[10]

Just as Payne was blossoming under Bonneau's tutelage and taking his place as the school's top pupil, his mother died. His great-aunt took him in, but his schooling ended. At twelve, he had to start earning his own way, first working in a shoe store and then in carpentry and tailoring. But he had already internalized the most important lesson: education was the way out of his situation. Rather than work to live, he worked to learn. As he wrote in his autobiography, he "resolved to devote every moment of leisure to the study of books, and every cent to purchase them." For the better part of a decade, he worked overtime crafting extra carpentry items that he could sell to finance his passion. If he wasn't building items or selling them at the market, he had his nose in a book. Nearly every moment not spent working, eating, or sleeping was reserved for reading. Work started at six in the morning, but he woke long before dawn to cram in two hours of reading before the day began. In the evenings, he would stay up until midnight to read more.[11]

By 1829, Payne was ready to follow in Bonneau's footsteps. The post-Vesey fervor had passed, and notwithstanding the firebrands, Charleston generally understood that it needed skilled and sometimes educated Black labor. Payne opened a school in the heart of Charleston just a few blocks from the harbor. He began with six students: three children during the day and three adults at night. His inexperience and the resource demands of a new enterprise, however, proved too much. He wrote that were it not for the generosity of an enslaved woman, he would have starved. At the year's end, he called it quits and returned to regular work.

A few months of reflection and the feeling that he had abandoned his God-given calling made him try again. In early 1830 he reopened the school, and this time it took off. The expanding roster of students quickly outgrew his little classroom, so he relocated to a second space but quickly outgrew that space as well. He needed a legitimate schoolhouse. Just as Holloway had built Bonneau a school on his personal property, Robert Howard stepped up to sponsor Payne, building him a school in his backyard. The Black world was coming full circle. The school stood at Anson Street, just west of Bay Street—the road Vesey's lottery tickets had helped finance.

Both the school and Payne's personal education remained works in progress. At the school's opening, he had a mastery of the basics—reading, writing, and arithmetic—but not much more. He learned the rest on the job, slowly teaching himself as he taught the students. First, he added geography to the curriculum, then grammar, then botany. Later he added chemistry, philosophy, astronomy, and Greek. For five years, the subjects he might learn and teach seemed endless. Not even book learning was enough.

Payne became a novice naturalist. He took his students on backwoods excursions to collect all manner of insects, reptiles, and plants. He dissected some, stuffed others, and examined the most interesting specimens while they were still alive, cutting open their chests while their organs were still moving. If he found something he could not identify, he canvassed the town for someone who could. That infectious zeal for knowledge soon made his school the most popular one in Charleston, drawing sixty children, most of whom came from the city's leading Black families.

This same zeal, however, also caused his school's fall from grace. Whether motivated by jealousy, ignorance, or both, white people began talking about Payne. They questioned why anyone would study the things that interested him. "He must deal with the devil," some said.[12]

Payne was largely oblivious. During the summer of 1834, he naively approached Lionel Kennedy, the author of the trial record in the Vesey affair. Payne wanted his students to examine a poisonous snake, a highland moccasin, and he thought Kennedy, who owned a farm outside the city, might have one or could catch one that he would sell. Kennedy agreed to help. Payne sent three students to the farm to fetch the viper. When they arrived, Kennedy's son interrogated the boys. He wanted to know why Payne wanted the snake and what he was teaching them. They answered directly and truthfully but couldn't pacify the man. He was convinced, as he remarked to his father, that "Payne is playing hell in Charleston."[13]

This questioning of his students unsettled Payne. When South Carolina passed legislation formally prohibiting the education of both enslaved and free persons of color in December 1834, Payne couldn't see his school surviving. He suspected the new law was aimed at him. The law's author, Whitemarsh Seabrook, had been campaigning for years to close Charleston's Black schools, and Payne's was the most prominent one in the state, maybe the entire South. Other schools could go underground, but there was no way Payne's could remain hidden.

He consulted his mentors and colleagues, white and Black, who assured him he couldn't stay in Charleston. A poem revealed the depths of his despair over leaving. He wrote of having helped his students "fly from earth where sinful pleasures blind" to ascend "the rugged hill of science." He was distraught that no one would "help op'ning wings to fly" once he was gone. If "tears of blood" could "revoke the fierce decree" or the "statesmen touch ... make my pupils free," he would shed those tears "til potent justice swayed the senate floor." But it was in God's hands. If he wanted to teach, he could do so only in the North.[14]

With the law set to go into effect in April 1835, Payne taught his last class in Charleston on March 31, closing the school "as it had begun—with singing and prayer." The law closed four other Black schools in the city too. A month later, on May 9, 1835, Payne left for New York.[15]

Payne was wise to get out. This educational crackdown was worse than the one following the Vesey affair. As tensions and rhetoric flared in the 1830s, even white people who taught Black people were in danger. Religious leaders and educators could not hold off the firebrands. The Catholic Church in Charleston had long ministered to the Black community and encouraged education, including among enslaved people. With Payne's departure and the closing of other Black-led schools, Bishop John England decided to open a formal school for free Blacks. He had eighty students within a few weeks.

Two months after Bishop England opened the school, the Charleston Post Office raid of July 1835 rekindled the city's worst instincts. Local concerns, however, went beyond postal policies. After the Charleston mob finished with the post office and burned the antislavery pamphlets, it proceeded to the Catholic seminary. All outward signs

Daniel Payne later in life. Courtesy of Library of Congress.

suggested that the crowd intended to lynch Bishop England and burn the church facilities. The city militia—or rather its sympathetic French and Irish branches—held off the mob but could not disperse it. Finally, a group of prominent citizens interceded, paving the way for an ad-hoc emergency committee to negotiate a compromise.[16]

The mob demanded that England close his school, but England would not let the Catholic school be singled out when other churches in the city were also educating Black people. He finally agreed to close his school if all the other churches agreed to close theirs. This stance salvaged a symbolic victory for Catholics, but it gave the mob even more than what it came for: the end of formal, church-sponsored schooling for Black people in Charleston.

Similar stories were already playing out across the South. Charles Colcock Jones, a white Presbyterian minister committed to Black education, characterized 1829 to 1835 as a period of revival in his religious community in carrying out its "duty" of "instruction of Negroes," but after the backlash to the Postal Campaign of 1835, "it was considered best to disband schools and discontinue meetings, at least for a season." By the end of 1835, as the historian Grey Gundaker writes, the Postal Campaign had pushed "the balance of white opinion over the top, leading to immediate anti-literacy legislation across the South and closure of virtually all schooling for blacks by 1835."[17]

In most places, the end was swifter and simpler than in Charleston. The politics were straightforward. Typically, a single petition or act of mob violence was enough to close Black schools permanently and force Black literacy underground. Savannah closed its Black schools half a decade before Charleston, and they stayed closed as far as any white person could see. The most important of those Savannah schools was run by Julian Froumontaine, Savannah's equivalent of Thomas Bonneau. After opening his first school around 1818, Froumontaine taught freely for a decade. But once Georgia passed its anti-literacy act in 1829, in the wake of David Walker's *Appeal*, Froumontaine went underground, teaching secretly for another half-decade. Several of his students followed his lead, operating a network of clandestine schools in Savannah for decades.[18]

Details on these schools are scant. Much of what survives comes from hints in oral family histories, a few passing references in isolated texts, and a single autobiography. The most vivid image they paint is of a few Black women running schools a short distance from Greene Square, one of Savannah's famous lush green spaces, brimming with giant oaks, ornamental fountains, and fine houses. The owners of those homes never knew that Black children were being secretly educated just steps from their opulent front doors.

Jane DeVeaux and her mother, Catherine, started one such school during the height of Savannah's anti-literacy sentiment. They were not deterred even when another Black teacher, James Simms, received a public whipping. Though Catherine would pass away, Jane and others operated their secret schools throughout the antebellum period and the Civil War. When Union troops captured Savannah in 1864, Jane finally stepped into the light, revealing a fully functioning school—one of several that had existed in the city for decades. Once he had fully grasped the extent of her efforts, the Union official in charge of starting more schools, John Alvord, was impressed, writing that she had been "instrumental" in the education of many Black people, who were now "scattered here and there through the south" and contributing to "the general elevation of the newly emancipated race."[19]

Heather Andrea Williams, in *Self-Taught*, explains just how much rested on the shoulders of women like DeVeaux. These teachers made lifelong sacrifices of time and money to teach Black children during slavery but were also integral to the success of Black education afterward. Though thousands of white teachers would eventually come south after the War, the "missionary" schools they taught in "could just as easily have been called freedpeople's schools. Certainly missionary employees taught in the schools," but most often "former slaves conceived of the school[s]" and made them work.[20]

The most intimate explanation of how these schools survived and flourished prior to the War, however, comes from an autobiographical account by one of the students, Susie King Taylor. She was born into slavery on an island thirty-five miles outside Savannah and apparently gained the affection of the woman who enslaved her. For reasons that are unclear, the mistress granted the girl permission to leave the plantation at age seven. Taylor was sent to live with her grandmother in Savannah.[21]

Taylor's grandmother sent her to a free woman of color, a Mrs. Woodhouse, to "learn to read and write" alongside twenty-five or thirty other students. Despite the group's size, Woodhouse avoided suspicion by pretending that the children coming and going from her house were learning a trade and helping her cook. She directed the students to wrap their books in paper. To all outward appearances, they were carrying kitchen supplies or tools and entering the back door to begin a day of labor. Some also carried buckets as though they were on some errand.[22]

Taylor arrived at nine in the morning each day, but others took pains to enter at different times. Unlike the typical schoolhouse, where the day began sharply with the ring of a bell, Woodhouse's school had students dribble in separately, one at a time throughout the morning. Neighbors never saw a group of students marching to school each morning. To avoid a discernable pattern or destination, students arrived by circuitous routes. At the day's end, they would similarly depart at different times in different directions, only to meet up in one of the city squares for innocent play.[23]

Susie King Taylor. Courtesy of Library of Congress.

Nothing indicates that the schools coordinated with one another, but collectively, they formed a rough system of education through which students could advance. Each schoolteacher had her strengths and knowledge. She would share what she knew and help a student master it, and once that knowledge was exhausted, any student whose family wanted more—and could afford it—would move to another teacher in another house. Taylor spent two years with Mrs. Woodhouse and then left for Mary Beasley's school, where she remained until Beasley announced that she "had better get some one else who could teach me more." By that time, at the age of twelve, she had advanced far enough that there was no obvious next stop. She stayed home until she braved the path of so many other enslaved people: she approached a white person whom she hoped she could persuade to discreetly give her lessons.[24]

Her first white teacher was a playmate who lived down the street and was receiving formal instruction at a local convent. For four months, the friend secretly guided Taylor through lessons every night. But when the girl took her station as a nun, Taylor had to find another teacher. Her grandmother risked approaching her landlord's son—a very friendly high school student—for help. He agreed to give Taylor lessons, which continued until 1861, when he was ordered to the front lines of the Civil War.

Education in the countryside presents a more varied picture, good and bad, because the law mattered less there. The legal culture of the nineteenth century bears little resemblance to today. Unified sets of laws that were known and applied throughout a state did not exist. Legislatures passed and printed new laws each year, but no state had a system for compiling and organizing prior and current laws together. Laws just heaped upon one another over decades, which explains the confusion during the Denmark Vesey affair over what rules actually governed the trials. Many people operated on lore. What the law required or prohibited was often as much a matter of cultural assumptions as it was the actual letter of the law.

Plantation life added another variable. There was necessarily a limit to how far the slave code, even if understood, could penetrate the culture of any given plantation. The plantation owner's word was, for all intents and purposes, final. Some of them quietly encouraged literacy, while others punished it with death. Either way, the law was irrelevant.

Escaped and formerly enslaved people regularly recounted extreme violence over literacy. Regardless of what the law might say, everything in their immediate environment told them reading and writing was completely off limits. Many whites didn't want enslaved people even to touch a book or open one out of curiosity. Spreading the desired level of terror involved making gruesome threats and occasionally carrying them out.

Gordon Bluford explained that he and the other 250 people whom Felix Calmes enslaved never learned to read because Calmes, who was particularly violent, said if he caught any of his slaves trying to learn he would "skin them alive." Another man said, "if they caught you trying to write ... they would cut your head off." Men missing fingers or hands and women stripped naked and burned with hot irons proved that these threats were serious. The swiftest punishment was for those enslaved people who dared to teach others. One man said his enslaver "hung the best slave he had" for teaching others to read. Another's father was whipped to death for teaching. Georgia Baker, who had been enslaved in Georgia, said examples like these made her enslaved community "more afraid of newspapers than they were of snakes."[25]

Where owners did not act, roaming patrols could mete out their own punishments. Even if an enslaver condoned literacy, the possibility of third-party violence lurked in many communities. Mere rumors about slave schools could bring horse riders in the night or a coffin box outside the door in the morning—a death warning not just to teachers but to any who persisted in learning. Patrols invaded plantations and Sunday schools in broad daylight and dragged grown adults into the yard to be whipped in front of their students.[26]

This terror did and did not work its intended effect. Reading and writing were the forbidden fruit that most dared not bite. But those who had already tasted literacy, or who understood what it might do for them, were not deterred. Hundreds of slave narratives and interviews document the extreme lengths to which people went to acquire literacy.

A federal writers' project in the 1930s preserved a massive oral history of formerly enslaved people, by then quite elderly, including interviews of more than two thousand people. Close to three hundred said they learned to read while enslaved. Two-thirds of these said they were taught, almost all as children, by white people. Black families were fully aware of prohibitions on Black literacy, but white children often were not, making them important, even if unwitting, allies in skirting the rules. Black parents encouraged their children to play with white children and ask what they were learning, or just to "play school," a game that could easily slip into regular lessons with time. Thinking little of it, some white children were eager to teach their Black playmates. In towns, other enslaved people bartered food and other items for lessons from loitering schoolboys. A number of Black children became literate by pure trickery and stealth, persuading white children to read aloud from the Bible, memorizing every word, and later matching those words to text in Bibles they had hidden away. Black children without trustworthy white playmates waited for white children to leave their schoolbooks behind and copied over already completed lessons.[27]

Acquiring literacy under these circumstances was slow work. A "stolen" lesson here and there provided an important boost. But learning to read typically occurred over long periods, in fits and starts, with many forced to figure it out entirely on their own—one letter, one syllable, eventually one word at a time. Those who could secretly lay their hands on a Noah Webster's *Blue-Back Speller*—the country's most popular text for teaching the alphabet, spelling, and grammar—found the process slightly easier. But even with this roadmap, it was a grueling process. One enslaved man recounted tearing one page or one scrap at a time from his spelling book. He carried it around in his front pocket, going over it until he memorized it before moving on to another scrap. Those without spellers looked over the shoulders of white men as they read the newspaper, later stealing a paper and matching what they overheard to the text.[28]

The other barrier was finding time to study. Between endless work, watchful eyes, and cramped quarters, privacy and time were in short supply. The footpath from one task or errand to another, the time when a white person left the room or the foreman left the worksite, and any small moment alone could provide a brief chance to study a line or two, but sustained opportunities tended to come only on evenings and weekends.

Putting aside the sacrifice of losing desperately needed rest, evening studying presented risk. A flickering candle in late evening could draw attention and suspicion, and a search of one's quarters or worse. To evade detection, enslaved people told of going deep into the woods and relying on the natural terrain to hide their efforts. One young man learned to read and write in the depths of a cave. Others located or dug holes in the ground and covered them with bushes and vines. In Mississippi, people told of holes large enough to accommodate a group. They called them "pit schools."[29]

For most, Sundays provided the safest time to learn. Whites deserted the plantation for church and generally left enslaved people to their own devices. Black people could hold their own religious services, rest, visit family and friends, or wander with relatively little risk, making it the perfect time to study, alone or in groups.

A single literate person could spread literacy widely throughout a family or community. Despite tightening restrictions, slave narratives tell a clear story of families keeping literacy alive, passing it on to their children and grandchildren over decades. A single hidden book or Bible could fuel those fires, even across family separation. Well-documented stories in Richmond, Virginia, tell of enslaved people who learned to read prior to Nat Turner's revolt—often with the explicit consent or help of whites—and desperately held on to that learning in the aftermath. They treated a single book as a family heirloom and huddled together with their children in the evenings to make sure the prized gift of literacy passed through the family.[30]

Reflecting on his youth, Elder Green, a formerly enslaved man, explained his family situation: "My father was a good man but I didn't see much of him because we belonged to different people. They let him come once a week to see us. I was always glad for him to come because he could read a little and he taught me about all I ever learned out of the Blue Back Speller." He eventually started asking his owner to let him visit his father's plantation, which "gave me a chance to learn more, for the slave children over there knew more than we did." New friends also presented an opportunity to socialize in a new circle, but the boy was more desperate to learn. As he later recalled, "there wasn't much playing for me."[31]

No matter the ingenuity or passion of secret learning, the larger legal and structural world still sharply limited its scope. Time, access to material, a safe space, or a teacher's knowledge all set limits on what an enslaved person could hope to learn. There were limits to how many children could learn at a time. Cities could mitigate those problems. City people like Susie Taylor could reach out for a tutor or new teacher; steal, buy, or barter for new materials; and move around with more freedom than people in the countryside. But the limits on time were unrelenting, and safety was never certain.

Yet, across all these geographies and stories, one thing remained constant—the human agency to persevere and learn. Closing formal schools did not end Black schooling. Black schools, though smaller, lived on in subterranean, camouflaged spaces. Violence and oppression did not eliminate Black literacy in the countryside either. It just retreated into darker, smaller spaces, sometimes just enough for a single person. Against all odds, a small core—individuals and groups—saved literacy for themselves and those who followed.

CHAPTER TWELVE

Black Literacy on Trial

WHILE LEGAL AND VIOLENT intolerance of Black literacy persisted in the South until the Civil War, ambiguities crept back in some places. Where the labor market required literacy, white culture tacitly accepted it. Religious communities also pushed it. Charleston, which had been the epicenter of Black literacy at the turn of the nineteenth century and then the locus of violent crackdowns in 1835, only temporarily eliminated Black schools. Once the anti-literacy fervor subsided, a few white Charlestonians quietly filled Daniel Payne's role. They never delivered education equal to what Payne provided, but they did resume literacy instruction—instruction that remained illegal no matter how limited. Operating on the ambiguous fringes of accepted norms, they kept their work as quiet as possible. Having secured a legal victory, many white Charlestonians were willing to turn a blind eye. And, of course, the already educated Black community continued to share literacy with others in more deeply concealed spaces.

The clash between explicit social expectations and practical reality brought yet another storm to Charleston in the late 1840s and early 1850s, when the anti-literacy cycle of the 1830s started up once again. By 1845, the religious community was pushing the boundaries of acceptable behavior. In May, Episcopal and Methodist leaders met for three days to discuss the subject of "Religious Instruction of the Negroes." Records of the meeting's discussion reveal that some religious instruction in the state included not just oral instruction but literacy.[1]

One of the state's Episcopal districts, Chester, reported that 22 of 213 Black congregants could "read and probably two-thirds of the whole number can spell and begin to try to read." Aiming to expand these efforts following that May meeting, religious leaders increasingly preached that it is the religious community's "duty" to support religious instruction for Black people. By 1848, one Charleston minister was holding separate services for Black people in the basement of St. Philip's Church. A year later, leaders were raising funds for the construction of Calvary Church—a building that would accommodate six hundred Black congregants in downtown Charleston.[2]

Whitemarsh Seabrook, as he had before, railed against the evils of Black literacy and the increased white leniency toward it. But now, as governor of South Carolina, he held even more sway. Convinced that illegal education was occurring in Charleston and elsewhere, he and his disciples targeted Calvary Church, or the "n***** church," as some took to calling it. As had been the case with the Vesey affair, men like Seabrook needed only a spark to set repressive events into motion.[3]

When a group of enslaved Black men escaped on July 13, 1849, from Charleston's workhouse, which was located just a few blocks from Calvary Church, the church's detractors had the excuse they needed. Though local authorities quickly recaptured the enslaved men and tried the lead instigator, Nicholas, on July 14, agitators turned the community's fear against Calvary Church. Just hours after Nicholas's trial concluded, hundreds of white people gathered at the church "with the intention of pulling it down." The city's military—established in response to the Vesey affair in 1822—arrived on the scene too but made no attempt to disperse the crowd. The mayor pled for law and order and promised to get to the bottom of the church's activities if the mob would just give him and other city leaders a little time to investigate. The mob finally relented and agreed to "postpone" the attack.[4]

The situation remained tense in the coming days. The white leaders who had spearheaded the church's construction issued public statements, assuring the community that they had meticulously followed the letter of the law and secured every necessary approval from local government. But newspaper editorials railed against the church, claiming that it was blatantly violating state law regarding "the management" of enslaved persons. Some charged the Episcopal leaders with trying to cover up "schemes generally pronounced destructive to the interests, even safety, of the community." Writing under a pseudonym of "Many Citizens,"

Andrew Gordon Magrath, a prominent attorney and former state representative, intentionally stoked "the fears of a community which had not forgotten the events of 1822."[5]

When the city leaders convened a meeting at City Hall on July 23, the recriminations finally began to subside. To quell suspicions of a cover-up, the city appointed fifty citizens to a committee tasked with investigating the church. More important, several agitators would serve leading roles on the committee. And to ensure nefarious activities were not afoot elsewhere—or coming Charleston's way—the committee was to send interrogatories to churches and religious authorities across the southeast—more than two hundred in total.[6]

The committee went to work immediately. Its interrogatories posed seventeen major questions, with various sub-questions. The first three questions were aimed at whether the church gave instruction to Black people, how much time was spent on instruction, and whether it was "oral or printed" and by "white or colored teachers, and preachers." The next questions went to the size of any "separate" meetings a church might hold for Black people and the level of white supervision. After that, the questions returned to Black literacy, asking, "Have you a Sabbath School for the colored people? Are the teachers white or colored, and the instruction oral or printed, the number of scholars, and what proportion of them read?" The final questions asked for information about how religion affected Black people: did it lead to "mischief against their masters" and other "disadvantages," or did enslaved people remain "docile and faithful to their duties?"[7]

On November 13, 1849, after four months of interviews, sixty-nine responses to its interrogatories, and making itself "minutely acquainted with what is done at Calvary Church," the committee released its findings in writing, along with an appendix that included individual responses to its questions. Whatever had been happening before July 14, the assault on Calvary had worked its intended effect. Its religious leaders ceased religious instruction for Black people and "dispersed" the congregation. Other nearby religious communities disavowed having ever held separate meetings or instruction for Black people. As Whiteford Smith, the pastor of the Methodist Episcopal Church on Cumberland Street for fifty years, flatly wrote in response to an interrogatory, "We do not teach colored persons to read." His church remembered too well, he assured the committee, "the insurrection of 1822."[8]

But the real matter to be settled was the future of Calvary. St. Philip's and St. Michael's, the churches that had financed Calvary, had sought to clear the air in their communications with the committee. The idea to construct Calvary, they wrote, only arose because constructing a separate balcony in St. Philip's for Black people was too expensive. And Calvary was never intended for Black people only. It was for white people too and would always have fifty or more in attendance to ensure compliance with the law. In separate correspondence, the minister of Calvary also assured the committee that he never held a " 'separate meeting' of colored persons" and his "instruction is altogether 'oral.' " As to "what proportion" of Black congregants "can read," he responded that "we have never inquired, as we should make distinction in consequence in our ways of teaching them."[9]

Under the premise that oral religious instruction at Calvary and elsewhere was, as all attested, improving "the moral condition, docility and submission to authority, of those slaves," the committee would allow the services at Calvary to proceed. But lest there be any backsliding or doubt, a subcommittee dedicated to the subject recommended three strict regulations for Calvary and other churches regarding Black religious instruction. First, religious instruction of Black people should not occur in separate facilities for Black people but only in places "dedicated ... for the use of some established congregation of white persons." Second, all religious instruction should be "imparted ... entirely and exclusively by white persons" and under the strict and close supervision of white people. Finally and crucially, "all teaching at such meetings should be oral."[10]

The final report was circulated as a pamphlet and, in the words of one historian, "went far toward dispelling fears that had lingered in Charleston since Denmark Vesey's time." Maybe more accurately, a mob and months of investigation reminded those in Charleston who had dared to expand Black literacy—or who might otherwise consider it—just how dangerous it still was. The city and the mob would always be looking over their shoulders.[11]

Two years later, agitators turned their attention elsewhere, running a prominent rural slave owner, Richard Fuller, out of the state for speaking freely on the topic of slavery and supporting Black literacy. Fuller, who enslaved between 150 and 200 people in Beaufort, a sea island south of Charleston, was unquestionably sympathetic to slavery as an institution. He led the Southern Baptist Convention after its split with the North over the slavery question. But as a minister, he insisted that everyone must have full access to God's word, and he intended to teach the people he enslaved to read the Bible no matter what.[12]

In 1850, he petitioned the state to exempt men like him from the state's anti-literacy law. When the state refused, Fuller declared that he was responsible to a higher authority than the state of South Carolina, and he continued to speak out and draw attention. The following year, the American Colonization Society, led by U.S. Senator Henry Clay, invited him to address its members in Washington, D.C. His typically righteous remarks on the subject of slavery and Black people's capacity to learn also revealed a man deeply conflicted—thoroughly Southern in many views and manners yet dismayed by how much the region had changed since the 1830s.[13]

He blamed the North and the South for the nation's struggle over slavery. Zealots on both sides were treating what he deemed to be mere political positions as though they were religious dictates. As a slaveholder, "I deeply deplore," he said, "the mischief which has been done by the fanatical agitation of this great question at the North. . . . They have fallen into the common error of enthusiasts, that of exaggerating their object, . . . and as if no guilt could be compared with that of countenancing and upholding it. The tone of their newspapers . . . has been fierce, bitter, and abusive."[14]

Yet the South, in his estimation, was overly sensitive to any discussion of slavery. "It was not so once," he said. Religious groups and political bodies "used formerly to discuss the subject freely. And we at the South ought still to discuss it." While the South was right "to repel all impertinent meddling, we owe it to ourselves," he said, "to not allow such impertinence to move us from a calm, generous, and conscientious discharge of our duty." He suggested that if the North would just stop denouncing all slaveholders as monsters and slaveholders would stop insisting that slavery was a blessing from God that ought to be extended, the nation might find a "middle ground." Yet, far from naive, he acknowledged—a decade before it would come—that civil war was dangerously close, putting a finger to his lips and refusing to utter the words "civil" and "war" together in a single breath for fear that he would hasten the event.[15]

Returning to his hometown of Beaufort shortly thereafter, he was, as the historian Janet Cornelius puts it, "informed that he was no longer welcome to speak." Fuller's contemporary biographer was only slightly more direct, writing that "extremists . . . commented with some severity on his propositions." Though no stranger to vitriol, Fuller knew that he could not safely remain in the South any longer. He left for Maryland and never returned.[16]

Still, the war on Black literacy and free thought was uneven across states and subject to contest. In South Carolina, men like Seabrook could lead high-profile charges against literacy, but that did not mean the progressive religious community went along. It continued its work, which provided fodder for his agitation. Outside South Carolina—and even in isolated areas of the South Carolina upstate—labor market demands, religious motivations, or ignorance of the law allowed some level of Black education to persist so long as no one made it their mission to persuade others to do the same and no anti-literacy crusader called attention to it.

Churches served as a primary locus of activity. No state entirely outlawed religious instruction. It could continue, as the Calvary Church incident demonstrated, in an oral form so long as it did not involve instruction in reading—and whites were present to oversee the instruction. Many churches operated in this area of ambiguity, while a few directly defied the law. A white person who believed in learning to read the Bible could easily slip from oral religious instruction into practices that taught or promoted literacy. Over time, whether intentionally or accidentally, religious instruction established new local norms with literacy as a central component.

An unspoken truce emerged in some communities where Black literacy was illegal but not that uncommon. Yet even where it was quietly tolerated, it remained an affront to Southern principles; the tolerance could be withdrawn in a moment. Margaret Douglass's ordeal in Norfolk, Virginia, in the 1850s perfectly captured the contradictions of the era.

A white woman born in the District of Columbia in 1822, Douglass grew up in Charleston following the Vesey affair. At one point, she held one or more enslaved people, who were perhaps given to her by her husband or parents—the details are unknown. But amid the harsh crackdown on Black life in the 1830s, the calls to ease anti-literacy by people like Fuller must have spoken to her. She later professed to have long been "a strong advocate for the religious instruction of the whole human family."[17]

After her son died—and apparently her husband—she left Charleston in 1845 and resettled in Norfolk with her surviving child, a daughter. One day in 1852, she noticed a Black shop owner's sons studying a spelling book and asked if they went to school. The man said he wished they did, but "there was no one who took interest enough in little colored children to keep a day school for them." She suggested he try Christ's Church, which offered Sunday school for Black children. He said they already went there, but the church did not teach much. For now, since he lacked an education himself, his two boys were mostly teaching themselves.[18]

Douglass volunteered her daughter, then about sixteen years old, to help. If the boys came by her house every day, the daughter could teach them. As she later wrote in her personal narrative detailing the ordeal that followed, Douglass "knew the laws of the Southern states did not permit the slaves to be educated," but she thought education for free Blacks was fully legal. As far as she could tell, all Norfolk's churches "were actually instructing" free persons, including some enslaved people, "and had done so for years without molestation." She often saw children carrying study books from the church. In her mind, she was just doing her Christian duty—like the church—but going a step further.[19]

A few days later, when the father arrived at her house, Douglass was surprised to see he had brought his two daughters, not his sons. He said he thought Douglass might prefer the girls because they were older and would give her daughter less trouble. The likely truth, however, was that the color line weighed heavily on his mind. He didn't dare ask for more than Douglass, a white woman he hardly knew, was offering. In fact, he was asking for less, probably hoping the girls could pass on their learning to their younger brothers. Douglass, however, volunteered what the father had not even imagined—that her daughter could teach all four children. The father replied that he needed the boys to work around his shop, but the girls came to Douglass's house every day. They studied hard and made "rapid progress." Within a month, they needed full-time instruction to progress further. Douglass's daughter could not teach them and also assist with her mother's sewing business.[20]

Margaret saw but two options: cut the girls loose or start a legitimate school to replace her sewing earnings with tuition. She put the choice to her daughter first. They were both in agreement; they would "open a school on the first of next month ... for free colored children." She asked the father to send all the kids he knew: tuition would be three dollars per academic quarter. Unwittingly tapping into a passion that went back generations, she was "overrun with applications." She took twenty-five students and went to work.[21]

Douglass made no pretense of hiding her school. She operated openly for the better part of a year, until one morning in spring 1853. The children were gathering around Douglass's daughter to begin their schoolwork when they heard a loud knock on the front door. Douglass opened the door to find a police officer wanting to know if she was Mrs. Douglass and if she kept a school. When she confirmed the allegation, he was incredulous. "A school for colored children?" When she confirmed that fact, he demanded to "see those children." Now he was asking for more than information. She dug in, asking what authority he had to barge into her house. When he said the mayor had sent him, she saw no choice but to let him in.[22]

Aware of the mortal danger white men posed, the students were terrified to see a policeman standing in their classroom. Some shrieked in fear. Others rushed to Douglass and clung to her side. Douglass's daughter sat paralyzed in her chair, hands covering her face. Minutes later, a second officer entered the house. They intended to take all the children into their custody, he said, and haul them before the mayor.

Douglass heatedly protested. "They were all free children," she insisted, and "members of the Christ's Church Sunday-school" too. She couldn't see the problem with having them study in her home. "It makes no difference, madam," the officer said, "it is a violation of the law to teach any person of color to read or write, slave or free, and punishable by imprisonment in the penitentiary." Brushing her pleas aside, the police marched the children off in a line, two by two, with one officer in front and another in the rear, each brandishing a club.[23]

The mayor was apparently more interested in making a point than punishing anyone. Once he had hauled everyone into court and scared them sufficiently, he was content to let the matter go. Satisfied that Douglass did not know she was breaking the law and had no ill intent, he dismissed the case. She was free to leave provided she permanently closed her school. But for the crowd waiting outside the courtroom, far more was at stake than Douglass's personal liberty. Spirits sank when she told them that the school was shuttered. They walked back to the schoolroom with the solemnity of a funeral procession.

The children gathered their supplies—books, chalk, writing slates. Milling about, not ready to go but with no reason to stay, they left one by one for the last time, their "wounded hearts" showing on their faces. Douglass tried to hide her own grief, worrying instead for the students who "must henceforth grow up in darkness and ignorance." The only solace in the tragedy was the community response. Unbeknownst to Douglass, she had earned a special place in the hearts and imagination of the Black community. For days, she received complete strangers who came to shed tears with her over "the breaking up of our little school."[24]

A few weeks later, a grand jury secretly indicted Douglass and her daughter. They received the formal summons in July, which charged them with violating the state's anti-literacy law and disturbing the "peace and dignity of the Commonwealth of Virginia." They were to appear for trial in November.[25]

Rejecting the notion that she had breached a norm that required defense counsel, Douglass decided to plead her own case. She couldn't imagine that anyone with a sense of justice would punish her. On one level, her instincts were right. Norfolk officials didn't even want to go to trial. They wanted her to leave this mess behind and flee north. That way, they could label her a fugitive of justice, decry her behavior, and not risk having their hypocrisy exposed. But she would not go quietly. Instead, she forced their hand, staying in Norfolk to confront her accusers.

On November 11, 1853, Douglass entered a packed courtroom, reveling in what was sure to be a spectacle. There was a ripple of excitement as the white audience caught its first glimpse of Douglass walking up the aisle alone. The very notion of a woman defending herself in open court, regardless of the crime, was a rarity. Clad in a black velvet dress trimmed with lace, white gloves, and a bonnet, Douglass took her place before the judge without event.

She held off speaking far longer than anyone anticipated, passing on the opportunity to cross-examine the state's witnesses. She had nothing to hide. She patiently listened to their stories one by one, not bothering to contradict them. She did not plan to fight the facts. Everything they said about her little school was true, but the jury could not fairly judge her without also considering what was going on at Christ's Church.

She planned to call and question witnesses from the church about what they and their families were teaching Black children on Sundays. A dozen or more of those in the courtroom could have served her purpose, including some sitting in the jury box. In the end, she called only three. She wanted them to admit that the books her students were using at her house were the same books they had been given at Sunday school. She also wanted to show that some of these witnesses were not just bystanders. Two had signed the court summons that brought her to court.

When she called the names of prominent white church members, the crowd stirred, sensing a scandal. But Douglass miscalculated with the first witness, Mr. Walter Taylor. Though she was sure his daughter taught Black people in the "lecture room" of Christ's Church, he denied having anything to do with the instruction of Black children at church.

Her second witness, Mr. John Williams, a lawyer and clerk of the court in which she stood, "took the stand with a pallid countenance, and quivering lip." Seeing how "extremely troubled" Williams was "by the position in which he found himself placed," Douglass later wrote that she could not bring herself "to convict" him or his "amiable daughter" and only asked him "a few unimportant questions" before dismissing him.[26]

She went after her last witness, Mr. Sharp, who was also a lawyer. After he denied teaching Black children in the Christ's Church lecture room, she pressed him, asking whether he was ever present in the room during Sabbath school for Black children. He admitted that he "occasionally" appeared in the room but chose his next words carefully. During his visits to the school, he said, he only "lectured to them." Douglass wouldn't let him go with that. Hadn't he given them books? "The ladies had all to do with that," he replied. Well, hadn't he taught them, she asked, to read and write out of those books? Absolutely not, he insisted. He offered only "religious and moral instruction," and quipped that he was not aware of the law prohibiting that. But he was being too coy. Douglass fired back: "If you, sir, who are engaged in the practice of law did not know it, how could it be expected that I should?" Stunned by the trap door she had opened beneath him, he asked the judge if he could address the jury rather than the question. The judge allowed it.[27]

Now speaking at liberty, Sharp ventured a creative rearticulation of his prior testimony. It was the preacher, he emphasized, who gathered Black children in the lecture room, and they were there strictly for "religious instruction," not reading and writing. It was true, he admitted, that he "found that some of them could read very well." But he denied doing anything during his lectures to advance their reading and writing. They might follow along in a book with his oral recitation of the text and recognize words they already knew, but when he spoke "hard words" or others they didn't recognize, "he allowed them to skip over them." And where they first learned to read, he had no idea.[28]

Douglass was willing to rest the substance of her case with Sharp. Regardless of what else happened in the church, he had confirmed that the books Douglass was charged with using for illegal teaching came from there. She began her closing argument by emphasizing that she could not be guilty of breaking a law of which she was ignorant. Just as important, the jury should not mistake her for an abolitionist or a fanatic. She had been a slaveholder in the past and "would be again, if I felt so disposed." Sounding much like Fuller in his speech to the Colonization Society, she told the jury she was "as strongly opposed as you are to the interference of Northern anti-slavery men with our institutions." But as to reading, she believed it was "the duty of every Southerner, morally and religiously, to instruct his slaves, that they may know their duties to their masters, and to their common God."[29]

On this basic point, she argued, there was no difference between her and Norfolk's religious community. White church leaders had put the reading primer in her students' hands, instructing one, she claimed, that "he must study his book, and attend the Sunday-school." She had only gotten those students "ready" for Sunday school. In her opinion, something the whole religious community supported could not be unlawful or improper. But if her ignorance, "good intentions, and the abundant examples set ... by your most worthy and pious citizens" did not absolve her, so be it. "Enforce" the laws "to the letter." Condemn her "to that cold and gloomy prison." She wouldn't hang her head and go "as a convicted felon, for I have violated no" law of the "Divine Decalogue." She would go as "a single sufferer under the operation of one of the most inhuman and unjust laws that ever disgraced the statute book of a civilized society." With that admonition, she left her fate to the jury.[30]

She clearly made it hard for them. Though the facts and law were undisputed, the jury deliberated for three days. It found her guilty but refused to imprison or punish her. Instead, it imposed a symbolic fine—a single dollar. The judge was less forgiving. He had the power to imprison her anyway and promised to sentence her for up to six months if necessary. Hoping she would finally take the easy way out and flee north, he gave her explicit permission to visit her daughter in New York for two weeks before he handed down her final sentence. She went to New York and, though nothing other than righteous indignation compelled it, freely returned to Norfolk.

Insulted that she had rebuffed the judge's grace, Virginia's newspapers took a harder stance this time. It was purely a matter of respecting law and order, not justice. Laws existed for a reason, said Norfolk's *Daily Southern Argus*, and it was not for her or anyone else to second-guess "the constitutionality or justice of the law." Douglass had returned, it claimed, simply to play the martyr. Hadn't Virginians already "suffered much from the aggression of Northern foes?" Virginia had to preserve "the majesty of laws necessary for the protection of our rights," along with "our firesides and homesteads." Douglass's "mischievous views" were "unworthy of a resident of the State, and in direct rebellion to our Constitution."[31]

Margaret Douglass. Courtesy of Library of Congress.

Back in the courtroom, the judge sentenced her to a month in the city jail—less than he had first threatened, but jail time nonetheless. He justified it with a stern written opinion. Douglass's "bold and open opposition" to the law, he wrote, "is not a matter to be slightly regarded." It was a threat to the Southern way of life. The South had adopted anti-literacy laws for "self-preservation and protection" against slave insurrections, and Douglass was making a "mockery" of those laws and drawing national attention. Such open disregard could not be ignored. If the South hoped to survive the dangers the laws were meant to subdue, he had to imprison her to send a clear message to "all others in like cases disposed to offend" the law.[32]

Douglass's ordeal was a capstone on another important chapter in the South's war on Black literacy. If Virginia—a state that had been open to abolition two decades earlier—would not relent on the most minor and innocent of infractions, neither would other states. The war on Black literacy had to be absolute, even if not consistent. Time would only harden this stance.

A single, crucially important question remains, however, regarding the hundreds of stories of secret learning, secret schools, and public resistance across half a century. Why would marginalized people risk life, limb, torture, and jail to learn to read and write? The simple answer is freedom. From freedom's smallest forms—simple acts of private defiance—to its largest form—physical freedom itself—literacy was bound up in enslaved people's idea of what it meant to be and become free.

The denial of literacy reinforced enslaved people's desire for it. When Frederick Douglass's enslaver discovered he was learning to read and ordered his wife to stop teaching him, he unwittingly shared exactly why Douglass had to persist in his studies. A "n*****" should know nothing," he said, "but to obey his master—to do as he is told to do. Learning would spoil the best n***** in the world. Now ... if you teach that n***** ... how to read, there would be no keeping him. It would forever unfit him to be a slave. He would at once become unmanageable, and of no value to his master. As to himself, it could do him no good, but a great deal of harm. It would make him discontented and unhappy." From that time onward, Douglass was willing to defy his enslavers and risk retribution to continue his learning.[33]

Booker T. Washington, who suffered any number of extreme deprivations during his enslavement, similarly placed education on a pedestal. Creature comforts were foreign to him; his bed was a "bundle of filthy rags laid upon the dirt floor." The first thing he knew of education was to walk "as far as the schoolhouse door with one of my young mistresses to carry her books." But the sight of "several dozen boys and girls in a schoolroom engaged in study made a deep impression upon me, and I had the feeling that to get into a schoolhouse and study in this way would be about the same as getting into paradise." He resolved that if he was going to do anything in life, it would be to learn to read.[34]

Reading was an immediate form of freedom. Whatever grand designs on physical freedom an enslaved person might harbor, the "written word," Heather Andrea Williams writes, "revealed a world beyond bondage," a world in which enslaved Blacks "could imagine themselves free to think and behave as they chose." Though still physically bound, an enslaved person could free their mind through reading and writing, journeying to places beyond anyone's control. That made the pursuit of literacy—and whatever ideas or experiences it might offer—one of the most important acts of defiance an enslaved person could make. It was a private assertion of freedom. An enslaved person could take pride in having claimed something. And in outsmarting the person who held them in slavery, they could also firmly crush the notion that the white man was intellectually superior. Ironically, some literate enslaved people lived under the thumb of illiterate enslavers.[35]

Once they crossed those boundaries, an insatiable conscious desire for full freedom tended to follow. As numerous personal narratives attest, it was the literate enslaved person who was so often "the first to run away." All enslaved people, of course, longed for freedom and did not need books to abhor their circumstances and dream of a different life. But mental freedom created new tensions that constantly pulled against the absence of physical freedom. As C. S. Hall remarked, "the more I read, the more I fought against slavery. Finally, I thought I would make an attempt to get free, and have liberty or death."[36]

Better than any, Frederick Douglass, in *My Bondage and My Freedom*, details the enlightenment and torture that literacy could bring to an enslaved person. He credited reading with giving "tongue to many interesting thoughts which had frequently flashed through my soul" and pouring "floods of light on the nature and character of slavery." The more he read, the more he "was led to abhor and detest slavery, and my enslavers." But at times, Douglass wrote, reading "made me gloomy and miserable," almost envious of "my fellow slaves in their ... contentment." When his mistress tried to end his reading, it strained their relationship, triggered depression, and "tempted" him to take his "own life."[37]

Even when life markedly improved on the surface, the tension remained. In 1835, Douglass was hired out to William Freeland, whom he described as "kind and gentlemanly" and affording him "favorable" conditions. Douglass also took up the most satisfying work of his life during this period: running a Sabbath school and teaching other people of color to read and write. But these new freedoms offered only a "temporary" reprieve before the emotional conflict returned stronger than ever. He "was now not only ashamed to be contented in slavery, but ashamed to seem to be contented ... under the mild rule" of his new master. It was then he made "a solemn vow ... to gain my liberty" within the next year—and he would use his literacy to attempt escape.[38]

For many other enslaved people, reading and writing had always been about acquiring the tools to secure physical freedom. Literacy was the means to plan insurrection, share information about the path to freedom, and forge written passes to freedom. Simply venturing to town, through woods, or to nearby plantations on an authorized errand was dangerous. A white person could question a Black person about their business at any time, and the only thing separating them from indiscriminate violence

Frederick Douglass as a young man. Courtesy of Wikimedia Commons.

was a written pass from their enslaver. The further away from home a Black person ventured, the greater the danger. Even a free person of color was assumed to be a runaway absent written evidence to the contrary. But given the prohibition on Black literacy (and the illiteracy of most white Southerners), whites had little reason or, often, ability to question a forged pass. In Savannah, where white people presumed they were the only ones who could write passes, Susie Taylor made a habit of writing passes that allowed her friends and family to freely traverse the city in the evenings. And as many slave narratives recount, forged passes allowed enslaved people to make it all the way to the North.

Successful escapes almost always required more than a pass. Frederick Douglass poignantly explained that fleeing a plantation was "making a leap in the dark." Innumerable challenges would immediately confront an enslaved person when they exited the familiar ground of their plantation or town and entered a world they only vaguely knew existed. Running blindly in unknown landscapes, past road signs and runaway slave notices, would almost certainly end poorly. But literacy could overcome those barriers, close information gaps, and more. Not only could it guide the path to freedom, it allowed enslaved people to transcribe and keep information and names that the memory might struggle to retain, and to absorb valuable new information along the way.[39]

Harriet Jacobs's autobiography is a masterclass in using literacy to gain the upper hand in the path to freedom. Well before she escaped, she used literacy in unique ways to preserve a modicum of autonomy. Most notably, she resisted the "love" letters of her infatuated enslaver, Dr. Norcom (whose name she changed to Dr. Flint in her book). Every word he wrote gave her a measure of leverage. She absorbed the information but feigned illiteracy. Never directly acknowledging the information in the letters, she thwarted his attempts at escalating the relationship without embarrassing or offending him.[40]

Later, during her escape, literacy facilitated safety, communication, and forethought. Unlike most, she did not go north. Instead, she hid at a nearby white woman's house, then in the swamps, and finally in the crawl space between the roof and ceiling of her grandmother's home. For Jacobs—and so many other enslaved people—escape was bittersweet. Freedom meant leaving family and loved ones behind. Jacobs, however, used literacy to maintain her family bonds and remain right under her pursuer's nose—or in this case, over his head. Her entire time on the run, she exchanged letters with family members, sharing life experiences, making plans, and staying apprised of dangers that awaited her. She even exchanged letters with her enslaver. With the spiderweb of information she collected, she could ferret out his lies, reject demands, and make her own.

For years she managed to stay a step ahead of him. The most dramatic example occurred after she had left her grandmother's attic and gone north to Philadelphia and then New York City. Dr. Norcom pursued her relentlessly, traveling north to search for her multiple times before and after she was actually there. Even after Norcom died, his family, particularly his son-in-law Daniel Messmore, hounded her. Long accustomed to the pursuit, Jacobs constantly scanned newspapers for runaway notices and the names of arrivals from out of town.

In New York, her diligent reading brought terror to her heart when she saw Mr. and Mrs. Messmore on a list of arrivals printed in the *Evening Express*. Jacobs immediately went into hiding, using literacy to cover her trail and alight on a new one. Having learned from reading the *Express* which hotel the Messmores were staying in, she sent a friend to engage them and delay their pursuit. Afterward, the friend wrote to Jacobs sharing what he had learned about their plans. Once she was completely safe, Jacobs began a correspondence with Mr. Messmore, eventually negotiating a truce that ended the days of looking over her shoulder. He agreed to end his pursuit in exchange for a small cash payment.[41]

Less dramatically, newspapers allowed countless enslaved people to keep a finger on the nation's pulse and offered a hedge against the informational silos of plantation life. Just as Denmark Vesey had followed the twists and turns of congressional debates in newspapers and pamphlets, other enslaved persons across the South stayed abreast of political developments at the state, local, and federal level. The Virginia General Assembly members who wanted to silence the papers during the 1831–32 debates on abolition—for fear that word might spread to enslaved people—were not mistaken about the possibilities. Literate free and enslaved people hung on to every word the papers published on the subject. Those words affected their thinking and built up expectations.

William Webb, for instance, recalled that he and other literate enslaved people "followed the John C. Fremont presidential campaign in 1856 and told others that his election would mean their freedom. When Fremont lost, the slaves were disappointed." Some urged rebellion, while others were willing to wait four more years, remaining "hopeful" that the next election would produce a different outcome.[42]

Not to be missed in his story is the essential way that literate people acted as conduits for the larger Black community. The phrase "I heard it through the grapevine" derives from enslaved people's practice of secretly passing information by word of mouth. Partly to protect the identity of the most recent link in the chain and partly because the original source might be unknown, enslaved people would say news came from the "grapevine" or "grapevine telegraph," particularly during the Civil War. Information passed through the grapevine with electric speed, traveling from one plantation to the next in a day and moving across states and regions in just days. Literate Blacks were the key to this speed: they could read the newspaper and plug the information into the local grapevine.

For a select few, literacy also became the means to publicly announce freedom and hopefully fuel the winds of freedom for others. The slave narrative, as David Blight writes, was Black authors' chance to declare to the world "I am here" and conclusively prove their humanity. Literacy, a central theme in many of these narratives, arises as its own sub-narrative, sometimes couched in drama and almost always presented as a turning point in the author's life. Frederick Douglass, for instance, knew that "a slave stealing knowledge and the power of the word from the residue of urban maritime life ... made a great story." At the same time, as Blight puts it, "words had become a reason" for Douglass "to live."[43]

Whatever the details, these stories disproved—in fact and theory—the South's narrative about Black people. By picking up the pen, these authors seized the power to define the world through their own eyes rather than someone else's. They were a living testament to the path David Walker urged years earlier in his *Appeal*. These men and women, though rarely calling for violence or rebellion, were the threat the South had spent decades trying to quash. But it could not quash them: they would live to write their literacy stories, and testify to the role literacy played in freedom. Literacy was more powerful than the slavocracy imagined. It did not just put "foolish" ideas in Black people's minds. It transformed them and their communities in ways that would never be fully controlled.

CHAPTER THIRTEEN

A Rebirth of Freedom
Black Schooling in the Midst of War

Just as black schooling and open dialogue had been the first casualties in the South's long march toward the Civil War, when war finally came, they were the first to be resurrected. What was underground would reemerge, and what was unspoken would be uttered. What education had long promised would bloom and spread life to a new freedom movement. When it came, it came fast and organically. And it began, of all places, on the same shores where enslaved people had first set foot in the country more than two centuries earlier.

In 1619, an English ship carrying twenty enslaved people from Angola landed at Point Comfort, Virginia, a small outcrop where the James River flows into Chesapeake Bay. Point Comfort later came to mark one of the corners of Fort Monroe, a massive military compound secured by walls high and thick enough to resist storms and cannons. Fort Monroe, effectively an island within an island, occupied the southwest tip of a stretch of land just off the Virginia coast. A narrow footbridge stretched across open water to provide the front gate's only access. To the south, across the mouth of the James River, lay Norfolk. Less than a hundred miles upriver was the Confederate capital, Richmond. Chesapeake Bay protected the fort's backside, offering free passage to D.C. and Maryland.

After Confederates took Fort Sumter, South Carolina, on April 13, 1861, Fort Monroe was the Union's only stronghold in the South. Its proximity to the nation's capital, robust fortifications, and size made it the best location from which to launch operations southward. President Lincoln was determined to hold it. On May 22, Major General Benjamin Butler arrived to take command of the fort.

Less than a day after arriving, Butler led his men on an expedition to the mainland. A fire set by fleeing Confederates on the footbridge stalled their progress. After rushing to extinguish it, Butler's men passed into what *The Atlantic* described as the "ancient village of Hampton," Virginia. With the white residents hiding or gone, Black people gathered excitedly around the troops to welcome them. When the troops passed into the countryside, they spotted enslaved people watching in the distance. They returned to the fort the same day.[1]

Three brave Black men, Frank Baker, James Townsend, and Shepard Mallory, having seen or heard about the troops, took the chance of a lifetime, escaped their enslavers, and followed Butler's path back to Fort Monroe. If they didn't return, they told their friends, it would mean they had found freedom. The three men approached under the cover of night, arrived at the fort's gates, and were allowed in. The next day Confederate Colonel John Cary came to demand their return on behalf of their enslaver, citing the federal Fugitive Slave Law for authority. The demand created a dilemma for Butler.[2]

At that point Lincoln remained, to all appearances, averse to Black freedom. Official Union policy dictated that, because slavery was still legal, enslaved people remained the property of their enslavers and the Union Army would not interfere. Yet turning these men away, which meant consigning them back to slavery, didn't sit well with Butler. A politician before ascending the military ranks, Butler, as the historian Willie Rose puts it, "was quick to read the signs of the time." He fashioned a way to turn the South's property arguments against it. During his expedition, Butler saw enslaved people forced into service for the Confederate cause—reinforcing military positions. If Black men were property, as the South claimed, and the South used that property to fight Union forces, Butler believed the normal rules of war applied. Enslaved people, like any other military property, could be confiscated as "contraband of war." On that logic, he rebuffed Colonel Cary and the men remained free.[3]

From that day forward, enslaved people called slavery's initial landing spot the Freedom Fort. News of Butler's action spread through the countryside. On May 26, eight more enslaved people arrived. The next

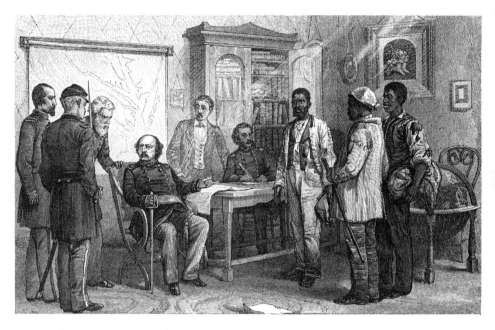

General Butler's meeting with enslaved men upon their escape to Fort Monroe. Courtesy of iStock by Getty Images.

morning it was forty-seven, and later that day another dozen. Slavery's empire, at least this corner of it, was collapsing without a shot being fired. On the 28th, Hampton radically changed in just moments. As Butler's men approached the village, white residents were in the process of abandoning it and ordered the people they enslaved to follow them. When Butler's troops came into sight from second-floor windows, white lookouts started yelling, "The Yankees are coming." Whites gathered whatever they could in coming moments, announced "I'm off," and urged those still remaining to "leave as soon as you can." But Black people feigned fright and confusion as whites fled. They tarried behind, saying, "I'm afraid to leave the house," they didn't want the Yankees to "catch them," and "Oh, master, won't you stay and protect us?" Out of spite, the last whites to flee set fire to Hampton on their way out. Whether Butler had come to claim the town is unclear, but as the buildings burned, Union troops hoisted the American flag and took the ground as their own.[4]

Mary Peake was among the free people of color watching the drama unfold. Though she cannot have imagined it, her secret life would soon

A Rebirth of Freedom

Burning of the village of Hampton by Confederates, in *Frank Leslie's Illustrated Newspaper*.

be splashed on the pages of pamphlets and papers across the country and mark a new chapter in American history and Black freedom. Born free in 1823 in Norfolk, Peake was shaped by Virginia's tumult over slavery. In 1829, as Walker's *Appeal* was arriving in Norfolk, Peake's mother sent her to be educated in Alexandria, which was then part of the District of Columbia. Black children, not bound by Virginia's laws, could pursue their studies in Alexandria relatively unmolested. With tensions escalating in Norfolk, Peake remained in Alexandria until she turned sixteen. She returned home in 1839 and eventually settled across the bay from Norfolk in Hampton.[5]

The pent-up demand for Black education soon called her to teach, just as it was calling many other literate people across the South. But the law was against her. A white woman like Margaret Douglass might escape with a fine or short stint in jail, but Peake, as a Black woman, was taking a far more serious risk. She started her school in secret and kept it going for years—even as the nearby Douglass trial warned of the state's continued opposition—until the day that General Butler's approach caused her white neighbors to set her town ablaze, taking her home with it.

With Hampton smoldering in the background, free and formerly enslaved people fell into formation behind the Union troops. Peake gathered what she could and followed them back to Fort Monroe. Those first days at the fort were chaotic. The Union had no plan for refugees—or contraband, as General Butler declared them. Food, shelter, and activity were all uncertain. While the immense fort could support a substantial population, there was only so much space. Similarly, the fatigue duty, previously assigned to soldiers, only required so many hands.

Having gained physical freedom, however, Black people wanted intellectual freedom. Literacy ranked alongside food and safety in importance. As one soldier wrote, looking back on those days, "There was a very general desire among the contrabands to know how to read." Some already had a little learning, having "been taught on the sly in their childhood by their white playmates." Now, with no legal prohibition, they wanted to put their minds to the task, with or without help. That same solider wrote of seeing "a young married woman, perhaps twenty-five years old, seated on a door-step with her primer before her, trying to make progress." Neither was aware that the perfect solution, Mary Peake, was already living among them. Peake's initial return to teaching was organic. A few kids asked for help and she gave it. By summer's end, she was a full-blown schoolmaster.[6]

As the number of refugees approached one thousand, Butler needed a plan. The outside world was watching, heavily vested in every move. Though neither Butler nor anyone of influence outside the fort knew her name, Peake would soon play an important role in shaping the future of her people. Lewis Tappan, the abolitionist leader who financed the pamphlet campaign in the 1830s, wrote to General Butler, suggesting that the American Missionary Association (AMA) could head off an impending crisis by sending agents to the fort to provide services and begin the process of resettling refugees in the North. Butler rebuffed him because the long-term legal status of contraband was still unclear. The last thing he wanted was to create a situation that looked like colonization, or invite a squad of missionaries closely aligned with abolitionists to mix with the newly freed people. Tappan was permitted to send a solitary visitor from the AMA.

Escaped men and women at the gates of Fort Monroe, in *Frank Leslie's Illustrated Newspaper*. Courtesy of Library of Congress.

Reverend Lewis Lockwood arrived at Fort Monroe a few weeks later. Grasping immediately that the AMA could gain a foothold by supporting education, he moved to open a Sabbath school. But just as Sabbath schools proved insufficient for Margaret Douglass's students, Lockwood's school couldn't meet the needs of Fort Monroe's children. A real school, however, needed a permanent teacher and resources. Lockwood eventually left Fort Monroe for D.C. and Maryland to drum up financial support for the project. Fortunately, he already had "a teacher of the choicest spirit, and of peculiar qualifications" in Peake.[7]

Two days after Lockwood opened his Sabbath school, Peake opened a formal school in a small brown house just outside the fort. The upstairs served as living quarters, the first floor as the classroom. A sketch in her 1863 biography showed the view from the school's back door—a large solitary oak tree a short walk away, with the banks of the James River sloping behind it and Fort Monroe in the distance.[8]

Mary Peake. Courtesy of Gutenberg Project.

Behind Union lines, Peake needed not fear prying eyes or heavy-handed laws. She gathered her students in the shade of the oak tree—Fort Monroe's ascending presence putting them at ease—and taught until the sun set or until their hearts were content. As war commenced around them, her first-of-a-kind school became its own little utopia. Black children passed through the school's doors and partook of what Booker T. Washington—and surely many others—had imagined as some kind of heaven on earth. Operating next door to the "Seminary"—a lavish house that had been a summer home to Presidents Tyler and Jackson—the school also symbolized the fundamental national change then taking place.[9]

Six students attended Peake's first day of classes. Word spread. Two weeks later, fifty or sixty children were enrolled. Peake quickly found that her students were not blank slates. Many children, not the ones she previously taught, had arrived already having some learning. A few were quite advanced. They were either self-taught or had come from secret schools like hers.

Her curriculum was traditional, yet it crackled with energy. On the one hand, she intermixed religion with formal education, believing that "school should aim to educate the children for eternity as well as for time." All of her instructional materials save the reading primer were religious. On the other hand, Peake's teaching went beyond religion and was more than the drill, kill, and brute-force learning typical of the era. She taught in ways that excited children—with songs, holiday festivities, outdoor activities, and intimate relationships—"awakening and developing," as Lockwood put it, the "heart and mind at once." Lockwood tried to capture her teaching with a poem:

And as a bird each fond endearment tries,
To tempt its new-fledged offspring to the skies,
She tried each art, reproved each dull delay,
Allured to brighter worlds, and led the way.[10]

Soon adults asked for help too, hoping to gain what oppression had robbed them of as children, so Peake started a school for adults in the evenings. As Lockwood observed, "several, who scarcely knew the alphabet before, now begin to read with considerable readiness."[11]

As the seasons changed, however, so too did Peake's health. Winter, overexertion, rampant sickness in the camps, and the normal progression of tuberculosis all took their toll. Rapidly declining and knowing the end was near, she labored throughout the holiday season to get the children ready for a Christmas Day festival, rehearsing a pageant, decorating the school, and constructing a stage.

On the appointed day, they drew a large audience—children, adults, soldiers, and officers. Lockwood marveled at the spectacle, writing that "a year ago, white children in Hampton could enjoy a scene of this kind, but colored children were excluded." Now, "the colored man's child is on the stage, and swell the choral song." He saw it as "a miniature picture of what will be. The present is prophetic of the future." Following the example of Peake's school, a million children, "on whom the sunlight of knowledge is yet to shine," would soon be learning "throughout the sunny South."[12]

A few weeks later, Mary Peake gave "up entirely, the charge to which she had clung with such tenacity." Her funeral commemorated the achievements of her life—all from that last year. A large concourse of students, families, and friends assembled in her schoolroom and processed to the live oak tree by the banks of the inlet, where they laid her to rest. No one would ever forget what she did under that tree. Just a few days after the first anniversary of her death, the Black community would gather again under the tree for what is said to be the first public reading in the South of Lincoln's Emancipation Proclamation. Five years later, the tree would mark the entrance to Hampton University, an institute of higher learning for freedmen. It still stands today as "the Emancipation Oak," one of the world's ten great trees.[13]

As Lockwood predicted, the freedmen's education story did not end with Peake or Fort Monroe. Instead, it went further south. Six weeks after Mary Peake started her school, the Union prevailed in the Battle of Port Royal in the South Carolina Sea Islands. Union ships, launched from Fort Monroe at the end of October, arrived in South Carolina waters on November 1, and began moving deeper into Port Royal. The battle commenced on November 7 and ran deep into the night. Having watched Union forces assemble in stages over several days, white landowners knew the battle was lost as soon as cannon fire lit up the night sky. By morning, the entire white population had disappeared.

Some of those who fled were foolish enough to think that the people they enslaved would willingly join them. Black survivors told of enslavers who shot and killed those who resisted. But most whites just loaded what few possessions they could carry on flat boats and headed for the mainland, leaving burning cotton bales behind them. In a single night, the Sea Islands were transformed from massive plantations overseen by white elites to a land of ten thousand formerly enslaved men, women, and children without a single enslaver in sight.[14]

These conditions offered the perfect location to rewrite the nation's narrative. Just south of Charleston and Fort Sumter, the Sea Islands' sprawling swamps, wooded expanses, and deep coastal waters were a geographic shield. The natural refuge offered the opportunity for a vast experiment deep in the heart of the Confederacy—something Fort Monroe and the adjoining Hampton village, where military officials were displacing refugees, could not match. Between harsh weather, limited supplies, makeshift shelters, and looming hostile forces, Fort Monroe and Hampton had begun to resemble a struggling refugee camp, particularly during the winter, when disease and exposure took scores of lives. But the Sea Islands could offer Black people their own land and the opportunity to develop a fully functioning social system outside the influence of white oppression.

In the first days after the Battle of Port Royal, however, Union officers were out of their depth. They knew how to win a naval battle but had no idea how to run Southern plantations and backwater villages. Agriculture, commerce, transport, and civic questions all weighed heavily. The Black families, now free, knew how to keep things running, so life, land, and work were theirs to decide in those first days. As much from the freedmen's design as from the Union's, Reconstruction would begin here three years before the War's end, and five years before Congress formally authorized it.

Port Royal's Sea Islands include three major islands: Paris Island in the center, Hilton Head Island to the south, and St. Helena Island to the north. St. Helena, the largest, held the most transformative activity. Six years before the battle, enslaved people had built a two-story brick church for whites, sinking their fingerprints deep in the bricks, which can still be seen today, as a testament to the forced blood, sweat, and tears they put into the church. Days after the Battle of Port Royal, the church became theirs.[15]

They knew exactly what they needed from the church building, and it wasn't religion. It was education. Even without a Mary Peake, the interest was overwhelming. Oral history, rather than written records, documents those early days when the students filled the church beyond its capacity. The motivations were clear. One woman told how her enslaver had tried to keep her ignorant. When he wanted to say something to his wife that he didn't want her to understand, "he used to spell it out. I could remember the letters, an' as soon as I got away I ran to uncle an' spelled them over to him, an' he told me what they meant." Her children were among the first to attend school in the Sea Islands. "They took to books as ducks take to water," and their expectations were immense. Some expected their babies to attend school as soon as they could walk. As soon as toddlers could talk, their parents expected them to start learning to read.[16]

Over the next several weeks, Union soldiers and Northern missionaries worked feverishly behind closed doors to speed up in the Sea Islands what had been impossible at Fort Monroe. They began to pave the way to real and permanent freedom and autonomy for Black people. Resuming normal day-to-day activity, including work, was part of that puzzle, but education was its centerpiece.

Brick Church on St. Helena Island converted into a school. Courtesy of Library of Congress.

On December 15, 1861, a *New York Tribune* correspondent in Beaufort, the largest town in the Sea Islands, wrote to Massachusetts senator Charles Sumner—the Senate's greatest orator and most powerful abolitionist—asking what the government could do to fund education in the Sea Islands for Black people, "whom this war must lift into freedom." Conversations were already under way in D.C. On December 20, Treasury Secretary Salmon Chase, another leading antislavery advocate, wired the man who had assumed control over all matters relating to contraband at Fort Monroe, Brigadier General Edward Pierce, and summoned him to the capital "at once." Pierce was sympathetic to Black people's plight, having eased the way for Peake's school and publicly expressed interest in larger issues pertaining to Black people's long-term welfare. His account of his time at Fort Monroe, published in the November 1861 issue of *The Atlantic*, had drawn national attention. And as a personal friend of Sumner and Chase, he was the perfect person to oversee what could be a huge pre-emancipation project in the Sea Islands.[17]

Pierce needed no persuasion. He rushed to D.C. in the middle of the Christmas holiday to talk with Chase. A few days later, he agreed to travel deep into enemy territory for the cause of freedom and humanity. Other duties called, but this, he wrote to Chase, was not a task he felt "at liberty to decline." Unlike at Fort Monroe, his mission would not be reconnaissance and making up plans on the fly. Pierce started plotting a strategy before he ever landed on Port Royal's shores. He alerted his Boston friends about his assignment and told them to get ready to send missionary teachers and supplies to Port Royal.[18]

He envisioned a project that would dwarf the AMA's work at Fort Monroe. The AMA had sent a single man, Lockwood, and funded a single resident teacher, Peake. The Sea Islands needed dozens of volunteers and a sizable budget. Pierce's Boston contacts reached out to similarly inclined people of influence in New York City and Philadelphia. Trusting they would be ready when he called, Pierce stepped aboard a steamer bound for Port Royal in New York on January 13, 1862. A week later, Lewis Tappan and another prominent AMA board member sent Reverend Mansfield French of New York, a friend of Secretary Chase, to meet Pierce in the Sea Islands. There, they would forge a partnership.[19]

When Pierce issued an official report to Secretary Chase on February 3, 1862, very little in it would have surprised Reverend French or the AMA. If anything, Pierce was probably just catching Chase up. His opening lines announced that shortly after landing in the Sea Islands, he posted letters to "benevolent persons in Boston" to ask for two things: clothing and a teacher. The next several pages were a status report, from the islands' population counts and geography to basic conditions, customs, and activities.[20]

Twenty-four pages of such details later, Pierce posed the key question: "What, then, should be the true system of administration here?" The first issue was labor. Some Northerners wanted to lease the "plantations and the people upon them," but Pierce warned that such a system would again pit humanity against profit and perpetuate "many of the worst vices of the slave system." Instead, he proposed that the Union pay superintendents to run each plantation. The formerly enslaved would receive wages and a patch of ground to grow vegetables. Their rights as laborers, parents, and persons would be respected. Treated well, "they may be hoped to become useful coadjutors, and the unconquerable foes of the fugitive rebels."[21]

Treating them well and gaining them as allies, Pierce continued, meant prioritizing education. He shared the details he had been priming for weeks: "The Government should ... provide some teachers specially devoted to teaching reading, writing and arithmetic, say some twenty-five, for the territory now occupied by our forces, and private benevolence might even be relied on for these." Education would fit the people of the Sea Islands "for all the privileges of citizens.... But whatever is thought best to be done, should be done at once."[22]

The freedmen, he promised, were ready for all this and more. They just needed help. Pierce had spoken with numerous parents and all "expressed a desire to have their children taught to read and write, and to learn themselves. On this point, they showed more earnestness than on any other." They so desperately wanted education for their children that Pierce believed "they might be willing to pay something" for it if necessary. The adults also wanted education for themselves and asked for "reading books ... daily."[23]

Pierce reported that a pastor had already established a school for children—possibly the Brick Church—with sixty students now attending. The secret learning that preceded it had resurfaced too. Three Black adults served as teachers, and some of the children were clearly no strangers to learning. The children were "rapidly learning their letters and simple reading." Impressed, Pierce briefly joined the teaching crew, leading the kids in their "letters for an hour or two."[24]

Pierce's allies were all on board with the plan. But they had to cross one major threshold to see the plan to fruition: the White House. An audacious plan laying the groundwork for freedom would have to have President Lincoln's assent. De facto freedom and preparation for citizenship were not the type of thing that Lincoln should learn about in the newspapers. Secretary Chase arranged for Pierce to meet with the president.

When Pierce entered the White House on February 15, 1862, the Lincoln he met was not the renowned story-telling, larger-than-life figure who awed and put you at ease at the same moment. As commander in chief, Lincoln labored under the weight of war. As a father, he struggled emotionally while his son, Willie, battled typhoid fever. He had lost one son a decade earlier, and Willie would soon follow.

Lincoln was impatient, if not confused, by the visit. He questioned why Chase—and now Pierce—was bothering him with contraband matters. Lincoln suspected they were "itching to get negroes into our lines." Pierce explained Port Royal was nothing like Fort Monroe. This was not a case of refugees fleeing behind federal lines for protection, but rather a vast region where Black people had remained in place and were now outside the reach of plantation owners or the Confederacy. With that clarification, Lincoln gave the plan as much attention and approval as he could muster under the circumstances. He referred the matter back to Chase, handing Pierce a card that said, "I shall be obliged if the Sec. of the Treasury will in his discretion give Mr. Pierce such instructions in regard to Port Royal contrabands as may seem judicious. A. Lincoln."[25]

Though not a ringing endorsement, the card was all they needed. Chase immediately approved Pierce's plan, authorizing him to receive teachers and oversee the education project. Port Royal's commanding officers, Flag Officer Samuel Du Pont and Brigadier General Thomas W. Sherman, were already on board. In mid-January, General Sherman had urged the War Department to send "suitable instructors" to the islands to teach "all the necessary rudiments of civilization." And on February 6, he issued General Order No. 9, calling on philanthropic societies to come to the "immediate" aid of the Sea Islands with teachers and clothing. Though stilted in its prose, the order revealed Sherman's thoughts about a radically different future. Disparaging the "ignorance" and "mental stolidity" that currently "preclude all possibility of self-government and self-maintenance" on the islands, he believed "competent instructors" could bring immediate improvement.[26]

Aid societies in Boston, New York, and Philadelphia had begun preparing for the mission before the request arrived. On February 7, the "Education Commission," comprised of friends and associates of Pierce and his allies, held its first official meeting. The Freedmen's Relief Association did the same in New York on February 20, followed by the Port Royal Relief Committee in Philadelphia on March 3. The message to attendees was simple. They needed superintendents and teachers to go south and men with resources to pay the way and salaries of those who volunteered. These meetings drew more than 150 applications to serve as teachers.[27]

On March 3, 1862, just six weeks after Pierce left for the Sea Islands and two weeks after the call for teachers went out, fifty-three men and women—some fresh from the campuses of Harvard, Yale, and Brown—took a leap of faith and stepped aboard a steamboat in New York Harbor bound for Beaufort, South Carolina. None had any real idea of what they would find there. Some may have been unsure where they were going, since similar ships sailed "under sealed orders" and the commanding officer refused to tell them more. All the passengers knew was that they would stop at Fort Monroe before crossing deep into the Confederacy and exchanging the safety and comfort of urban New York for undeveloped backwaters and marshes. While their intent was to help, the passengers would depend on people only a few months removed from slavery as much as those people would depend on them.[28]

The passengers also did not know how long their mission would last, or what end it would ultimately serve. The formal acknowledgment of Black people as contraband had been contentious in Washington. There was no assurance that Lincoln would not end the War by returning Black people as property to the Confederates.

Some of those who boarded in New York would succumb to sickness and other challenges in the islands, and never return. But they all believed the sacrifice they intended to make was worth it. They might be cogs that tipped the scales of justice. If they could bring full freedom and citizenship to Black people in the Sea Islands, surely Lincoln could not be so callous as to return them to bondage. When they disembarked at Beaufort's docks on March 9, Pierce christened them as history makers, declaring that their work would "cheer or dishearten good men to settle, perhaps, one way or the other the social problem of the age." Their voyage south, he assured them, eclipsed the importance of any other in American history, even the pilgrims landing at Plymouth Rock. For their efforts, they would receive the highest recognition, "in this life or the next."[29]

The missionaries wasted no time getting to work. They fanned out over the islands' two hundred plantations, home to nearly ten thousand Black people, taking up posts in different communities, finding shelter in abandoned homes, and starting schools anywhere they could host an audience. Within two weeks, a dozen schools had opened. Beaufort's three schools drew between sixty and ninety students each. More remote areas drew a dozen or so. The missionaries serving these students traveled between plantations to reach multiple groups.

The first interactions between teachers and students revealed how deep the connection ran, both practically and psychologically, between enslaved people and education. One of the first teachers to arrive, Elizabeth Hyde Botume, recounted that what she expected to be a simple process—calling the roll—turned into self-professions of freedom. Students initially announced themselves by their first names only. When Botume pressed for last names, the children insisted that they had no last names, because the last names their "masters" had given them were now dead to them. One boy said his "ole rebel master" was "nothing to me now. I don't belong to he no longer, an' I don't see no use in being called for him." Some students named themselves after people who had been kind to them or simply adopted the name "Freeman." Reflecting on moments like this, Botume called the days after the first shots in Port Royal "the beginning of time for these poor freed people."[30]

Parents who visited the schools made their priorities clear. After having been completely denied the chance to learn anything, parents explained that their children "mus' go to school" and "learn eberyting dey can." They and their children had, as one mother put it, been kept in "darkness too long" and desperately needed to step into the "light." These schools "seemed a fulfillment of an old slave dream," which the islands' people expressed in a spiritual:

I would like to read,
Like to read,
Like to read dat sweet story ob ole,
I would like to read.[31]

Many parents sat alongside their children or attended school in the evenings. Both the children and their parents treated it as an "honor" to be counted among a school's "scholars." Being part of the enterprise gave them, as Botume wrote, "a new consciousness of their own individuality and personal dignity."[32]

Those early days were challenging; there were too many students and not enough schools or teachers. When students found a teacher, they treated her like royalty. They would arrive at the teacher's home in the morning and escort her to school. Botume reported students crossing rivers by boat each morning, even in the worst weather, to get to school, and begging teachers to take them in their school or travel to their community to start another. One morning, a student "smuggled" herself into Botume's school, taking in most of the day's lessons before Botume realized she was there. Some families relocated from other communities solely to send their children to school. Going to school was such a privilege that some families sent notes when their children couldn't make it, asking the teacher to excuse their absence. And when holidays came, they had no interest in taking a vacation from school.[33]

The biggest and most successful school was on St. Helena Island—the one Black people had started in the Brick Church at their own initiative just days after the Battle of Port Royal. When Pierce visited on

March 25, the enrollment stood at 145 students. The challenge, as it had been in slavery, was time, not interest. Teachers often had to work around older children's schedules. Rather than a way to escape work, schooling was something that happened in between work. School at the Brick Church, like other schools around plantations, opened at noon, after the morning's fieldwork was complete, and closed at three to leave time for the day's remaining chores.[34]

Those three hours each day bore sweet fruit. Pierce ducked into a class of twelve students reading an essay aloud from their textbook. Though the essay was unfamiliar, they made their way through it without hesitation or spelling out words in lieu of reading. Others recited the thirty pages from a spelling book and their multiplication tables through fives. They ended the day with a rendition of "My Country, 'Tis of Thee" and finished with a "song of praise for these little children, chattles no longer," on "sweet St. Helen's Isle," where "none in all the world before were ever glad as we," because now "We're free on Carolina's shore, We're all at home and free!"[35]

After surveying all the islands' schools, Pierce was even more confident in his plan. They had planted seeds, he thought, that would change history, and there was no turning back now. The Sea Islands' people had learned "that the world is not bounded north by Charleston, south by Savannah, west by Columbia, and east by the sea," and that New York was not on some other planet. "They are acquiring the knowledge of figures with which to do the business of life" and "singing the songs of freemen." Even if the Union abandoned the islands and shuttered their schools, the people would "pursue self-instruction" anyway.[36]

It was stunning, Pierce said, to remember that a year ago it had "been a crime to teach their race," and now to see "a scene which prophets and sages would have delighted to witness." It was incomparable to any other time or place in history that he could recall. He had "never looked on St. Peter's, or beheld the glories of art which Michel Angelo has wrought," but what he now beheld surely "transcend[ed] in moral grandeur anything that has ever come from mortal hands."[37]

Pierce told the aid societies that he could use three times as many teachers as they had first sent. He didn't get that many, but the next waves brought the handmaidens of an education legacy that would persist across generations. The first, Laura Matilda Towne, boarded *The Oriental* in New York on April 9, 1862, three weeks short of her thirty-seventh birthday.

Writing in her diary on April 17 of her first moments in Beaufort, she described sights and sounds that spoke to her spirit. She looked past the signs of war and marveled at the beauty of the flat grassy marshes, the fiddler crabs scurrying along in the sand, children trying to snatch them, and others carrying their catch home in tubs on their heads. But it was the sounds that most captivated her. The deep rhythmic songs of formerly enslaved people carried across the waters, announcing residents long before their slowly rowing boats came into sight. Some coded, some explicit, the songs told of life and culture unique to this place.[38]

Towne reserved her gripes for the white people. The Confederates had vacated the Sea Islands, but they had left behind the vestiges of slavery. Her antislavery sentiments, she mused, would have excited "the animosity of Union soldiers," who, in ways big and small, continued to leverage racial power over the islands' people—idly threatening, for instance, to return people to their owners for punishment when some demand was not met. Towne moderated her voice in their presence to preserve the "anti-slavery work" that drew her there. It was "noble work," she said, and "we mean to do it earnestly."[39]

In one of her first talks with Pierce, when she asked him about the school "system," he told a much humbler story than what appeared in the newspapers. "Oh, Miss Towne," he said, "we have no systems here." Triage consumed the days, not formal plans. Some of the teachers who preceded Towne had yet to start teaching because they didn't know where to go. And those who were teaching were not, in Towne's estimation, always of the highest caliber. Thinking that a woman of Towne's skill would be more valuable calming the chaos than diving into it, Pierce tapped Towne to work directly with him as a clerk—though her gender apparently placed housekeeping on her list of responsibilities, too. Nonetheless, working alongside Pierce, Towne grew well-acquainted with the Sea Islands' needs, faults, and potential. She eventually grew into an all-purpose contributor, filling roles that ranged from nurse to teacher.[40]

The church offered the first opportunity to step into a teaching role. Her diary entry for May 4, 1832, tells of an overflowing church service with three hundred inside and another four hundred outside. There were nowhere near enough people to teach Sunday school. She taught an impromptu class for a group of twenty or thirty children, beginning with exhortations of Christ's love and how to get to Heaven and then transitioning into teaching letters and words. After that morning, she resolved to return to her calling. Pierce was not ready to let her go entirely, but she began to assist at regular schools during the week and fill in when teaching vacancies occurred. By fall, her passion for teaching had overtaken Pierce's immediate needs.[41]

Towne settled into "The Oaks," a plantation house two islands away and about five miles east of Beaufort. The towering home, nestled on the banks of the creek separating St. Helena Island from Ladies Island, had more space than she could use. She and another woman, Ellen Murray, started a school in the house's back room. Towne quickly built a reputation as one of the finest teachers in the area, and within a month, she and Murray had eighty students—or as they called them, scholars.[42]

Such popularity inspired jealousy from nearby teachers. Students abandoned their original schools and traversed distances—sometimes by land, other times across open water—to study under Towne. There were more than enough students to go around—some 1,200 on St. Helena and Ladies Island alone—but other teachers complained. One even marched to the Oaks plantation and demanded that Towne return "her" students—as though Towne had stolen them. She had already recommended that they return, and even turned some away entirely, but she was torn. The teacher's students reported that she "did not keep school half the time and never did more than hear them a little reading-lesson, while they wanted to learn to write and cipher." Now that the woman had forced the issue, Towne confronted her, asking whether "she would teach them, for if she would not, we would."[43]

When the plantation house's back room could no longer accommodate Towne's popularity, she looked for a new location. The Brick Church was just three miles east of the plantation, in the heart of St. Helena Island. Whether the families invited Towne or she invited herself, she moved her school to the church and taught there for decades. Children were proud to be her students and to meet her high standards. She was proud to be their teacher and to see them do it.

Towne was later joined by Charlotte Forten, the first African American teacher the AMA ever sent south. As a Black woman, she was acutely aware that she was a target: "a band of guerillas" would "seize and hang" her if they got the chance. Yet, she steeled herself. Together, she and Towne would go on to offer formal, regimented schooling. Forten's years of teaching experience in Northern schools helped tremendously, but both she and the children had to adapt.[44]

It was not always easy for restless children to adjust, but, Forten wrote, "I never before saw children so eager to learn.... Coming to school is a constant delight and recreation to them. They come here as other children go to play." Even older children, tired from hot summer-day toil, arrived "as anxious to learn as ever." The Sea Island people, she remarked, had "been so long crushed to the earth ... among the most degraded negroes of the South," but they rose, desiring to learn, and did so "with wonderful rapidity."[45]

Forten took it as her job to offer not just a standard education but one adapted to the world these formerly enslaved children would surely face. In her deep analysis of Forten's various writings, Mollie Barnes explains how Forten "positions teaching and editing [of existing narratives and language] as strategic acts of resistance and recovery." Sensing the special "significance" of her first moments in the Sea Islands, she taught her students "John Brown's Body," an ode to a white abolitionist who had fought and died for them before any Union solider ever raised a rifle in their defense. In the coming years, she had the children sing it with her again and again, on holidays and when the Emancipation Proclamation finally arrived in Beaufort. The immense power of what they were learning and doing "in the very heart of Rebeldom" was undeniable. "I wish their old 'secesh' [secessionist] masters," she wrote, "could hear their former chattels singing the praises" of John Brown. She similarly shared stories meant to empower her students. They were not, she told them, a people suffering or rising at the whim of others, but a people no less capable than white people of seizing their destiny. To prove her point, she taught them about men like Toussaint Louverture, who had led the Haitian Revolution. It was important, she said, that they should know what "one of their own color had done for his race. They listened attentively and seemed to understand."[46]

Others also recognized that something extraordinary was happening on St. Helena Island. A year or so into Towne's work, someone sent a photographer to the school, a rare thing at the time given the nascent technology and the difficulty of photographing people outside a portrait studio. (Even pictures of Lincoln show some blurring due to motion.) But someone thought it important to capture Towne's school. One sharp image shows twenty-nine students, all probably younger than thirteen, sitting in a circle of wooden chairs around Towne. Dense Spanish moss hangs from the oak trees sheltering them from the sun. Girls in dresses, boys in formal shirts, all with their noses buried in texts, reading. One girl, probably the youngest, stands before Towne, who leans forward as if to offer direct instruction.

Charlotte Forten. Courtesy of The New York Public Library.

Eventually even the church and its grounds couldn't support the size and scope of the school Towne was building. And some Baptists were unhappy that Towne, a non-Baptist, was teaching there at all, though they tried to hide their true objection by emphasizing the physical toll her growing population of students was taking on the church facility. In March 1864, Towne wrote to the Education Commission of Philadelphia, asking for the construction of a new school. Not only was she at risk of expulsion from the church building, she had more students than it could accommodate—sometimes as many as two hundred. She and her fellow teachers had multiple large groups studying in a single room. The cacophony made effective communication and order difficult. The church also lacked the basic instruments of learning—it had no blackboards, no places for students to write, no desks, and probably no bookshelves.

That fall, something previously unimaginable happened on this quiet island in the heart of the Confederacy. For four decades, South Carolina had waged war on Black education and literacy. Whatever learning man-

Newly constructed Penn School on St. Helena Island. Courtesy of Library of Congress.

aged to persist moved in secret. Even as it reemerged at Fort Monroe, Port Royal, and elsewhere, it happened in makeshift places—the back room, the back porch, the backyard. There were never enough rooms or supplies. But shortly after Towne's request, men in Boston began prefabricating walls for an expansive schoolhouse, large enough to accommodate all her students—and in separate rooms. It would be the first freestanding, purpose-built Black schoolhouse in the South. When the walls finally arrived and stood in place on St. Helena Island, Towne believed it needed one final touch before she christened it the Penn School. She asked the commission to send her a large bell, which she placed in a steeple above the front doors. It was a replica of the one hanging in Independence Hall in Philadelphia, bearing the inscription "Proclaim Liberty." Each day, the massive bell could be heard a mile and a half away. Some of Towne's students negotiated much greater distances—five and six miles—but they heard the bell as they neared the school each morning and knew it was time to hurry.[47]

At the time, Towne had little inkling of the legacy she was building, but surely it settled in over the years, making it impossible for her to leave. She spent the rest of her life, nearly four more decades, at the Penn School, building an education and social justice institution that continues to operate to this day. During her lifetime, government dignitaries, generals, and educational leaders—from Secretary of War Edwin Stanton and General Oliver Howard to Booker T. Washington—came to see the Penn School and then support it. Civil rights icons like Martin Luther King Jr. have come to pay honor, sojourn, and add to the legacy. In the final days of his presidency, Barack Obama officially declared the Penn School and the surrounding community a national monument (now known as Penn Center).

Those early visits by powerful men helped shape life beyond the Sea Islands, and maybe even influenced federal policy during Reconstruction. Secretary Stanton, in an early visit to Port Royal, asked countless questions. "Do you really think the contrabands can learn?" he asked Botume. "I know they can," she assured him. "I believe so," he replied. "You are doing great work here, and I honor you for it." General Howard, who later directed the Freedmen's Bureau and its vast education efforts, fully appreciated what the Penn School represented. Soon after his arrival he assembled the students to ask them questions and eventually offered a short speech. He proffered a short motto for them, one born of what he knew was possible: "try hard." When he was leaving, he asked them what news he should pass on to their friends in the North. The kids said to report that they were going "to try hard."[48]

The Sea Islands consistently drew Northern volunteers. But they also drew other enslaved people from across South Carolina and Georgia, who thought that if they could just make it to the Sea Islands, they would find a whole new world. By the end of 1863, teachers and formerly enslaved people were operating thirty schools on the islands.[49]

Although something special was happening in Port Royal, its people and their desires were not unique. They inspired similar projects elsewhere, as well as official policies that would take shape after the War. After General Ulysses S. Grant led the Union to victory in the Battle of Vicksburg in 1863 and seized the Mississippi River valley, James Yeatman, the president of a private organization that provided medical care and services to wounded Union soldiers, set out on an expedition of the Union-controlled territory along the Mississippi to survey the condition of the freedmen and issue a formal report. Like Pierce at Fort Monroe and Port Royal, Yeatman found a long-suppressed desire among Black people to learn, and enough secret learning to speed it along.

One of the most poignant stories in Yeatman's report involved a missionary teacher, a Mrs. Porter, who was stationed at a freedmen's camp just south of Memphis. When she first arrived, "an old negro came out to meet her." His "head had been whitened by the frosts of ninety winters," and he was "almost blind." He stood "supporting himself by his staff," greeted her warmly, and said, "Well, you have come at last, I'se been 'spectin you, lookin for you, for de last twenty years. I knowed you would come, and now I rejoice." Porter replied that she had "come to teach you," to which he said, "Yes, yes, I know it, and I thank de Lord."[50]

Just as in the Sea Islands, schools sprang up, with or without teachers, wherever the Union took new land. The missionaries who followed the Union armies never ceased to be surprised. Remembering those days, one missionary in Savannah wrote that the "freedmen here betook themselves to education" with "speed and energy" unlike anything he had seen. It was the very first thing they wanted to do—almost like a ritual cleansing that might wash away what they had been through and mark their mental rebirth into a new life. Soon, schools were operating in nearly every Confederate state. As Major General Wager Swayne said in Mississippi, "to open a school has been to have it filled." By the War's end, close to 100,000 freedmen were attending around 700 schools, run by more than 1,000 teachers.[51]

Whereas secret learning had been a tool to resist slavery, carve out mental autonomy, and maybe even escape, open learning offered something distinct. Attending school in broad daylight and acquiring literacy for everyday use represented a sharp break from slavery. As Christopher Span writes, "Becoming literate proved to be as much a psychological victory for many freedpeople as it was an intellectual one. Illiteracy was a vestige of slavery, a reminder of the blatant denial of one's rights to self-advancement; it served as a badge of inferiority and societal impotence. To become literate challenged this status." Thus, it was the schoolhouse where Black people could put their past behind them and "learn how to be something other than a slave."[52]

CHAPTER FOURTEEN

Public Education for All

For all the progress places like Port Royal achieved in the midst of war, Black people's access to education—and the full freedom it might open—remained tenuous without a national policy and the commander in chief's full support. Government officials like Edward Pierce were supportive, but elsewhere, indifference, if not hostility, often prevailed. Union officials sometimes forced children back into the field rather than sending them to the schoolhouse. One Black father who enlisted in the Union Army was upset that his children were kept on a plantation, purportedly for their own good. The father wanted his children brought to the Union camp so that he could "send them to school." When the commanding officer resisted, the father rebuked him: "I am in your service; I wear military clothes; I have been in three battles; I was in the assault at Port Hudson; I want those children; they are my flesh and blood."[1]

North Carolina's military governor, Edward Stanly, was worse. According to one report, he insisted that the state's pre-War prohibition on Black literacy remained valid, forcing the school superintendent for New Bern in the spring of 1862 to close a school he had recently opened. Incensed, the superintendent and the students' parents reached out to Senator Charles Sumner, who took the matter straight to President Lincoln. As with Pierce's visit about schooling in the Sea Islands, Lincoln met Sumner gruffly. The War was not going well—Union forces had seen narrow wins and a string of large losses—and abolitionists were constantly pressuring him to emancipate and enlist Black people to turn the tide.

Lincoln was considering it, but on his own time. Sumner's visit struck him as petty by comparison. According to Sumner's memoirs, Lincoln snapped: "Do you take me for a school-committee-man?"[2]

Sumner dressed down the commander in chief: "Not at all. I take you for President of the United States; and I come with a case of wrong, in attending to which your predecessor, George Washington, if alive, might add to his renown." Lincoln, however, was hesitant to override a military officer without more information. Sumner left disappointed and turned up the pressure by raising the matter on the Senate floor and apparently prodding his House colleagues to do the same.[3]

The House was the first to act, pressing the president to explain the situation. A formal House resolution, adopted with unanimous consent on June 2, 1862, requested "that the President of the United States ... communicate to the House: 1. What powers have been conferred upon Hon. Edward Stanly, as military governor of North Carolina, or as the agent of the government under the appointment of the President. 2. Whether the said Edward Stanly has interfered to prevent the education of children, white or black, ... and if so, by what authority if any. 3. If the said Edward Stanly has been instructed ... to prevent such education, to what extent, and for what purpose were such instructions given." To question the military's authority on this issue communicated the sense in Congress that Black people had a right to learn and that the government had a duty to secure this right. But Congress was also upset that Lincoln had unilaterally appointed military governors in the first place, a practice that Lincoln discontinued after the resolution.[4]

Coming on top of the Sea Islands' experiment, the North Carolina fiasco must have made an impression on Lincoln. Or maybe he remembered his childhood and more peaceful days early in his career. Growing up on the frontier, Lincoln could have only dreamed of an actual schoolhouse— though a nearby school wouldn't have helped much. His father discouraged his education. Were it not for the later intercession of his stepmother, Lincoln's name might very well have been lost to history. If any high official had personal knowledge of how literacy could change a person's life, it was Lincoln. That experience also carried over into his early political life. Campaigning for the state legislature in Illinois, he urged his audience to see that formal education was "of vital importance." It allowed people to understand history and "appreciate the value of our free institutions." Thus, he believed it was necessary to make access to education "much more general than at present."[5]

Freedmen's school in New Bern, North Carolina. Photograph by John Heywood, ca. 1868. Courtesy of the Smithsonian National Museum of African American History and Culture.

After lying seemingly dormant in his national politics and early presidency, Lincoln's sentiments about education suddenly and forcefully resurfaced in 1863, a year after the North Carolina controversy. In a letter to the commanding officer in Louisiana, General Nathaniel Banks, Lincoln demonstrated a radically different perspective from what he had expressed to Pierce and Sumner. Now that the Union controlled Louisiana, he wrote, its people needed to call a constitutional convention to "adopt some practical system by which the two races could gradually live themselves out of their old relation to each other, and both come out better prepared for the new." He would not dictate that new government's details, but on one thing he was sure: "Education for young blacks should be included in the plan."[6]

By late fall, Lincoln would go public with his thoughts: he announced terms for peace in his Proclamation of Amnesty and Reconstruction on December 8, 1863. This would effectively grant Confederate states amnesty if 10 percent of their white citizens swore an oath to the Union. Those who took the oath would get a full pardon. Amnesty also, however, required that Confederate states accept the abolition of slavery. As significant as that term was, any requirement for Black citizenship or suffrage was noticeably absent. But the president did speak to education. Perhaps seeing it as an alternate pathway to citizenship, he mentioned education alongside the requirement that new state governments "recognize and declare [freed people's] permanent freedom." States seeking amnesty should "provide for their education."[7]

The proclamation attracted no takers among Confederate states, but General Banks took Lincoln's education concerns to heart. Banks issued a general military order that restructured Louisiana's government until the people could establish a new one. Among other things, Banks divided the state into school districts, appointed superintendents, and mandated that they establish a system of schools. In a second order, he granted the districts taxing power, ensuring resources for the schools.[8]

Two years later when the schools were up and running, federal officials, in an effort to save money, temporarily shuttered the Louisiana schools. The freedmen responded with one of the South's first acts of mass political activity by Black citizens—a petition drive to maintain the schools. People who had long been voiceless refused to "consent to have their children sent away from study." A federal official wrote that one petition was "at least 30 feet in length, representing 10,000 negroes.... It was affecting to examine it and note the names and marks of such a long list of parents, ignorant themselves, but begging that their child might be educated, promising that from beneath their present burdens, and out of their extreme poverty, they would pay for it" even if the government would not. Black people had stopped asking for education and were now demanding it.[9]

As the War came to an end, Black literacy entered yet another phase. The arrival of Union forces had allowed the education of Black children to step out from the shadows. Missionary teachers expanded individual learning into group learning. But education was not yet an official public program, nor was it permanent or uniform. It remained absent in many communities. If Black leaders hoped to put their people on a path from dehumanization to citizenship, education was the gateway.

That made public education, not just private or benevolent education, an exigency. Black leaders made their case to both Congress and newly reconstituting state governments. In many states they came together in what they called "colored people's conventions"—more than a dozen were held in 1865 alone—to make their case. Most of these, however, were held in the North.

Abraham Lincoln School for Freedmen in New Orleans, in *Harper's Weekly*. Courtesy of Wikimedia Commons.

The most important convention to meet in the former Confederacy may have been the Colored People's Convention of the State of South Carolina, which opened on November 20, 1865. South Carolina, or more precisely Charleston, had fostered Black leadership since the days of Vesey. The state's majority-Black population, now free, gave those leaders power, and Port Royal's three-year-old freedom project had given them experience and resources. They chose an auspicious place: Zion Church, the very same congregation where Vesey had hatched his plan for Black liberation some four decades earlier. This time, the attendees did not need to hide their ambitions or lower their voices. They invited reporters and commentators, reserving special seats for them to listen to the debates.

The convention ran for six days, producing a "declaration of rights and wrongs," a petition to the legislature, and a memorial to Congress. Fifty-two official delegates, hailing from Greenville, Chester, Charleston, and everywhere in between, attended. Charleston, unsurprisingly, sent nearly half of the entire convention's delegates. Several of the Charlestonians were members of the Brown Fellowship and other Black societies

Jonathan Jasper Wright, in *Harper's Weekly*. Courtesy of Internet Archive.

that had kept Black education going through years of repression. In later years, these men would go on to wield enormous official influence—as lieutenant governor, congressmen, state senators and representatives, and a host of other elected and appointed positions.[10]

The brightest of these future stars was Jonathan Jasper Wright. Pennsylvanian by birth, he answered the American Missionary Society's call for teachers in early 1865, a job for which he was better equipped than most of his white counterparts who came south. He had attended common schools in Pennsylvania until he was fifteen, then left for college in Ithaca, New York. What he studied isn't clear, but after graduating in 1860, he taught in Pennsylvania, studying law on the side under the tutelage of local attorneys. But he put his legal career on hold to teach in Beaufort, in South Carolina's Sea Islands. He taught Black soldiers during the day, Sabbath school on the weekends, and part-time classes in the evening.[11]

Wright's time in Beaufort showed him what was possible, but also how far the state had to go. He regularly struggled with inadequate resources, often teaching without books or compensation. The inspiration of teaching freedmen, however, outweighed the challenge. And he knew that his predecessors had labored under even worse conditions. Wright's hope was to take all the experience and wisdom he had gathered in the Sea Islands and use it to inform policies that would support education across the state.

With delegates like Wright, education rose to the convention's fore. Elections, committee assignments, and rules of order consumed the first day's business. The convention's first resolution, proposed on the second day, advanced the same thesis David Walker had offered three decades earlier. Education was a weapon—or a defense—against slavery. The delegates unanimously approved the declaration that " 'Knowledge is power' and an educated and intelligent people can neither be held in, nor reduced to slavery." The resolution continued:

> We insist upon the establishment of good schools for the thorough education of our children throughout the State; that, to this end, we will contribute freely and liberally of our means, and will earnestly and persistently urge forward every measure calculated to elevate us to the rank of a wise, enlightened and Christian people.
>
> Resolved, That we solemnly urge the parents and guardians of the young and rising generation, by the sad recollection of our forced ignorance and degradation in the past, and by the bright and inspiring hopes of the future, to see that schools are at once established in every neighborhood; and when so established, to see to it that every child of proper age, is kept in regular attendance upon the same.
>
> Resolved, That we appreciate, with hearts overflowing with gratitude, the noble and self-sacrificing spirit manifested by the various philanthropic and Christian Associations of the North, in providing teachers and establishing schools among us; and that we can only best testify such gratitude by heartily co-operating with them in this their great work of love and humanity.

With that flourish, the convention retired for the evening.[12]

The third day was more complex. The convention had to say something about the institution of slavery and its passing, but what? How could they fairly capture the freedmen's relationship to slavery and those who had perpetuated it? The men framing the answer had mixed relationships with the institution. While some delegates had been enslaved, many had not, and the free-born men were the most influential. Northern transplants like Wright knew only slavery's aftermath. And while the Charleston delegation had lived in the proximity of slavery, most had not lived fully under its thumb. One of the delegates, Robert DeLarge, came from a family that had enslaved people.

If the delegates had better represented South Carolina's demographics, its statement about slavery might have been different. But in these halls, the convention outwardly resolved that "the old institution of slavery has passed away [and] we cherish in our hearts no hatred or malice toward those who have held our brethren as slaves." Instead, "we extend the right hand of fellowship to all, and make it our special aim to establish unity, peace and love amongst all men." Immediate practical matters were more important than looking backward. They hoped to "encourage amongst the freedmen, education, industry, and economy." Education came up again that evening when the group reconvened for dinner and remarks from the convention's leading orators, most notably James Ransier, soon to be a dominant political force. He caught the crowd's attention with his prediction that Black people were on the verge of citizenship and political power. Education, he emphasized, would pave the way.[13]

The next two days produced debates and resolutions on voting and the right to live free from discrimination. The final day encapsulated everything in a memorial to Congress that made four requests: that Congress enforce the rule of law; keep its land pledges to the freedmen; guarantee equal suffrage; and ensure "that the three great agents of civilized society—the school, the pulpit, the press—be as secure in South Carolina as in Massachusetts or Vermont."[14]

Conventions in other states took similar education stances, situating education as a pillar of democracy. The Convention of Colored Citizens in Arkansas, for instance, demanded that the state grant them citizenship, "clothe us with the power of self protection" through "suffrage," and "provide for the education of our children." In Alabama, the convention called for "a thorough system of common schools throughout the State, and indeed of the Union, for the well-being of such ensures to the advantage of all." The conventions wanted assurances against the backsliding, half-commitments, and unreliable education resources the freedmen often encountered during the War. And they wanted a government partner, not a handout.[15]

Black people had already put a lot into their schools themselves and would continue to do so. In 1865 in Arkansas, for instance, freedmen formed a society to raise funds to support free schools in Little Rock, not merely supplemental funds but enough to keep the schools operating throughout the year. Self-help and initiative were common. New to the market economy and mostly living hand to mouth, freedmen prized education so highly that they were willing to bear a financial burden to get it. A later federal report indicated that nearly thirty thousand freedmen had been paying some level of tuition to send their kids to school, enough to cover 40 percent of the cost of delivering education. Having invested so much labor and so many resources in their schools, Black communities in places like Mobile, Alabama, jealously guarded them and worried what would become of their children's education if authority over their schools changed hands.[16]

As the nation transitioned from war, responsibility for supporting education fell to Congress, which, like the president, wavered at times but came through in the end. Its first major legal step to support the freedmen came in March 1865, in the form of the Freedmen's Bureau. The final bill charged the bureau with supplying "provisions, clothing, and fuel, as . . . needful for the immediate and temporary shelter and supply of destitute and suffering refugees and freedmen and their wives and children." But Congress faltered in its first attempt at passing the bill, in the summer of 1864. Disagreements over whether the bureau should be part of the War Department, the Treasury Department, or an entirely independent agency divided the House and the Senate. Some legislators thought the bureau was a bad idea altogether because it would perpetuate permanent dependency on the federal government.[17]

The final bill gave the Freedmen's Bureau a tenuous home in the War Department. Congress set its operations and resources to terminate one year after the end of the War. Allen Guelzo, the only three-time winner of the Lincoln Prize, speculates that Lincoln, motivated by the lessons and instincts learned through his own personal journey from poverty, may have made a significant impact on public education had he lived to oversee the bureau and Reconstruction. In fact, in his last speech, Lincoln "raised" education "to a level equal in importance to that of voting." Lincoln believed that the ballot was not enough to secure a man's

National Colored People's Convention in Washington, D.C.
Courtesy of Library of Congress.

freedom. To be free in any meaningful sense, Black people—and white people, too—needed economic independence. "Free labor," Lincoln bluntly said, "insists on universal education."[18]

Lincoln's assassination, just six weeks after he signed the bill, placed the bureau's and education's future in jeopardy. Andrew Johnson, who had opposed the bureau, would name its leader. But at least on this matter, Johnson stayed the course Lincoln had set. He chose a good man: General Oliver Howard.

Howard was military through and through—a graduate of West Point who experienced the Civil War's ravages from start to finish. He had commanded troops in the First Battle of Bull Run, Antietam, and Chancellorsville. He served under General William T. Sherman in the "scorched earth" march to the sea from Atlanta to Savannah. Yet war had not hardened him to the plight of the freedmen. His visit to Port Royal in January 1865 had been his own idea, and he was affected by what he saw there. The "zealous, self-denying Christian teachers" working across several schools drew his immediate attention. Writing in his autobiography a half century later, he still remembered Laura Towne and Charlotte Forten's school on St. Helena Island. These "maiden ladies of wealth . . .

from New England," he remarked, had "started a school with all the appliances of object teaching and all the neatness of a Northern academy."[19]

While Congress had envisioned the bureau as helping to ensure the freedmen's daily subsistence, Howard focused on securing their lasting freedom and citizenship through education. On May 15, 1865, days after receiving his commission to lead the bureau, Howard wrote to John Alvord, a missionary who had been working with and supporting the freedmen in the Sea Islands and Savannah. Howard informed him of his new position and requested that Alvord "give me all the ideas and suggestions you have drawn from your experiences and observations to be pursued in dealing with the freedmen. I want you to write me particularly in regard to schools." A few weeks later, Howard called Alvord to Washington to help him construct an education plan. Soon after, Alvord assumed an official government post as head of the bureau's education efforts.[20]

In October, Howard wrote to the American Freedmen's Aid Commission, the umbrella organization for all the missionary and humanitarian groups supplying relief support in the South, announcing his vision. "Education," he said, "underlies every hope of success for the freedman." With it, "the fearful prejudice and hostility against blacks can be overcome. They themselves will be able to demand and receive both privileges and rights that we now have difficulty to guarantee." Howard would go on to devote "more attention" to expanding schools for the freedmen "than to any other branch of my work" and spent more than two-thirds of the bureau's budget on education in most years, allowing bureau officers to secure, lease, build, and repair countless school facilities. They also coordinated with missionaries and local communities to staff the schools with teachers. Lawmakers must have been impressed. In 1868, when funding for the Freedmen's Bureau came up for reauthorization, Congress refused to extend the bureau's general subsistence work but authorized it to continue its education programs for another four years.[21]

From the start, Howard envisioned an education effort so expansive that it required a large leadership and bureaucracy to administer day-to-day activities. In half a decade, he and his subordinates helped establish and maintain 4,239 schools, hire 9,307 teachers, and provide instruction to 247,333 students. His urgency was propelled by his early recognition that the federal role in the South was temporary. Well before it came, he foresaw a day when Congress would abandon the freedmen and their hopes would rest on states' willingness to provide education. He was determined to create the conditions for education to outlive and outgrow the bureau.[22]

Children reading outside a freedmen's barracks in Alexandria, Virginia. Courtesy of Library of Congress.

Writing in 1865 to the freedmen and missionaries working on the ground, Howard assured them that the bureau's purpose was neither to displace their work nor to become a permanent fixture. It was a bridge that would support and expand education efforts "until a system of free schools can be supported by the re-organized local governments." A year later, in his second semi-annual report to Congress as general superintendent for schools, John Alvord echoed this idea: "If the several States will inaugurate and sustain a system of public instruction for all, though imperfect at first, we should give it warmest encouragement."[23]

Two years after creating the Freedmen's Bureau, Congress was prepared to force those state systems into existence. While Southern oppression of Black literacy had worked its own special sin, poor whites had also been victims of the South's hostility to education. In their opposition to educating anyone other than their own children, elites of the slavocracy had blocked any meaningful moves toward public education. In the words of the education historian Lawrence Cremin, "all effort to go beyond a patchwork quilt of public, quasi-public, religious, and pauper schools on the elementary levels [had] failed." White illiteracy rates were four times higher in the South than in the North.[24]

Some in Congress argued that lack of education in the South had precipitated the War. Southern elites had seen public education as a threat to the status quo. Its suppression had allowed elites to dominate society and government, and eventually to persuade ordinary citizens to support a war that was against their interests. Senator Charles Sumner imagined, albeit naively, that with better education, the War could have been averted:

> In a republic Education is indispensable. A republic without education is like the creature of imagination, a human being without a soul, living and moving blindly, with no just sense of the present or the future. ... It is not too much to say that had these States been more enlightened they would never have rebelled. ... A population that could not read and write naturally failed to comprehend and appreciate a republican government.[25]

Given the North's own uneasy relationship with abolition, there is plenty of reason to doubt that the South would have ever willingly given up slavery. The exponential growth of the cotton plantations in the nineteenth century, and the wealth they generated for the ruling class, had made the entire South economically and psychologically dependent on slavery in a way the North had never been—though months of debate in the Virginia General Assembly in 1831 and 1832 suggested that the possibility of abolition was not entirely fantastical. Regardless, Congress saw education as an indispensable step in remedying slavery and reconstructing democracy. As Senator Oliver Morton bluntly remarked on the Senate floor, until the disadvantaged were educated, "the political power will remain almost entirely in the hands of the present rebel-educated classes."[26]

The task of legally enshrining access to education in the South, however, had to fall on the states. Congress prodded them along by making education a requirement for readmission to the Union. The Reconstruction Act of 1867 set three major conditions on Southern states' readmission: extend the vote to Black men; ratify the Fourteenth Amendment; and rewrite their state constitutions to guarantee a republican form of government. A republican government meant, among other things, ensuring public education. Many of those most in need of education were too poor to pay for it for themselves. If the state did not provide it, Senator Morton argued, those people "will remain uneducated. . . . Republican government may go on for a while with half the voters unable to read or write, but it cannot long continue."[27]

With Congress backing them, Black people leveraged the local political process at home. In the fall of 1867, they elected as many friendly delegates as possible to the conventions that would rewrite each state constitution a few months later. South Carolina's convention, where Black delegates comprised a majority, stood out. Among them were men who well appreciated the role education had to play if the state and its people were to secure a different future.

Many of the South Carolina delegates had been leading figures at the Colored People's Convention three years earlier. Men like Alonzo Ransier, Robert DeLarge, and Jonathan Jasper Wright had already placed stakes in the ground for education. By the time the constitutional convention opened, Wright had been teaching for seven years and was an expert on how other states ran their education systems. His political stock had also risen dramatically. He had taken a brief leave from Beaufort to finish the process of being admitted to the Pennsylvania bar, becoming the first Black lawyer in his Pennsylvania county and, upon his return to Beaufort, the only one in South Carolina. General Howard offered him the opportunity to use his legal skills where they were most needed: providing legal advice to refugees and freedmen in Beaufort. For three years, he wielded power and influence that no Black man ever had in the state, with a style marked by grace and intellect rather than force. As the official reporter of the Colored People's Convention remarked, Wright had "a light and graceful hand ... and, like the humming-bird, extracted nectarine sweets from every opening flower."[28]

Wright arrived at the Constitutional Convention of South Carolina in January 1868 primed for leadership and was quickly chosen as one of two Black vice presidents (out of five). William Beverly Nash was the other. Though Nash had also attended the Colored People's Convention in 1865, his path to leadership had been more unlikely. Unlike Wright or the Charleston power brokers, he had been born to enslaved parents in Virginia. His enslaver separated him from his family at thirteen, selling him to a politician in Columbia, South Carolina. Working a variety of hotel jobs serving the state's politicians, Nash absorbed the tricks of their trade. Although it was only a daydream before the War, the jump to politics was natural afterward. But education was also key to climbing that steep curve. Peering at all the papers shuffled around offices and read aloud, Nash saw the power of words and secretly learned to read and write.

Men like Wright, Nash, and their colleagues anchored public education within the convention's explicit charge to create a republican form of government. To ensure that education wouldn't get drowned out by the mundane aspects of constitution making—delineating branches of government, elections, state debts, taxation and so on—the convention created a standing Education Committee. Before naming any members, however, the convention paused to host South Carolina's military governor, James Orr, who directed the delegates' attention to what he believed were the most pressing issues. His speech dripped with Confederate sympathy, but he struck a chord when he linked voting, citizenship, and education together. On that score, Black and white people had a common interest. "Education," he urged, "is now the great desideratum of all the colored people of South Carolina." The state had once tried to "exclude the slave population from the benefits and advantages of education," but now, providing education to Black people was "of the utmost importance." It would expand their opportunities and appreciation of the rule of law. Conversely, "profound ignorance, almost universally couples with it crime and vice. Hence, the education of the black population—and, I am sorry to say, of many of the white population of the State—should command the earnest attention of this body."[29]

After Orr's speech, the convention announced the various committee members. Wright would have been a natural for the Education Committee, but as the sole Black lawyer, he was needed on the Judiciary Committee. Francis Cardozo, a stalwart advocate, took his place on the Education Committee. Born free in Charleston just months after the postal raid of 1835, he received a solid education through the worst of the city's crackdowns on Black literacy. But finding no opportunities to pursue advanced education in the United States, he left for England in 1858. When he returned, in 1864, he made Connecticut his home. The War's end finally gave him a chance to settle in South Carolina on his own terms, as a teacher for the American Missionary Association. For three years he led what later became Charleston's first accredited secondary school for Blacks, the Avery Normal Institute. If there was an equal to Wright on education, it was probably Cardozo. He later became the first Black person to hold statewide office in the country, winning election as secretary of state.[30]

Cardozo dug into the Education Committee's work from day one and defended it until the end. Others, however, were not content to wait on the committee. An early draft from the Bill of Rights Committee included an education guarantee, and the full convention also considered proposed resolutions for the Education Committee from the floor. Fortunately, everyone was on the same page, looking to the Massachusetts Constitution as a model, which made sense given the number of missionary teachers from Boston in freedmen's schools and the singular efforts of Massachusetts senator Charles Sumner to remake the South. The influence was so heavy that one delegate, perhaps mistaking Cardozo for a Northerner, complained that the Education Committee had too many men from Massachusetts and not enough from South Carolina. Cardozo simply responded that "there is but one Massachusetts man on the Committee" and refused to dignify the slight beyond that. The real measure of merit, he added, was whether the committee's proposals made "good sense."[31]

Massachusetts made a good jumping-off point. The state's 1780 constitution was the first in the nation to include an education mandate. The Education Committee's proposals mirrored the Massachusetts education clause, declaring that a "diffusion of education . . . is the surest guarantee of the enhancement, increase, purity and preservation of the great principles of republican liberty," and thus, it "shall be the duty of the General Assemblies, in all future periods of this commonwealth, to establish, provide for, and perpetuate a liberal system of free public schools." But the South Carolina convention sought to improve on Massachusetts's original idea by mandating that public schools be "open to all the children and youths of the State, without regard to race or color." That addition reflected an amendment Charles Sumner had proposed to the Reconstruction Act of 1867—an amendment that had failed by the narrowest of margins, 20 to 20, not on substance but because some questioned the prudence of dictating specific terms in advance rather than letting the state conventions come to them on their own.[32]

The Education Committee's task was not just to mandate the provision of public education or articulate its general value, but to work out the details. The committee's proposal specified everything from school funding and taxes to compulsory education and teacher training. Some of these details—ranging from how best to raise money for education to whether the constitution should compel school attendance and mandate racially equal access—were more radical than the Massachusetts Constitution. The problem of school funding was ever present. Though the governor, in his opening speech, had implored the convention to put education at the forefront, he also warned that the "Treasury is empty" and plummeting property values eliminated any immediate hope of an improved financial situation.[33]

No clear path marked the way out. The War had claimed thousands of lives and devastated the state's infrastructure—including warehouses, railroad depots, and manufacturing. Even the state capitol building and library had been consumed by fire. The cotton plantations, which produced the state's most important export, had lost the unpaid labor that made them so lucrative. Although no one opposed a constitutional education obligation in principle, many delegates believed the state needed time to regain its economic footing. They preferred an open timetable for implementing education.

But the majority pushed in the opposite direction, arguing that education was the one thing that could not wait. Despite the immense cost of building an education system from scratch, the Finance Committee's chairman insisted that it was an expense the state must bear: "We who make the Constitution are deeply interested in advancing [the cause of financing it], for upon this rests our hope of perpetuating the Government we ordain. To realize the greatest practical benefit from the new Government we create, we must adopt such measures as will sustain such Government. . . . We are not legislating for today." Another delegate put it more simply: the state needed "a system of free schools at as early a day as possible."[34]

The Education Committee offered a plan it hoped would force an education system into existence. Knowing a tax bill had recently failed in the legislature, the committee proposed constitutional language that required the General Assembly to "levy at each regular session after the adoption of this Constitution an annual tax on all taxable property throughout the State for the support of public schools." But knowing that property taxes would not cover the full cost, the committee also identified a supplemental source of funding: poll taxes.[35]

Black delegates supported the measure in the belief that Black voters would gladly pay a poll tax that went exclusively to their children's education. If recent years had shown anything, it was their willingness to make enormous sacrifices for their children's education. Yet Black delegates also appreciated the practical effect of imposing a poll tax and included a caveat: "no person shall ever be deprived of the right of suffrage for the nonpayment of the said tax." When the convention finally took a vote on poll taxes, Black delegates supported it at a higher rate than whites—73 percent versus 62 percent.[36]

The more controversial issues were compulsory education and segregation. Compulsory education divided the Black delegates on practicality; segregation united them on principle. The Education Committee's proposed constitutional language would have required not just that the General Assembly provide public education but that it compel all students to attend. Delegate DeLarge moved to strike the word "compulsory." It couldn't be enforced, he warned, and schoolmasters would waste time chasing families who did not want education. He and others argued that parents had the right to choose labor over learning for their children.

Alonzo Ransier rebuked these notions as simplistic and selfish: "The success of republicanism depends [on] the progress which our people are destined to make. If parents are disposed to clog this progress by neglecting the education of their children, for one, I will not aid and abet them." Another delegate added that liberty does not include a license to trample on republicanism: "Men, living in a savage, uncivilized state are perfectly free.... But the first thing, when a man goes into society, is to concede certain individual rights necessary for the protection and preservation of society." Republicanism, they argued, demands education regardless of what an individual parent might want.[37]

Buoyed by the support, Ransier offered one of the convention's longest speeches. From the ashes of a society that had left education to chance for some and legally prohibited it to others, he argued, it was the government's duty to compel education, and a citizen's duty to accept it. Without education, government and individuals would struggle in their most basic functions.

> I appeal to gentlemen of the Convention to know whether they desire to see a state of anarchy, or a state of confusion in South Carolina in the future. I desire to know whether they wish to see an independent people, engaged in industrious pursuits, living happy and contented. The child that remains in ignorance until grown up will never learn the first duty that ought to be learned by every man, which is to love his country and to love his State. If a man is so ignorant as to know nothing of political economy of his State or country, he can never be a good citizen.... If you give a man the privilege of remaining in ignorance, it is anti-republicanism to punish him. You must compel them to learn. Do that and you will have peace in the future. If you neglect

to do this, you must expect confusion, vice, and everything of the sort....

It is the sacred, solemn, and imperative duty of the State to vouchsafe to all its citizens all their rights, and all their privileges, [but] I also maintain that it is just as much its bounden duty to check and restrain the abuse of those rights and privileges, that the government has the prerogative to assume to act as the regulator, and monitor, as well as the faithful defender and preserver of liberty. No one will deny that individual rights should and ought to be subservient to the great interests of the common weal and prosperity. "No one has a right to do as he pleases, unless he pleases to do right."....

In the present relationships of our mixed population in the United States, this law of compulsion is called for as a defence of our liberties. We have in our country more than a million children between the ages of five and sixteen who can neither read nor write! Do you ask what we are going to do with them? That is not the question. The question is, what are they going to do with us? Think of their future power at the ballot-box![38]

Ransier's speech drew but a single response, surprisingly from Jonathan Jasper Wright—an objection born of experience, not principle. What might seem plausible in Charleston or Columbia, Wright explained, made little sense in the countryside and backwaters. He had seen firsthand just how hard it was for some children to attend school. Even where schools existed, many children faced long journeys to get there. In other places, there were no schools at all, and none coming anytime soon. Forcing attendance on these children was either cruel or impossible. Wright offered a lawyerly solution: direct the legislature to provide for compulsory attendance but give it the discretion to adjust the law to meet the circumstances.

The prospect of children of all races and classes sitting next to each other in school was the next hurdle. White families would refuse mixing with Black kids; wealthy families would object to mixing with poorer ones; and biases like these could doom the whole project. White families might turn against education altogether. Add compulsory education to that, and the education system could turn into a powder keg of emotions.

The Black delegation, however, wouldn't divide or budge on discriminatory enrollment. Democracy's new pillar could not be built with slavery's bricks. Segregated education would perpetuate slavery's vestiges, continue Black oppression, and show that the state was not committed to righting its wrongs. John Chestnut, also a former delegate to the Colored People's Convention of 1865, said equal education was a first-order principle that would admit no compromise:

> Republicanism has given us freedom, equal rights, and equal laws. Republicanism must also give us education and wisdom. It seems that the great difficulty in this section is in the fact that difficulty may arise between the two races, in the same school, or that the whites will not send their children to the same schools with the colored children. What of that? Has not this Convention a right to establish a free school system for the benefit of the poorer classes? Undoubtedly. Then if there be a hostile disposition among the whites, an unwillingness to send their children to school, the fault is their own, not ours.

His Black colleagues agreed.[39]

Robert Elliott was one of the strongest voices for education. Well-educated, the son of Caribbeans, and a former British sailor, Elliott was the type of man to whom South Carolina closed its ports after Vesey's revolt. He had lived in the state for only a year, but he already commanded respect at the convention. "It is republicanism to reward virtue. It is republicanism to educate the people, without discrimination," he boomed. The principles on which the convention stood would reverberate across time, tilting the balance of the state's future. He was "astonished" at the arguments raised against the education proposal. The answer to the most important question was straightforward. It "is not white or black united or divided, but whether children shall be sent to school or kept at home. If they are compelled to be educated, there will be no danger of the Union, or a second secession of South Carolina from the Union."[40]

Elliott was surely correct on some level, but those counting the votes worried that the issue could imperil the entire constitution. The convention, a white delegate argued, had produced a string of good ideas that "no power in the State can by any possibility defeat," but this provision was "odious to a large class of people in the State." Resist the temptation of drafting a perfect constitution, he urged his colleagues, and settle for a great one that the people will condone. The time had come to compromise within the realm of possibility—"for heaven's sake have sense enough to leave ... out" what the people would vote down. When the final votes were tallied, principle prevailed. Both compulsory attendance (as modified by Wright) and non-discriminatory enrollment passed with easy margins. A full 80 percent supported the prohibition on discrimination.[41]

At the convention's close, its president called its work a rebirth of republicanism, with education at its center:

> Here we have made every needful arrangement for the free education of our people, so that if future legislators shall carry out in good faith the provisions which we have ordained on this vital subject, in a few years the stain of ignorance which now pollutes our history will be forever obliterated, and the happy period will have arrived when no son or daughter of South Carolina will be unable to read and write. Thus have we broadly sown the seeds of public education, and thus shall we, in no distant time, reap the rich harvest of public virtue. Crime and ignorance are inseparable companions. We have stricken a heavy blow at both, and may look for the natural and inevitable result in the elevation of all our people to a social, political and religious eminence, to which, under the former Constitution and laws of the State, they had never attained.[42]

Other state constitutional conventions similarly vindicated the precious human freedom that had previously been denied based on race. They decreed that this injustice had to be rectified for all, without regard to race. Nine of the ten states readmitted under the Reconstruction Act included an affirmative education clause in their state constitutions. Although their language varied, they all created systems of schools aimed at extending statewide access to education. And though whites in state conventions proposed separate schools for white and Black students, the overall delegations, even those with far less Black representation than South Carolina, beat back those proposals. Southern constitutions would commit to schools "open to all."[43]

Access, however, was not enough. Several conventions included additional specific mandates that education be "uniform" or "thorough"—a concept first adopted in Ohio's education clause in 1851. Ohio delegates used the phrase "thorough and efficient" education, by which they meant "a system of schools as perfect as could be devised" that would "improve so as to keep pace with the most rapid progress of the most rapid element of our social or political constitution." Some states, like Florida, also added safeguards for the system, indicating that providing for education was "the paramount duty of the State" and expressly reserving funds for it. Alabama, for instance, required that all proceeds from state lands "be inviolably appropriated to educational purposes" and that one-fifth of the state's general revenues "be devoted exclusively to the maintenance of public schools."[44]

Voter ratification of these constitutions and the election of legislators would take a couple of years. By 1870, however, the legislative process was in full swing, leading to major education legislation in most of the states. The new constitutions and laws implementing them created the foundation and bureaucracy to set up and manage schools on a statewide basis. They established offices that still govern education today—state and local superintendents of education, state and local boards of education, and, of course, school districts. Prior to this legislation, the few schools that existed were randomly located, and they operated outside any formal governance structure. The new laws specified the geographic parameters for districts and mandated local bodies to form them.

Public education governance began taking shape from the top down. A state superintendent or state board of education appointed local superintendents or boards (unless an election was required). Those local officers then took the lead in starting schools within their districts, which meant exercising any taxing or spending power the state delegated, hiring teachers, and securing facilities. Some communities had to start from scratch, whereas others incorporated missionary, Freedmen's Bureau, or private schools, as well as their teachers.

Regardless of the circumstances, one thing was radically different. The new public schools would be free and open to all. This defining element, as W. E. B. Du Bois emphasized in his seminal book, *Black Reconstruction*, was a Black idea. "The first great mass movement for public education at the expense of the state, in the South," he wrote, "came from Negroes."[45]

Most of what has been written of this period is critical. Some criticisms arise from racism, others from dashed expectations and urgent needs delayed. Mismanagement and corruption by officials both Black and white no doubt undermined public education's full potential. Ill-equipped teachers and ill-conceived curricula sometimes created controversy and propagated bias. Black and white illiteracy remained too high, and access to schooling too low. Much blame rests with legislatures that never allocated enough funds to meet all children's needs. Although war had laid waste to the South's financial capacity, the legislators could have done much more.

But it is undeniable, and ultimately more important, that real and meaningful progress occurred. The states laid the foundations upon which education growth could occur, and still occurs today. The numbers don't lie. Prior to the War, no schools—save secret ones in larger cities, educating a handful of students—existed for the education of enslaved children, and very few accepted even free children of color. During the War, schools opened and, in places like Port Royal, served thousands of children, but only behind Union lines.

After the War, the Freedmen's Bureau expanded schooling throughout the South. In 1867 it reported 1,641 teachers operating under its protection and help—about one thousand white teachers and five hundred Black teachers. Just three years later, the total number of teachers had nearly doubled, and the number of Black teachers more than tripled. They served 115,000 students. During that period, the bureau spent the equivalent of nearly $100 million on those students—far from sufficient, but enough, particularly in combination with tuition and the resources that the Black community raised, to put a serious dent in the education debt slavery had created.[46]

The new public schools absorbed most of these teachers and students and drew many more. In his first official report, Justus Jillson, South Carolina's newly established state superintendent of education, wrote that 16,000 students—just 7 percent of the state's children—were attending 381 state schools in 1869. That number rose to 30,000 students and 769 schools the next year. When he left office in 1876, the public schools enrolled 123,000 students and served more than half of the state's children. The state was providing one teacher for every forty to forty-five students.[47]

Other states made similar progress. After taking office under an 1870 law, Georgia's state commissioner for education collected extensive data about the law's implementation. The legislation provided for one school commissioner per county, and he found that 133 of 136 counties had, in fact, appointed one. Similarly, all but twenty-five of the required 1,291 county school board members had taken their places, as had more than 3,600 school trustees. In ten years, public school enrollment went from 6,000 students to 86,000.[48]

Although it was among the last to reenter the Union, Mississippi's public school enrollment was even larger when they opened: 86,399 stu-

Black delegates at the Virginia Constitutional Convention of 1867–68, in *Frank Leslie's Illustrated Newspaper*. Courtesy of Library of Virginia.

dents. North Carolina, an early mover, apparently trumped them all. In 1869, the state had roughly 330,000 students who were eligible to attend school, and by 1872, more than half of them were enrolled. Half may seem like a failure to us today, but it was extremely high under the circumstances, especially given that parents expected teenagers to work in the fields. Despite its agricultural base, Southern school attendance exceeded Northern attendance in some places during this period. For Black children in particular, enrollment dramatically rose throughout the 1870s, from 91,000 in 1866 to 150,000 in 1870 to a staggering 572,000 in 1877.[49]

Franklin Moses, South Carolina's governor from 1872 to 1874, may have summarized the era best:

> Popular instruction is the most sacred duty of the Commonwealth. ... In a republic like ours, ... it is essential to the very existence of the Government that education should be widely diffused.... No greater eulogy can be written about the reconstructed administration

of government in South Carolina than that when it came into power it was a statutory offense ... to impart even the rudiments of a common school education to a South Carolinian, *because, forsooth, he was black*, while the reconstructed government has made it a stator offense to hinder or prevent any child in the State, of whatever color, from obtaining a common school education. Nay, we have even gone further, and demanded, by our Constitution, that their attendance at school be compulsory.[50]

CHAPTER FIFTEEN

Burning Down the Schoolhouse

THE IDEOLOGICAL AND VIGILANTE elements that oppressed Black literacy for decades before the War did not disappear with the Confederacy's fall. In many places, Black education remained as dangerous as it had been before the War. During slavery, literacy might foment rebellion, but many white leaders were convinced that rebellions would always be isolated and could be quickly subdued. Violence was a cost of doing business. But when slavery ended, Black education signaled that Black people might be on a path to equality with white people. Educated Black people would have the real potential to seize the reins of political power.

"As soon as the freed people began to act on the dream" of education as the pathway out of their current conditions, white violence followed in multiple forms. Sometimes the violence was economic. Former enslavers threatened to turn their former charges and their families out of their homes and terminate their "employment" if they sent their kids to school. Others hurled verbal threats and even physically attacked families walking their kids to school.[1]

Teachers began reporting problems as early as 1865. Shortly after he withdrew his troops from middle Tennessee, Major General Richard Johnson reported that white citizens "have caused the colored schools to be closed and the teachers ordered to leave." He promised to "post colored troops there to enforce the laws, and protect the schools," but stopping random attacks was more than the military could guarantee. It was one thing to declare schools open, and quite another to stop violent opposition aimed at preventing children from attending.[2]

White resistors also employed means beyond the military's purview. One strategy was simply to make life inhospitable for teachers. One teacher wrote that "being the teacher of a colored school has, as it were, isolated me from the rest of the world. I have communication with but a few beyond the limits of my domicile." Another, in Lexington, Virginia, reported that threats of tar and feather were "not uncommon, while petty insults and indignities are freely and boldly offered." Other communities refused to rent accommodations to teachers, leaving them nowhere to stay.[3]

Thousands of teachers—white and Black, Northern and Southern—worked in communities in fear and isolation. Their students faced even worse. Terror remained ever present for Black people, most of whom had nowhere to flee. White vigilantes did not need an overwhelming force. They just needed to shift the atmosphere, from a feeling that the time was pregnant with opportunity to one in which Blacks once again feared white power. This was hard to do when the South was occupied by half a million Union soldiers, but as those troops withdrew, violence against Black education seemed to increase each year.

It is impossible to pin down the level of terrorism Black schools and people suffered in any given year. Most violence went unreported, at least in any form available today. The Freedmen's Bureau is somewhat to blame for the information gap. Many officials did not consider violence worthy of study or systematic reporting. They were living in war zones, where extralegal violence and retribution from both sides were often the norm.

The same officials likely wished to paint a favorable picture of progress. Bringing education to the South was the most vivid and concrete symbol of democratic transformation. The bureau needed all the support it could get for its programs—governmental and philanthropic funding, as well as volunteers—and schooling was one thing that people in the North could easily feel good about. Teachers fleeing their schoolhouses or carted away dead was not the story those on the ground wanted to tell.

The best information scholars have about the violence comes from newspapers, Freedmen's Bureau records, and personal correspondence, all of which generally identify just one incident at a time. Ronald Butchart's book *Schooling the Freed People* identified thousands of instances of terrorism. Much of it involved attacks on individual teachers that would have been enough to make anyone quit then and there—shattered windows in the middle of the night, mock funerals, and the sound of bullets speeding by as they missed their target. Vigilantes dragged one teacher from his bed, miles into dark woods, and threatened to "blow your damned Yankee brains out" if he kept teaching "n———." Some teachers were, in fact, murdered, while others suffered repeated attacks over one, two, and three years. One reported that her life was "threatened again and again."[4]

With no one to write home to and very few bureau agents collecting their stories, Black students and families endured violence that is less well documented. But teachers often recounted their students' experiences in their diaries. Philena Carkin, a teacher in Charlottesville, reported that University of Virginia students routinely disrupted Black children at her freedmen's school. The college students, she wrote, "had a habit of climbing upon the top of" train cars, with their "pockets filled with stones," to "throw these missiles left and right as they pleased" through the school windows. In Hickman, Tennessee, one of Jennie Mead's students was murdered, and "the parents of her pupils menaced until the attendance has been diminished to nearly one-half of the original number." Reverend T. K. Noble, a Freedmen's Bureau superintendent of education, wrote that he would "not be surprised any day to learn that the school has been broken up by a mob." For Black people, the terror surely ran deep. They knew from experience that the threats they faced were not empty—and that they had little recourse against white violence.[5]

The most widespread terror-inducing and destructive violence was the burning of schools themselves, an action that was at once brazen, public, and tangible and also anonymous, nearly unstoppable, and broadly symbolic. Burning a school destroyed the immediate tools and venue for Black education, and the schools represented Black freedom more openly than any other aspect of social life. Burning them was a visceral announcement of white supremacy: the power it still held and refused to concede. Like the burning of abolitionist pamphlets in Charleston, the burning of schools was a communal act symbolic of absolutist white Southern power. The education historian Campbell Scribner called school burnings "a signal act of rebellion"—renewed and ongoing. As a signal act, they drew a national audience.[6]

On May 26, 1866, a school burning in Memphis, Tennessee, was reported on the front page of *Harper's Weekly*, then the country's most widely read journal. The imagery, which took up almost the entire page,

Burning of a freedmen's schoolhouse in Memphis, in *Harper's Weekly*.
Courtesy of Library of Congress.

was savage. Three dozen men gloried in their work: a large school consumed by flames and billowing smoke. The heat of the fire forced vigilantes back some thirty feet, but there they raised fists in triumph, fired rifles into the sky, ran about in glee, and conversed in relaxed solidarity. Their party carried on into the night.

The terrorist act had started with a dispute between a white policeman and a group of Black soldiers, who the officer claimed were drunk and disorderly. Whatever the truth, police officers and a white mob used it as the justification for a full-out assault on the Black community. They killed forty-six Black people, injured another seventy-five, raped five women, and destroyed eight schools. Although they burned churches too, the big schoolhouse was the crescendo of the two-day massacre—"an excitement," *Harper's Weekly* explained, "unequaled since the close of the war."[7]

On the surface, Tennessee was a surprising place for this level of violence. It was one of the few Southern states that had not criminalized

Black education during slavery. Though never supportive of Black education, it had not taken an absolutist approach. Several important institutions had openly taught Black students throughout the antebellum period. But after the War, the state turned against them. The Memphis massacre was only the first of many in the state.

Campbell Scribner, scouring newspapers and other remaining sources, documented 631 attacks on Black schools during Reconstruction. In Tennessee, white people destroyed seventy-six Black schools, some 9.2 percent of all the Black schools in the state. Such burnings occurred more often, on a per capita basis, in Tennessee than anywhere else. The formation of the Ku Klux Klan in Pulaski, Tennessee, in 1865 surely contributed to those numbers. But Tennessee was no outlier.[8]

Mississippi and Alabama saw more total school burnings—158 in Mississippi—in part because they had more Black schools to target. But burnings were curiously uneven across states. Of all the known burnings of Black schools in sixteen states, 80 percent occurred in seven of them: Alabama, Georgia, Louisiana, Mississippi, South Carolina, Tennessee, and Texas. Nine other states reported just five burnings each—though the level of unreported violence is anyone's guess.[9]

Aggregate numbers, whatever they were, understate the lived reality. A school burning could bring a full and permanent stop to education both in the community where it occurred and anywhere in the vicinity. A string of burnings in a single county sent the message that Black education would not be tolerated anywhere in the jurisdiction. When a community rebuilt a school, vandals often torched it again. The net result was to shut down Black education in many areas. The only thing that kept Black schools operating in many places was either soldiers or armed Black community members standing constant guard.

Violence against freedmen's schools peaked around 1868. Then it subsided somewhat, though it persisted throughout Reconstruction. The beginning of formal Reconstruction, its terms, the pro-Black and pro-Union political activity it sparked, and the schoolhouse as its symbol, gave the Klan and others an immediate target. But when that violence didn't stop the larger education project, much of that vitriol morphed into traditional resistance, through the political process and advocacy.

Much of the white opposition was aimed at undermining the public education initiatives passed by the constitutional conventions and legislatures. Opponents of those measures did not show up at the conventions, either because they engaged in boycotts or because they refused to swear

Political cartoon in *Harper's Weekly* depicting violent suppression of Black enfranchisement and education during Reconstruction. Thomas Nast, *Worse than Slavery*, 1874. Courtesy of Library of Congress.

allegiance to the Union and were thus ineligible to attend. But outside the conventions, they were a constant presence in public fora and eventually the statehouses.

Southern newspapers amplified those hostile positions, in both the editors' commentary and in the essays they published. These voices rejected the basic principle that the state was responsible for Black children's education. Black education was the wedge with which these papers tried to turn voters against the new state constitutions. Arkansas's *Des Arc Weekly Citizen*, for instance, called the state's new constitution a "misera-

Practical Illustration of the Virginia Constitution (So Called) to discourage its ratification. Courtesy of Library of Virginia.

ble document," with the unacceptable requirement that "a tax shall be levied to establish and maintain schools, in which no distinction shall be made on account of race or color." It was an outrage that "the white man shall be taxed to educate the [Black]."[10]

If white people started paying to educate Black people, Georgia's *Weekly Constitutionalist* argued, the extraction of white wealth for the benefit of Black people would never stop. Black people, the argument went, did not possess enough taxable property or pay enough in poll taxes to support their schools "for a week, and so for the rest of the year ... [the tuition bill] ... must be footed out of the school fund raised by a uniform *ad valorem* tax upon all of the property of the whites." Worse, they would be supporting the salaries of "New England teachers" whose practical effect, if not express aim, was to "increase the hatred between the races."[11]

The widely repeated trope about New England teachers was reminiscent of the attack on Northern literature during the antebellum period. Any idea not of the South was inherently suspicious, and any effort to educate Black people was inherently subversive of the racial order. Rather than concede the civic capacity of an educated Black populace, many critics resorted to the same premise that once propped up slavery—the notion of Black inferiority. Any dollar spent on Black education, papers across the South argued, was a dollar wasted.[12]

More sophisticated yet equally racist arguments went after the thesis behind education—that it was the foundation of republican government. The new public education system, according to its detractors, was an attempt to socially reengineer the South. Rather than expand freedom and democracy for white people, public education posed an inescapable dilemma: send one's children to school with Black children or keep them home and pay taxes for others' education. Parents who chose the former would see their children fed a steady diet of "social equality" indoctrination. Those who chose the latter would hand Black people a monopoly on public education resources. Wrapping anti-tax, anti-Black, and Confederate sympathy all into one, these voices argued that public education was anti-republican. As the *Daily Phoenix* in South Carolina wrote, "The white man is taxed, without a vote, to school a black man's child, while the black man pays no tax at all, unless he owns property."[13]

The only remedy for this supposed injustice was to scuttle the entire public education project. Otherwise, white people would be "compelled to pay taxes for the support of schools inuring to the exclusive benefit of negro children." But since scuttling the project was beyond their immediate reach, opponents of public education chipped away at it year after year.[14]

True to the warnings at South Carolina's 1868 constitutional convention, some white people did refuse to send their children to public schools. They faced little resistance. State officials never seriously enforced the compulsory attendance or "open to all" laws that delegates had bravely defended a few years earlier. Even in South Carolina and Louisiana, where the conventions explicitly required non-discriminatory enrollment, state officials looked the other way—and sometimes directly violated the law. No sooner had the ink dried on South Carolina's constitution than its governor pushed for and implemented segregated education. School systems in states with less powerful constitutional language than South Carolina's never stood a chance.[15]

Once integrated schooling was put to rest, the white opposition began to attack school finances. The edifice of public education, they claimed, was "gigantic," its costs "excessive," and the financial burden one-sided. The more politically astute factions did not advocate boycotting or scuttling the education system but controlling its finances until the opposition regained full power. In the decade after the War, that meant finding a middle ground. The opposition's political representatives sought to tame the beast as best they could, never funding public education at the level it needed but never completely starving it either.[16]

Education expenditures generally increased every year during early Reconstruction, but those increases were grossly inadequate compared with the growing number of students the system served. Florida's annual public education budget, for instance, grew from $75,000 to $158,000 between 1860 and 1876, but the student population ballooned from 4,500 students to 28,000. This meant the amount the state spent per student plummeted by two-thirds. The story was the same elsewhere. South Carolina, which by 1876 had increased its education appropriation to $457,000, spent far less per pupil than Florida.[17]

The 1876 presidential election marked a turning point. Voters cast roughly eight million ballots in the contest between Republican Rutherford B. Hayes and Democrat Samuel Tilden. Tilden reportedly won the national popular vote by around 250,000, but rampant fraud and voter intimidation in the South made any tally unreliable. The presidency hung on three states where the margins were razor-thin: Louisiana, Florida, and South Carolina. A new election was probably in order, but instead, the Republican and Democratic parties brokered a truce. If the Democrats conceded the election, Hayes would withdraw Union troops from the South and end Reconstruction.

The deal sealed education's fate for the rest of that century and much of the next. Much that had been accomplished in the past decade either vanished or transformed into a shell of its former self. The Jim Crow era was beginning: white people would now exclude Black people from all decision-making and attempt to reduce them to second-class citizenship—a status that was not slavery but not far removed from it. Their strategy was to undermine the governmental structures of voting and schooling that elevated Blacks into the body politic. Blacks would formally retain their citizenship but lose many of its rights and privileges.

Some states had taken steps in that direction before 1876. In North Carolina, as soon as Democrats regained control of the legislature (though not the governor's mansion) in 1870, the state began subverting the constitution's education clause. Democrats left in place the broad language describing a "uniform" system of public education but amended the constitution to require that "the children of the white race and the children of the colored race shall be taught in separate schools." Though they added that "there shall be no discrimination in favor of, or to the prejudice of either race," after 1876 the state heaped abuse upon abuse on Black schools.[18]

With the end of Reconstruction, the voices that had once criticized Black education from the sidelines took center stage everywhere, exerting enormous political leverage. Their message was simple: public education was a threat to the racial and economic status quo. It would "inflate the economic and political expectations of workers" and "spoil good field hands." The more education Blacks got, the more they would push for equality. The rallying cry to reinstate the supposed natural order reached the highest levels of state government. Georgia's governor proclaimed: "God made them negroes and we cannot make them white. We are on the wrong track. We must turn back." South Carolina's governor claimed that "the greatest mistake the white race has ever made was to educate the free Negro." Mississippi's governor said money spent on Black education was "money thrown away."[19]

Public education made for an easy target because it required taxation. And even though white students benefited from it as much as Black students, Black lawmakers and Black students bore the blame for high taxes. Newspaper editors and politicians made sure the public got a steady stream of stories leveraging the intersection of racism and anti-tax sentiment. The talking points were simple: education spending was excessive and wasteful, particularly on Black students.[20]

This narrative fueled a movement to defund and restructure public education. The white South had no interest in supporting public education if it symbolized Black freedom and empowerment, even though that system was designed for all children. With the fall of Reconstruction, public education budgets stagnated across the South. In Georgia, the state appropriation for public education had risen to $265,000 in 1874 but fell to $149,000 in 1876 and remained well under $200,000 for the rest of the decade.[21]

How education was financed and managed also changed. During Reconstruction, Southern states had sought to create a unified system of schools under state leadership. After Reconstruction, states began devolving authority to the local level. This allowed local districts to run two systems of education—one white and one Black—while freeing the state of any formal responsibility for them. Local officials could more effectively segregate and disparately fund schools than state officials, and

Members of the South Carolina legislature ca. 1876, many of whom had been delegates to the state's constitutional convention of 1868 (detail). Courtesy of Library of Congress.

their actions were less likely to draw the attention of federal officials or courts.

One method of localizing education was to authorize "special" or "independent" school districts. Local communities could petition the legislature for permission to tax themselves for separate districts. To assuage fears that some communities might try to perpetuate education radicalism, states placed caps on the amount of taxes these districts could levy. They also limited the voters who could approve those levies. Only those who paid property taxes—meaning property owners—were eligible to vote.

These districts were highly racialized. Some were created as one-race districts. In others, local trustees segregated the schools under their own authority, dividing funds between Black and white schools however they saw fit. Black communities could petition for their own districts, too, but the state reserved the power to appoint local trustees to manage schools in keeping with the state's desired outcomes.

Some states went so far as to divide local tax dollars by race. In 1881, a North Carolina law required that taxes "collected from ... white persons, shall be expended" on "public school for" white persons, and taxes "collected from colored persons, shall be expended for the benefit of the colored schools." Two years later, the state required that voters approve these local tax levies for schools, but it precluded Black citizens from voting. Though the North Carolina Supreme Court struck down the system under the state constitution, racist forces had by then consolidated so much power that they ignored the court's ruling and continued segregating school tax dollars. Other states followed. In 1888, a South Carolina law gave each taxpayer in a special school district "the right to designate to which school in his district he wishes the money paid by him to go." Two years later, Governor Bill Tillman called for the state to come up with a permanent solution: standard-sized districts in each county but "one white and one colored school in each" district, with "each tax payer" having the right to designate "the school to which his additional tax shall go."[22]

By the 1890s, states were beginning to etch these patterns of Jim Crow discrimination into their constitutions. It was not enough to oppress Black people and citizens through statutes: the Reconstruction constitutions had to be overthrown. As James Underwood wrote in his multivolume treatise on the South Carolina Constitution, men like Bill Tillman had long viewed the constitution of 1868 as an "alien document unsuitable to local conditions." It represented a world in which Black people might aspire to opportunities equal to those of whites. The time had come to conclusively right that wrong and "dismantle" Reconstruction once and for all.[23]

An anti-Black constitutional agenda spread across the South just as surely as the pro-democracy agenda had spread at the close of the War. The agenda had two prongs: disenfranchise Black voters, and segregate and underfund Black education. Having run roughshod over Black rights for a decade and a half, Mississippi's leaders didn't mince words. Their constitutional convention in 1890 opened with the convention president, Solomon S. Calhoon, saying what everyone already knew: "We came here to exclude the negro. Nothing short of this will answer." At the South Carolina constitutional convention in 1895, the chair stated that its purpose was to "blot out" the "despotism" of the 1868 constitution, which was "framed by a body that did not represent the people of South Carolina" and "perpetuated the reign of ignorance and vice over wisdom and virtue." A slew of other state constitutional conventions followed, similarly aiming, in the words of a contemporary observer, "to eliminate the negro from political life."[24]

To disenfranchise Black voters, the conventions added constitutional clauses that made "understanding" the laws and constitutions a condition for voting. This gave local officials broad discretion to exclude unwanted voters. White citizens, even if illiterate, could gain permission to vote by satisfying sympathetic officials that they "understood" the constitution when someone else read it to them. But Black voters, even if literate and well educated, would be cross-examined until they got something wrong or simply said something that a local official thought lacking. A Mississippi newspaper slyly assured whites that this new provision would work devious wonders in the hands of racist officials: "there might be honest differences of opinion between a corn-field n—— and inspectors of the election." Three state constitutions also added moral character clauses to their constitutions, allowing officials an even more subjective basis for excluding voters.[25]

New approaches to poll taxes took an additional toll on Black voters. During Reconstruction, state constitutions adopted poll taxes to fund public education but did not exclude voters for nonpayment. Mississippi's 1890 convention changed that. Not only did it make the payment mandatory, it doubled the tax and required back payment of all prior poll taxes. These changes put voting out of most Black people's economic reach, especially those already trapped in debt by white planters' exploitative and often illegal sharecropping tactics. The new constitution in Mississippi disenfranchised more than one hundred thousand Black voters. Black voter turnout in the state fell from 29 percent in 1888 to 2 percent in 1892 to 0 percent in 1895. In Louisiana, Black voter registration fell from 95.6 percent prior to an 1896 law to 1.1 percent in 1904.[26]

In both white and Black people's minds, however, education remained a gateway to freedom, citizenship, and voting. Black leaders, though alarmed by voting changes, continued to believe that as long as educational opportunities remained open, Black people could overcome the barriers before them. White delegates to the constitutional conventions agreed, and saw education suppression as integral to political suppression. As Dorothy Pratt writes, Mississippi's delegates fully understood that "the future of disenfranchisement depended on an illiterate African American population." Lest anyone doubt it, the newspapers sounded the alarm: "As soon as all the negroes in the state shall be able to read and write they will become qualified to vote," and then "they will demand their rights."[27]

Voluntary special districts and local tax machinations were not enough. The point of the new constitutional convention was to remove any possibility of Black equality. The Mississippi Constitution of 1890 required that "separate schools shall be maintained for children of the white and colored races." South Carolina's 1895 constitution was more emphatic: "Separate schools shall be provided for children of the white and colored races, and no child of either race shall ever be permitted to attend a school provided for children of the other race." States also expanded opportunities for local officials to entrench inequality in other ways. From financing and leadership to the academic calendar and educational quality, the states got out of the education business. Local communities, not the states, would pick up the cost of education expansion and improvement. Local communities, not the states, would decide how many days a year children should attend school. Local officials, not the states, could figure out the ways to ensure that Black people did not get the education—or the idea—to assert their political rights.[28]

The surest way to do this was to eliminate public education altogether. That idea did cross some convention delegates' minds. They questioned whether public education was even an appropriate subject for state constitutions, noting that education mandates had been forced on the Southern states by Reconstruction. But too many white families wanted public education for their own children for its elimination to gain any traction. Delegates overwhelmingly favored the new system of mandated segregation.

During Reconstruction, state funding for public education had been similarly inadequate for both Black and white schools. In some places, that parity persisted until 1880. In North Carolina and Alabama, the Reconstruction-era funding structures even produced slightly higher funding for Black schools than for white schools. But after the Jim Crow constitutional conventions, the retribution on Black schools was as vicious as that on Black voters.[29]

States forced Black schools to operate under conditions as impoverished as in the first days of freedom, during the War, when families relied on voluntary funding for their children's education. Reconstruction spurred plenty of school construction, but as time passed, those facilities deteriorated and became too small. Black students still had physical structures to attend, but there was barely enough money to staff or maintain them.

Shortly after Mississippi's new constitution passed, one school district spent eleven times as much on white students as on Black students. When Black property owners in Jackson, Mississippi, challenged a bond referendum to build a new white school—even though there was no school for Black students—the Mississippi Supreme Court dismissed the notion that there was any limitation on the state's authority to operate segregated schools and called the prior constitution's language requiring uniform schools "absurd." When the city built a Black school a year later, the salaries for Black teachers were 30 percent lower than for their white peers and their student ratios nearly twice as high.[30]

Such inequalities and indignities only worsened over time. Two decades after South Carolina's Jim Crow convention, the state spent twelve times as much on white students. Florida, which operated one of the least discriminatory regimes, still spent more than twice as much on white students as on Black students. In *Simple Justice*, the seminal account of the NAACP's litigation strategy to bring down segregation, Richard Kluger writes that "fifty years after ratification of the Fourteenth Amendment, 'equal protection' in Southern schools meant that scarcely one-third as much was spent on the education of each black child as on each white one."[31]

Inequality this stark was not simply a function of wealth differences between white and Black taxpayers. If states had simply left Black communities to their own devices, they would have managed better for themselves. But state and local policymakers actively reduced Black education to the lowest level they could without being accused of denying it altogether. In 1906, Mississippi governor James Vardaman told the legislature to stop "wasting" half a million dollars a year—money generated by "toiling white men and women"—and spending it on "the vain purpose of trying to make something of the negro which the Great Architect of the Universe failed to provide for in the original plan of creation." Some local districts later took the idea to heart, refusing to even fully use the small state appropriations they received for Black schools. Three out of four districts allowed much of the money simply to sit in the treasury. Half of the districts spent 75 percent or less of what the state gave them. In short, they would not even fund Black education at no cost to them.[32]

Segregated school in Clarendon County School District, South Carolina, which was one of the four school districts involved in the *Brown v. Board of Education* court decision. Courtesy of University of South Carolina, South Caroliniana Library.

Both teachers and students suffered. Black teachers were overworked and grossly underpaid, while black students attended dilapidated schools, often in a single room that lumped students of different ages and grades together. Inequality was the starkest at the high school level. When high school education began to take hold in white communities, states denied it to Black children. Black teenagers, it was thought, should be working in the field, not pursuing education that could take them out of it. In the early 1900s, some Southern states refused to operate even a single high school for Black students. Even those states that opened Black high schools refused to operate more than a few statewide. Older Black students could remain in a one-room school with elementary students or travel long distances each day to a district that had a Black high school. Most chose to end their education altogether.[33]

By the turn of the century, what had begun as public education for all—a Black idea—had become public education for some. What was conceived as a means to eradicate the vestiges of slavery had become a tool for perpetuating them. As Mississippi's state superintendent proudly said in 1899, "It will be readily admitted by every white man in Mississippi that our public school system is designed primarily for the welfare of the white children of the state, and incidentally, for the negro children."[34]

Yet, even segregation and inequality were not enough to satisfy the most strident redeemers of the old way of life in the South. They insisted on rewriting the history through which the region had recently passed. In 1892, the United Confederate Veterans appointed a committee to vet "every text-book on history and literature in Southern schools." Northern educators and authors, the group believed, had perpetrated lies about the South and slavery that had to be corrected. The committee aimed to root out these texts and replace them with others that explained the Civil War was the North's fault, it was not fought over slavery, and "slaves were not ill-treated." All the South had ever "desired," the veterans claimed, was "peace." Vetting all the books, however, would be a process. As an immediate start, the committee issued a twenty-three-page text by Mildred Lewis Rutherford, *A Measuring Rod to Test Text Books, and Reference Books in Schools, Colleges and Libraries*, that set out rigid ideological standards for book adoptions.[35]

Over the next several years, the United Confederate Veterans released several more reports singling out inappropriate books, promoting appropriate ones, and articulating a historical narrative of an unjustly treated South. The veterans' organization also joined forces with other groups like the United Daughters of the Confederacy, the Sons of the Confederate Veterans, and local groups in the effort to ensure that "every textbook so teaches our children" that "Confederate soldiers were ... justified in their construction of constitutional rights."[36]

This propaganda movement proved more successful than the one of the 1840s and 1850s. Whereas the South had previously lacked the institutions, authors, and professors necessary to generate its own textbooks, the South's colleges and professorial ranks had since grown, allowing the new movement to produce a wide range of books lamenting the passing of the antebellum era and extolling Southern values. Some of these new history textbooks, the scholar Fred Bailey writes, "entirely ignored slavery," while others "justified it through appeals to white fears, most boldly calling it a virtuous institution."[37]

Recalling the "old plantation system" in his history of Arkansas, John Reynolds wrote, "we often regret that we cannot see it as it used to be." In his telling, "simple-minded" slaves "endeared themselves to their masters by their faithfulness" and "went to their work cheerfully." No one "returned from a day's labor a happier or jollier crowd than the Southern negroes." Though he allowed that a master might occasionally be "cruel to his darkies," Reynolds insisted that most were "kind" and slaves "in turn loved their master." Numerous other textbooks told similar narratives. But old Southern virtue was not their only focus. They painted Reconstruction as a period of grossly flawed policy, Northern cruelty, and illegitimate political control, from which Southern heroes had finally redeemed the South. These texts led subsequent Southern generations to absorb, as Bailey put it, a "veneration for the Confederate cause, an intense resistance to black civil rights, and a deferential spirit toward their 'proper' leaders."[38]

This rebirth of the anti–Black literacy and white-propaganda movement would last longer and be more pervasive than the one that followed Vesey, Walker, and Turner. The pause in between the two phases—Reconstruction and its education missions and manifestos—lasted but a decade. Jim Crow would last three-quarters of a century. Even the aftermath of *Brown v. Board of Education* was a sad testament to how hard old habits are to break—habits that preceded war, survived war, and flourished as though little had happened. The time between the *Brown* decision and congressional action to enforce it was longer than the entirety of Reconstruction. Congress stalled *Brown*'s mandate for a decade, from 1954 until it finally passed the Civil Rights Act of 1964. By comparison, its formal commitment to Black education lasted only six years, from 1866 to 1872, when it ended the education efforts of the Freedmen's Bureau.

Yet Black people's struggle for education was equally persistent. They had struggled against legal opposition to learn to read for at least four decades prior to the War, forced schools into existence when they got their first glimmers of freedom in the early 1860s, mobilized constitutional conventions to expand public education from 1868 through 1870, and taken their seats in legislatures to implement rapid change through 1876. They laid the groundwork for what would become the modern public education project. With the fall of Reconstruction, these hopes remained frustrated for generations, until they could be revived in the modern era.

CHAPTER SIXTEEN

Our Chance to Break the Cycle

I<small>N LEGAL TERMS, THE</small> war on Black literacy ended when Jim Crow finally fell. Ending a war, however, is not the same as repairing the damage or resolving the conflicts that perpetuated it. It may not even amount to a meaningful truce. The Civil War ended formal slavery but did not remedy the conditions slavery had perpetuated for centuries. Reconstruction began as a remedy but was abandoned while far from complete. The same is true of the second reconstruction—the Civil Rights Movement. School desegregation, for instance, lasted only a decade in most places before it ended. Nonetheless, formal segregation and opposition to Black equality died as an acceptable public policy.

Brown v. Board of Education and its progeny fundamentally altered the way society thinks about education, not just of Black children but of all children. Laws prohibiting discrimination against students based on sex, language status, ethnicity, alienage, disability, poverty, and homelessness all grew out of the foundation *Brown* laid. For the past half century, the federal legal apparatus as well as several state regimes have aimed to deliver equal educational opportunity. The pursuit of racial equality, not just the prohibition of intentional discrimination, is embedded in any number of education policies. Education bureaucracy disaggregates every aspect of education by race—from basic attendance, test scores, and graduation rates to suspensions, expulsions, advanced placement opportunities, access to qualified teachers, and more. This data fuels a national conversation about closing the achievement gap that began in the 1960s.

Both sides of the political spectrum have, surprisingly, found a good deal of agreement about closing this gap—an important testament given the nation's racial track record. In 2001, 90 percent of Congress voted in favor of the No Child Left Behind Act and its mandate to close gaps in achievement and teacher access for every racial and ethnic group in our public schools. The mechanism for achieving this goal proved flawed, but Congress still pursued the goal. At the end of 2015, a moment when Republicans and Democrats could not agree on the time of day and their mutual opposition was crossing all historical lines of decency, Congress rewrote the No Child Left Behind Act. Nearly 85 percent of its members voted for the bill, restyled as the Every Student Succeeds Act, which retained the goal of closing achievement gaps.[1]

Yet, tragedy abounds in American schools. Despite consensus agreements and commitments, stubborn biases persist beneath the surface in our schools, communities, and legislatures. And for all its lofty goals, the country has left problematic aspects of the status quo relatively untouched—the way states fund schools, allocate teachers, assign students to classes, discipline students, and build educational communities. As a result, national policy hasn't translated into full equal educational opportunity for any disadvantaged student group, including Black students. The enormous legislative and judicial push of the 1960s was not enough to do the most basic thing—fully desegregate schools. School integration hit its high-water mark in the 1980s and consistently slid backward from there, leaving schools nearly as racially isolated today as they were in the late 1960s.

The slippage was not happenstance. Successful school desegregation, which required aggressive desegregation, triggered a political backlash in the early 1970s. As a presidential candidate, Richard Nixon explicitly campaigned against court-ordered school desegregation and, as president, appointed Supreme Court justices he knew would limit or reverse school desegregation remedies. One of his appointees, William Rehnquist, had been a clerk on the Supreme Court when it decided *Brown*. Rehnquist authored a memo to Justice Jackson that made the case for upholding school segregation. Another Nixon appointee, Lewis Powell, had served on the Richmond School Board when it resisted desegregation, and on the Virginia State Board of Education when it facilitated private school vouchers for white parents fleeing desegregation. These justices shifted the balance of power on the court and soon reversed school desegregation's course.[2]

This backlash, however, was less explicit than those in prior eras. Neither the court nor any public law or agenda affirmatively subjugated Black children. *Brown* had provoked vicious political hostility, official state recalcitrance, and private violence, but by the 1970s, openly racist talk and opposition had become socially unacceptable. Public leaders no longer said Black children were inferior, integration was immoral, or that it made sense to treat children differently. Rather than advocate for discrimination and segregation, the court stopped doing its job—stopped remedying the effects of past discrimination. It distinguished between what it called private and public discrimination—ignoring the former and remedying the latter only when unassailable evidence afforded no other option. As a result, old habits returned.

Equity advocates often say that the second reconstruction—like the first—failed and the South once again won the long war, reimposing its values slowly over time. (To be clear, on many metrics, the North was even worse than the South.) A decade or so ago, that conclusion felt persuasive. While the country maintained legislative commitments to equality and the Supreme Court still professed its belief in diversity and equality, the numbers told a different story. School desegregation and funding equality had been flat or retreating in most places for some time. The second reconstruction was, at best, surviving with a faint heartbeat. Even the most optimistic observers could not point to a time when the remedies for racial discrimination had finished the job in a way that they would call success. But most could name a time or event when schools started moving in the wrong direction.

Then, as had happened often before, racial violence upended conventional thinking. Police and private violence took the lives of Trayvon Martin, George Floyd, Breonna Taylor, and others. Those events triggered a racial reckoning that indicated America might not be content with its backward slide. When video cameras forced the country to look at itself, many were unhappy with what they saw. We could have framed those events as aberrations or limited our view to police brutality. Instead, substantial portions of American society and government began to question racial disparities in all quarters. Rather than hide behind outdated legal standards and old habits that perpetuated discrimination, many began taking proactive steps.

Schools were a natural location for change. That is not to say America rethought the foundations of schooling, mandated integration, or diverted adequate resources to schools, but our educational institutions proved far more receptive to change than they had been in the past. Many were willing to try things that might make a difference. Restorative justice programs accelerated. Diversity, equity, and inclusion programming became a norm. Culturally inclusive curricula, not just along lines of race but in terms of sex, gender, disability, and more, filtered into classrooms. The books students read, the ways teachers communicated, the events schools sponsored, the ways students were encouraged to interact with one another, and the things schools stopped doing all spoke to a consistent effort to identify the shortcomings of the second reconstruction and find renewed progress. In some places, to be sure, these new initiatives were window dressing meant to assuage guilt without changing much. But globally, the ethos of schooling was changing rapidly.

These changes do not align with a narrative of failure that depicts the Civil Rights Movement as only a temporary deviation from a status quo of racism and bias. That large portions of American society were receptive to a racial reckoning suggests that the Civil Rights Movement did change the country in important ways. The change did not ensure equity, then or now, but it moved society to the point where it might never again be comfortable with sustained, systemic inequality—even if it was not always quick to appreciate and acknowledge inequality. The slowness surely reflects a nation that had been naive from the start about its sins. But caveats and nuances aside, America was awakening—without war, without a single new law or court decision, and without mass violence.

Yet this hopeful narrative is attached to another one. Something dangerously reminiscent of the pre–Civil War South is happening in education today. The rising paranoia over critical race theory, curricular transparency, "socialist" teachers, and diversity, equity, and inclusion in public schools strikingly resembles the South's paranoia over Northern textbooks, Northern teachers, Northern universities, and Northern popular literature in the decades before the Civil War. Today's insistence that these new trends in public education make students uncomfortable and paint white people as irredeemably racist sounds a lot like John Calhoun's Senate speeches about abolitionist literature injuring Southerners' pride and character. When modern politicians insist their states will set their own academic standards and teach history and values that align with their way of life, rather than the professional judgments of "woke" outsiders, they sound like pre–Civil War Southerners insisting that Southern students need a Southern education that promotes Southern values. They sound like champions of the Lost Cause who claimed to be redeeming Southern education from Northern lies about slavery and the War following Reconstruction. When states and school boards ban books from libraries and threaten legal consequences for teachers who say the wrong thing, their tactics resemble those of Southern states that banned abolitionist newspapers, pilfered mailbags for offending materials, and ran people out of the state. They resemble the United Confederate Veterans who issued rigid guidelines by which to purge Southern schools and libraries of unflattering history.

Embedded in these resemblances is a dangerously broad exercise of power. The sweep of antebellum laws covered not only immediate actual threats but anything that might remotely be connected to a potential threat. As far as the law was concerned, regular religious gatherings were the same as insurrectionary meetings and Black seamen doing their job the same as insurrectionary conspirators. Discussing the economics of slavery was as dangerous as discussing abolition and acknowledging Northern virtue the same as harboring anti-Southern animus. The breadth of the South's anti-literacy laws and censorship left its people at the whim of arbitrary power.

Many of today's reactionary laws and policies place educators in the same position. New laws broadly prohibit instruction that "espouses, promotes, advances, inculcates, or compels" objectionable ideas. The ideas in question are described in vague terms, as "divisive concepts," for example, or as nebulous academic fields of study like critical race theory. "Vagueness," according to free expression advocates, "is the point." It gives those enforcing the law enormous discretion, complaining parents enormous leverage, and teachers very little clue as to what they can or cannot teach, other than that they should not discuss anything perceived as or somehow related to objectionable content. As the attorney for a terminated teacher remarked in August 2023, "after two days of trial, we still do not know … where the lines are drawn when it comes to sensitive, controversial, or divisive concepts."[3]

Placing these current events against the map of the Confederacy is equally disturbing. Among states that were part of the Union prior to the Civil War, ten of the twelve that have passed anti-critical-race-theory legislation are below the Mason-Dixon line. Among newer states, another pattern jumps out. All seven that have passed such legislation—North Dakota, Idaho, South Dakota, Iowa, Montana, Utah, and Oklahoma—have overwhelmingly white populations. In six of these seven states, the white population exceeds 85 percent. The Black population is 2 percent or less in all but two of these states. Bills repressing free speech relating to gender and LGBTQ students map out similarly. As of summer 2023, with the sole exception of Arizona, the states advancing or passing those bills were all Southern or predominantly white, western states.[4]

Also returning is the Southern fascination with privatizing education. The private school voucher movement started in the South as a way to avoid desegregation, but it died in a 1964 case, *Griffin v. Prince Edward County*, that declared Virginia's attempt to subvert desegregation through vouchers unconstitutional. The South's ambivalence toward the public education project itself—a long hangover from Jim Crow—remained. Today, Southern states still fail to properly fund their public schools. A 2022 study that normalized funding levels across all states (to account for differing costs) showed that all but one former Confederate state was funding public education below the national average. Most were far below the average—in one case (North Carolina) by $4,655 per pupil.[5]

Rather than address those deficits, the South is recommitting to vouchers, particularly since the 2020 presidential election. Until the closing months of Donald Trump's presidency, his administration's voucher agenda had gone nowhere fast. Then the intersection of COVID frustrations, critical race theory allegations, and wokeness paranoia reset the playing field. Public schools—or government schools, as some derisively called them—went from the institutions the nation desperately needed to the enemy that had refused to reopen and was indoctrinating children, persecuting people of faith, and denying freedom to disadvantaged students.

These attacks on public education, however, were less about improving education policy than about symbolic outrage. Attacking public schools is a way to signal displeasure with the willingness in national civic culture to redeem America from its cultural flaws. Pete Hegseth, a Fox News commentator with no background in education, captured the fervor with his bestselling 2022 book *Battle for the American Mind: Uprooting a Century of Miseducation*. He and his co-author, David Goodwin, offer "a revolutionary road map to saving our children from leftist indoctrination" that threatens "the very survival of the American Republic." Public education, according to the authors, was "an invention of Progressives," better thought of as "a plot" that now teaches students to hate America. They describe the history of American education as akin to "the Bolshevik Revolution as told by Lenin."[6]

Their cultural outrage is mixed with a large measure of military metaphors. Hegseth brought Goodwin to the project because his "experience in military counterinsurgency" allows him to "see what needs to be done." They write that "Marxist" educators have seized "fortified high ground" and conservatives must fight back. Neither "nerf guns," nor traditional methods of reform, will "work" in a war in which they find themselves "outnumbered, and outgunned." Concluding that the "only option is insurgency," they lay out three phases. The first involves a "campaign to discredit the public school system" while simultaneously building their own "alternate" system of private schools. Phase two is a political mobilization for universal private school tax credits that "drive a stake through the heart of government schools" and trigger a "mass exodus." The final phase replaces the current system with Christian education.[7]

Though most politicians avoid this type of militaristic language, an agenda to end the public school system as we know it is well under way. Private school vouchers have become a way for politicians to facilitate the most disaffected persons' divorce from the public system. As the former lobbyist for charters and vouchers—now whistleblower—Charles Siler says, the goal is to "dismantle public schools" and "there's virtually no other initiative in the education space that's a bigger priority for the right today than creating and expanding unaccountable, unrestricted, universal voucher programs."[8]

This anti-public-education thinking has made it all the way to the highest levels of government. After spending decades funding "privatization efforts across the country," often millions in a single election cycle alone, Betsy DeVos ascended to the office of U.S. secretary of education in 2017 with the goal of continuing her "life's work." Though initially skeptical of her policies, Congress is now following her lead. After winning the majority in the House of Representatives in 2022, the new Republican leadership announced that the Committee on Education and the Workforce, which for half a century had worked to bolster public education, would henceforth move in a different direction. Its first hearing, on April 18, 2023, was on school choice.[9]

The majority invited three witnesses to testify at the hearing. Their message was emphatic. They decried the public school "monopoly," questioned the motives of public education itself, and advocated public financing of private schools instead. One of the hearing's most dramatic moments came when a minority member, Congressman Jamal Bowman, asked each of the witnesses whether they supported the U.S. Department of Education. The first two said they would abolish it. The third had worked at the department earlier in her career but refused to answer the question. In full disclosure, I was the fourth witness (on invitation from the minority) and offered my unqualified support for the department as the nation's primary enforcement mechanism of anti-discrimination in education.[10]

The chair of the committee, Virginia Foxx, has been blunt about her agenda, saying her "top issue is education freedom. Education freedom is just crucial to our country. We've had a government-run monopoly on education for a long time, but it's outdated. It has failed students. And students deserve the opportunity to learn in the environment that works best for them. ... We don't want to see students ... be controlled by the government." Her second "high-level priority" is "protecting parental rights."[11]

As rhetoric, educational freedom sounds good. As a practical matter, it falls well short of freedom for all. It does not even attempt to ensure that private education works for children. At best, it is agnostic toward the school environments students enter. At worst, it uses public funds to facilitate patterns and values that America has spent the last half century trying to tame. Of course, some private schools offer an excellent education. But those schools aren't particularly interested in expanding to serve large numbers of new students, much less disadvantaged students who would arrive with additional needs. And while some private schools attract students for good reasons, the education freedom movement speaks most directly to families who want to leave public schools for the wrong reasons—such as rage over values like anti-discrimination, inclusiveness, free thinking, and equal playing fields.

Some state legislators are now giving public money to private schools with no strings attached. Fewer than half of the states operating private school tuition programs prohibit race discrimination in admissions. Fewer than one in four prohibit disability discrimination or sex discrimination. An even smaller percentage prohibits sexual-orientation discrimination. On top of that, states afford religious schools an affirmative tool to cull students—the right to deny enrollment to students based on their beliefs. LGBTQ students and families, in particular, have borne the brunt of this religious exception.[12]

The problems do not stop at enrollment. Some of the private schools participating in Florida's tuition program—the largest in the nation—are teaching students that dinosaurs and humans lived together, that God intervened to prevent Catholics from dominating North America, that slavery benefited its victims by exposing them to Jesus Christ, and that Black and white Southerners lived in harmony. Investigative reporting has revealed disturbing curricula in many private schools in other states too. Schools are trafficking in conspiracies, white nationalism, anti-science, and bigotry. One proposed school in South Carolina, aiming to provide a "pro-American education" that would shield students from "LGBTQ, CRT, or 'woke' teachings," would go so far as to have its "students wear a military-inspired uniform" and "encourage parents, grandparents, and mentors to participate by wearing the uniform" too.[13]

Public schools, to be sure, are far from perfect. They have never fully met the needs of all students and all communities. But those shortcomings are clearly understood as problems to fix. They are seen as bugs, not features, of public education, which has operated for two centuries on the premise that public schools are the place where children—regardless of status—share a common experience, come to appreciate the public good, and prepare for equal citizenship. The purpose of public education has always been to sustain a republican form of government. And public schools are the only place in society premised on bridging the gaps that normally divide us—race, wealth, religion, disability, sex, culture, and more.

The founders of the American public education system believed that rather than inhibiting liberty, a common public education is essential to it. The Arkansas Constitution of 1874 declared that public education is one of the surest "safeguards of liberty, and the bulwark of a free and good government." South Carolina's 1868 constitutional delegation, standing in the ashes of the worst kind of oppression, similarly recognized that public education is "the surest guarantee of . . . republican liberty." As the Indiana Constitution had explained half a century earlier, in 1816, public education could not be left to chance or the market: "Knowledge and learning, generally diffused through a community . . . [are] essential to the preservation of a free government."[14]

Policy agendas that encourage people who rage against public schools to exit them are coded calls for disunion. That is not to say that all politicians authorizing vouchers consciously understand their actions in such terms. But the policies they advocate would undermine a foundational pillar of democracy that has long worked to bring and hold the Union together. The loudest voices in their movement are using language that promotes disunion and are funding people and institutions with anti-democratic motives, spreading anti-democratic ideas. At a moment when our nation desperately needs our schools to serve their animating function and heal our division, states are funding programs that seem entirely uninterested in that goal.

As if disunion were not enough, legislatures are littering their laws with a new form of orthodoxy. New bills would require schools to post the Ten Commandments in every classroom, allow schools to hire chaplains instead of counselors, give parents the effective right to censor the instruction that teachers offer, and ban certain discussions of race and gender. These restrictions cross constitutional lines while also narrowing the scope of knowledge available to students. Many of the proposals coming from politicians are so patently unconstitutional that they don't warrant a response, but one is worth mentioning for its audacity.[15]

In Virginia's 2023 state senate primary, one candidate campaigned on abolishing the public education system and giving every parent $10,000 to secure education on their own. To achieve that end, he proposed to amend the state constitution to remove its education mandate. This would violate the express terms of Virginia's readmission to the Union in 1870—terms necessary to ensure a republican form of government in the state. Though the candidate was initially unaware of the problem, he was not dismayed when he learned of it, believing the audacity of his position would increase his election chances. And it is not just prospective candidates who treat outrage as sport.[16]

In 2023, Rick Scott, a U.S. senator from Florida and a former governor of the state, issued a statement "warning socialists and communists not to travel to Florida. They are not welcome in the Sunshine State." He tried to inject a measure of levity, saying their attempts to spread their message "will be met with laughter and mockery," but he also warned that anyone who believes in "big government" should "think twice" about coming to the state. For a U.S. senator to suggest that his state is for some people but not others is not far removed from the talk of disunion that surfaced in the Negro Seamen Act, the postal raid, and the Virginia abolition debates.[17]

Repeated over decades, talk of disunion has a corrosive effect. Even if more subtle, disunion-like politics in the very field upon which we have built freedom and democracy is corrosive too. The current movements against public schooling, if they fester long enough, may undo what has brought democracy together. Public education has long been described as the fourth branch of government—the one on which the others lean. What does the intentional erosion of confidence in public education portend for the other branches? What would its failure do to American democracy?

The upshot is not that the United States is headed for armed conflict or cataclysmic democratic failure. Too much has changed since the Civil

War, and since the Civil Rights Movement. As polarized as the current moment is, the South is more diverse on many more metrics now than it was even twenty years ago. This diversity makes unifying the region—or any other region—against democracy a steep hill to climb. Instead of driving away moderates or progressives, the South has been attracting outsiders in droves. Look no further than the 2008 and 2012 presidential results in North Carolina and Virginia, or the 2020 results in Georgia, to appreciate the effect.

These shifts place a limit on how far disunion politics can go. The values that disunionists oppose are not those of distant Northerners. They are the values of next-door neighbors—neighbors who are not inclined to leave. And the more radical the reactionary talk becomes, the more it alienates neighbors who simply want peace, order, and decent public schools. The likelihood that the nation staves off disunion, however, does not mean the future will lack chaos.

Our hopes of avoiding that chaos have long rested on our ability to leverage wisdom in the face of complexity, to wrestle justice from conflict. The story of Black literacy, from slavery until today, cannot fairly be reduced to a singular narrative. Though this book is surely guilty of telling too little too simply, that was never its aim. The instinct toward simplicity is at least in some part to blame for today's polarization. Each competing faction claims that the others have left something crucial out of the national narrative. Worse, some factions insist that there is but one story to tell. To concede anything to the other side is a sign of weakness rather than virtue.

This book, like its subject, asks us to hold several oppositions in mind at once: white repression of literacy and the resistance to that repression in the antebellum period; the conflict between slaveholders and abolitionists, as well as the competing ideologies within each of their camps; redemptive reconstruction and vocal, violent white resistance, which ultimately triumphed in the system of racial hierarchy known as Jim Crow; school desegregation and the changing politics that prevented its full realization; and, in our current moment, a push for a more substantive form of equality and what too often looks like a movement to revive old divisions. The closer one gets to each of these periods, the more complex these tensions appear and the more difficult it is to define the main narrative. Is it one bending toward justice or pulling the nation backward?

One could see the current backlash as a recurrence of the old battle over literacy and free thought. Yet another vision suggests that after persisting for two centuries, the old ways are lashing out because they are on their last gasps. Although this book spends most of its time on repression that refused to submit even after the Civil War, its story is one of justice prevailing. Justice was never the overwhelming force, but with each encounter it shrank the forces of evil and continually reached for more. By slow steps, each era marshalled a new majority—rarely an overwhelming consensus, but enough to tip the scales slightly more toward justice.

The moral stance of Black literacy drew adherents under the most difficult circumstances—white and Black people willing to break the law to keep literacy alive during the antebellum period; a significant number of slave owners speaking for some form of abolition in Virginia and teaching a more just form of Christianity in South Carolina; thousands of volunteers flocking to the South to eradicate the vestiges of slavery through education when the War's outcome was still in doubt; teachers making the South their permanent home and facing life-threatening violence when Union forces retreated. There is no Civil War, no Reconstruction, no literacy or education movement, and no Civil Rights Movement without a moral movement just as tenacious as the forces of oppression.

In his first inaugural address, given just five weeks before the opening shots of the Civil War, Abraham Lincoln spoke of the world as he hoped it would be: "We are not enemies, but friends. We must not be enemies. Though passion may have strained it must not break our bonds of affection." The speech—overoptimistic in the moment—was prescient of the future Lincoln would not live to see: "The mystic chords of memory, stretching from every battlefield and patriot grave to every living heart and hearthstone all over this broad land, will yet swell the chorus of the Union, when again touched, as surely they will be, by the better angels of our nature." Those better angels have visited us too often to be mere strangers.[18]

But to reduce the story of literacy and the fight to control information to a moral tale about the Union is to do it a disservice. Though it is a functional skill, literacy is much more than that. Enslaved and freed people's literacy journeys are stories of becoming—becoming whatever it was they hoped and dreamed to be and had the capacity to be. They are stories of people taking full ownership of their personal destiny.

These stories give the lie to modern notions of education as merely a market commodity responding to individual preferences. Learning that prepared Black people for work but not personal autonomy would have only been half an education. And learning that satisfied individual desires without preparing Black children for the new social world they were entering would not have been education for freedom or citizenship. It is precisely the goal of preparing people for civic life and freedom that makes public education a common public good rather than a private good.

That's why government has played such an enormous role. It has been a guarantor of educational opportunity, not a market player. Before the Civil War, the free market of education had failed to deliver opportunity to huge groups of children, Black and white, rural and urban, Northern and Southern. Private actors lacked the capacity or desire to do more. When government decided to act in the aftermath of the War, it was to lift a race of people out of slavery, not deliver fungible commodities. Government proved that only public education could expand schooling from individual institutions into a system that would eventually reach everyone, or nearly so. Only government could mandate and fund education for every student. And in that unique role, it was government that insisted that schools overcome society's basest instincts.

Also embedded in these literacy stories is the awesome power of the written word—a power seen at every turn. For Black people, the written word was a means to fight back, resist, subvert, and escape their conditions. They shared and circulated crucial information, reinterpreted religious and political texts, stayed abreast of war and government, and wrote manifestos. Sometimes the object was to plot rebellion—other times, to stay one step ahead of slaveholders or just survive with no clear end in sight. For the abolitionist, the written word was the means to lift up an issue, provoke a fight, prod a government, and ultimately galvanize like-minded communities across space and time.

For the antebellum South, too, the written word was a tool in the struggle for political and cultural power. Fearing the power of the Northern word, the South, though far from successful, tried to replace it with its own. The power of words, however, was always bounded by literacy itself, which left the South in a double bind. Southern elites restricted the literacy of Black people for fear of what they might do with it. They restricted public education for fear of what white people might demand. But those restrictions also limited the South's capacity to generate its own ideas and institutions to counter the North. Because words had less power in the South, the South had less power in the nation.

Today, the word is both less powerful than it could be and more dangerous than it should be. It is less powerful because literacy and education gaps still plague students of color and white students in rural communities, limiting their prospects of full citizenship and economic self-sufficiency. Recent litigation involving the Detroit public school system was a sad reminder. Students alleged before the federal district court and then the U.S. Court of Appeals that they had been deprived "of a basic minimum education, meaning one that provides a chance at foundational literacy." They suffered from "missing or unqualified teachers, physically dangerous facilities, and inadequate books and materials." In addition to providing voluminous data, the students told shocking stories, like of "an eighth grade student ... put in charge of teaching seventh and eighth grade math classes for a month because no math teacher was available."[19]

In its opinion, the Sixth Circuit Court of Appeals connected these students' literacy story to slavery. Americans, the court wrote, are apt to "take for granted that state-sponsored education will be provided for their children as of right." But access to basic literacy and education has long been a fight because of the "substantial relationship between access to education and access to economic and political power.... Slaveholders and segregationists used the deprivation of education as a weapon, preventing African Americans from obtaining the political power needed to achieve liberty and equality." Although the facts have changed dramatically since the era of slavery, students in Detroit still face "serious injustices, ones that conflict with our core values as a nation."[20]

Detroit students are not alone. According to the National Assessment of Education Progress, reading proficiency rates for Black students are nearly 60 percent lower than for white students. And at this late date in history, a startling number of children of all races do not have access to a basic literacy resource: library books. Thirteen million students attend schools where there are less than ten library books available per student. Two and a half million students attend schools that have no library at all. Even those who have a library can't find a trained adult to guide and inspire them to pick out a book. Roughly one in three students attend a school that lacks a librarian.[21]

On the banks of the Mississippi River, not far from where that ninety-year-old freedman stood to meet that white missionary teacher in 1863, to tell her that he had been waiting for her to come teach his people for twenty years, fifteen hundred students, half of whom are poor and

90 percent of whom are students of color, are still waiting for a library in their Coahoma County School District.[22]

These critical shortcomings have gone all but unnoticed in the dozens of states banning books. And in Congress, a bill that would begin to address the problem has languished with just two cosponsors since 2021. In short, the power of the word has yet to be fully realized not only for Detroit's students but across America.[23]

At the same time, an undereducated citizenry is making the power of words more dangerous than it should be. In an age where information travels at the speed of light and the people receiving it too often lack the means to sort fact from fiction, opinion from news, or science from fantasy, the nation is awash in questionable information that divides rather than enlightens. Citizens struggle to hold government accountable to their interests, while algorithms and political opportunists play a dangerously outsized role in setting the nation's course.

Detailed solutions for our public schools and democratic structures are beyond the scope of this book, but less information, less public education, less conversation across lines of division, and more calls for silence are not the path forward. The South pursued that course—a course of totalitarianism—to maintain its way of life. Through its literature bans, postal raid, censorship, and silencing of the public commons, the South made life inhospitable to anyone who saw things differently. Black people had long fled Southern totalitarianism and slavery, but whites who refused to fully adopt Southern ideology eventually fled too—or were run out. Many who remained either converted or learned to live double lives. Eventually, the South spoke with but one voice and lost the capacity to deliberate. It preached to itself and moved beyond the reach of others.

The Southern totalitarianism, ironically, strengthened its opposition. Northern abolitionists initially faced violence and opposition from their own neighbors, including high-ranking public officials. But the more the South pressed the North to adhere to its totalitarian strictures, the more sympathy it created for the abolitionists. Regardless of the merits of abolition, most Northern leaders were unwilling to violate free speech rights. Southern radicalization helped transform abolitionists from rabble-rousers to victims.

Had Southerners just burned Northern pamphlets in their fireplaces when they received them rather than raiding the post office, lighting bonfires, and swearing death to men like Tappan and Garrison, abolitionists might have stopped wasting postage and printing costs. Without Southern aggression, abolitionist papers certainly would have been thinner. *The Liberator* did not just rehash its ideological sermon week after week. It reported on the fight for liberation, and its lifeblood was the continuing stream of Southern acts of aggression. The more the South lashed out, the stronger the opposition grew, eventually placing people in elected positions of power and convincing others of their cause.

Today, the insistence of many in the South's political class on drawing sharp ideological lines, adhering to irrationally polarizing politics, and shaping historical narratives to fit a desired current political outcome should serve as a warning. Moreover, both sides of the current political debate are guilty of refusing to see the other's point of view, refusing to concede the complexity of issues, the complexity of history, and the impassible gulf between ideas and reality. Though their positions are not morally equivalent, both sides succumb to the temptation to control historical narratives and mistake historical interpretations for facts. As camps align around their narratives, nuance fades, free thinking shrinks within each camp, and the ability to concede anything to the competing point of view vanishes amid fear of losing ground.

This is the lesson I hope we might take with us about disunion—that we have to think harder, listen harder, and try harder to see the nuances. We must afford ourselves, our friends, and our estranged neighbors the grace to explore ideas and solutions free from the burden of ideological conformity. It is these skills that we must value in our leaders and instill in our children. The story of Black literacy is full of rewarding, though often uncomfortable, lessons. To avoid a repetition of the past, we must resist the urge to shrink the bounds of the human mind and the categories we use to think of one another. For good or bad, this is the work of the public education project. Prior eras have left much for us to finish.

Notes

Introduction

1. John R. Rachal, "Gideonites and Freedmen: Adult Literacy Education at Port Royal, 1862–1865," *Journal of Negro Education* 55, no. 4 (Autumn 1986): 456; Abraham Lincoln, "The Gettysburg Address, November 19, 1863," *Abraham Lincoln Online*, accessed December 6, 2023, https://www.abrahamlincolnonline.org/lincoln/speeches/gettysburg.htm.
2. Rachal, "Gideonites and Freedmen," 456.
3. Abraham Lincoln, "Letter to Horace Greeley, Friday, August 22, 1862," *Abraham Lincoln Online*, accessed December 6, 2023, https://www.abrahamlincolnonline.org/lincoln/speeches/greeley.htm.
4. Edward L. Pierce, "The Contrabands at Fortress Monroe," *Atlantic Monthly*, November 1861, https://www.theatlantic.com/magazine/archive/1861/11/the-contrabands-at-fortress-monroe/628956/.
5. For a discussion of a later trip from New York to Beaufort via Fort Monroe, see Elizabeth Hyde Botume, *First Days Amongst the Contrabands* (Boston: Lee and Shepard, 1893), 26, https://library.missouri.edu/confederate/items/show/1708.
6. Edward L. Pierce, "The Freedmen at Port Royal," *Atlantic Monthly*, September 1863, https://cdn.theatlantic.com/media/archives/1863/09/12-71/132121222.pdf.
7. William C. Gannett and E. E. Hale, "Education of the Freedmen," *North American Review* 101, no. 209 (October 1865): 533.
8. Botume, *First Days*, 6, 7; "Letter from W.C. Gannett, April 28, 1865," *Freedmen's Journal* 1 (1865): 91.
9. Botume, *First Days*, 63.
10. Ibid., 17, 57.
11. Edward A. Pollard, *The Lost Cause: A New Southern History of the War of the Confederates*, 2nd ed. (New York: E. B. Treat, 1867), ii, 750, 752, https://tile.loc.gov/storage-services/public/gdcmassbookdig/lostcausenewsout03poll/lostcausenewsout03poll.pdf.

12. Brown v. Board of Education of Topeka, 347 U.S. 483 (1954).
13. Bettina L. Love, *We Want to Do More Than Survive: Abolitionist Teaching and the Pursuit of Educational Freedom* (Boston: Beacon Press, 2019).
14. Gareth Davies, "Richard Nixon and the Desegregation of Southern Schools," *Journal of Policy History* 19, no. 4 (2007): 367, 369, https://doi.org/10.1353/jph.2008.0003.
15. Keyes v. School District No. 1, Denver, 413 U.S. 189 (1973); Milliken v. Bradley, 418 U.S. 717 (1974); Freeman v. Pitts, 503 U.S. 467 (1992); Gary Oldfield and Chunmei Lee, "*Brown* at 50: King's Dream or *Plessy*'s Nightmare?," Civil Rights Project, January 2004, https://civilrightsproject.ucla.edu/research/k-12-education/integration-and-diversity/brown-at-50-king2019s-dream-or-plessy2019s-nightmare/orfield-brown-50-2004.pdf.
16. Parents Involved in Community Schools v. Seattle School District, 551 U.S. 701 (2007); Students for Fair Admissions v. Harvard, No. 20–1199 (2023), https://www.supremecourt.gov/opinions/22pdf/20-1199_hgdj.pdf; "Remarks by President Trump at the White House Conference on American History," National Archives Museum, September 17, 2020, https://trumpwhitehouse.archives.gov/briefings-statements/remarks-president-trump-white-house-conference-american-history/.
17. "ALA Statement on Book Censorship," American Library Association (ALA), November 29, 2021, https://www.ala.org/advocacy/statement-regarding-censorship; Arika Herron, "Indiana HB 1134 Approved by House, Would Limit What's Taught in Classrooms," *Indy Star*, updated February 1, 2022, https://www.indystar.com/story/news/education/2022/01/26/hb-1134-indiana-critical-race-theory-schools-crt-bill/9225989002/; Bekah McNeel, "While Campaigning on 'Parental Control,' Top State Officials Champion School Vouchers," *Texas Monthly*, September 8, 2022, https://www.texasmonthly.com/news-politics/school-vouchers-texas-parental-control-abbott/; "The War on DEI," *Insight into Diversity*, accessed December 6, 2023, https://www.insightintodiversity.com/the-war-on-dei/; "Governor Ron DeSantis Signs Legislation to Protect Floridians from Discrimination and Woke Indoctrination," on Ron DeSantis's website, April 22, 2022, https://www.flgov.com/2022/04/22/governor-ron-desantis-signs-legislation-to-protect-floridians-from-discrimination-and-woke-indoctrination/#:~:text=The%20bill%20authorizes%20discussion%20of,the%20principles%20of%20individual%20of%20freedom; Christopher F. Rufo, "Laying Siege to the Institutions," *Imprimis* 51, no. 4/5 (April/May 2022), https://imprimis.hillsdale.edu/laying-siege-to-the-institutions/.
18. "CRT Forward Tracking Project," CRT Forward, accessed December 6, 2023, https://crtforward.law.ucla.edu/map/; Brendan Clarey, "School Choice Bills Have Swept the Nation. Where Does Your State Stand on the Issue?," *ChalkboardNews*, updated August 28, 2023, https://www.chalkboardnews.com/issues/school-choice/article_95aeb6bb-356a-51e5-86c8-dbdb5ae9ce34.html#Signup; Meghan Collins Sullivan, "ALA: Number of

Unique Book Titles Challenged Jumped Nearly 40% in 2022," NPR, April 24, 2023, https://www.npr.org/2023/04/24/1171570138/number-of-books-banned-or-challenged-up-in-2022-ala#:~:text=Banned%20and%20 Challenged%3A%20Restricting%20access,titles%20were%20banned%20 or%20challenged.

19. Gabriella Borter, Joseph Ax, and Joseph Tanfani, "School Boards Get Death Threats Amid Rage Over Race, Gender, Mask Policies," *Reuters Investigates—School Under Siege*, February 15, 2022, https://www.reuters.com/investigates/special-report/usa-education-threats/#:~:text=School%20 board%20members%20across%20the,teaching%20of%20America's%20 racial%20history; Hannah Natanson, "A White Teacher Taught White Students About White Privilege. It Cost Him His Job," *Washington Post*, December 6, 2021, https://www.washingtonpost.com/education/2021/12/06/tennessee-teacher-fired-critical-race-theory/.

20. "Who We Are," Moms for Liberty, accessed December 6, 2023, https://www.momsforliberty.org/about/; "The Year in Hate and Extremism 2022," SPLC (Southern Poverty Law Center), accessed December 6, 2023, https://www.splcenter.org/year-hate-extremism-2022; Linda Jacobson, "Chiefs Out in Half of Districts Where Moms for Liberty Flipped Boards Last Year," Yahoo!News, October 5, 2023; Maddy Quon Mquon, "New Berkeley County School Board Fires Superintendent, Bans Critical Race Theory in First Meeting," *Post and Courier*, November 16, 2022, https://www.postandcourier.com/news/new-berkeley-county-school-board-fires-superintendent-bans-critical-race-theory-in-first-meeting/article_e10a688c-64f3-11ed-895b-8321c1eaod51.html.

21. Pete Hegseth with David Goodwin, *Battle for the American Mind: Uprooting a Century of Miseducation* (New York: HarperCollins, 2022), 19, 20, 225; "President Trump's Plan to Save American Education and Give Power Back to Parents," Trump 2024 campaign website, June 30, 2023, https://www.donaldjtrump.com/news/e8800793-143f-4660-ac9d-5c19895bf6c2.

22. Itzel Luna, "New Slavery Curriculum in Florida Is Latest in Century of 'Undermining History,'" *USA Today*, updated July 27, 2023, https://www.usatoday.com/story/news/nation/2023/07/27/historian-warns-against-floridas-slavery-curriculum/70463676007/.

Chapter One. The Spark

1. Population data is notoriously imprecise during the colonial period, as formal and reliable data is not available until the U.S. Census begins in 1790. Compare Walter Edgar, *South Carolina: A History* (Columbia: University of South Carolina Press, 1998), 78, with *1790 Census: Return of the Whole Number of Persons Within the Several Districts of the United States* (Philadelphia: J. Phillips, 1793); Powhatan's Mantle: Indians in the Colonial Southeast, Charleston Museum.

2. "Two Views of the Stono Slave Rebellion, South Carolina, 1739," National Humanities Center Resource Toolbox, accessed November 14, 2023, http://nationalhumanitiescenter.org/pds/becomingamer/peoples/text4/stonorebellion.pdf (reprinting an interview from WPA Federal Writers' Project).
3. The Negro Act of 1740 was formally titled "An Act for the Better Ordering and Governing of Negroes and Other Slaves in this Province"; Edgar, *South Carolina*, 77 (both Blacks and whites "disregarded [the law] ... almost immediately").
4. Edgar, *South Carolina*, 78.
5. John Oliver Killens, *The Trial Record of Denmark Vesey* (Boston: Beacon Press, 1970), 40.
6. James Hamilton Jr., "An Account of the Late Intended Insurrection Among a Portion of the Blacks of the City of Charleston, South Carolina, Biography of Denmark Vesey 1822," in *The Denmark Vesey Affair: A Documentary History*, ed. Douglas R. Egerton and Robert L. Paquette (Gainesville: University Press of Florida, 2017), 2; Thomas Wentworth Higginson, "The Story of Denmark Vesey, *The Atlantic*, June 1861, accessed November 15, 2003, https://www.theatlantic.com/magazine/archive/1861/06/denmark-vesey/396239/; Douglas R. Egerton, *He Shall Go Out Free: The Lives of Denmark Vesey* (Lanham, Md.: Rowman and Littlefield, 1999), 20.
7. Egerton and Paquette, *Denmark Vesey Affair*, 36 n.1; Robert L. Paquette, "Revisiting Denmark Vesey's Church," in *Fugitive Movements: Commemorating the Denmark Vesey Affair and Black Radical Antislavery in the Atlantic World*, ed. James O'Neil Spady (Columbia: University of South Carolina Press, 2022), 181. Douglas Egerton posits that Denmark Vesey developed his reading and writing doing clerical work for Joseph Vesey's business. Egerton, *He Shall Go Out Free*, 33. Exactly how Denmark Vesey earned the money is unknown. Based on prevailing practices and anecdotal evidence regarding others, it is reasonable to infer that Joseph Vesey permitted him to work on the side for money. Ibid., 61–74.
8. Joseph Vesey's wife, Mary Clodner, was, however, listed as Denmark Vesey's actual owner at the time. Ibid., 72.
9. Lionel H. Kennedy and Thomas Parker, "Narrative of the Conspiracy and Intended Insurrection, October 1822," in Egerton and Paquette, *Denmark Vesey Affair*, 75 (lamenting the number of pamphlets brought into Charleston—a "consequence of the unrestricted intercourse allowed to persons of color between different states").
10. "Our History," Charleston Library Society, accessed November 14, 2023, https://charlestonlibrarysociety.org/our-history/; Edward A. Pearson, ed., *Designs Against Charleston: The Trial Record of the Denmark Vesey Slave Conspiracy of 1822* (Chapel Hill: University of North Carolina Press, 1999), 92.
11. William Paul, "Testimony, June 19, 1822," in Pearson, *Designs Against Charleston*, 168; "Witness No. 7, June 19, 1822," in Killens, *Trial Record of Denmark Vesey*, 47.

12. Pearson, *Designs Against Charleston*, 121 ("several rebels alluded to Vesey's library"); see also "Copy of Letter from the Governor of the State of South Carolina," *Niles Register*, September 7, 1822, in Pearson, *Designs Against Charleston*, 346 (indicating there were "abundant materials" that affected their machinations); Kennedy and Parker, "Narrative," 78–79 (Denmark had a "variety of papers and books relating to this transaction, which he burnt when the discovery of the intended attempt was made"); Egerton and Paquette, *Denmark Vesey Affair*, 180 (Denmark had "the resources to build a small library of his own"). No specifics exist as to the precise texts Vesey read. The statement regarding his reading habits is an inference based on knowledge he acquired and conversations he had about books he was purportedly reading.

    Though no direct reference to New Orleans exists, Vesey seems to have been aware of the New Orleans slave revolt of 1811 as well, which at the time was a frontier city—a place from which news did not easily travel. Two other witnesses specifically reference it. Egerton and Paquette, *Denmark Vesey Affair*, 286, 298 (Hammet Bacchus Confession and William Paul testimony).

13. Pearson, *Designs Against Charleston*, 103.

14. Egerton, *He Shall Go Out Free*, 50, 78; Pearson, *Designs Against Charleston*, 75, 98–99; see sections 7–9 of Act No. 1745, "An Act respecting Slaves, Free Negroes, Mulattoes and Mestizoes; for enforcing the more punctual performance of patroll [sic] duty; and to impose certain restrictions on the emancipation of slaves," ratified on December 20, 1800, in *The Statutes at Large of South Carolina*, ed. David J. McCord, vol. 7 (Columbia, S.C.: A. S. Johnston, 1840), 440–43.

15. Pearson, *Designs Against Charleston*, Appendix, 286–87; "Charleston City Ordinance, June 11, 1818," in Egerton and Paquette, *Denmark Vesey Affair*, 27; Pearson, *Designs Against Charleston*, Appendix, 286–87; "Grand Jury Presentment, November 1819," in Egerton and Paquette, *Denmark Vesey Affair*, 11.

16. Haitian Const. of 1801, Title II, arts. 3, 4, 5; Haitian Const. of 1805, art. 1; ibid., art. 12.

17. Bernard E. Powers, "Denmark Vesey, South Carolina, and Haiti: Borne, Bound, and Battered by a Common Wind," in Spady, *Fugitive Movements*, 21, 22; "*City Gazette and Daily Advertiser*, October 9, 1793," in Egerton and Paquette, *Denmark Vesey Affair*, 6; Pearson, *Designs Against Charleston*, 90; Egerton and Paquette, *Denmark Vesey Affair*, 75–76.

18. Powers, "Denmark Vesey, South Carolina, and Haiti," 27; Egerton, *He Shall Go Out Free*, 43.

19. "Communication from the Secretary General of the Haytian Republic, *New York Commercial Advertiser*, October 10, 1818," in Egerton and Paquette, *Denmark Vesey Affair*, 13; Letter from Joseph Balthazar Inginac to James Tredwell, November 21, 1817; Pearson, *Designs Against Charleston*, 289; Leonora Sansay, *Secret History; or, The Horrors of St. Domingo and Laura*, ed.

Michael Dexter (Peterborough, Ontario: Broadview Press, 2007), 50. Boyer apparently did not formalize this offer in writing, however, until after Vesey's death. In 1823, Boyer wrote he would give them land if they came. Egerton and Paquette, *Denmark Vesey Affair*, 14; "City Gazette and Commercial Daily Advertiser, February 14, 1822," in Egerton and Paquette, *Denmark Vesey Affair*, 71.

20. "Jack, Confession," in Egerton and Paquette, *Denmark Vesey Affair*, 214; Pearson, *Designs Against Charleston*, 85, 203, 220.
21. "Monday Gell, Testimony in Trial of Saby Gaillard, July 16, 1822," in Egerton and Paquette, *Denmark Vesey Affair*, 220.
22. Julius S. Scott, *The Common Wind: Afro-American Currents in the Age of the Haitian Revolution* (London: Verso Books, 2020); Egerton, *He Shall Go Out Free*, 110; Egerton and Paquette, *Denmark Vesey Affair*, 18.
23. "Southern Patriot, and Commercial Advertiser, June 8, 1818," in Egerton and Paquette, *Denmark Vesey Affair*, 26; Spady, *Fugitive Movements*, 193; Egerton and Paquette, *Denmark Vesey Affair*, 26; Egerton, *He Shall Go Out Free*, 122; "Southern Patriot, and Commercial Advertiser, June 10, 1818," in Egerton and Paquette, *Denmark Vesey Affair*, 26.
24. "Confession of Rolla Bennett, Official Report," in Egerton and Paquette, *Denmark Vesey Affair*, 182; "Benjamin Ford Testimony, June 26, 1822," in Pearson, *Designs Against Charleston*, 191; "Smart Anderson Confession, July 16, 1822," in Pearson, *Designs Against Charleston*, 217.
25. "Petition, To the Honorable the Speaker, and Members of the House of Representatives of the Said State, 1820," in Egerton and Paquette, *Denmark Vesey Affair*, 32; "Letter to the House of Representatives, October 16, 1820," in Pearson, *Designs Against Charleston*, 319; Paquette, "Revisiting Denmark Vesey's Church," 194.
26. Ephesians 6:5; Colossians 3:22; 1 Peter 2:18.
27. Matthew 5:38–40; Mark 12:17.
28. Kennedy and Parker, "Narrative," 74.
29. "Examination of Rolla Bennett, June 25, 1822," in Egerton and Paquette, *Denmark Vesey Affair*, 295; Kennedy and Parker, "Narrative," 75.
30. Exodus 21:16; Paquette, "Revisiting Denmark Vesey's Church," 187; see also "Fourth Version of Bacchus Hammet's Confession, Senate Transcript," in Egerton and Paquette, *Denmark Vesey Affair*, 323 (indicating Vesey directed them to question white ministers as to why they did not teach certain parts of the Bible).
31. "Benjamin Ford Examination, June 26, 1822," in Egerton and Paquette, *Denmark Vesey Affair*, 296.
32. "Bacchus Hammet Confession, July 12," in Pearson, *Designs Against Charleston*, 329.
33. Ibid.
34. "Witness No. 1, Official Report, June 19, 1822," in Egerton and Paquette, *Denmark Vesey Affair*, 164.

35. William G. Thomas III, *A Question of Freedom: The Families Who Challenged Slavery from the Nation's Founding to the Civil War* (New Haven, Conn.: Yale University Press, 2020), 35; The Honourable Rufus King, *The Substance of Two Speeches, Delivered in the Senate of the United States, on the Subject of the Missouri Bill* (Philadelphia: Clark and Raser, 1819), accessed November 15, 2023, https://www.loc.gov/resource/gdcmassbookdig.substanceoftwospooking/?sp=6&st=pdf&r=-0.345%2C0%2C1.691%2C1.691%2C0&pdfPage=6.
36. King, *Substance of Two Speeches*.
37. Ibid.
38. Paquette, "Revisiting Denmark Vesey's Church," 183; Egerton and Paquette, *Denmark Vesey Affair*, 178, 183; Kennedy and Parker, "Narrative," 75; Paquette, "Revisiting Denmark Vesey's Church," 189.
39. Pearson, *Designs Against Charleston*, 163; "*Liberator*, August 25, 1837," in Egerton and Paquette, *Denmark Vesey Affair*, 726 (recounting a conversation with Rolla Bennett, one of the persons involved in the planned revolt).
40. "*Liberator*, August 25, 1837," 726; "Petition, October 1820," in Egerton and Paquette, *Denmark Vesey Affair*, 56.
41. Robert Olwell, *Masters, Slaves, and Subjects: The Culture of Power in the South Carolina Low Country* (Ithaca, N.Y.: Cornell University Press, 1998), 130; Jean Comaroff, *Body of Power, Spirit of Resistance: The Culture and History of a South African People* (Chicago: University of Chicago Press, 1985), 143; Benedict Anderson, *Imagined Communities: Reflections on the Origin and Spread of Nationalism* (London: Verso Books, 1991), 7, 26, 35; Brian V. Street, *Social Literacies: Critical Approaches to Literacy in Development, Ethnography and Education* (Abingdon, U.K.: Routledge, 1995), 124–27.
42. *Charleston Courier*, February 1822 (multiple dates).
43. Paulo Freire, *Pedagogy of the Oppressed*, trans. Myra Bergman Ramos (Freiburg: Herder and Herder, 1972), 45–46, 52–53, 56–57; Paulo Freire and Donaldo Macedo, *Literacy: Reading the Word and the World* (Westport, Conn.: Praeger, 1987), 50–51, 35, 120–23, 145–49, 156–59; Pearson, *Designs Against Charleston*, 18.
44. Higginson, "Story of Denmark Vesey."
45. "An Act to Restrain the Emancipation of Slaves, December 20, 1820," in Egerton and Paquette, *Denmark Vesey Affair*, 63.
46. "Witness No. 1, Official Report, June 19, 1822," 163.
47. Egerton and Paquette, *Denmark Vesey Affair*, 121; "Mary Lamboll Beach to Elizabeth Gilchrist, July 5, 1822," in Egerton and Paquette, *Denmark Vesey Affair*, 374.
48. Pompey, "Testimony, Evidence Document B," in Egerton and Paquette, *Denmark Vesey Affair*, 280; Spady, *Fugitive Movements*, 38 ("merely talking about rebellion ... was highly dangerous"); "Israel Nesbitt on Great-Grandfather Robert Nesbitt," in Egerton and Paquette, *Denmark Vesey Affair*, 792. The Negro Act of 1740, of course, punished talk of rebellion with death.

49. Thomas Wentworth Higginson, "The First Black Regiment, *Outlook*, July 2, 1898," in Egerton and Paquette, *Denmark Vesey Affair*, 777.
50. Pearson, *Designs Against Charleston*, 110; Frank Ferguson, "Testimony," in Egerton and Paquette, *Denmark Vesey Affair*, 182; "Rolla Bennett Confession, June 25, 1822," in Pearson, *Designs Against Charleston*, 186.
51. "Confession of Bacchus, July 17, 1822," in Egerton and Paquette, *Denmark Vesey Affair*, 302; "Examination of Frank Ferguson, Official Report," in Egerton and Paquette, *Denmark Vesey Affair*, 183.
52. "Confession of Bacchus Hammet, Official Report," in Egerton and Paquette, *Denmark Vesey Affair*, 234.
53. John Enslow, "Confession, Senate Transcript," in Egerton and Paquette, *Denmark Vesey Affair*, 324; Monday Gell, "Second Confession, Official Report," in Egerton and Paquette, *Denmark Vesey Affair*, 191.
54. "Fourth Version of Bacchus Hammet's Confession," 321.
55. Whether Vesey could actually ride a horse is unclear, but he had paid great attention to recruiting draymen to his movement and others who had easy access to and experience with horses. See, e.g., "Senate Transcript," in Egerton and Paquette, *Denmark Vesey Affair*, 324, 327, 330, 333, 336, 350. William Garner claimed to have "procured twelve or thirteen horses." Ibid., 336.
56. Kennedy and Parker, "Narrative," 87; Egerton, *He Shall Go Out Free*, 161–62.
57. Pearson, *Designs Against Charleston*, 297–309, 310–11.
58. Egerton and Paquette, *Denmark Vesey Affair*, 185 n.2.
59. "Official Report," in Egerton and Paquette, *Denmark Vesey Affair*, 159; Egerton and Paquette, *Denmark Vesey Affair*, 137–44 (reprinting letters that detailed the dispute between the tribunal and Justice William Johnson).
60. "Governor Thomas Bennett Jr. to Attorney General Robert Young Hayne, July 1, 1822," in Egerton and Paquette, *Denmark Vesey Affair*, 147–48; "Attorney General Robert Y. Hayne to Governor Thomas Bennett Jr., July 3, 1822," in Egerton and Paquette, *Denmark Vesey Affair*, 148–52.
61. Crawford v. Washington, 541 U.S. 36 (2004) (discussing the historical background); Virginia Declaration of Rights §8 (1776); Pennsylvania Declaration of Rights §IX (1776); Delaware Declaration of Rights §14 (1776); Maryland Declaration of Rights §XIX (1776); North Carolina Declaration of Rights §VII (1776); Vermont Declaration of Rights ch. I, §X (1777); Massachusetts Declaration of Rights §XII (1780); New Hampshire Bill of Rights §XV (1783).
62. "Official Report," 184; Higginson, "Story of Denmark Vesey."
63. "Official Report," 184; "Extract of a Letter, *Connecticut Mirror*, September 2, 1822," in Egerton and Paquette, *Denmark Vesey Affair*, 488 (discussing the appeal of two other free persons of color to the Court of Common Pleas).
64. If we are to believe the trial record, which indicates he shed "tears" after receiving his sentence. Ibid. On the day of his execution, however, he was resolute. "Mary Lamboll Beach to Elizabeth Gilchrist, July 5, 1822," in Egerton and Paquette, *Denmark Vesey Affair*, 374.

65. Lionel Kennedy and Thomas Parker, "An Official Report of the Trials of Sundry Negroes Charged with an Attempt to Raise an Insurrection in the State of South Carolina," in Pearson, *Designs Against Charleston*, 279.
66. Spady, *Fugitive Movements*, 39.
67. David W. Blight, *Frederick Douglass: Prophet of Freedom* (New York: Simon and Schuster, 2018), 395.

Chapter Two. The Quarantine

1. Richard C. Wade, "The Vesey Plot: A Reconsideration," *Journal of Southern History* 30, no. 2 (1964): 143–61; Douglas R. Egerton, "Forgetting Denmark Vesey; Or, Oliver Stone Meets Richard Wade," *William and Mary Quarterly* 59, no. 1 (January 2002): 144; Michael P. Johnson, "Denmark Vesey's Church," *Journal of Southern History* 86, no. 4 (2020): 805–48.
2. James O'Neil Spady, "Denmark Vesey and the 1822 Charleston Antislavery Uprising: New Themes and Methods," in *Fugitive Movements: Commemorating the Denmark Vesey Affair and Black Radical Antislavery in the Atlantic World*, ed. James O'Neil Spady (Columbia: University of South Carolina Press, 2022), 38–60; Manisha Sinha, "Foreword," in Spady, *Fugitive Movements*, xii; Douglas R. Egerton, " 'To See What He Could Do for His Fellow Creatures': Enslaved Women, Families, and Survivors in North American Slave Conspiracies," in Spady, *Fugitive Movements*, 199. For another new book affirming the core narrative in the Vesey affair, see Jeremy Schipper, *Denmark Vesey's Bible: The Thwarted Revolt That Put Slavery and Scripture on Trial* (Princeton: Princeton University Press, 2022), 24.
3. Spady, "Denmark Vesey and the 1822 Charleston Antislavery Uprising," 38–60.
4. Thomas Wentworth Higginson, "The Story of Denmark Vesey, *The Atlantic*, June 1861, accessed November 15, 2003, https://www.theatlantic.com/magazine/archive/1861/06/denmark-vesey/396239/; John Oliver Killens, *The Trial Record of Denmark Vesey* (Boston: Beacon Press, 1970), 40 (indicating Charleston was on the verge of "the most horrible catastrophe with which [South Carolina] has been threatened since it has been an independent state"); "Thomas Bennett to John C. Calhoun, July 15, 1822," in Pearson, *Designs Against Charleston*, 330.
5. Nicholas May, "Holy Rebellion: Religious Assembly Laws in Antebellum South Carolina and Virginia," *American Journal of Legal History* 49, no. 3 (July 2007): 238–39; John Locke, *Political Writings*, ed. David Wootton (Indianapolis: Hackett Publishing, 2003); Bell v. Graham, 10 S.C.L. 278 (1818); E. Jennifer Monaghan, *Reading for the Enslaved, Writing for the Free: Reflections on Liberty and Literacy* (Worcester, Mass.: American Antiquity Society, 2000), 319. In 1819, Virginia slave code also took up literacy, but more indirectly. Rather than prohibiting literacy, Virginia barred "meetings or assemblages of slaves, or free negroes or mulattoes mixing and associating

with such slaves at any meeting-house or houses ... in the night; or at any SCHOOL OR SCHOOLS for teaching them READING OR WRITING, either in the day or night." The concern was not necessarily with literacy per se but with the meetings where insurrection and education might comingle.

6. "*Niles Weekly Register,* Saturday, September 14, 1822," in *The Denmark Vesey Affair: A Documentary History,* ed. Douglas R. Egerton and Robert L. Paquette (Gainesville: University Press of Florida, 2017), 499.
7. "Circular of Governor Thomas Bennett Jr., Saturday, August 10, 1822," in Egerton and Paquette, *Denmark Vesey Affair,* 469.
8. James Hamilton Jr., *Negro Plot. An Account of the Late Intended Insurrection Among a Portion of the Blacks of the City of Charleston, South Carolina* (Boston: Joseph W. Ingraham, 1822), accessed November 15, 2023, https://docsouth.unc.edu/church/hamilton/hamilton.html.
9. Higginson, "Story of Denmark Vesey"; Killens, *Trial Record of Denmark Vesey,* xxii.
10. Achates, "Reflections, Occasioned by the Late Disturbances in Charleston," in Egerton and Paquette, *Denmark Vesey Affair,* 553, 554.
11. Ibid., 569; A Columbian, "A Series of Numbers Addressed to the Public, on the Subject of the Slaves and Free People of Colour" (Columbia, S.C.: State Gazette Office, 1822), 20, accessed November 15, 2023, https://reader.library.cornell.edu/docviewer/digital?id=may891711#mode/1up.
12. Ulrich B. Phillips, ed., *Plantation and Frontier Documents: 1649–1863,* vol. 2 (Cleveland, Ohio: Arthur H. Clark Co., 1909), 103–15, https://books.google.com/books?id=zoley-snvSkC&printsec=frontcover&source=gbs_ge_summary_r&cad=0#v=onepage&q&f=false.
13. Lacy K. Ford, *Deliver Us From Evil: The Slavery Question in the Old South* (New York: Oxford University Press, 2009), 273–74.
14. Ibid., 279.
15. "Extinction of the Church in South Carolina," in Daniel A. Payne, *History of the African Methodist Episcopal Church,* ed. Charles Spencer Smith (Nashville, Tenn.: A. M. E. Sunday School Union, 1891), 31, https://docsouth.unc.edu/church/payne/payne.html#p31.
16. Brandon Boyle, "The Causes and Consequences of the South Carolina Negro Seamen's Act," *Bridges: A Journal of Student Research* 13, no. 13 (2020): 1, 6, cdc.gov/tobacco/sgr/50th-anniversary/pdfs/fs_smoking_youth_508.pdf.
17. "An Act for the Better Regulation and Government of Free Negroes and Persons of Color, Saturday, December 21, 1822," in Egerton and Paquette, *Denmark Vesey Affair,* 594–95.
18. U.S. Const. art. I, § 8.
19. U.S. Const. art. IV, § 1.
20. Hal Goldman, "Black Citizenship and Military Self-Presentation in Antebellum Massachusetts," *Historical Journal of Massachusetts* 25, no. 1 (Winter

1997): 157–83, https://www.westfield.ma.edu/historical-journal/wp-content/uploads/2018/06/Hal-Goldman-winter-97-combined.pdf.
21. Michael Alan Schoeppner, "Navigating the Dangerous Atlantic: Racial Quarantines, Black Sailors and United States Constitutionalism" (PhD diss., University of Florida, 2010), 46, 51.
22. Ibid., 10; Robert Alderson, "Charleston's Rumored Slave Revolt of 1793," in *The Impact of the Haitian Revolution in the Atlantic World*, ed. David P. Geggus (Columbia, S.C.: University of South Carolina Press, 2002), 93–111.
23. "Memorial of Sundry Masters of American Vessels Lying in the Port of Charleston, S.C.," *Niles Weekly Register*, March 15, 1823.
24. "Free People of Color," *Niles Weekly Register*, March 15, 1823, 32; Philip M. Hamer, "Great Britain, the United States, and the Negro Seamen Acts, 1822–1848," *Journal of Southern History* 1, no. 1 (February 1935): 4, https://doi.org/10.2307/2191749; Calder v. Deliesseline, 16 S.C.L. 186 (Harp. 1824).
25. Stratford Canning to John Adams, February 15, 1823, in "Correspondence, 1–2," in Schoeppner, "Navigating the Dangerous Atlantic," 55; "John Quincy Adams, Letter to Stratford Canning, Tuesday, June 17, 1823," in Egerton and Paquette, *Denmark Vesey Affair*, 642; Schoeppner, "Navigating the Dangerous Atlantic," 60.
26. "Rules of the South Carolina Association Adopted in the City of Charleston on the Fourth Thursday in July Being the 25th Day, A.D. 1823," in Egerton and Paquette, *Denmark Vesey Affair*, 604–5; Alan F. January, "The South Carolina Association: An Agency for Race Control in Antebellum Charleston," *South Carolina Historical Magazine* 78, no. 3 (July 1977): 191–201, https://www.jstor.org/stable/27567452. "Memorial of the South Carolina Association to the Senate, November 1823," in Egerton and Paquette, *Denmark Vesey Affair*, 605.
27. Elkison v. Deliesseline, Brunn. Coll. C. 431, 494, 495 (August 1, 1823).
28. "Caroliniensis No. 5," *Charleston Mercury*, August 22, 1823, in Michael Schoeppner, "Peculiar Quarantines: The Seamen Acts and Regulatory Authority in the Antebellum South," *Law and History Review* 31, no. 3 (August 2013): 565 n.8, https://www.jstor.org/stable/23489503?seq=7; Schoeppner, "Navigating the Dangerous Atlantic," 83.
29. "Letter from William Johnson to Thomas Jefferson, July 3, 1824," in Egerton and Paquette, *Denmark Vesey Affair*, 648.
30. "John Quincy Adams, Diary, Thursday, September 4, 1823," in *The Diaries of John Quincy Adams 1779–1848*, ed. David Waldstreicher (New York: Library of America, 2017); Hamer, "Great Britain, the United States, and the Negro Seamen Acts," 10.
31. "*Southern Patriot (Charleston)*, Dec. 7, 1824," in Hamer, "Great Britain, the United States, and the Negro Seamen Acts," 11 n.30; "Sentiments of the South," *Eastern Argus (Portland ME)*, Thursday, December 30, 1824.

32. Hamer, "Great Britain, the United States, and the Negro Seamen Acts," 11, 12.
33. Schoeppner, "Navigating the Dangerous Atlantic," 6, 9.
34. Annals of Congress, House of Representatives, 18th Cong., 1st Sess., 1399, February 6, 1824, https://memory.loc.gov/cgi-bin/ampage?collId=llac&fileName=041/llac041.db&recNum=696.
35. "William Johnson Jr. Letter to John Quincy Adams, July 3, 1824," in Egerton and Paquette, *Denmark Vesey Affair*, 648.
36. Ibid.
37. Whitemarsh B. Seabrook, *A Concise View of the Critical Situation and Future Prospects of the Slave-Holding States, in Relation to Their Coloured Population*, 2nd ed. (Charleston, S.C.: A. E. Miller, 1825), 3–4, https://babel.hathitrust.org/cgi/pt?id=dul1.ark:/13960/t4sj52947&view=1up&seq=9.
38. Ibid., 7.
39. Ibid., 13.
40. Ibid., 15, 17.

Chapter Three. The Word

1. Peter Thompson, "David Walker's Nationalism—and Thomas Jefferson's," *Journal of the Early Republic* 37, no. 1 (2017): 47, 61.
2. Peter Pringle Hinks, "'We Must and Shall Be Free': David Walker, Evangelicalism, and the Problem of Antebellum Black Resistance" (PhD diss., Yale University, 1993), xiv, 242; Thompson, "David Walker's Nationalism," 62; Frederick Douglass, "Address on the Twenty-First Anniversary of Emancipation in the District of Columbia," April 16, 1883, *Wikisource*, https://en.wikisource.org/wiki/Address_on_the_Twenty-First_Anniversary_of_Emancipation_in_the_District_of_Columbia.
3. Robert S. Levine, *Dislocating Race and Nation* (Chapel Hill: University of North Carolina Press, 2008), 67.
4. Peter P. Hinks, *To Awaken My Afflicted Brethren: David Walker and the Problem of Antebellum Slave Resistance* (University Park: Penn State University Press, 2010), 7.
5. Ibid., 21.
6. Thompson, "David Walker's Nationalism," 63.
7. *A History of the African Methodist Episcopal Church*, ed. Charles Spencer Smith (Nashville, Tenn.: A. M. E. Sunday School Union, 1891), 14, https://docsouth.unc.edu/church/payne/payne.html#p31.
8. Hinks, *To Awaken My Afflicted Brethren*, 75; Levine, *Dislocating Race and Nation*, 71.
9. Martin E. Dann, ed., *The Black Press, 1827–1890: The Quest for National Identity* (New York: G. P. Putnam's Sons, 1971); "To Our Patrons," *Freedom's Journal*, March 16, 1827, https://jim-casey.com/enap/files/original/f2eab

c00599ba510a934b1e3c13d1df3.pdf; Levine, *Dislocating Race and Nation*, 71; Hinks, *To Awaken My Afflicted Brethren*, 102, 103.
10. Dann, *Black Press*, 17; Hinks, *To Awaken My Afflicted Brethren*, 90.
11. David Waldstreicher, *In the Midst of Perpetual Fetes: The Making of American Nationalism, 1776–1820* (Chapel Hill: University of North Carolina Press, 1997), 142.
12. Paul Starr, *Entrenchment: Wealth, Power, and the Constitution of Democratic Societies* (New Haven, Conn.: Yale University Press, 2019), 58.
13. David Walker, *David Walker's Appeal, in Four Articles; Together with a Preamble, to the Coloured Citizens of the World, But in Particular, and Very Expressly, to Those of the United States of America*, Written in Boston, State of Massachusetts, September 28, 1829, 3rd ed. (Boston: David Walker, 1830), 9, https://www.jstor.org/stable/10.5149/9780807869482_walker.4. Stephen H. Marshall, *The City on the Hill From Below: The Crisis of Prophetic Black Politics* (Philadelphia: Temple University Press, 2012), 29.
14. Walker, *David Walker's Appeal*, 8.
15. Annals of Congress, Senate, 16th Cong., 2nd Sess., 109, 111, 636, 637, accessed November 16, 2023, https://memory.loc.gov/cgi-bin/ampage?collId=llac&fileName=040/llac040.db&recNum=2. Levine, *Dislocating Race and Nation*, 76, 77, 78; Kate Masur, *Until Justice Be Done: America's First Civil Rights Movement, From the Revolution to Reconstruction* (New York: W. W. Norton, 2021), 63–65. Senator Charles Pinckney of South Carolina, a former delegate to the Constitutional Convention of 1787, claimed that he had authored the constitution's privileges and immunities clause and that he knew "what I meant by it. . . . At the time I drew that constitution, I perfectly knew that there did not exist such a thing in the Union as a black or colored citizen, nor could I then have conceived it possible such a thing could ever have existed." Annals of Congress, 16th Cong., 2nd Sess., February 1821, 1124.
16. Melvin L. Rogers, "David Walker and the Political Power of the Appeal," *Political Theory* 43, no. 2 (2015): 208–33.
17. Ibid., 208, 213.
18. Thomas Jefferson, *Notes on the State of Virginia* (Boston: Lilly and Wait, 1832), 115, https://www.google.com/books/edition/Notes_on_the_State_of_Virginia/FlEVAAAAYAAJ?hl=en&gbpv=1&pg=PP7&printsec=frontcover.
19. Ibid., 153, 154. Walker, *David Walker's Appeal*, 31.
20. Ibid., 18, 20.
21. Marshall, *The City on the Hill*, 34; Walker, *David Walker's Appeal*, 42.
22. Alex Zamalin, *The Struggle on Their Minds: The Political Thought of African American Resistance* (New York: Columbia University Press, 2017), 57; Marshall, *The City on the Hill*, 31; Walker, *David Walker's Appeal*, 13, 49.
23. Walker, *David Walker's Appeal*, 20.
24. Ibid., 40, 42, 43.

25. Ibid., 23, 44.
26. Ibid., 9.
27. Ibid., 74, 75.
28. Ibid., 26, 61.
29. Ibid., 9.
30. Ibid., 35, 52 (quoting Elias B. Caldwell), 53, 57, 58.
31. Marshall, *The City on the Hill*, 31; Walker, *David Walker's Appeal*, 34, 35.
32. Walker, *David Walker's Appeal*, 35.
33. "James Madison to W. T. Barry, August 4, 1822," https://founders.archives.gov/documents/Madison/04-02-02-0480; Thompson, "David Walker's Nationalism," 70–71; Walker, *David Walker's Appeal*, 35.
34. Walker, *David Walker's Appeal*, 62.
35. Ibid.; *Boston Daily Courier*, March 22, 1830.
36. *The Liberator*, January 29, 1831.
37. "Letter from Boston Mayor Harrison Gray to the Mayor of Savannah, William T. Wiliams, February 10, 1830," *Richmond Enquirer*, February 18, 1830, 3, https://chroniclingamerica.loc.gov/lccn/sn84024735/1830-02-18/ed-1/seq-3/; Walker, *David Walker's Appeal*, 70.

Chapter Four. Arresting the Word

1. Kim Tolley, "Slavery and the Origin of Georgia's 1829 Anti-Literacy Act," in *Miseducation: A History of Ignorance-Making in America and Abroad*, ed. A. J. Angulo (Baltimore, Md.: Johns Hopkins University Press, 2016).
2. Ibid.
3. Glenn M. McNair, "The Elijah Burritt Affair: David Walker's Appeal and Partisan Journalism in Antebellum Milledgeville," *Georgia Historical Quarterly* 83, no. 3 (1999): 455 (quoting Gov. Gilmer).
4. *Acts of the General Assembly of the State of Georgia, Passed in Milledgeville at an Annual Session in November and December, 1829* (Milledgeville: Camak and Ragland, 1830).
5. Ibid.
6. *Niles Register*, vol. 38, March 27, 1830, 87.
7. "Walker's Appeal," *The Liberator* 1, no. 2, January 8, 1831.
8. *Niles Register*, vol. 38, March 27, 1830, 87; "Walker's Appeal," *The Liberator* 1, no. 2, January 8, 1831; Henry Highland Garnet, *Walker's Appeal, with a Brief Sketch of His Life* (New York: Tobitt, 1848), https://www.gutenberg.org/files/16516/16516-h/16516-h.htm; "Death of Walker," *The Liberator* 1, no. 4, January 22, 1831, 14.
9. Garnet, *Walker's Appeal*, 7; Peter P. Hinks, *To Awaken My Afflicted Brethren: David Walker and the Problem of Antebellum Slave Resistance* (University Park: Penn State University Press, 2010), 270.
10. *Southern Recorder* (Milledgeville, Ga.), July 31, 1830, 3.
11. Ibid.

12. McNair, "Elijah Burritt Affair," 457.
13. Ibid.
14. Ibid.
15. *Niles Register*, vol. 38, March 27, 1830, 87.
16. Ibid.
17. Ibid., 88.
18. Ibid., 87–88.
19. William H. Pease and Jane H. Pease, "Walker's *Appeal* Comes to Charleston: A Note and Documents," *Journal of Negro History* 59, no. 3 (July 1974): 289, https://www.jstor.org/stable/2716768.
20. Ibid., 287, 288, 291.
21. "Benjamin Faneuil Hunt to Mayor Harrison Gray Otis (Boston, Massachusetts), October 4, 1831," in *The Denmark Vesey Affair: A Documentary History*, ed. Douglas R. Egerton and Robert L. Paquette (Gainesville: University Press of Florida, 2017).
22. Clement Eaton, *Freedom of Thought in the Old South* (Durham, N.C.: Duke University Press, 1940), 2; Hinks, "We Must and Shall Be Free," 223. Though the pamphlet wasn't specifically named, it was presumably Walker's *Appeal*. Charles Edward Morris, "Panic and Reprisal: Reaction in North Carolina to the Nat Turner Insurrection, 1831," *North Carolina Historical Review* 62, no. 1 (1985): 45. Deverly Daniel to New Bern Intendant of Police, 20 September 1830, General Correspondence and Miscellaneous Materials, 1771–1868, Records of Department of the Adjutant General, AG 77, North Carolina State Archives.
23. Eaton, *Freedom of Thought*, 123; Clement Eaton, "A Dangerous Pamphlet in the Old South," *Journal of Southern History* 2, no. 3 (1936): 331 n.31 (discussing L. D. Henry to Governor Owen, September 3, 1830, Executive Papers of North Carolina); ibid., 331 n.32 (citing J. Burgwyn to Governor Owen, November 15, 1830, Letter Book of the Governors of North Carolina, 1829–1830, 247–49); Marshall Rachleff, "David Walker's Southern Agent," *Journal of Negro History* 62, no. 1 (1977): 101 (reprinting letter from Wilmington Police).
24. *Journals of the Senate and House of Commons of the General Assembly of the State of North Carolina, at the Session of 1830–31*, 161.
25. Eaton, *Freedom of Thought*, 125.
26. Ibid., 124; *Acts Passed by the General Assembly of the State of North Carolina* (New Bern, N.C.: Arnett and Hodge, 1831), 10, https://digital.ncdcr.gov/Documents/Detail/acts-passed-by-the-general-assembly-of-the-state-of-north-carolina-1830-1831/1955764?item=2080281.
27. *Acts Passed by the General Assembly of the State of North* Carolina, 10; *Greensborough Patriot*, March 20, 1833, 3.
28. *Acts Passed at a General Assembly of the Commonwealth of Virginia, Begun and Held at the Capitol, in the City of Richmond* (Richmond, Va.: Thomas Ritchie, 1831), https://babel.hathitrust.org/cgi/pt?id=osu.32437123259513&view=1up&seq=114&skin=2021&q1=slave.

Chapter Five. The Fire

1. Stephen B. Oates, *The Fires of Jubilee: Nat Turner's Fierce Rebellion* (New York: Harper and Row, 1975), 81; David F. Allmendinger Jr., *Nat Turner and the Rising in Southampton County* (Baltimore: Johns Hopkins University Press, 2014), 2.
2. Oates, *Fires of Jubilee*, 77; Vincent Harding, "Symptoms of Liberty and Blackhead Signposts," in *Nat Turner: A Slave Rebellion in History and Memory*, ed. Kenneth S. Greenberg (New York: Oxford University Press, 2003), 98.
3. Ibid., 100 (quoting letter).
4. Allmendinger, *Nat Turner and the Rising*, 4; Oates, *Fires of Jubilee*, 7, 116.
5. Allmendinger, *Nat Turner and the Rising*, 5.
6. "*Lynchburg Virginian*, September 8, 1831," in *The Southampton Slave Revolt of 1831: A Compilation of Source Material*, ed. Henry Irving Tragle (Amherst: University of Massachusetts Press, 1971), 73–74.
7. Allmendinger, *Nat Turner and the Rising*, 244–55 (analyzing Gray and his role in the confession).
8. Anthony Santoro, "The Prophet in His Own Words: Nat Turner's Biblical Construction," *Virginia Magazine of History and Biography* 116, no. 2 (2008): 140.
9. Allmendinger, *Nat Turner and the Rising*, 254 and 255.
10. Thomas R. Gray, *The Confessions of Nat Turner: The Leader of the Late Insurrection in Southampton, Va.* (Baltimore: Lucas and Deaver, 1831), 2.
11. Ibid., 2.
12. Ibid., 3.
13. Ibid., 2, 3, 4.
14. Ibid., 15.
15. Oates, *Fires of Jubilee*, 12; Santoro, "Prophet in His Own Words," 116; James Sidbury, "Reading, Revelation, and Rebellion: The Textual Communities of Gabriel, Denmark Vesey, and Nat Turner," in *Nat Turner: A Slave Rebellion in History and Memory*, ed. Kenneth S. Greenberg (New York: Oxford University Press, 2003), 122, 128.
16. Gray, *Confessions of Nat Turner*, 3, 4, 9.
17. Oates, *Fires of Jubilee*, 7, 20, 21. Oates, however, indicates that the Black community also played a role in this expectation. Ibid., 21.
18. Ibid., 20; Harding, "Symptoms of Liberty," 84.
19. David Walker, *David Walker's Appeal, in Four Articles; Together with a Preamble, to the Coloured Citizens of the World, But in Particular, and Very Expressly, to Those of the United States of America*, 3rd. ed. (Boston: David Walker, 1830), 70, accessed November 16, 2023, https://docsouth.unc.edu/nc/walker/title.html.
20. The precise language in the Bible is, "But seek first the kingdom of God and His righteousness, and all these things shall be added to you." Matthew 6:33.

21. Gray, *Confessions of Nat Turner*, 4.
22. Ibid., 4–5.
23. Ibid., 5.
24. Ibid.
25. Ibid., 9.
26. Ibid., 6.
27. Ibid., 7.
28. Marion D. deB. Kilson, "Towards Freedom: An Analysis of Slave Revolts in the United States," *Phylon* 25, no. 2 (1964): 175–87.
29. Sidbury, "Reading, Revelation, and Rebellion," 119.
30. Ibid., 122.
31. Jeremiah 1:5; for a detailed examination of all this, see Santoro, "Prophet in His Own Words."
32. Gray, *Confessions of Nat Turner*, 18.
33. Ibid., 51.
34. Oates, *Fires of Jubilee*, 105.
35. Santoro, "Prophet in His Own Words," 122.
36. William W. Freehling, *The Road to Disunion*, vol. 1, *Secessionists at Bay 1776–1854* (New York: Oxford University Press, 1990), 273, 286, 316; Lacy K. Ford, *Deliver Us From Evil: The Slavery Question in the Old South* (New York: Oxford University Press, 2009), 4.

Chapter Six. The South's Last Slavery Debate

1. Lacy K. Ford, *Deliver Us From Evil: The Slavery Question in the Old South* (New York: Oxford University Press, 2009), 6–12; Clement Eaton, *Freedom of Thought in the Old South* (Durham, N.C.: Duke University Press, 1940), 167–95.
2. Erik S. Root, ed., *Sons of the Fathers: The Virginia Slavery Debates of 1831–1832*, (Lanham, Md.: Lexington Books, 2010), 77 (republishing the legislative debates in their entirety).
3. Ibid.
4. Joseph Clarke Robert, *The Road from Monticello: A Study of the Virginia Slavery Debate of 1832* (Durham, N.C.: Duke University Press, 1941).
5. Charles H. Ambler, *The Life and Diary of John Floyd, Governor of Virginia, an Apostle of Secession, and the Father of the Oregon Country* (Richmond, Va.: Richmond Press, 1918), 158–59, https://babel.hathitrust.org/cgi/pt?id=loc.ark:/13960/t1cj8p7of&seq=168&q1=defend+their+masters.
6. Ibid., 160.
7. Ibid., 170.
8. *The Liberator*, vol. 1, January 1, 1831.
9. Ibid.
10. Ambler, *Life and Diary of John Floyd*, 161–62.
11. Ibid., 89–90.

12. Ibid., 90.
13. "Governor Floyd's Message to the General Assembly, December 6, 1831," in *Journal of the House of Delegates of the Commonwealth of Virginia* (Richmond, Va.: Thomas Ritchie, 1831), 9, 10, 13, 14, https://babel.hathitrust.org/cgi/pt?id=nyp.33433014925501&view=1up&seq=17&skin=2021.
14. Ibid., 9, 10.
15. Ibid., 10.
16. Patrick S. Brady, "The Slave Trade and Sectionalism in South Carolina, 1787–1808," *Journal of Southern History* 38, no. 4 (1972): 601, 603–4.
17. *Journal of the House of Delegates of the Commonwealth of Virginia*, 15–16.
18. Alfred L. Brophy, *University, Court, and Slave: Pro-Slavery Thought and Southern Colleges and the Coming of Civil War* (New York: Oxford University Press, 2016), 24.
19. Ambler, *Life and Diary of John Floyd*, 172.
20. "Excerpt from the *Richmond Enquirer* (January 12, 1832)," in *Encyclopedia Virginia* (Charlottesville: Virginia Humanities, 2007), https://encyclopediavirginia.org/entries/excerpt-from-the-richmond-enquirer-january-7-1832/.
21. Ibid.
22. *Richmond Whig*, January 10, 1832.
23. Louis P. Masur, "Nat Turner and Sectional Crisis," in *Nat Turner: A Slave Rebellion in History and Memory*, ed. Kenneth S. Greenberg (New York: Oxford University Press, 2003), 156.
24. *Journal of the House of Delegates of the Commonwealth of Virginia*, 93; Root, *Sons of the Fathers*, 37; *Richmond Enquirer*, January 19, 1832, https://virginiachronicle.com/?a=d&d=RE18320119&e=-------en-20--1--txt-txIN--------.
25. Root, *Sons of the Fathers*, 25–27.
26. Ibid., 25; William W. Freehling, *The Road to Disunion*, vol. 1, *Secessionists at Bay 1776–1854* (New York: Oxford University Press, 1990), 182.
27. Root, *Sons of the Fathers*, 28.
28. Ibid., 29, 30, 32, 35.
29. Ibid., 40–41.
30. Ibid., 43.
31. Ibid., 45.
32. Ibid., 47.
33. Ibid., 58–59.
34. Ibid., 82, 83, 87.
35. Ibid., 62–65.
36. Ibid., 65–66.
37. Ibid., 67.
38. Ibid.
39. Ibid., 68.
40. Ibid., 75–76.
41. Ibid., 79.
42. Ibid., 82.

43. Ibid., 86.
44. Ibid., 91–92.
45. Ibid., 106.
46. Brophy, *University, Court, and Slave*, 28; Root, *Sons of the Fathers*, 117 n.2.
47. Root, *Sons of the Fathers*, 125.
48. Ibid., 137.
49. Ibid., 158, 196–97.
50. Ambler, *Life and Diary of John Floyd*, 175.
51. Root, *Sons of the Fathers*, 217.
52. Ibid., 218.
53. Ibid., 287.
54. Ibid., 291; Brophy, *University, Court, and Slave*, 30.
55. Brophy, *University, Court, and Slave*, 31.
56. Ambler, *Life and Diary of John Floyd*, 175, 177.
57. *Journal of the House of Delegates of the Commonwealth of Virginia*, 759.
58. Ibid., 759, 760.
59. Ibid., 764.
60. The one exception was Maryland, which did have a relatively subdued slavery debate following Virginia's. Maryland, however, was distinct in that slavery "was decaying" quickly as the free Black population was increasing. Freehling, *Road to Disunion*, 201; Junko Isono Kato, "Slaves and Education: Tennessee as a Slave State Where the Instruction of Slaves Was Not Prohibited," *Tennessee Historical Quarterly* 77, no. 2 (Summer 2018): 123.
61. *Journal of the Convention of the State of Tennessee, Convened for the Purpose of Revising and Amending the Constitution Thereof* (Nashville: Laughlin and Henderson, 1834), 87–88, https://babel.hathitrust.org/cgi/pt?id=uc1.$b45911&seq=1.

Chapter Seven. The Blockade

1. The first public printed use of the term "slavocracy" appears to have been in 1839 in *The Emancipator*. For a discussion of the evolving characterization of the South, see Rod Farmer, "Maine Abolitionists View the South: Images in Maine Antislavery Newspapers, 1838–1855," *Maine History* 25, no. 1 (1985), 9, https://digitalcommons.library.umaine.edu/cgi/viewcontent.cgi?article=1511&context=mainehistoryjournal; Nicholas May, "Holy Rebellion: Religious Assembly Laws in Antebellum South Carolina and Virginia," *American Journal of Legal History* 49, no. 3 (July 2007): 237, 255.
2. Lacy K. Ford, *Deliver Us From Evil: The Slavery Question in the Old South* (New York: Oxford University Press, 2009), 466; Whitemarsh B. Seabrook, *A Concise View of the Critical Situation and Future Prospects of the Slave-Holding States, in Relation to Their Coloured Population*, 2nd ed. (Charleston, S.C.: A. E. Miller, 1825), 16, https://babel.hathitrust.org/cgi/pt?id=dul1.ark:/13960/t4sj52947&view=1up&seq=9 (quoting the synod's committee).
3. Ford, *Deliver Us From Evil*, 463–67.

4. Daniel Alexander Payne, *Reflections of Seventy Years*, comp. and arr. Sarah C. Bierce Scarborough, ed. Rev. C. S. Smith (Nashville, Tenn.: A. M. E. Sunday School Union, 1888), 15–16, https://docsouth.unc.edu/church/payne70/payne.html.
5. Ibid., 20; Bernard E. Powers, "Denmark Vesey, South Carolina, and Haiti: Borne, Bound, and Battered by a Common Wind," in *Fugitive Movements: Commemorating the Denmark Vesey Affair and Black Radical Antislavery in the Atlantic World*, ed. James O'Neil Spady (Columbia: University of South Carolina Press, 2022), 43.
6. Whitemarsh B. Seabrook, *An Essay on the Management of Slaves, and Especially on Their Religious Instruction* (Charleston, S.C.: A. E. Miller, 1834), https://babel.hathitrust.org/cgi/pt?id=uiug.30112062900748&seq=5.
7. Larry E. Tise, *Proslavery: A History of the Defense of Slavery in America, 1701–1840* (Athens: University of Georgia Press, 1987), 308.
8. Seabrook, *An Essay*, 3.
9. Ibid., 4.
10. Ibid., 6.
11. Ibid., 12, 14.
12. Ibid., 15.
13. Ibid., 18, 19.
14. Ibid., 24.
15. Ford, *Deliver Us From Evil*, 471.
16. *Acts and Resolutions of the General Assembly of the State of South Carolina* (Columbia: E. F. Branthwaite, 1834), 13, https://www.carolana.com/SC/Legislators/Documents/Acts_and_Resolutions_of_the_General_Assembly_of_the_State_of_South_Carolina_1834.pdf.
17. "The Petition of Sundry Citizens of Chester District Praying an Alteration of the Law in Relation to Slaves and Free Persons of Color," 1834, in *Born a Child of Freedom, Yet a Slave: Mechanisms of Control and Strategies of Resistance in Antebellum South Carolina*, ed. Norrece T. Jones Jr. (Middletown, Conn.: Wesleyan University Press, 1990), 140–41.
18. Edward R. Laurens, *A Letter to the Hon. Whitemarsh B. Seabrook, of St. John's Colleton in Explanation and Defence* (Charleston, S.C.: Observer Office Press, 1835), 8, https://babel.hathitrust.org/cgi/pt?id=loc.ark:/13960/t48p64025&seq=14&q1=ameliorate.
19. Ibid., 9.
20. *The Constitution of the American Anti-Slavery Society: with the Declaration of the National Anti-Slavery Convention at Philadelphia, December, 1833* (New York: American Anti-Slavery Society, 1838), 3, 7, https://www.loc.gov/item/2001615799/.
21. Ibid., 3.
22. Ibid., 10, 11.
23. Ibid., 12.

24. David M. Reese, *A Brief Review of the "First Annual Report" of the American Anti-Slavery Society* (New York: Howe and Bates, 1834), 42, https://www.loc.gov/resource/gdcmassbookdig.briefreviewoffiro1rees/?sp=7&r=-0.638,-0.003,2.275,1.424,0.
25. Bertram Wyatt-Brown, "The Abolitionists' Postal Campaign of 1835," *Journal of Negro History* 50, no. 4 (October 1965): 228, https://doi.org/10.2307/2716246.
26. Susan Wyly-Jones, "The 1835 Anti-Abolition Meetings in the South: A New Look at the Controversy over the Abolition Postal Campaign," *Civil War History* 47, no. 4 (December 2001): 290–91, https://muse.jhu.edu/article/9026; Wyatt-Brown, "Abolitionists' Postal Campaign," 229; Clement Eaton, *Freedom of Thought in the Old South* (Durham, N.C.: Duke University Press, 1940), 119.
27. *Niles Register*, October 29, 1831; "Letter from U.S. Senator Robert Y. Hayne (South Carolina) to Mayor Harrison Gray Otis (Boston, Massachusetts) Oct 14, 1831," *The Nat Turner Project*, https://www.natturnerproject.org/sen-hayne-to-mayor-otis.
28. *Charleston Southern Patriot*, July 29, 1835.
29. Frank Otto Gatell, ed., "Postmaster Huger and the Incendiary Publications," *South Carolina Historical Magazine* 64, no. 4 (October, 1963): 194, https://www.jstor.org/stable/27566483 (reprint of Huger's letter).
30. *Southern Patriot (Charleston)*, Thursday Afternoon, July 30, 1835; *Charleston Courier*, July 30, 1835.
31. Richard R. John, *Spreading the News: The American Postal System from Franklin to Morse* (Cambridge, Mass.: Harvard University Press, 1998), 266, https://www.jstor.org/stable/j.ctvjf9zgq; Gatell, "Postmaster Huger," 195.
32. *Southern Patriot*, August 4, 1835.
33. *Richmond Enquirer*, August 11, 1835.
34. Ibid.
35. Andrew Jackson to Amos Kendall, August 9, 1835, https://www.loc.gov/resource/maj.01091_0264_0264/?st=text.
36. *Charleston Courier*, August 11, 1835.
37. Ford, *Deliver Us From Evil*, 486; Wyly-Jones, "1835 Anti-Abolition Meetings," 291.
38. Robert Gage to James Gage, August 31, 1835, Wilson Special Collections Library, 01812 #folder 1, #1, University of North Carolina Library, https://finding-aids.lib.unc.edu/01812/#folder_1#1; Wyly-Jones, "1835 Anti-Abolition Meetings," 293.
39. Robert Gage to James Gage, August 31, 1835, Wilson Special Collections Library; "An Abolitionist Caught," *Nashville Republican*, August 11, 1835.
40. "Public Meeting in Sparta, Hancock County," *Milledgeville Southern Recorder*, November 20, 1835; Wyly-Jones, "1835 Anti-Abolition Meetings," 302, 303.
41. *Richmond Enquirer*, August 14, 1835.

42. Gerhard Peters and John T. Woolley, "Andrew Jackson, Seventh Annual Address to Congress, December 8, 1835," *The American Presidency Project*, accessed November 22, 2023, https://www.presidency.ucsb.edu/documents/seventh-annual-message-2.
43. Cong. Globe, December 8, 1835, 10.
44. Ibid.
45. Incendiary Publications, Register of Debates, 24th Cong., 1st Sess. (February 4, 1836), 73, https://memory.loc.gov/cgi-bin/ampage?collId=llrd&fileName=025/llrd025.db&recNum=510.
46. Ibid.
47. Ibid., 74
48. Ibid., 77.
49. Richard R. John, "Hiland Hall's 'Report on Incendiary Publications': A Forgotten Nineteenth Century Defense of the Constitutional Guarantee of the Freedom of the Press," *American Journal of Legal History* 41 no. 1 (January 1997): 94–125.
50. Ford, *Deliver Us From Evil*, 497.
51. 5 Stat. 80, 24th Cong., Sess. 1, Chapter 270 (July 2, 1836).

Chapter Eight. A Gag in the Halls of Congress

1. U.S. Constitution, Amendment I.
2. *Petition from the Pennsylvania Society for the Abolition of Slavery to the First Congress (1790)*, accessed November 22, 2023, https://constitutioncenter.org/media/files/10.5_Primary_Source_Petition_from_the_Pennsylvania_Society_for_the_Abolition_of_Slavery_to_the_First_Congress_%281790%29_.docx_.pdf.
3. U.S. Const. art. I, § 8.
4. Cong. Globe, 24th Cong., 1st Sess. 24 (December 16, 1835).
5. Reg. Deb., Congress, 24th Cong., 1st Sess. 1962 (December 16, 1835).
6. Reg. Deb., 24th Cong., 1st Sess. 1963 (December 16, 1835).
7. Cong. Globe, 24th Cong., 1st Sess. 27 (December 18, 1835).
8. Ibid., 27.
9. Ibid., 28.
10. Ibid., 28.
11. Ibid.
12. Gerald Sorin, *The New York Abolitionists: A Case Study of Political Radicalism* (Westport, Conn.: Praeger, 1971), 32; Cong. Globe, 24th Cong., 1st Sess. 29 (December 18, 1835).
13. Ibid., 34.
14. Ibid., 75.
15. Ibid., 77.
16. Reg. Deb., House of Rep., 24th Cong., 1st Sess. 2241 (January 21, 1836).
17. Ibid., 2242.

18. Ibid., 2245.
19. Cong. Globe, 24th Cong., 1st Sess. 128 (January 21, 1836).
20. Cong. Globe, 24th Cong., 1st Sess. 128 (January 21, 1836).
21. Cong. Globe, Senate, 24th Cong., 1st Sess. 238 (March 9, 1836).
22. Ibid., 239.
23. Reg. Deb., Senate, 24th Cong., 1st Sess. 805, 810 (March 11, 1836; March 14, 1836).
24. William W. Freehling, *The Road to Disunion*, vol. 1, *Secessionists at Bay 1776–1854* (New York: Oxford University Press, 1990), 328.
25. Reg. Deb., House of Rep., 24th Cong., 1st Sess. 2534 (February 15, 1836).
26. Reg. Deb., House of Rep., 24th Cong., 1st Sess. 3757 (May 18, 1836).
27. Freehling, *Road to Disunion*, 330.

Chapter Nine. The Tragedy of Silence

1. Michael Kent Curtis, "The Curious History of Attempts to Suppress Antislavery Speech, Press, and Petition in 1835–37," *Northwestern University Law Review* 89, no. 3 (1995): 804; *Niles Weekly Register*, October 3, 1835, 65 (quoting Columbia *Telescope*); *Acts Passed by the General Assembly of the State of North Carolina at the Session of 1834–1835* (Raleigh, N.C.: Philo White, 1835), 121, https://www.gilderlehrman.org/collection/glc00267064.
2. Curtis, "The Curious History," 837 (listing statutes).
3. Ibid., 802, 823; *New York Evening Post*, January 11, 1836, 2; William Jay, *Miscellaneous Writings on Slavery* (Boston: John P. Jewett, 1853).
4. *The Trial of Reuben Crandall, M.D., Charged with Publishing and Circulating Seditious and Incendiary Papers, etc. in the District of Columbia, with the Intent of Exciting Servile Insurrection* (New York: H. R. Piercy, 1836), https://tile.loc.gov/storage-services/service/rbc/rbcmisc/lst/lst0090/lst0090.pdf; Commonwealth v. Barrett, 36 Va. 665, 665 (Va. 1839); Bacon v. Commonwealth, 48 Va. 602 (Va. 1849).
5. *Journal of the Senate of the Commonwealth of Pennsylvania*, vol. 2 (Harrisburg, Penn.: Crabb and Barrett, 1835–36), 138–39, https://babel.hathitrust.org/cgi/pt?id=chi.74612312&view=1up&seq=7.
6. Ibid., 141.
7. Register of Debates, Senate, 24th Cong., 1st Sess. 1147 (1836).
8. Debates of Congress, Senate, 25th Cong., 2d Sess. 578 (1838).
9. *Writings and Speeches of Alvan Stewart, on Slavery*, ed. Luther Rawson Marsh (New York: A. B. Burdick, 1860), 55, www.loc.gov/resource/gdcmassbookdig.writingsspeeches00stew/?sp=9&r=-0.295,1.149,1.604,0.624,0.
10. Leonard L. Richards, *"Gentlemen of Property and Standing": Anti-Abolition Mobs in Jacksonian America* (London: Oxford University Press, 1970), 156, 157.
11. Samuel J. May, *Some Recollections of Our Antislavery Conflict* (Boston: Fields, Osgood, 1869), 164, 166, 169 (printing Gerrit Smith's reflections on the "Riot at Utica").

12. Lewis Tappan, *The Life of Arthur Tappan* (New York: Hurd and Houghton, 1870), 170, 209, https://tile.loc.gov/storage-services/public/gdcmassbookdig/lifeofarthurtappootapp_2/lifeofarthurtappootapp_2.pdf.
13. Eugene Portlette Southall, "Arthur Tappan and the Anti-Slavery Movement," *Journal of Negro History* 15, no. 2 (April 1930): 193; Tappan, *Life of Arthur Tappan*, 223.
14. Tappan, *Life of Arthur Tappan*, 201, 217, 222, 229.
15. *The Boston Mob of "Gentlemen of Property and Standing": Proceedings of the Anti-Slavery Meeting Held in Stacy Hall, Boston, on the Twentieth Anniversary of the Mob of October 21, 1835* (Boston: R. F. Walcutt, 1855), 125.
16. Ibid., 26.
17. Ibid., 27.
18. Paul Simon, *Freedom's Champion: Elijah Lovejoy* (Carbondale: Southern Illinois University Press, 1994), 30.
19. *Missouri Republican*, May 26, 1836; Simon, *Freedom's Champion*, 52.
20. "Abraham Lincoln, Speech to the Young Men's Lyceum of Springfield (1838)," National Constitution Center, accessed November 22, 2023, https://constitutioncenter.org/the-constitution/historic-document-library/detail/abraham-lincoln-speech-to-the-young-mens-lyceum-of-springfield-1838.
21. Richards, *"Gentlemen of Property and Standing,"* 157–59.
22. *History of Pennsylvania Hall, Which Was Destroyed by a Mob, on the 17th of May, 1838* (Philadelphia: Merrihew and Gunn, 1838), 5, 97; "Destruction of Pennsylvania Hall," *The Liberator*, May 25, 1838; *History of Pennsylvania Hall*.
23. Gordon E. Finnie, "The Antislavery Movement in the Upper South Before 1840," *Journal of Southern History* 35, no. 3 (August 1969): 319.
24. Ibid., 328, 336–67.
25. Frank Friedel, "Francis Lieber, Charles Sumner, and Slavery," *Journal of Southern History* 9, no. 1 (February 1943): 75.
26. Robert Y. Hayne et al., *Appeal in Behalf of the South-Carolina College* (Charleston, S.C.: A. E. Miller, 1835), 14, 20, https://www.loc.gov/resource/gdcmassbookdig.appealinbehalfofo1hayn/?sp=16&st=image&r=-0.02,0.165,1.245,0.87,0.
27. Hartmut Keil, "Francis Lieber's Attitudes on Race, Slavery, and Abolition," *Journal of American Ethnic History* 28, no. 1 (Fall 2008): 13, 22.
28. Thomas Sergeant Perry, ed., *The Life and Letters of Francis Lieber* (Boston: J. R. Osgood, 1882), 230–31.
29. Ibid., 234.
30. Ibid., 235.
31. Friedel, "Francis Lieber, Charles Sumner, and Slavery," 84.
32. Ibid., 87–88.
33. Ibid., 91–92.

34. Clement Eaton, *Freedom of Thought in the Old South* (Durham, N.C.: Duke University Press, 1940), 202.
35. Willis P. Whichard, *A Consequential Life: David Swain, Nineteenth-Century North Carolina, and Their University* (Chapel Hill: University of North Carolina Chapel Hill Library), xvi, 217, 220; Eaton, *Freedom of Thought*, 205.
36. Curtis, "The Curious History," 846.
37. Perry, *Life and Letters of Lieber*, 236.
38. Bernard Schwartz, *The Bill of Rights: A Documentary History*, 2 vols. (New York: Chelsea House Publishers, 1971), 2:1032.
39. Ibid., 2:1034; Curtis, "The Curious History," 794.

Chapter Ten. Southern Propaganda

1. *Southern Literary Messenger*, August 1834, 1, 2.
2. Lucian Minor, "An Address on Education, as Connected with the Permanence of Our Republican Institutions," September 24, 1835, https://babel.hathitrust.org/cgi/pt?id=hvd.hn58kc&seq=7.
3. Thomas Jefferson, Letter to General James Breckenridge, February 15, 1821, https://founders.archives.gov/documents/Jefferson/03-16-02-0516.
4. Albert G. Brown, "An Address on Southern Education Delivered Before the Faculty, Trustees, Students, and Patrons of Madison College" (July 18, 1859), 3, 8.
5. "Southern School-Books," *DeBow's Review* 13 (1852): 260; Joseph Story, "Story's Commentaries," *Southern Quarterly Review* 2, no. 4 (October 1842): 420–21.
6. *DeBow's Review* 13 (1852): 265; *DeBow's Review* 23 (1857): 23.
7. John S. Ezell, "A Southern Education for Southrons," *Journal of Southern History* 17, no. 3 (August 1951): 306.
8. Brown, "An Address on Southern Education," 5.
9. *DeBow's Review* 20 (1856): 75.
10. *DeBow's Review* 23 (1857): 340–41, 342.
11. Ezell, "Southern Education for Southrons," 306.
12. *DeBow's Review* 16 (1854): 551; *DeBow's Review* 22 (1857): 68.
13. C. K. Marshall, "Southern Authors, School Books, and Presses," *DeBow's Review* 21, no. 5 (November 1856): 520, 521, 522, https://quod.lib.umich.edu/m/moajrnl/acg1336.1-21.005/524:10?page=root;rgn=full+text;size=100;view=image.
14. *Southern Literary Messenger* 25 (1857): 318, 319.
15. Brown, "An Address on Southern Education," 6.
16. *DeBow's Review* 15 (1853): 268.
17. Brown, "An Address on Southern Education," 11.
18. William H. Stiles, "Southern Education for Southern Youth, An Address before the Alpha Pi Delta Society of the Cherokee Baptist College," July 14, 1858, 8, 9, 10, 11.

19. *DeBow's Review* 10 (1851): 362.
20. "A Brief Enquiry into the True Nature and Character of Our Federal Government," *Southern Quarterly Review* 3, no. 6 (April 1843): 306.

Chapter Eleven. Secret Learning

1. Heather Andrea Williams, *Self-Taught: African American Education in Slavery and Freedom* (Chapel Hill: University of North Carolina Press, 2005), 12.
2. Antonio T. Bly, " 'Pretends He Can Read': Runaways and Literacy in Colonial America, 1730–1776," *Early American Studies* 6, no. 2 (Fall 2008): 261–94, https://www.jstor.org/stable/23546575; Grey Gundaker, "Hidden Education Among African Americans During Slavery," *Teachers College Record* 109, no. 7 (July 2007): 1601, https://journals.sagepub.com/doi/abs/10.1177/016146810710900707.
3. Bernard E. Powers Jr., *Black Charlestonians: A Social History, 1822–1885* (Fayetteville: University of Arkansas Press, 1994).
4. C. W. Birnie, "Education of the Negro in Charleston, South Carolina, Prior to the Civil War," *Journal of Negro History* 12, no. 1 (January 1927): 15, https://www.jstor.org/stable/2714159; Janet Cornelius, " 'We Slipped and Learned to Read': Slave Accounts of the Literacy Process, 1830–1865," *Phylon* 44, no. 3 (1983): 171–86, https://www.jstor.org/stable/274930; Janet Duitsman Cornelius, *When I Can Read My Title Clear: Literacy, Slavery, and Religion in the Antebellum South* (Columbia: University of South Carolina Press, 1991), 26, 81.
5. Cornelius, *When I Can Read*, 26; Powers, *Black Charlestonians*, 52–53; Birnie, "Education of the Negro."
6. Cornelius, *When I Can Read*, 39.
7. "Memorial Regarding Schools and Employment for Persons of Color, 1826," in *The Denmark Vesey Affair: A Documentary History*, ed. Douglas R. Egerton and Robert L. Paquette (Gainesville: University Press of Florida, 2017), 631.
8. Ibid.
9. Birnie, "Education of the Negro," 16.
10. Daniel Alexander Payne, *Reflections of Seventy Years*, comp. and arr. Sarah C. Bierce Scarborough, ed. Rev. C. S. Smith (Nashville, Tenn.: A. M. E. Sunday School Union, 1888), 15–16, https://docsouth.unc.edu/church/payne70/payne.html.
11. Ibid., 18.
12. Ibid., 25.
13. Ibid., 26.
14. Ibid., 31, 33.
15. Ibid., 36.
16. Cornelius, *When I Can Read*, 43–44.

17. Charles Colcock Jones, *The Religious Instruction of the Negroes in the United States* (Savannah, Ga.: Thomas Purse, 1842): 97–98, https://docsouth.unc.edu/church/jones/jones.html; Gundaker, "Hidden Education," 1596–97.
18. Richard R. Wright, *A Brief Historical Sketch of Negro Education in Georgia* (Savannah, Ga.: Robinson Printing House, 1894), 21, https://www.google.com/books/edition/A_Brief_Historical_Sketch_of_Negro_Educa/hxE-AQAAMAAJ?hl=en&gbpv=1&pg=PA1&printsec=frontcover.
19. Janice L. Sumter-Edmond, "Free Black Life in Savannah," in *Slavery and Freedom in Savannah*, ed. Leslie M. Harris and Daina Ramey Berry (Athens: University of Georgia Press, 2014), 134, https://www.google.com/books/edition/Slavery_and_Freedom_in_Savannah/mOXZCgAAQBAJ?hl=en&gbpv=1&pg=PA1&printsec=frontcover; Williams, *Self-Taught*, 98.
20. Williams, *Self-Taught*, 16–17.
21. Susie King Taylor, *Reminiscences of My Life in Camp with the 33d United States Colored Troops Late 1st S. C. Volunteers* (Boston: published by the author, 1902), 1–2, https://docsouth.unc.edu/neh/taylorsu/taylorsu.html.
22. Ibid., 5–6; Whittington B. Johnson, "Free African-American Women in Savannah, 1800–1860: Affluence and Autonomy Amid Adversity," *Georgia Historical Quarterly* 76, no. 2, (Summer 1992): 278.
23. Taylor, *Reminiscences of My Life*, 5–6; Johnson, "Free African-American Women," 277–78.
24. Taylor, *Reminiscences of My Life*, 6.
25. Federal Writers' Project, *Slave Narratives: A Folk History of Slavery in the United States from Interviews with Former Slaves*, vol. 14 (Washington, D.C.: Library of Congress, 1941) (interview subject: Project 1885-1-District #4Spartanburg, S. C. June 7, 1937), https://www.gutenberg.org/files/18912/18912-h/18912-h.htm; Jermaine Fowler, *The Humanity Archive: Recovering the Soul of Black History from a Whitewashed American Myth* (Irvine, Calif.: Row House Publishing, 2023); Hazel Arnett Ervin and Lois Jamison Sheer, eds., *A Community of Voices on Education and the African American Experience: A Record of Struggles and Triumphs* (Newcastle upon Tyne, U.K.: Cambridge Scholars Publishing, 2025), 47 (excerpting Cornelius); Williams, *Self-Taught*, 30; Cornelius, "We Slipped," 174; Fowler, *The Humanity Archive*.
26. Ervin and Sheer, *A Community of Voices*, 46, 76.
27. Federal Writers' Project, *Slave Narratives;* Cornelius, "We Slipped," 171; Gundaker, "Hidden Education," 1600; Ervin and Sheer, *A Community of Voices*, 42.
28. Christopher M. Span, *From Cotton Field to Schoolhouse: African American Education in Mississippi, 1862–1875* (Chapel Hill: University of North Carolina Press, 2014), 43.
29. Williams, *Self-Taught*, 20.
30. New England Freedmen's Aid Society, *The Freedmen's Record*, vol. 1 (1865): 95–96, https://catalog.hathitrust.org/Record/006784897.

31. Gundaker, "Hidden Education," 1600; George P. Rawick, ed., *The American Slave: A Composite Autobiography*, vol. 19 (Westport, Conn.: Greenwood, 1972), 148.

Chapter Twelve. Black Literacy on Trial

1. *Proceedings of the Meetings in Charleston, S.C., May 13–15, 1845, on the Religious Instruction of the Negroes* (Charleston, S.C.: B. Jenkins, 1845), https://tile.loc.gov/storage-services/service/rbc/rbaapc/04710/04710.pdf.
2. Ibid., 15.
3. Robert F. Durden, "The Establishment of Calvary Protestant Episcopal Church for Negroes in Charleston," *South Carolina Historical Magazine* 65, no. 2 (April 1964): 72.
4. Ibid., 71–72; *The Commercial (Charleston)*, July 19, 1849.
5. *Mercury*, July 23, 1849; *Charleston Courier*, July 16, 1849.
6. *Public Proceedings Relating to Calvary Church, and the Religious Instruction of Slaves* (Charleston, S.C.: Miller and Browne, 1850), 2, https://lcdl.library.cofc.edu/lcdl/catalog/lcdl:89214?tify={%22pages%22:[0,1],%22panX%22:0.92,%22panY%22:0.799,%22view%22:%22scan%22,%22zoom%22:0.448}1.
7. Ibid., 6, 7.
8. Ibid., 8, 26, 38, 43.
9. Ibid., 29, 30.
10. Ibid., 9, 15.
11. Ibid., 82.
12. Janet Duitsman Cornelius, *When I Can Read My Title Clear: Literacy, Slavery, and Religion in the Antebellum South* (Columbia: University of South Carolina Press, 1991), 115.
13. Ibid.
14. Richard Fuller, *Our Duty to the African Race: An Address Delivered at Washington, D.C., January 21, 1851* (Baltimore: W. M. Innes Press, 1851), 7, https://tile.loc.gov/storage-services/public/gdcmassbookdig/ourdutytoafricanoofull/ourdutytoafricanoofull.pdf.
15. Ibid., 7, 10; J. H. Cuthbert, *Life of Richard Fuller, D.D.* (New York: Sheldon, 1878), 200, https://babel.hathitrust.org/cgi/pt?id=hvd.hx2pgn&seq=13.
16. Cornelius, *When I Can Read*, 138; Cuthbert, *Life of Richard Fuller*, 201.
17. Margaret Douglass, *Educational Laws of Virginia; The Personal Narrative of Mrs. Margaret Douglass, a Southern Woman* (Boston: John P. Jewett, 1854), 7, https://www.loc.gov/resource/gdcmassbookdig.educationallawsooodoug/?st=pdf&pdfPage=6.
18. Ibid.
19. Ibid., 9.
20. Ibid., 10.
21. Ibid., 10, 11.

22. Ibid., 14.
23. Ibid., 15.
24. Ibid., 20.
25. Ibid., 22.
26. Ibid., 30–31.
27. Ibid., 31.
28. Ibid., 31–32.
29. Ibid., 33.
30. Ibid., 33, 34, 36.
31. Ibid., 41 (quoting *Daily Southern Argus*, February 9, 1854); ibid., 42–43.
32. Ibid., 47, 49.
33. Frederick Douglass, *Life of an American Slave* (Boston: Anti-Slavery Office, 1845), 36, http://utc.iath.virginia.edu/abolitn/abaufda8t.html.
34. Booker T. Washington, *Up from Slavery* (New York: Doubleday, 1901), 4, 7, https://docsouth.unc.edu/fpn/washington/washing.html.
35. Heather Andrea Williams, *Self-Taught: African American Education in Slavery and Freedom* (Chapel Hill: University of North Carolina Press, 2005), 7.
36. John W. Blassingame, ed., *Slave Testimony: Two Centuries of Letters, Speeches, Interviews, and Autobiographies* (Baton Rouge: Louisiana State University Press, 1977), https://www.google.com/books/edition/Slave_Testimony/EJBbh7oNZkkC?hl=en&gbpv=1&printsec=frontcover. Ishmael Reed, in his fictional account of one enslaved person's escape, said it more eloquently, albeit less precisely: "the slave who learned to read and write was the first to run away." Ishmael Reed, *Flight to Canada* (New York: Random House, 1976).
37. Frederick Douglass, *My Bondage and My Freedom* (New York: Miller, Orton and Mulligan, 1855), 158, 159, 160, 163, https://docsouth.unc.edu/neh/douglass55/douglass55.html.
38. Ibid., 273.
39. Ibid., 422.
40. Jacobs published her narrative under the pseudonym Linda Brent, and under the title *Incidents in the Life of a Slave Girl. Written by Herself*, ed. L. Maria Child (Boston: published for the author, 1861), https://gel.sites.uiowa.edu/sites/gel.sites.uiowa.edu/files/wysiwyg_uploads/jacobs_incidents_in_the_life.pdf.
41. Ibid., 295–98.
42. John W. Blassingame, *The Slave Community: Plantation Life in the Antebellum South*, rev. and enlarged ed. (New York: Oxford University Press, 1979), https://openlibrary.org/books/OL21278835M/The_slave_community.
43. David W. Blight, *A Slave No More: Two Men Who Escaped to Freedom, Including Their Own Narratives of Emancipation* (Orlando: Harcourt, 2007), 162; David W. Blight, *Frederick Douglass: Prophet of Freedom* (New York: Simon and Schuster, 2018), 55.

Chapter Thirteen. A Rebirth of Freedom

1. Edward L. Pierce, "The Contrabands at Fortress Monroe," *Atlantic Monthly*, November 1861, https://www.theatlantic.com/magazine/archive/1861/11/the-contrabands-at-fortress-monroe/628956/.
2. Edward L. Pierce, *Enfranchisement and Citizenship: Addresses and Papers*, ed. A. W. Stevens (Boston: Roberts Brothers, 1896), 22, https://babel.hathitrust.org/cgi/pt?id=yale.39002002289479&seq=38; "Monthly Record of Current Events," *Harper's New Monthly Magazine*, vol. 23, June–November 1861, 257, https://babel.hathitrust.org/cgi/pt?id=mdp.39015056090312&seq=7.
3. Willie Lee Rose, *Rehearsal for Reconstruction: The Port Royal Experiment* (Athens: University of Georgia Press, 1964), 13, 14.
4. Lewis C. Lockwood, *Mary S. Peake, The Colored Teacher at Fortress Monroe* (Boston: American Tract Society, 1862), 16–23, https://www.gutenberg.org/cache/epub/20744/pg20744-images.html.
5. Ibid., 5–9.
6. Pierce, "The Contrabands."
7. Lockwood, *Mary S. Peake*, 31.
8. Ibid., 57.
9. Ibid., 16.
10. Ibid., 32, 33, 34.
11. Ibid., 34.
12. Ibid., 37.
13. Ibid., 39; Jaweed Kaleem, "For 156 Years, a Mighty Oak in Virginia Has Stood as a Symbol of Freedom Across the Nation," *Los Angeles Times*, September 26, 2019, https://www.latimes.com/world-nation/story/2019-09-26/emancipation-oak-tree-hampton-university-virginia.
14. Rose, *Rehearsal for Reconstruction*, xvi (Introduction by C. Vann Woodward).
15. Orville Vernon Burton, *Penn Center: A History Preserved* (Athens: University of Georgia Press, 2014), 28, https://www.google.com/books/edition/Penn_Center/Kr-NBAAAQBAJ?hl=en&gbpv=1&printsec=frontcover.
16. Elizabeth Hyde Botume, *First Days Amongst the Contrabands* (Boston: Lee and Shepard, 1893), 7, https://library.missouri.edu/confederate/items/show/1708.
17. Rose, *Rehearsal for Reconstruction*, 21 (quoting Smalley to Charles Sumner, December 15, 1861); Pierce, *Enfranchisement and Citizenship*, 54; Pierce, "The Contrabands."
18. "Edward Pierce to Chase, December 29, 1861," in *The Salmon P. Chase Papers*, vol. 3, Correspondence 1858–March 1863, ed. John Niven (Kent, Ohio: Kent State University Press, 1996), 115.
19. Pierce, *Enfranchisement and Citizenship*, 67.
20. *The Negroes at Port Royal. Report of E. L. Pierce, Government Agent, to the Hon. Salmon P. Chase, Secretary of the Treasury* (Boston: R. F. Wallcut, 1862), 3, https://www.loc.gov/item/12001839/.

21. Ibid., 13, 25.
22. Ibid., 28.
23. Ibid., 12, 18, 32.
24. Ibid., 32.
25. Pierce, *Enfranchisement and Citizenship*, 87.
26. Ray Allen Billington, ed., *The Journal of Charlotte L. Forten* (New York: Dryden Press, 1953), 22, https://books.google.com/books?id=hBZBAAAAI AAJ&printsec=frontcover&source=gbs_ge_summary_r&cad=0#v=onepage &q&f=false; *Brief History of the New York National Freedmen's Relief Association* (New York: N.Y.N.F.R.A., 1866), 161–62; Botume, *First Days*, 17 (reprinting Sherman's Order).
27. *The Negroes at Port Royal*, 36 (attaching Educational Commission, Appeal of the Educational Commission, March, 14, 1862, as an appendix).
28. Botume, *First Days*, 26.
29. Pierce, *Enfranchisement and Citizenship*, 92.
30. Botume, *First Days*, 49.
31. Ibid., 55, 57; "Charlotte Forten, Life on the Sea Islands," in Lewis C. Lockwood, *Two Black Teachers During the Civil War* (New York: Arno Press, 1969), 77; Elizabeth Jacoway, *Yankee Missionaries in the South: The Penn School Experiment* (Baton Rouge: Louisiana State University Press, 1980), 30.
32. Botume, *First Days*, 57, 62.
33. Ibid., 66, 92, 255.
34. Pierce, *Enfranchisement and Citizenship*, 109.
35. Ibid., 109, 304.
36. Ibid., 115 (citation covers the entire paragraph).
37. Ibid., 115, 116.
38. Rupert Sargent Holland, ed., *Letters and Diary of Laura M. Towne: Written from the Sea Islands of South Carolina, 1862–1884* (Cambridge, Mass.: Riverside Press, 1912), 3–9, https://babel.hathitrust.org/cgi/pt?id=coo1.ark:/13960/t82j7197m& seq=13.
39. Ibid., 8.
40. Ibid., 9.
41. Ibid., 32–37.
42. Jacoway, *Yankee Missionaries in the South*, 29–30.
43. Holland, *Letters and Diary of Laura M. Towne*, 95, 106.
44. Mollie Barnes, "Teaching to Resist, Teaching to Recover: Charlotte Forten's Sea Islands Archives Across Private and Public Forms," *Legacy: A Journal of American Women Writers* 37, no. 2 (2020): 241 (quoting letter of October 28, 1862).
45. Charlotte Forten Grimké, "Life on the Sea Islands, Part I," *The Atlantic Monthly*, May 1864, 591.
46. Barnes, "Teaching to Resist," 236, 245; Grimké, "Life on the Sea Islands, Part I," 591.

47. Jacoway, *Yankee Missionaries in the South*, 30.
48. Botume, *First Days*, 112, 114.
49. "Timeline of Penn Center History," Penn Center, accessed November 30, 2023, https://www.penncenter.com/history-timeline; Luana M. Graves Sellars, "Penn Center and the Port Royal Experiment," *Hilton Head Monthly*, January 30, 2017, https://www.hiltonheadmonthly.com/living/4078-penn-center-the-port-royal-experiment (recounting the Penn Center's history); Robert C. Morris, *Reading, 'Riting, and Reconstruction: The Education of Freedmen in the South, 1861–1870* (Chicago: University of Chicago Press, 1981), 7.
50. James E. Yeatman, *A Report on the Condition of the Freedmen of the Mississippi* (Saint Louis: Western Sanitary Commission Rooms, 1861), 3, https://bkbb philly.org/report-condition-freedmen-mississippi.
51. Maxine D. Jones, "The American Missionary Association and the Beaufort, North Carolina, School Controversy, 1866–67," *Phylon* 48, no. 2 (1987): 103, https://www.jstor.org/stable/274774 (describing the opening of a school in North Carolina); Yeatman, *A Report*, 11 (reporting on new schools erected in Mississippi); "Letter from W.C. Gannett," *Freedmen's Record*, April 28, 1865, 91; American Missionary Association, *History of the American Missionary Association* (New York: Bible House, 1891), 14–15; Joe M. Richardson, *Christian Reconstruction: The American Missionary Association and Southern Blacks, 1861–1890* (Tuscaloosa: University of Alabama Press, 1986), 37–40 (noting stories from Virginia, Tennessee, Louisiana, South Carolina, Florida, North Carolina, Arkansas, Missouri, and Mississippi about the African American desire for education following the Civil War); Peter Kolchin, *First Freedom: The Responses of Alabama's Blacks to Emancipation and Reconstruction* (Tuscaloosa: University of Alabama Press, 2008), 84; J. W. Alvord, *First Semi-Annual Report on Schools and Finances of Freedmen January 1, 1866* (Washington, D.C.: U.S. Government Printing Office, 1868).
52. Christopher M. Span, *From Cotton Field to Schoolhouse: African American Education in Mississippi, 1862–1875* (Chapel Hill: University of North Carolina Press, 2014), 43.

Chapter Fourteen. Public Education for All

1. Heather Andrea Williams, *Self-Taught: African American Education in Slavery and Freedom* (Chapel Hill: University of North Carolina Press, 2005), 70 (emphasis omitted).
2. Edward L. Pierce, *Memoir and Letters of Charles Sumner*, vol. 4, *1860–1874* (Boston: Roberts Brothers, 1894), 78, https://upload.wikimedia.org/wikipe dia/commons/8/89/Memoir_and_letters_of_Charles_Sumner_%28IA_ memletterssumner04pierrich%29.pdf.
3. Ibid.

4. *Journal of the House of Representatives of the United States*, vol. 59 (Washington, D.C.: U.S. Government Printing Office, 1862): 781, https://memory.loc.gov/cgi-bin/ampage?collId=llhj&fileName=059/llhj059.db&recNum=780&itemLink=r?ammem/hlaw:@field(DOCID+@lit(hjo591 26))%230590781&linkText=1; Pierce, *Memoir and Letters*, 78 n.2.
5. Abraham Lincoln to the People of Sangamon County, March 9, 1832, Papers of Abraham Lincoln Digital Library, https://papersofabrahamlincoln.org/documents/D200008.
6. "Letter from Abraham Lincoln to Nathaniel Banks (Aug. 5, 1863)," in Abraham Lincoln Association, *The Collected Works of Abraham Lincoln*, ed. Roy P. Basler, vol. 6, *1862–1863* (New Brunswick, N.J.: Rutgers University Press, 1953), 365, https://abrahamlincolnassociation.org/abraham-lincoln-collected-works/.
7. Ibid.
8. "General Orders, No. 23 (Feb. 3, 1864)," in Robert N. Scott, *The War of the Rebellion: A Compilation of the Official Records of the Union and Confederate Armies*, vol. 34 (Washington, D.C.: U.S. Government Printing Office, 1891), 227–29, https://babel.hathitrust.org/cgi/mb?a=listis;c=106642625; "General Orders, No. 38 (Mar. 22, 1864)," in Elihu Root, *The War of the Rebellion: A Compilation of the Official Records of the Union and Confederate Armies*, vol. 4 (Washington, D.C.: U.S. Government Printing Office, 1900), 193–94, https://babel.hathitrust.org/cgi/pt?id=hvd.hwsk39;view=1up;seq=209.
9. James D. Anderson, *The Education of Blacks in the South 1860–1935* (Chapel Hill: University of North Carolina Press, 1988), 9–10.
10. *Proceedings of the Colored People's Convention of the State of South Carolina* (Charleston: South Carolina Leader Office, 1865), https://docs.google.com/viewerng/viewer?url=https://omeka.coloredconventions.org/files/original/fb7ce2e02cc45786fb4530926135de24.pdf.
11. Richard Gergel and Belinda Gergel, "'To Vindicate the Cause of the Downtrodden': Associate Justice Jonathan Jasper Wright and Reconstruction in South Carolina," in *At Freedom's Door: African American Founding Fathers and Lawyers in Reconstruction South Carolina*, ed. James Lowell Underwood and W. Lewis Burke (Columbia: University of South Carolina Press, 2000), 38.
12. *Proceedings of the Colored People's Convention*, 10.
13. Ibid., 13, 15.
14. Ibid., 22, 30.
15. Philip S. Foner and George E. Walker, eds., *Proceedings of the Black National Conventions, 1865–1900*, vol. 1 (Philadelphia: Temple University Press, 1986), 194; Hilary Green, *Educational Reconstruction: African American Schools in the Urban South, 1865–1890* (New York: Fordham University Press, 2016), 49; see also "Alabama Colored Convention," *19th Century U.S. Newspapers*, accessed December 1, 2023, https://omeka.coloredconventions.org/

items/show/1690 (calling for the creation of tax-supported schools); Foner and Walker, *Proceedings of the Colored People's Convention*, 9–10 (adopting a rule that calls for the establishment of schools in every neighborhood).

16. J. W. Alvord, *First Semi-Annual Report on Schools and Finances of Freedmen January 1, 1866* (Washington, D.C.: U.S. Government Printing Office, 1868), 11; J. W. Alvord, *Fourth Semi-Annual Report on Schools for Freedmen* (Washington, D.C.: U.S. Government Printing Office, 1868), 3–4; Green, *Educational Reconstruction*.

17. Freedmen's Bureau Act of March 3, 1865, ch. 90, 13 Stat., 507, 508; Eric Foner, *Reconstruction: America's Unfinished Revolution, 1863–1877* (New York: HarperCollins, 1988), 144 ("Education probably represented the greatest success [of the Freedmen's Bureau] in the postwar South"); Freedmen's Bureau Act of March 3, 1865, § 2, 13 Stat., 508.

18. Allen C. Guelph, *Our Ancient Faith: Lincoln, Democracy, and the American Experiment* (New York: Alfred A. Knopf, 2024), 157.

19. Oliver Otis Howard, *Autobiography of Oliver Otis Howard: Major General United States Army*, vol. 2 (New York: Baker and Taylor, 1908), 192, https://www.google.com/books/edition/Autobiography_of_Oliver_Otis_Howard_Majo/nZw3AQAAMAAJ?hl=en&gbpv=1&pg=PR3&printsec=frontcover.

20. Letter from General Oliver Howard to Rev. John W. Alvord, May 15, 1865, Letters of Rev. John W. Alvord, A Project of University of Virginia Library, https://fromthepage.com/uvalibrary/letters-of-rev-john-w-alvord/1865-05-15-letter-a-howard-to-alvord/display/25198198.

21. "Letter from General O. Howard, War Department, Bureau of Refugees, Freedmen, and Abandoned Lands," *Freedmen's Record* (1865): 177; Howard, *Autobiography of Oliver Otis Howard*, 368; Eric Schnapper, "Affirmative Action and the Legislative History of the Fourteenth Amendment," Virginia Law Review 71, no. 5 (1985): 780–81; Paul Skeels Peirce, *The Freedmen's Bureau: A Chapter in the History of Reconstruction* (Iowa City: University of Iowa, 1904), 76–77 (discussing the multiple ways in which the funds were raised for and expended on education, including through discretionary acts of the bureau); Robert C. Morris, *Reading, 'Riting, and Reconstruction: The Education of Freedmen in the South, 1861–1870* (Chicago: University of Chicago Press, 1981), 36–37, 43–44, 49 (noting congressional funds for "repairs and rent of schoolhouses"); George R. Bentley, *A History of the Freedmen's Bureau* (Philadelphia: University of Pennsylvania, 1955), 171–74, https://babel.hathitrust.org/cgi/pt?id=mdp.39015002382383&seq=9 (discussing the acquisition of buildings, which were given free of rent for schools, and the creative financing to support the schools); *Records of the Field Offices of the Freedmen's Branch, Office of the Adjutant General, 1872–1878* (Washington, D.C.: United States Congress and National Archives and Records Administration, 2006), https://www.archives.gov/files/research/microfilm/m2029.pdf.

22. J. W. Alvord, *Tenth Semi-Annual Report on Schools for Freedmen* (Washington, D.C.: Government Printing Office, 1870), 4; Alan Brinkley, *American History: Connecting with the Past*, vol. 2, *From 1865* (New York: McGraw-Hill Education, 2014), 409. To be clear, however, African Americans made huge contributions on their own behalf—both financially and through in-kind services. Alvord, *Fourth Semi-Annual Report*, 3–4 (indicating 28,068 freedmen paid tuition and covered about 40 percent of the bureau's monthly statewide costs in some instances and the entire cost of some schools); "Letter from General O. Howard," 130 (indicating the bureau's role was to act "until a system of free schools can be supported by the re-organized local governments").

23. "Letter from General O. Howard," 130 (indicating the bureau's role was to act "until a system of free schools can be supported by the re-organized local governments"); J. W. Alvord, *Second Semi-Annual Report on Schools and Finances of Freedmen* (Washington, D.C.: Government Printing Office, 1866), 13.

24. Lawrence A. Cremin, *American Education: The National Experience, 1783–1876* (New York: HarperCollins, 1980), 149.

25. Cong. Globe, 40th Cong., 1st Sess. 167 (March 16, 1867); Susan P. Leviton and Matthew H. Joseph, "An Adequate Education for All Maryland's Children: Morally Right, Economically Necessary, and Constitutionally Required," *Maryland Law Review* 52, no. 4 (1993): 1155; Wythe W. Holt, *Virginia's Constitutional Convention of 1901–1902* (New York: Routledge, 1990), 254; *Proceedings of the Constitutional Convention of South Carolina 1868* (Charleston, S.C.: Denny and Perry, 1868), 695, https://www.google.com/books/edition/Proceedings_of_the_Constitutional_Conven/YfQoAAAAYA AJ?hl=en&gbpv=1&bsq=ignorance. Only after the Civil War had ended elites' political dominance did public education become possible, even in a relatively moderate state like Maryland. Leviton and Joseph, "An Adequate Education," 1155.

26. Cong. Globe, 40th Cong., 1st Sess. 168 (1867), https://memory.loc.gov/cgi-bin/ampage?collId=llcg&fileName=078/llcg078.db&recNum=303.

27. Reconstruction Act of 1867, ch. 153, 14 Stat. 428 (March 2, 1867); Cong. Globe, 40th Cong., 1st Sess. 168 (1867), https://memory.loc.gov/cgi-bin/ampage?collId=llcg&fileName=078/llcg078.db&recNum=303.

28. R. H. Woody, "Jonathan Jasper Wright, Associate Justice of the Supreme Court of South Carolina, 1870–77," *Journal of Negro History* 18, no. 2 (April 1933): 115, https://www.journals.uchicago.edu/doi/10.2307/2714290; *Proceedings of the Colored People's Convention*, 15.

29. *Proceedings of the Constitutional Convention of South Carolina 1868*, 51.

30. "Avery Institute History," Avery Institute, accessed December 1, 2023, http://www.averyinstitute.us/history.html.

31. *Proceedings of the Constitutional Convention of South Carolina 1868*, 74.

32. Ibid., 264.

33. Ibid., 51, 264.
34. Ibid., 173.
35. Ibid., 873.
36. Ibid.; Underwood and Burke, *At Freedom's Door*, 9–10.
37. *Proceedings of the Constitutional Convention of South Carolina 1868*, 688, 696.
38. Ibid., 695, 696–98.
39. Ibid., 692.
40. Ibid., 695.
41. Ibid., 695, 703. The specific "yeas" and "nays" for compulsory education were not counted, as it passed as part of the overall education provisions. The convention held a separate vote as to whether to include affirmative language indicating that all schools would be "free and open to all the children and youth of the State, without regard to race or color." S.C. Const. of 1868, art. 10, § 10. This even more controversial measure still passed with 80 percent voting in favor. Underwood and Burke, *At Freedom's Door*, 15.
42. *Proceedings of the Constitutional Convention of South Carolina 1868*, 925.
43. Ala. Const. of 1867, art. XI, § 6; Ark. Const. of 1868, art. IX, § 1; Fla. Const. of 1868, art. IX, § 1; Ga. Const. of 1868, art. VI, § 1; La. Const. of 1868, tit. VII, art. 135; Miss. Const. of 1868, art. VIII, § 1; N.C. Const. of 1868, art. IX, § 2; S.C. Const. of 1868, art. X, § 3; Tex. Const. of 1868, art. X, § 7; William Preston Vaughn, *Schools for All: The Blacks and Public Education in the South, 1865–1877* (Lexington: University Press of Kentucky, 1974), 55–60.
44. Ga. Const. of 1868, art. VI, § 1 ("The general assembly ... shall provide a thorough system of general education"); Miss. Const. of 1868, art. VIII, § 1 ("As the stability of a republican form of government depends mainly upon the intelligence and virtue of the people, it shall be the duty of the legislature to ... establish[] a uniform system of free public schools"); N.C. Const. of 1868, art. IX, § 2 ("The general assembly ... shall provide, by taxation and otherwise, for a general and uniform system of public schools."); S.C. Const. of 1868, art. X, § 3 ("The General Assembly shall ... provide for a liberal and uniform system of free public schools throughout the State."); *Report of the Debates and Proceedings of the Convention for the Revision of the Constitution of the State of Ohio* (Columbus, Ohio: S. Medary, 1851), 698, https://www.google.com/books/edition/Report_of_the_Debates_and_Proceedings_of/emWlAQjEci4C?q=%22schools+as+perfect+as+could+be+devised,+and+to+see+it+improve+so%22&gbpv=1#f=false; Fla. Const. of 1868, art. IX, § 1 ("It is the paramount duty of the State to make ample provision for the education of all the children residing within its borders"); Ala. Const. of 1868, art. XI, § 10 (providing that proceeds from all new and old state lands "shall be inviolably appropriated to educational purposes"); ibid. art. XI, § 11 (requiring that one-fifth of general annual state revenues "be devoted exclusively to the maintenance of public schools"); Fla. Const. of 1868, art. VIII, §§ 4, 7 (devoting resources to an education fund and requiring per-capita distribution among counties); see also John Mathiason Mat-

zen, "State Constitutional Provisions for Education: Fundamental Attitude of the American People Regarding Education as Revealed by State Constitutional Provisions, 1776–1929" (master's thesis, Columbia University, 1931), 129–39 (tracking the new common school funds in state constitutions).

45. W. E. Burghardt Du Bois, *Black Reconstruction in America: An Essay Toward a History of the Part Which Black Folk Played in the Attempt to Reconstruct Democracy in America, 1860–1880* (New York: Harcourt Brace, 1935), 638.

46. Du Bois, *Black Reconstruction in America*, 648. The number of formerly enslaved children would have exceeded one million. The 1850 census estimated that Southern states enslaved nine-hundred thousand children between the ages of five and fifteen—and the overall enslaved population increased in the subsequent decade. *Compendium of the Seventh Census* (1854), 88, https://www2.census.gov/library/publications/decennial/1850/1850c/1850c-04.pdf.

47. Ibid., 650; *Journal of the House of Representatives of the State of South Carolina for the Regular Session of 1873–74* (Columbia, S.C.: Republican Printing, 1874), 85–86 https://www.carolana.com/SC/Legislators/Documents/Journal_of_the_House_of_Representatives_of_the_State_of_South_Carolina_1873_1874.pdf (surveying education data and progress).

48. J. R. Lewis, *First Annual Report of the State School Commissioner of the State of Georgia* (Atlanta: New Era Steam Printing Establishment, 1871); Richard R. Wright, *A Brief Historical Sketch of Negro Education in Georgia* (Savannah, Ga.: Robinson Printing House, 1894), 21, https://www.google.com/books/edition/A_Brief_Historical_Sketch_of_Negro_Educa/hxE-AQAAMAAJ?hl=en&gbpv=1&pg=PA1&printsec=frontcover.

49. Du Bois, *Black Reconstruction*, 652; David Tyack and Robert Lowe, "The Constitutional Moment: Reconstruction and Black Education in the South," *American Journal of Education* 94, no. 2 (February 1986): 236–56.

50. *Journal of the House of Representatives of the State of South Carolina for the Regular Session of 1873–74*, 86–87.

Chapter Fifteen. Burning Down the Schoolhouse

1. Ronald E. Butchart, *Schooling the Freed People: Teaching, Learning, and the Struggle for Black Freedom, 1861–1876* (Chapel Hill: University of North Carolina Press, 2010), 154.

2. "Burning Freedmen's School-Houses," *New York Times*, September 14, 1865, 2, https://www.nytimes.com/1865/09/14/archives/burning-freedmens-schoolhousesburn.html.

3. Butchart, *Schooling the Freed People*, 158, 162.

4. Ibid., 167; John W. Alvord, *Seventh Semi-Annual Report on Schools for Freedmen* (Washington, D.C.: U.S. Government Printing Office, 1869), 44.

5. Philena Carkin, "Reminiscences of My Life and Work Among the Freedmen of Charlottesville Virginia from March 1st 1866 to July 1st 1875," vol. 1, Papers of Philena Carkin, University of Virginia Library, 42, accessed December 4, 2023, https://xtf.lib.virginia.edu/xtf/view?docId=2005_Q3_2/uvaGenText/tei/z000000523.xml; Alvord, *Seventh Semi-Annual Report*, 44.
6. Campbell F. Scribner, *Surveying the Destruction of African American Schoolhouses in the South, 1864–1876, Journal of the Civil War Era* 10, no. 4 (December 2020): 469–94, https://searchworks-lb.stanford.edu/articles/edsgus__edsgcl.641359673.
7. House Select Committee on the Memphis Riots, *Memphis Riots and Massacres, 25 July 1866*, 39th Cong. 1st Sess. (New York: reprinted by Arno Press, 1969); "Burning a Freedmen's School-house," *Harper's Weekly*, May 26, 1866.
8. Scribner, *Surveying the Destruction of African American Schoolhouses*.
9. Ibid., 475.
10. "The Constitution," *Des Arc Weekly Citizen*, February 22, 1868.
11. Albus, "The Situation: IX," *The Weekly Constitutionalist*, March 11, 1868; Albus, "The Situation: Number VII," *The Weekly Constitutionalist*, February 26, 1868 (suggesting that, under the "constitution proposed," "the whites will never cease paying for educating" Black students); B. H. Hill, "The Relief Iniquity Exposed," *The Cuthbert Appeal*, April 9, 1868. In 1874, Georgia legislatively attempted "[t]o ensure that white tax dollars were not used to support black schools" by "requiring separate tax returns" for both races. Kamina A. Pinder and Evan R. Hanson, "De Jure, De Facto, and Déjà Vu All Over Again: A Historical Perspective of Georgia's Segregation-Era School Equalization Program," *John Marshall Law Journal* 3, no. 2 (2010): 172 n.42 (citing Oscar H. Joiner et al., eds., *A History of Public Education in Georgia, 1734–1976* [Columbia, S.C.: R. L. Bryan, 1979], 86).
12. Leon O. Beasley, "A History of Education in Louisiana During the Reconstruction Period, 1862–1877" (PhD diss., Louisiana State University, 1957), 167 (quoting *Livingston Herald*, February 16, 1870).
13. Malcom Cook McMillan, *Constitutional Development in Alabama, 1798–1901: A Study in Politics, the Negro, and Sectionalism* (Chapel Hill: University of North Carolina Press, 1955), 160, https://onlinebooks.library.upenn.edu/webbin/book/lookupid?key=ha004422469 (quoting Montgomery *Daily Mail*, writing that the board of education will "force all white children, to go into all the free public schools upon terms of social equality with all sorts of negro children or else to surrender the schools as a monopoly to the negroes" and complaining about school taxes); "Public Education—Negro Equality," *Wilmington Journal*, March 13, 1868 (calling "attention to this diabolical scheme to *force negro social equality* upon the poorer classes of our people"); "To the Freedmen of South Carolina," *The Daily Phoenix*, April 12, 1868, supp.
14. "Letter from Col. E.Y. Clarke," *Weekly Intelligencer*, April 22, 1868.

15. J. O. Lewis, "Educational," *Keowee Courier*, May 29, 1868 (suggesting whites not participate in public education).
16. Dorothy Overstreet Pratt, *Sowing the Wind: The Mississippi Constitutional Convention of 1890* (Jackson: University Press of Mississippi, 2018), 55 (citing a newspaper article criticizing "excessive" government spending on Black education); "Why the People of the South Are Arrayed in a Body Against Radicalism," *Daily Clarion*, April 9, 1868 (complaining about "a gigantic 'school system' (so called) which ... the white people ... will necessarily pay the bulk of").
17. W. E. Burghardt Du Bois, *Black Reconstruction in America: An Essay Toward a History of the Part Which Black Folk Played in the Attempt to Reconstruct Democracy in America, 1860–1880* (New York: Harcourt Brace, 1935), 650, 654–55.
18. North Carolina Constitution of 1875 art. IX, § 2.
19. James D. Anderson, *The Education of Blacks in the South 1860–1935* (Chapel Hill: University of North Carolina Press, 1988), 81; Michael J. Klarman, *Unfinished Business: Racial Equality in American History* (New York: Oxford University Press, 2007), 44; James K. Vardaman, "Negro Education," *Commonwealth (Greenwood)*, June 30, 1899, 4, https://chroniclingamerica.loc.gov/lccn/sn89065008/1899-06-30/ed-1/seq-4.pdf.
20. Pratt, *Sowing the Wind*.
21. Anderson, *Education of Blacks*, 101; Gustavus J. Orr, *Third Report of the State School Commissioner* (Atlanta: W. A. Hemphill, 1874), table no. 7, https://dlg.galileo.usg.edu/data/dlg/ggpd/pdfs/dlg_ggpd_y-ga-be300-b-pa1-b1874.pdf; Gustavus J. Orr, Fourth Report of the State School Commissioner (Savannah: J. H. Estill, 1875), table no. 7, https://dlg.galileo.usg.edu/data/dlg/ggpd/pdfs/dlg_ggpd_y-ga-be300-b-pa1-b1875.pdf; Gustavus J. Orr, Sixth Report of the State School Commissioner (1877), table no. 6; Gustavus J. Orr, Seventh Report of the State School Commissioner (Atlanta: Jas P. Harrison, 1878), table no. 6, https://dlg.galileo.usg.edu/data/dlg/ggpd/pdfs/dlg_ggpd_y-ga-be300-b-pa1-b1878.pdf.
22. Riggsbee v. Town of Durham, 93 N.C. 800 (1886); Puitt v. Gaston County Commissioners, 94 N.C. 709 (1886); Jeff Lingwall, "Educational Gerrymanders: Creating Unequal School Districts in North Carolina," *North Carolina Central Law Review* 40, no. 1 (2017): 8 (discussing the "surprising" decision in *Puitt* and the ways that conservatives continued to get around its requirements); An Act to Provide for a Graded School in the Town of Hendersonville, North Carolina, ch. 266, 1895 Public Laws, https://www.carolana.com/NC/Education/1895_03_11_Act_to_Provide_for_a_Graded_School_in_Hendersonville.html (example of a graded school legislation's continuing use of the exact sort of system struck down in *Riggsbee* almost a decade later); Act of December 24, No. 18, § 4, 1888 S.C. Acts 49, 50, https://babel.hathitrust.org/cgi/pt?id=nyp.33433007186806&view=1up&seq=80&skin=2021; "Governor Tillman's Inaugural Address," *The Watchman and Southron*, December 10, 1890, 3.

23. James Lowell Underwood, *The Constitution of South Carolina*, vol. 2, *The Journey Toward Local Self-Government* (Columbia: University of South Carolina Press, 1988), 2:68.
24. Neil R. McMillen, *Dark Journey: Black Mississippians in the Age of Jim Crow* (Urbana and Chicago: University of Illinois Press, 1989), 41; *Journal of the Constitutional Convention of the State of South Carolina* (Columbia, S.C.: Charles A. Calvo, 1895), 10; Ralph Clipman McDanel, *The Virginia Constitutional Convention of 1901–1902* (Baltimore: Johns Hopkins University Press, 1928), 25, https://archive.org/details/TheVirginiaConstitutionalConventionOf1901-1902.
25. Albert D. Kirwan, *Revolt of the Rednecks: Mississippi Politics, 1876–1925* (Lexington: University of Kentucky Press, 1951), 69–70; James Lowell Underwood, *The Constitution of South Carolina*, vol. 4, *The Struggle for Political Equality* (Columbia: University of South Carolina Press, 1994), 4:134–35.
26. John Hope Franklin, *From Slavery to Freedom: A History of African Americans*, 3rd ed. (New York: Alfred A. Knopf, 1967), 339; Michael J. Klarman, *From Jim Crow to Civil Rights: The Supreme Court and the Struggle for Racial Equality* (New York: Oxford University Press, 2004), 32.
27. Pratt, *Sowing the Wind*, 117; Anderson, *The Education of Blacks*, 95.
28. Miss. Const. of 1890, art. VIII, § 207; S.C. Const. of 1895, art XI, § 7.
29. Pratt, *Sowing the Wind*, 114.
30. Franklin, *From Slavery to Freedom*, 387; Chrisman v. Town of Brookhaven, 12 So. 458, 460 (Miss. 1893); Charles C. Bolton, *The Hardest Deal of All: The Battle over School Integration in Mississippi, 1870–1980* (Jackson: University Press of Mississippi, 2005), 27.
31. Richard Klarman, *From Jim Crow to Civil Rights*, 45; Franklin, *From Slavery to Freedom*, 387; Richard Kluger, *Simple Justice: The History of* Brown v. Board of Education *and Black America's Struggle for Equality*, 1st Vintage Books ed. (New York: Vintage, 2004).
32. Bolton, *The Hardest Deal of All*, 28, 53.
33. Cumming v. Richmond County Board of Education, 175 U.S. 528 (1899); Bolton, *The Hardest Deal of All*, 49 (By 1950, white teachers made an average of $1,806 per year while their Black counterparts collected 39 percent of that total, or roughly $711 per year); Klarman, *From Jim Crow to Civil Rights*, 46–47.
34. A. A. Kincannon, "Manner of Apportioning the Common School Fund" *in Biennial Report of the State Superintendent of Public Education to the Legislature of Mississippi* (Jacksonville, Fla.: Vance Printing, 1900), i.
35. Mildred Lewis Rutherford, *A Measuring Rod to Test Text Books, and Reference Books in Schools, Colleges and Libraries* (Athens, Georgia, 1919), 2–4.
36. Ibid.; Fred Arthur Bailey, "The Textbooks of the 'Lost Cause': Censorship and the Creation of Southern State Histories, *Georgia Historical Quarterly* 75, no. 3 (1991): 514.

Notes to Pages 273–281

37. Bailey, "Textbooks of the 'Lost Cause,' " 521.
38. John Hugh Reynolds, *Makers of Arkansas History* (New York: Silver, Burdett and Company, 1905): 177–80; Bailey, "Textbooks of the 'Lost Cause,' " 521–27, 533.

Chapter Sixteen. Our Chance to Break the Cycle

1. Alyson Klein, "No Child Left Behind: An Overview," *EducationWeek*, April 10, 2015, https://www.edweek.org/policy-politics/no-child-left-behind-an-overview/2015/04; Derek W. Black, "Abandoning the Federal Role in Education: Every Student Succeeds Act," *California Law Review* 105, no. 5 (2017): 1309.
2. Derek W. Black, *Schoolhouse Burning: Public Education and the Assault on American Democracy* (New York: PublicAffairs, Hachette Book Group, 2020), 179–89.
3. Florida HB 7 (2022) Individual Freedom, https://legiscan.com/FL/text/H0007/2022; Jonathan Feingold and Joshua Weishart, "How Discriminatory Censorship Laws Imperil Public Education," National Education Policy Center, November 30, 2023, http:// nepc.colorado.edu/publication/censorship; Jeffrey Sachs et al., "For Educational Gag Orders, the Vagueness is the Point," PEN America, April 28, 2022, https://pen.org/for-educational-gag-orders-the-vagueness-is-the-point/; "Statement on Cobb County School Board Decision to Uphold Termination of Katherine Rinderle," Southern Poverty Law Center, August 17, 2013, https://www.splcenter.org/presscenter/statement-cobb-county-school-board-decision-uphold-termination-katherine-rinderle.
4. Sarah Schwartz, "Map: Where Critical Race Theory Is Under Attack," *EducationWeek*, updated June 13, 2023, https://www.edweek.org/policy-politics/map-where-critical-race-theory-is-under-attack/2021/06; "Mapping Attacks on LGBTQ Rights in U.S. State Legislatures," ACLU, last updated December 1, 2023, https://www.aclu.org/legislative-attacks-on-lgbtq-rights?impact=speech&state=#categories.
5. Griffin v. County School Board of Prince Edward County, 377 U.S. 218 (1964); Danielle Farrie and David G. Sciarra, *2022 Making the Grade: How Fair Is School Funding in Your State?* (Philadelphia: Education Law Center, 2022), https://edlawcenter.org/assets/files/pdfs/publications/Making-the-Grade-2022-Report.pdf.
6. Pete Hegseth and David Goodwin, *Battle for the American Mind: Uprooting a Century of Miseducation* (New York: HarperCollins, 2022), xii, 219; HarperCollins, "Battle for the American Mind," www.harpercollins.com, December 6, 2023, https://www.harpercollins.com/products/battle-for-the-american-mind-pete-hegsethdavid-goodwin?variant=40819073417250.
7. Hegseth and Goodwin, *Battle for the American Mind*, 27, 42, 225, 232, 233, 235.

8. Ralph Mipro, "Kansas Republicans Justify Private School Handouts with Fear of 'Woke Ideology,'" *The Pitch*, May 17, 2023, https://www.thepitchkc.com/kansas-republicans-justify-private-school-handouts-with-fear-of-woke-ideology/; Valerie Strauss, "Former Lobbyist Details How Privatizers Are Trying to End Public Education," *Washington Post*, April 16, 2021, https://www.washingtonpost.com/education/2021/04/16/former-lobbyist-details-how-privatizers-are-trying-to-end-public-education/.

9. Strauss, "Former Lobbyist Details How Privatizers Are Trying to End Public Education"; Tyler Kingkade, "A Betsy DeVos-Backed Group Helps Fuel a Rapid Expansion of Public Money for Private Schools," NBC News, March 30, 2023, https://www.nbcnews.com/politics/politics-news/betsy-devos-american-federation-children-private-school-rcna76307; "Betsy DeVos' Record: Privatizing Education and Undermining Public Schools," AFT American Federation of Teachers, accessed December 5, 2023, https://allin.rtp.aft.org/files/devos_educ_record_121316.pdf; "School Choice: Expanding Educational Freedom for All": Hearing before the Subcommittee on Early Childhood, Elementary, and Secondary Education, Committee on Education and the Workforce, April 18, 2023, https://edworkforce.house.gov/calendar/eventsingle.aspx?EventID=409046.

10. "School Choice: Expanding Educational Freedom for All."

11. Libby Stanford, "Ending 'Government-Run Monopoly' on Schools Is Top Priority for Rep. Virginia Foxx," *EducationWeek*, February 14, 2023, https://www.edweek.org/policy-politics/ending-government-run-monopoly-on-schools-is-top-priority-for-rep-virginia-foxx/2023/02.

12. Derek W. Black, "When Religion and the Public-Education Mission Collide," *Yale Law Journal Forum* 132 (2022): 559; Bayliss Fiddiman and Jessica Yin, "The Danger Private School Voucher Programs Pose to Civil Rights," Center for American Progress, May 13, 2019, https://files.eric.ed.gov/fulltext/ED596183.pdf.

13. Leslie Postal, Beth Kassab, and Annie Martin, "Private Schools' Curriculum Downplays Slavery, Says Humans and Dinosaurs Lived Together," *Orlando Sentinel*, June 1, 2018, https://www.orlandosentinel.com/2018/06/01/private-schools-curriculum-downplays-slavery-says-humans-and-dinosaurs-lived-together/; Rebecca Klein, "The Rightwing US Textbooks that Teach Slavery as 'Black Immigration,'" *Guardian*, August 12, 2021, https://www.theguardian.com/education/2021/aug/12/right-wing-textbooks-teach-slavery-black-immigration; Rebecca Klein, "These Textbooks in Thousands of K-12 Schools Echo Trump's Talking Points," *Huffington Post*, January 15, 2021, https://www.huffpost.com/entry/christian-textbooks-trump-capitol-riot_n_6000bce3c5b62c0057bb711f; Adam Gabbatt, "Outrage Over Alleged Nazi Homeschooling Group in Ohio," *Guardian*, February 1, 2023, https://www.theguardian.com/us-news/2023/feb/01/nazi-homeschooling-group-ohio-condemned; Leonardo Blair, "Pastor Mark Burns Plans to Open $200 a Month Military Christian Academy to Fight 'Woke' Agenda," *Christian*

Post, October 25, 2023, https://www.christianpost.com/news/mark-burns-plans-to-open-200-a-month-military-christian-academy.html.

14. Ark. Const. of 1868, art. IX, § 1; *Proceedings of the Constitutional Convention of South Carolina 1868* (Charleston, S.C.: Denny and Perry, 1868), 264; Ind. Const. of 1851, art. VIII, § 1.
15. Robert Downen, "Bill Requiring Ten Commandments in Texas Classrooms Fails in House After Missing Crucial Deadline," *Texas Tribune,* May 24, 2023, https://www.texastribune.org/2023/05/24/texas-legislature-ten-commandments-bill/.
16. Dwayne Yancey, "One State Senate Candidate Wants to Abolish the Mandate for a Public School System. Here's Why He Can't," *Cardinal News,* June 19, 2023, https://cardinalnews.org/2023/06/19/one-state-senate-candidate-wants-to-abolish-the-public-school-system-heres-why-he-cant/; Act of January 26, 1870, ch. 10, 16 Stat. 62, 63 (providing that Virginia would be admitted to the Union so long as its constitution "shall never be so amended or changed as to deprive any citizen or class of citizens of the United States of the school rights and privileges secured by the [state] constitution").
17. Hanna Panreck, "GOP Lawmaker Angers Liberals with 'Socialists and Communists' Travel Advisory for Florida: 'Totally Normal,'" Fox News, June 27, 2003, https://www.foxnews.com/media/gop-lawmaker-angers-liberals-socialists-communists-travel-advisory-florida-totally-normal.
18. Abraham Lincoln, "First Inaugural Address of Abraham Lincoln," *The Avalon Project,* March 4, 1861, https://avalon.law.yale.edu/19th_century/lincoln1.asp.
19. Gary B. v. Whitmer, 957 F.3d 616, 620–21, 625 (6th Cir. 2020), *reh'g en banc granted, opinion vacated,* 958 F.3d 1216 (6th Cir. 2020).
20. Ibid., 624, 650, 652.
21. NAEP Report Card: Reading, available at https://www.nationsreportcard.gov/reading/nation/achievement/?grade=8; U.S. Department of Education, Access to Reading Materials, https://www2.ed.gov/datastory/bookaccess/index.html.
22. U.S. Department of Education, Access to Reading Materials.
23. Right to Read Act of 2022, H.R. 9056, https://www.congress.gov/bill/117th-congress/house-bill/9056/text.

Acknowledgments

This book, unexpectedly, became the greatest challenge of my professional career. The path to publication involved twists, turns, ups, and downs in so many instances that I doubt I would have seen it through were it not for the faith of my agent, Matthew Carnicelli, and the perseverance of my editor, Bill Frucht. I could not ask for a more supportive and thoughtful partner than Matthew. Trust is hard to earn in today's impersonal marketplace, but he has mine. I never imagined that Bill would, or could, invest as much into a book as he did this one. His contributions to the prose were simultaneously sharp and graceful. His historical knowledge is deep and his substantive edits were uncanny.

When I struggled to find the proper voice for this book, my wife, Claire, gave me a private space where I might abandon the search and then the strength and encouragement to renew the search and ultimately capture what I had found so elusive. My son, Rohan, offered youthful but wise reflections that enabled me to step back from my absorption in the moment and adopt a healthier perspective.

My colleague Bob Bockman was my muse. Our regular conversations about my research discoveries were often more thrilling and insightful than the research itself. If there is any wisdom in this book, I surely derived a portion of it from Bob. And the books he so generously shared and recommended made an imprint on both this book and me.

At the University of South Carolina, Inge Lewis and Ashley Alvarado were the first and last readers of the full manuscript. Inge was actually part of the genesis of the book. It was her attraction to a passage about "secret learning" in my first draft of *Schoolhouse Burning* that prompted a full chapter in that book. That chapter then came to inspire this book. Ashley helped me structure and streamline the initial chapter drafts of this book, some of which were an otherwise unmanageable size. Inge and Ashley also helped polish the text and citations several times. Vanessa McQuinn provided help on that front too and took the lead on ensuring the book's illustrations were in order and properly sourced.

The librarians at University of South Carolina School of Law, particularly Michael Mounter and Candle Wester, introduced me to genuine historical research and proved that good librarians make good history books possible. Michael's ability to locate obscure documents regularly amazed me. When I failed to find or devise an internet search that could generate a mere lead on what I needed, Michael always found a way. He connected dots, archives, and texts that were beyond me. His experience and skill proved more valuable than any artificial aid.

At Yale University Press, Amanda Gerstenfeld effectively coordinated everyone and kept the book on schedule. Once I had submitted the manuscript and thought it near perfect, Erica Hanson carefully proofed it and offered yet more suggestions that enhanced the quality of the writing. Working long hours, Margaret Otzel carried the book to its final production.

When I was wandering aimlessly to grasp an understanding of early nineteenth-century Charleston, Bernard Powers, author of *Black Charlestonians*, generously set my bearings. Vaughnette Goode-Walker did the same in Savannah when I was exploring secret learning there, literally walking me through the city.

William Hubbard, Ned Snow, and the University of South Carolina School of Law supported my research from start to finish. Though the pace of researching and writing this book was more measured than my previous ones, there was never a suggestion that my attention or determination was any less dedicated or complete. Their patience was integral to making a longer and better book possible.

Index

Abolition debate, in Virginia General Assembly, 101–16
Abolitionists, 24, 53, 54, 70, 111, 117, 120, 123, 124, 128, 132, 134, 138, 143, 144, 149, 152, 154, 155, 162, 163, 175, 212, 232, 285, 289
Adams, John Quincy, 47, 48, 49, 50, 51, 135, 146
African Methodist Episcopal Church, 57, 178, 179
African Methodist Episcopal Zion Church, 16
Allen, Bishop Richard, 57, 70
Alvord, John, 184, 242–43
American Anti-Slavery Society, 123, 124, 125, 138, 139, 152
American Colonization Society, 68, 194, 199
American Freedman's Aid Commission, 242
American Literary Company, 171
American Missionary Association (AMA), 2, 212, 219, 246
American Missionary Society, 237
anti-critical-race-theory legislation, 279
The Anti-Slavery Record, 125
antislavery sympathizers, 132
Appeal to the Coloured Citizens of the World, 55, 61, 70, 72, 77, 80

Arkansas Constitution of 1874, 283
Atlantic (military steamship), 1–2
Avery Normal Institute, 246

Bailey, Fred, 273, 274
Baker, Frank, 209
Baker, Georgia, 187
Baldwin, James, 55
Banks, General Nathaniel, 234–35
Barnes, Mollie, 227
Barrett, Lysander, 149
Battle of Port Royal, 216–17, 223
Beach, Mary, 26
Beardsley, Samuel, 141, 152
Beaufort, South Carolina, 2, 193, 218, 221, 225, 226, 227, 237, 245
Bennett, Rolla, 27
Bennett, Governor Thomas, 40, 42–43
Black education, 5, 43, 178, 183, 184, 195, 211, 228, 237, 257, 258, 259, 261, 262, 264, 266, 268, 271, 274; Black schools: during slavery (prior to bans), 15, 38, 44, 118–19, 123, 131, 177–83; freedmen schools, 4–5, 212–31; secret schools, 183–89; violence against, 257–61
Black Masonic Lodge, Prince Hall, 57
Black preachers, 101, 122
Black Reconstruction, 253

Black seamen, 72, 73, 77, 115, 279, see also Negro Seamen Act of 1822
Blight, David, 207
Blue-Back Speller, 188
Bluford, Gordon, 186
Bly, Antonio, 176
Bonneau Library Society, 179
Bonneau, Thomas, 177–79, 180, 183
Boston Courier, 161
Boston Daily Courier, 70
Botume, Elizabeth Hyde, 222–23, 230
Bowman, Congressman Jamal, 281
Boyer, President Jean-Pierre (Haiti), 18, 28, 39
Breckenridge, General James, 168
Brodnax, William, 107, 108, 109, 112
Brophy, Alfred, 114
Brown Fellowship Society, 177, 236
Brown v. Board of Education, 6, 7, 272, 274, 275, 276, 277
Brown, Governor Albert (Mississippi), 170, 172, 173
Brown, John, 227
Brown, Reverend Morris, 43, 57
Bruce, James, 110
Bruce, Captain Jared, 47
Bryce, James, 61
Buchanan, James, 145
burning of schools, 259–61
Burritt, Elijah, 76–77
Butchart, Ronald, *Schooling the Freed People*, 258
Butler, Major General Benjamin, 209, 210, 212

Calhoon, Solomon S., 268
Calhoun, Senator John, 134, 135, 136, 138, 142, 144, 145, 146, 151, 159, 160, 162, 163, 171, 173
Calmes, Felix, 186
Calvary Church, 191–93, 195
Cardozo, Francis, 246–47
Carkin, Philena, 259
Caroliniensis, 49

Cary, Colonel John, 209
Charles Town Negro School, 38
Charleston Courier, 15, 41, 127
Charleston Southern Patriot, 126
Charleston workhouse, 25, 27, 31, 191
Chase, Salmon, 2, 218–19, 220–21
Chestnut, John, 251
Christ's Church, 195, 197, 198, 199
Citadel, 43, 127
City Gazette, 18
Clay, Henry, 57, 144–45, 194
colonization movement, 58, 69, 105, 108, 212
Colored People's Convention of the State of South Carolina *1865*, 236, 245, 251
Columbia Telescope, 148, 158
Columbian Centinel, 55
Columbian Orator, 177
Commercial Gazette (Boston), 154
common schools, 168, 173, 237, 239
Common Sense, 55, 67
Constitutional Convention of South Carolina *1868*, 245, 264, 267
contraband of war, 1, 2, 209, 212, 218, 220, 222
Convention of Colored Citizens in Arkansas, 239
Cornelius, Janet, 194
Cornish, Samuel, 58
courts, x, 6–8, 17, 31–33, 38, 40, 47–49, 54, 78–79, 85, 132, 134, 154, 197–99, 201, 268, 271, 276–77, 288
Cowen, Jacob, 80
Cox, Samuel, 128
Crandall, Reuban, 149
Cremin, Lawrence, 243
critical race theory, ix, x, 8, 9, 278, 279, 280

Daily Phoenix (South Carolina), 264
Daily Southern Argus (Norfolk, Va.), 200
Daley, Amos, 51
de Tocqueville, Alexis, 61

Index

DeBow, Charles, 169, 170, 171, 173, 174
DeBow's Review, 169–70
DeLarge, Robert, 239, 245, 249
Des Arc Weekly Citizen (Arkansas), 262
DeSaussure, Judge Henry William, 41
DeVeaux, Catherine, 183, 184
DeVeaux, Jane, 183, 184
DeVos, Betsy, 281
Douglass, Frederick, 35, 55, 202, 204, 207; *My Bondage and My Freedom*, 203–05, 207
Douglass, Margaret, 195–201, 211–12
Du Bois, W. E. B., 253
Du Pont, Flag Officer Samuel, 221

Eaton, Clement, 125, 161
economic violence, 257, 269
Education Commission (for the coordination of southern missionary teachers), 221, 228
educational crackdown, 181
Egerton, Douglas, 14, 36, 37
Elkison, Henry, 48–49
Elliott, Robert, 251
Emancipation Oak, 216
Emancipation Proclamation, 216, 227
The Emancipator, 117, 125, 149
Encyclopedia Americana, 158, 160
England, Bishop John, 181–82
Eppes, Richard, 85
Eustis, Representative William, 63
Evening Express (New York), 206
Exodus, 21

Fairfield, Congressman John, 139
Faulkner, Charles, 110–111, 112
federal writers' project, 187
Ferguson, Frank, 27
Finnie, Gordon, 157
Floyd, George, 277
Floyd, Virginia Governor John, 98–103, 112, 114–15
Ford, Lacy, 43, 96
Forsythe, Senator John, 75

Fort Monroe, 2, 208, 213, 214, 216, 217, 218, 219, 220, 221, 229, 230
Forten, Charlotte, 226–28
Foxx, Representative Virginia, 282
Francis, Nathaniel, 83–84
Franklin, Benjamin, 138, 142
Free people of color, during slavery, 17, 18, 38, 41, 44, 45, 46–48, 49, 57, 63, 68, 73–74, 77–80, 97, 100, 101–02, 109, 116, 118, 119, 131, 144, 177, 179, 181, 183–84, 196–97, 206, 210
Freedmen's Bureau, 230, 240, 242, 243, 253, 254, 258, 259, 274
Freedmen's Relief Association, 221
Freedmen's schools, 4–5, 212–31. *See also* Black schools
freedom of speech, 124, 165
freedom of the press, 54, 135, 136, 165
Freedom's Journal (New York), 58–59
Freehling, William W., 105, 145
Freeland, William, 203
Fremont, John C., 160, 161, 206
French, Reverend Mansfield, 219
Froumontaine, Julian, 183
Fugitive Slave Law, 209
Fuller, Richard, 193–95, 199

Gag Rule debates, 139–47
Gage, Robert, 132
Garnet, Henry Highland, 75
Garrison, William Lloyd, 70, 99, 100, 101, 125, 128, 152, 153, 154, 155, 289
Gayle, Alabama Governor John, 149
Gell, Monday, 18, 23, 28
General Order No. 9 (calling for educators to come to the Sea Islands), 221
Genius of Universal Emancipation, 99, 153
Georgia-South Carolina Synod, 117, 121
Gholson, James, 106, 107, 108, 173
Gideonites, 1
Giles, Virginia Governor William B., 77
Gilmer, Georgia Governor George, 73, 74, 75, 76
Goode, William, 104, 105, 115

Grant, General Ulysses S., 230
Grapevine (transfer of secret information through), 85, 93, 206
Gray, Thomas, 86–87, 94
Green, Duff, 171
Green, Elder, 189
Griffin v. Prince Edward County, 280
Guelzo, Allen, 240
Gundaker, Grey, 183

Haiti/St. Domingo/Saint-Domingue, 14, 17, 18, 22, 28, 30, 63, 106, 118
Hall, C. S., 203
Hall, Hiland, 136
Hamilton, Charleston Intendant/South Carolina Governor James, 42, 43, 44, 47, 100, 101
Hammond, Congressman James, 140–42, 143, 144, 145, 146, 169
Harding, Vincent, 83
Hayes, Rutherford B., 265
Hayne, Senator Robert Y., 125
Hedrick, Sherwood, 161
Hegseth, Pete, and David Goodwin: *Battle for the American Mind*, 9, 10, 280
Henry, Patrick, 103
Hercules and the Wagoner, 21–22
Herrisse, Henri, 161
Higginson, Thomas Wentworth, 27, 33, 40,
Hillard, George Stillman, 161
Hinks, Peter, 55, 75
Hoar, Representative Samuel, 144
Holloway, Richard, 177, 180
Horton, Gilbert, 63
Howard, General Oliver, 230, 241–43, 245
Howard, Robert, 119, 180
Huger, Postmaster Alfred, 126, 129–30
Human Rights (abolitionist paper), 125

Indiana Constitution of 1816, 283

Jack, Gullah, 19, 28
Jacobs, Harriet, 205–06

Jackson, Andrew, 130, 133–34, 136–38, 214
Jay, Justice John, 63
Jay, William, 63
Jefferson, Thomas, 49, 64–65, 69, 94, 105, 110, 135, 161, 168, 177
Jemmy, 13
Jillson, Justus, 254
Johnson Jr., Justice William, 48–49, 51
Johnson, Andrew, 241
Johnson, Major General Richard, 257
Johnson, Michael, 36
Jones, Charles Colcock, 117, 118, 165, 183

Kendall, Postmaster General Amos, 126
Kennedy, Lionel, 40, 180
King Jr., Martin Luther, 55, 230
King, Senator Rufus, 22–23, 59
Kluger, Richard, *Simple Justice*, 271
Ku Klux Klan, 261

Laurens, Representative Edward, 122
Lawless, Judge Luke, 155
legal culture of the nineteenth century, 185
Levine, Robert, 56
The Liberator, 70, 99, 100, 149, 153, 290
Lieber, Francis, 158–60, 163, 165, 169
Lincoln Prize, 240
Lincoln, Abraham, 1, 2, 156, 209, 220–21, 222, 227, 232–34, 240–41, 286
Literacy bans, debates, and restrictions, 3, 7, 13, 37–38, 41, 44, 73, 76, 77–78, 80–81, 96, 107, 116–17, 119, 121–23, 178, 183, 194–95, 198, 201
literacy: role of in escape from slavery, 176–77, 202, 203–06, 287; role of in freedom and citizenship, 1, 70, 231, 235, 288; role of in mental autonomy, 24–25, 203, 205, 207, 287; role of in revolt, 13, 15, 24, 27–28, 35, 37, 86–87, 92–95, 106–07, 287; intersection with religion, 16, 19–21, 26–27,

85–87, 89, 91–93, 100–01, 115, 117–19, 121–23, 176, 178, 181, 183, 187–88, 190–195, 199–200, 215
Lockwood, Revered Lewis 213–16, 219
Louverture, General Toussaint, 17, 227
Lovejoy, Elijah, 155–56, 165
Lynch Men (vigilance society), 126
lynching, 155, 152

Madison, James, 64, 70, 135, 164, 165
Magrath, Andrew Gordon, 192
Malcolm X, 55
Malcolm, Howard, 161
Mallory, Shepard, 209
Marcy, New York Governor William, 149
Marshall, Reverend C. K., 171–72, 173
Marshall, Stephen, 61
Marshall, Thurgood, 6
Martin, Trayvon, 277
Massachusetts Constitution, 247
May, Nicholas, 117
Mead, Jennie, 259
Messmore, Daniel, 205–06
Minor, Lucian, 167–68
Minors Moralist Society, 177, 179
missionaries, 2, 3, 4, 6, 24, 38, 67, 78, 102, 176, 212, 217, 222, 231, 242, 243
Mississippi Constitution of 1890, 270
Missouri Compromise and Debates, 22–27, 45–47, 59, 53–54, 59, 63, 99, 123, 148
Moms for Liberty, 9
Monroe, James, 48, 50, 64
Moore, Representative Samuel McDowell, 105
Moore, Thomas, 88
Morril, Representative David, 63
Morton, Senator Oliver, 244–45
Moses, South Carolina Governor Franklin, 255
Murray, Ellen 226

Nash, William Beverly, 245–46
national compact, 133, 149, 150, 163
Negro Act of 1740, 13, 14, 24, 31, 32, 37
Negro Seamen Act of 1822, 44–54, 63, 75, 97, 115, 119, 136, 178, 284
Nero, 83
newspapers: abolitionist, 70, 99, 100, 117, 124–25, 130, 149, 153, 155, 279, 290; Black newspapers, 57–59; censorship and blockade of, 3, 10, 76–77, 126–32, 133–34; importance of, 15, 16, 18, 22, 24, 57, 72, 206
New York Tribune, 218
Niles Weekly Register (Baltimore), 18, 39
Nixon, Richard, 7, 8, 276
Noble, Superintendent T. K., 259
non-interference principle, 150
Norcom, Dr., 205
North Carolina Manumission Society, 157
Notes on the State of Virginia, 65, 97

Oates, Stephen B., 87, 88
Obama, Barack, 230
Orr, Military Governor James, 246
Otis, Boston Mayor Gray, 74–75

Paine, Thomas, 55, 67
Parker, Thomas, 40, 180
Paul, William, 30
Payne, Daniel, 43, 118–19, 179–81, 190
Peake, Mary, 210–16, 217, 219
Pearson, Edward, 25
Penn School (Penn Center), 229–30
Petition Campaign, 138, 143, 148, 156, 162
Peyton, Representative Balie, 140–41
Pickens, Congressman Francis, 143–44
Pierce, Brigadier General Edward, 218–25, 230, 232, 234
Pinckney, Congressman Henry, 145–46
Pinckney, South Carolina Governor Thomas, 41
pit schools, 188
Point Comfort, Va., 208
Polk, Speaker James K., 140, 145, 146

Pollard, Edward, *The Lost Cause*, 5
Port Royal Relief Committee, 221
Porter, Mrs., 230–31
Postal Campaign, 124, 126, 128, 131, 132
Postal Raid, 126–28
Postal Service, 39, 125, 130, 131, 134, 136
Powell, Justice Lewis, 276
Powers, Bernard, 10, 336
Pratt, Dorothy, 269–70
Preston, William, 111
Prichett, E. C., 156
Proclamation of Amnesty and Reconstruction, 216, 227, 234
Prosser, Gabriel, 39, 91–92, 93
public education: creation of in South, 5, 243–56; campaign against, 261–64; defunding and segregation of, 264–72. *See also* common schools

Quakers, 103, 144

Randolph, Thomas Jefferson, 105–07, 109, 112, 113, 114
Ransier, Alonzo, 245, 249, 250
Ransier, James, 239
Reconstruction Act of 1867, 147, 244, 252
Rehnquist, Justice William, 276
religious instruction, 38, 115, 117, 118, 119, 120, 121, 122, 123, 190, 191, 192, 193, 195, 199
Revolutionary War, 16, 63
Reynolds, John, 274
Richards, Leonard, 152
Richmond Enquirer, 103, 133
Richmond Whig, 77
The Rights of All, 58
Rives, William M., 107
Roane, Delegate William, 103, 111
Robert, Joseph Clarke, 98
Rogers, Melvin, 64
Roman slaves, 65
Rose, Willie, 209

Ross, D. Barton, 172
Ruffin, Edmund, 169
Rufo, Chris, 9
rule of law, 51, 120, 165, 239, 246
Rush, Dr. Benjamin, 99
Russwurm, John, 58
Rutherford, Mildred Lewis: *A Measuring Rod to Test Text Books, and Reference Books in Schools, Colleges and Libraries*, 273

Schoeppner, Michael, 46, 50
Scott, Julius, 18
Scott, Senator Rick, 284
Scribner, Campbell, 259, 261
Sea Islands, 1, 2, 4, 5, 216, 217, 218, 219, 220, 221, 222, 224, 225, 227, 230, 231, 232, 233, 237, 242
Seabrook, Whitemarsh, 52–54, 119–22, 152, 162, 173, 181, 191, 195
second reconstruction, 275, 277, 278
secret schools and learning, 176–85, 187–89, 202–05
Sherman, Brigadier General Thomas W., 4, 221
Sherman, General William T., 241
Sidbury, James, 91
Siler, Charles, 281
Simms, James, 183
Sinha, Manisha, 37
Slade, William, 139–40
slave revolts, 2–3, 13–14, 19, 28, 30, 37–40, 82–84, 90–93
Slavery Report, 124, 125
The Slave's Friend, 125
slavocracy, 111, 117, 140, 163, 166, 172, 207, 243
Smith, Edward, 78–79
Smith, Whiteford, 192
South Carolina Association, 48, 51, 126
Southern Commercial Convention, 171, 173
Southern education movement, 167, 169, 171–74, 177, 286

Index

Southern Literary Messenger, 167, 172
Southern Speaker, 172
Southern Quarterly Review, 169, 170, 175
Spady, James O'Neil, 36, 37
Span, Christopher, 231
St. Helena Island, South Carolina, 4, 217, 218, 223, 226, 227, 229, 241
St. Louis Observer, 155
Stanly, Military Governor Edward, 232–233
Stanton, Edward, 230
Starr, Paul, 60
Stewart, Alvan, 151
Stiles, William, 174
Stokes, General Montfort, 80
Stono Rebellion, 13, 37, 53
Story, Justice Joseph, 158, 169
Summers, George, 112
Sumner, Senator Charles, 159, 161, 218, 232, 233, 234, 244, 247
Supreme Court, x, 7–8, 276–77
Swayne, Major General Wager, 231

Tappan, Arthur, 128, 152, 153, 289
Tappan, Lewis, 152, 212, 219
tar and feather threats, 151, 154, 258
Taylor, Breonna, 277
Taylor, Susie King, 184–85, 189, 204
Taylor, Walter, 198
teachers: censorship of, 8–9, 10, 278–79; current, 7, 275–76, 278–79, 288; during segregation, 271–72; during slavery, 16, 25, 183–85, 187, 189, 192; missionary, 1–4, 24, 38, 119, 176, 184, 212, 219, 222–31, 235, 237–38, 241–42, 246–47, 253–54, 257–59, 263, 288; opposition to northern educators, 168, 172–73
Telescope, 158, see also *Columbia Telescope*
terrorism, 186, 258–59
Thompson, George, 154
Thompson, Peter, 70
Thurmond, Strom, 8

Tilden, Samuel, 265
Tillman, Governor Bill, 268
Tise, Larry, 119
Tolley, Kim, 72
Towne, Laura Matilda, 224–29, 241
Townsend, James, 209
Tranquillus, 159
Travis, Joseph, 82
Trinity Methodist Church, 19
Trump, Donald, 8, 10
Turner, Ben, 88
Turner, Nat, 82–95, 98, 99, 109, 119, 120, 121, 123, 174, 274

Underwood, James, 268
United Confederate Veterans, 273, 279

Van Buren, Martin, 145
Vardaman, James, 271
veil of silence, 162
verbal violence, 257
Vesey, Denmark, 14–35, 36, 37, 39, 40, 42, 43, 45, 47, 48, 54, 55, 56, 57, 60, 61, 63, 72, 85, 86, 91, 92, 93, 94, 96, 100, 109, 117, 118, 121, 123, 126, 127, 148, 162, 174, 178, 179, 180, 181, 185, 191, 195, 206, 236, 274
Vesey, Joseph, 14, 15
Vigilance Association of Columbia, 125
violence: against abolitionists, 152–56, 289; against enslaved people, 85, 88, 93, 105, 187, 189, 203; against schools, teachers, and students, 7, 9, 183, 257–61; by mob, 127, 132, 152, 156, 183, 260; by police, 277; disavowal of, 99–100, 12; in response to slavery, 13, 34, 60, 75, 94, 104; in support of disunion, 50

Wade, Richard, 36
Waldstreicher, David, 59
Walker, David, 55–71, 72, 74, 75, 76, 77, 79, 80, 83, 86, 88, 93, 94, 96, 101, 105, 117, 120, 123, 144, 160, 207, 237, 274

Warren court, 8
Washington, Booker T., 202, 214, 230
Webb, William, 206
Weekly Constitutionalist (Georgia), 263
Williams, Heather Andrea, 176, 184, 202
Williams, John, 199
Williams, Robert, 149
Williams, Savannah Mayor William T., 74, 75, 76

Wilson, South Carolina Governor John, 50
Wirt, Attorney General William, 50
workhouse (for enslaved people), 25, 27, 31, 191
Wright, Jonathan Jasper, 237, 238, 239, 245, 246, 250, 252
Wyly-Jones, Susan, 131, 132

Yeatman, James, 230